THE
SHAMROCK
AND
THE LILY

PETER LANG
New York • Washington, D.C./Baltimore • Bern
Frankfurt am Main • Berlin • Brussels • Vienna • Oxford

Mary C. Kelly

THE SHAMROCK AND THE LILY

The New York Irish
and the Creation of a
Transatlantic Identity,
1845–1921

PETER LANG
New York • Washington, D.C./Baltimore • Bern
Frankfurt am Main • Berlin • Brussels • Vienna • Oxford

Library of Congress Cataloging-in-Publication Data

Kelly, Mary C.
The shamrock and the lily: the New York Irish
and the creation of a transatlantic identity, 1845–1921 / Mary C. Kelly.
p. cm.
Includes bibliographical references and index.
1. Irish Americans—New York (State)—New York—History. 2. Irish Americans—
New York (State)—New York—Ethnic identity.
3. New York (N.Y.)—History. I. Title.
F128.9.I6K45   974.7'10049162073—dc22   2004010422
ISBN 978-0-8204-7453-3

Bibliographic information published by **Die Deutsche Bibliothek**.
Die Deutsche Bibliothek lists this publication in the "Deutsche
Nationalbibliografie"; detailed bibliographic data is available
on the Internet at http://dnb.ddb.de/.

Cover design by Joni Holst

The paper in this book meets the guidelines for permanence and durability
of the Committee on Production Guidelines for Book Longevity
of the Council of Library Resources.

Peter Lang Publishing, Inc., New York
29 Broadway, 18th Floor, New York, NY 10006
www.peterlang.com

Printed in the United States of America

To Mike and Eileen

Contents

Illustrations

Figure 6.1 | 172
"The Irish Party." Edward Brown, "The Irish Party," p. 422;
Harper's New Monthly Magazine Vol. 75, Issue 447 (August 1887), pp. 496–514.
Courtesy of Cornell University Library, Making of America Digital Collection.

Foreword

The boundaries between everyday realities and idealistic otherworlds occasionally blur. These distinct spheres largely retain their precincts, but at specific junctures they collide and may even merge. Such confluences tend not to occur solely at the behest of profound change, but dramatic turning points highlight influences of romanticism, patriotism, and other intellectualized affiliations paving the way for subscription to a variety of cultural and political agendas. Such crossroads heighten connection with the symbolic and the emblematic; with the artifacts best reflecting the figments of the imagination. Although persons do not typically dwell exclusively within such realms, their motifs help elucidate the episodes and agendas under construction. The Irish men and women who undertook the serious business of creating a new home across the Atlantic employed badges of nationality to bridge two versions of their identity. Inspired variously by history, heritage, politics, and religion, the gamut of cultural association housed in the words, buildings, lapel pins, insignia[d] letterhead and banner headlines nurtured the hopes and dreams of generations as they emblazoned their transatlantic identity.

Acknowledgments

It is a pleasure to thank those whose assistance helped shape this book. The notion of tackling post-Famine Irish New York could not have moved beyond casual consideration were it not for the scrupulous direction of Margaret Susan Thompson at Syracuse University. Peggy adeptly guided me through a research process often challenging and always rewarding. I appreciate her time and attention and warmly thank her for continual encouragement then and thereafter. I am grateful to J. Scott Strickland for his insight and assistance throughout; also to David Bennett and William Stinchcombe for their helpful contributions. Other Syracuse University sages enriched the research stages more than they know; they include Daniel Field, Elisabeth Lasch-Quinn, Fred Marquardt, Peter Marsh, Michael Miller, J. Roger Sharp, and Walter Ullmann. Paul Archambault and Richard Grant proved supportive, as did Mary Lindemann at Carnegie Mellon University. My peers at Syracuse steered me from initial delusions and toward better things; for intellectual comradeship and the many instances that merit remembrance, I thank Shafiq Ahmed, Sue Bergeron, Eric Estes, Sherri Klassen, Michael L. Oberg, Vincent Puma, and Alan Willis.

Keepers of history located hidden seams and veins along the way that enriched my research. The staff at Bird Library at Syracuse University proved unfailingly patient. Christopher Cahill at the American Irish Historical Society in New York welcomed me into a mine of Irish-American riches. Then-Director Alec Ormsby deserves special mention for his interest in my work and help with research material, and I thank him most sincerely. I found AIHS staff invariably helpful, and I enjoyed fruitful conversation with fellow-travelers and Society members there. Archivists at the New York Public Library, the New York Historical Society, Columbia University, Trinity College Dublin, and the National Library of Ireland, in particular, eased a complex research process. I thank Fiona Patrick and the staff at Olin Library, Cornell University, who facilitated usage of the illustrations. I am grateful for permission to reproduce "The Irish Party," "In the Gallery at the Theater," "Walker's Pillar, Londonderry," and "Career of a Politician" from *Harper's New Monthly Magazine*, courtesy of Cornell University Library, Making of America Digital Collection. I also wish to express my thanks to the Picture Collection, The Branch Libraries, The New York Public Library, Astor, Lenox and Tilden Foundations, for permission to reproduce Image 818074: Roberts, "Favorite Investments," 1852 [print] (source, *Harper's Magazine*).

My thanks to Dean Robert Reilly for permission to quote from Friendly Sons of St. Patrick material. I am grateful to the Director of the Rare Book and Manuscript Library at Columbia University for permission to include material from the Meloney-Mitchel Papers Collection, Rare Book and Manuscript Library, Columbia University, and from the Edwin Patrick Kilroe Papers, also at the Rare Book and Manuscript Library, Columbia University. Permission granted by the American Irish Historical Society to quote from the following collections is much appreciated: The Seamas O'Brien Papers; The Irish Emigrant Society Papers; The Papers of the Society of the Friendly Sons of Saint Patrick; Rose McDermott, Diary; The Irish National Volunteers Certification; The Daniel J. Cohalan Papers; Records of the Catholic Club of the City of New York; The Jeremiah O'Donovan-Rossa Papers; and the Friends of Irish Freedom Papers. I am similarly indebted to the Curator of Manuscripts at the New-York Historical Society for permission to quote from William H. Bell, Diary, 1850–1851, The New-York Historical Society, and John Burke, Reminiscences, 1839–1891, Misc. Mss. Burke, John, The New-York Historical Society. I thank most sincerely the Librarian at the Manuscripts Department, Trinity College Library, Dublin, University of Dublin, for permission to reproduce quotations from TCD MS 9576/7 1901 Record Book, and TCD MS 9397/1485 Michael Davitt Papers. From the Office of Special Collections at the New York Public Library, I am grateful for permission to use material from John J. Sturdevant. Recollections of a Resident of New York City 1835–1905, Manuscripts and Archives Division, The New York Public Library, Astor, Lenox and Tilden Foundations; Sophie C. Hall. Diary kept during a visit to New York, 1879, Manuscripts and Archives Division, The New York Public Library, Astor, Lenox and Tilden Foundations; James Stephens Diary, 1858–1860, Manuscripts and

Archives Division, The New York Public Library, Astor, Lenox and Tilden Foundations; William Bourke Cockran Papers, Manuscripts and Archives Division, The New York Public Library, Astor, Lenox and Tilden Foundations.

Numerous individuals at Franklin Pierce College provided much-appreciated guidance and encouragement. Provost Suzanne Buckley and Dean Paul Kotila have been solicitous and motivational regarding my research interests. I am indebted to many of my colleagues at Franklin Pierce, in particular, to the Humanities Division faculty and staff who daily generate a warmhearted scholarly environment within which to teach and write. I want to express my thanks to them for continued support over several years. My colleagues in the History Department merit my specific appreciation. As a teacher and historian of distinction, Douglas Ley has inspired me since I came to Franklin Pierce. I have benefited much from his fount of erudition and his commitment to the value of good scholarship, and I owe him many thanks. I acknowledge with gratitude the encouragement and guidance of Nickolas Lupinin through several stages of the process. Thanks also to Mary Beth Connolly for her generous assistance with sources.

My introduction to history under the formidable guidance of Gearoid O'Tuathaigh, Nicholas Canny, and the late T. P. O'Neill at National University of Ireland, Galway, continues to invigorate and motivate. Since then, I thank the numerous others who played key roles in the process, including Phyllis Korper, Lisa Dillon, Ace Blair, and the staff at Peter Lang whose care in preparing the manuscript for publication is much appreciated. I also want to acknowledge the input of scholarly audiences I interacted with over the past several years concerning specific sections of the book; particularly members of the American Conference for Irish Studies. For hospitality and much support in New York and Ireland, I thank Angela Ruane-Carty, Michael Ruane, and Phyllis Ruane. Special thanks to Mairead and Roy Heaney, Nancy Rainey, and the Ruane family. I am grateful for the insight and motivation of Maire Kirrane, Canon James Kelly, and Rev. Patrick Kelly at various junctures.

In memory of Joanne Barrett, and for making me so welcome and demonstrating much-appreciated interest in my work, I wish to thank Jim Barrett and my sisters-in-law Beth, Kathy, and Lora. For quite a while now, my family in Ireland has endured my protracted academic career path and my divided attention; and the persistence of that endurance has proven remarkably valuable for me throughout. Growing up in a home crowded with books where my parents John and Kathleen Kelly prioritized the life of the mind has stood me in good stead. For their continual foundation of support I remain forever grateful. I am indebted to my sisters Eileen, Jane, and Susan Kelly and my brother James Kelly for their tremendous and unflagging encouragement, and I thank them one and all. Finally, my husband Mike

Barrett and our little daughter Eileen have journeyed alongside me and shepherded me through much of the writing process. For all manner of forbearance and cooperation, I thank them from the heart. Words fail to convey how vital Mike's luminous generosity has proven, but I hope the Dedication at least suggests the extent of my gratitude.

Mary C. Kelly

Αϐϐreviαtions

American Historical Review | AHR
American Irish Historical Society | AIHS
The Ancient Order of Hibernians | AOH
Friends of Irish Freedom | FOIF
Irish Historical Studies | IHS
The Journal of American Ethnic History | JAEH
Journal of American History | JAH
Journal of Interdisciplinary History | JIH
Metropolitan Toronto Reference Library | MTRL
National Library of Ireland | NLI
New York Historical Society | NYHS
New York Public Library | NYPL
Pamphlets in American History Series | PAH
The Protestant Friends of Ireland | PFI
Trinity College, Dublin | TCD
United Irish League | UIL
United Irish League of America | UILA

Introduction

O n February 24, 1915, New York lawyer John Quinn drafted a letter to the playwright Seamus O'Brien. Visiting from Ireland, O'Brien had written to Quinn the previous day seeking formal introductions to high-profile literary clubs and societies with Irish connections.[1] O'Brien aspired toward a series of lectures on the Irish arts patronized by affluent Gaelic-minded literati, followed by flattering press reviews celebrating his valuable contribution to the city's Irish cultural scene. In order to assure John Quinn's full comprehension of his request, O'Brien enclosed an assortment of newspaper clippings documenting past achievements and showcasing his ability to lecture publicly in the field. But the reply was surprising in its brusqueness. Quinn proved unwilling to make introductions, sponsor activities, or even meet the playwright personally. Fuming that too many visitors hounded him for this type of service, he castigated the unsuspecting O'Brien for his imposition. Still irritated eight months after the troublesome organization of a lecture tour for Dr. Douglas Hyde (later first President of Ireland) the previous summer, Quinn charged that his precious time and energy could not be spent shepherding motley contingents of Irish visitors around the halls and clubrooms of the city.

Singled out as an example of the type of visitor he respected, typically the man or woman who resisted the urge to impose on him, Padraig Colum's recent arrival for a series of poetry readings moved Quinn to note that the poet "told a common friend that he had not looked me up or called upon me during the first two or three months of his stay here, lest I might feel that he had in the back of his head that I should aid him in his lecturing or literary work." Calling Colum's restraint "a bit of tact and real consideration . . . which was not lost upon me," the lawyer expressed frustration at the speediness with which total strangers sought out his services the moment they docked into the city. His concluding thoughts were delivered without concern for the veneer of civility that often veiled stronger passions in the early twentieth century:

> Lest you may think that this letter is churlish, I may add that the demands upon my time are such that every moment of my time outside of my professional work is taken up for the winter, and that even if you were a personal friend of mine, and I had known you for years, I could not undertake to advise you as you request. I return you herewith the clippings which you ask me to return. Whether or not you may take offense at this letter, I have come to the point where I am going to write frankly. If my frankness offends you, I must endure it. Yours very truly, John Quinn.[2]

The tone here jars with popular stereotypes associated with Irish settlement in urban America. That a hectic schedule and bombardment with requests for assistance would prove annoying to prominent individuals like John Quinn may be understandable, but rejection of his compatriot flies in the face of standard depictions of the networks of cooperation and alliance broadly characteristic of the Irish-American experience. While no one expects to plumb the depths of Ireland's immigrant culture by means of a lone example, the disquieting quality of the exchange illuminates a dimension of the experience often overshadowed in the historical record. The most cursory glance through the Irish-American canon confirms as its backbone a series of stock themes involving a teeming world built on Famine escape to harsh tenement conditions, close-knit immigrant communities, and the establishment of institutions paving the road to settlement. Such themes inform most of the histories of Irish America and constitute the popular perception of the settlement.

As befitting an experience of the magnitude of the Irish exodus to America, vivid images arising from a compelling historical drama command center stage. Ranging from depictions of peasantry fleeing oppressive forces and braving the cruel Atlantic under Middle-Passage conditions to portrayals of survival within urban ghettos that seemed to damn even as they salvaged; the imagery has provoked emotional resonance over the decades. Titles like "Uprooted," "Transplanted," or "Exodus" headlining the historical scholarship exert a similar effect.[3] Dramatic power is intensified by contrasting the grimness of early settlement with the prosperity of subsequent generations.[4] But beneath the flashpoints, the basic themes have persisted. The story of close-knit communities that empowered transformation "from proletarian pioneers of the American urban ghetto to prosperous, well-educated, influential, middle-class suburbanites"[5] anchors a narrative that recently encompassed some of the more private dimensions of the immigrant psyche and the role of the Great Famine as a high-water mark.[6]

Within the field, much of value has stood the test of time. Rooted in the framework of advancement from survival to prosperity within a few generations, the Irish-American historical experience incorporates the wide spectrum of settlement from the clanging mill towns of New England to the rough-hewn streets of Butte. Within this purview, Democratic affiliation and local political involvement loom large.[7] The shadowy bosses acting out the rough-and-tumble of ward politics inculcated a sense of expanding agency, the excitement of power, and much local color into the mid-century political scene.[8] Beyond the ward-heeling world-within-a-world, another reliable stands to rival Irish-Democratic identity within the Irish-American canon. The historical powerhouse of Ireland's struggle for independence addressed via a one-label-fits-all "nationalism" rubric found expression in a plethora of outlets. Influenced by French and American Revolutionary heritage and the legacy of Wolfe Tone and later high priests of republicanism, the fate of Ireland prioritized within a variety of political agendas intertwined with the evolution of Irish-American identity throughout the nineteenth century, and particularly during the tumultuous years prior to 1921 and the establishment of the Irish Free State.[9] The competing strands agitating for the winning independence formula in key respects epitomized the nerve center of the Irish-American urban experience.[10]

Equally prominent in the narrative is the role of the Catholic Church, and no discussion of significant themes within the Irish ethnic enclave can afford to exclude the Catholic power. Under the shadow of the institution Lawrence McCaffrey called "a vast Irish spiritual empire," immigrants gained a valuable foothold in America on the strength of their parochial, clerically controlled Catholicism.[11] Despite the fact that Ireland's formalized Church administration was itself still undergoing significant reconstruction in the mid-century decades, the clear identification of "Catholic" with "Irish" rapidly achieved cornerstone status in the United States.[12] Stresses and strains notwithstanding, as McCaffrey noted, "those who complain of the intellectual limitations, the dogmatism, and peasant quality of Irish Catholicism fail to appreciate just how well it fit the United States. The Irish Catholic experience produced a dedicated, pastoral clergy, close to and respected by the people."[13] As "Devotional"-era Catholicism diffused throughout America during the later nineteenth century, the fusion of nationality and religious identification culminated in the rooting of the "Irish-Catholic" linkage as a deep-set cultural identikit. The correlation and its rapid entrenchment within the broad spectrum of American culture have long been recognized by historians as central to the Irish immigrant experience.[14]

Settlement conditions facing Irish men and women differed according to location, and case studies progressing beyond the generalized approaches have lately addressed sources and points of distinction within the narrative. As Timothy J. Meagher noted for one community, "Though Irish Americans in all parts of the country had much in common at the turn of the century, the specific environment of turn of the century Worcester clearly had a profound effect on the experience of its Irish people." The stock themes that used to depict the Irish-American "community" in a more or less standardized way are now being reworked in light of the new case studies. In some instances, the old reliables have been reconfigured to reflect localized conditions, but occasionally even replaced by radically new points of reference. "The contrast between the Butte and Worcester Irish points up, once again," Meagher summarizes, "that there was no typical Irish American experience—as the experiences of the Irish in all the other 'untypical' cities like New York, Chicago, Lowell, or Denver also make clear."[15] As one of the most prominent of the "untypical" cities, New York's post-Famine Irish culture encapsulated the distinct experience explored here in the following chapters. Different from Boston, or Chicago, Worcester or Philadelphia, or elsewhere in the United States, the identity that developed in New York certainly embodied the stock Irish-American themes while institutionalizing a powerful transatlantic cultural force. As John Quinn's curt response to Seamus O'Brien stands out as uncharacteristic of typical Irish-American practice, but helps illuminate previously shadowy depths, a closer look at the post-Famine Irish New York world beyond the usual framework of assimilation and integration reveals rich veins under explored in the history of Irish America to this point.[16]

For decades now, the relationship between immigrant and host cultures has played out meticulously underneath the "cultural-studies" umbrella.[17] Instead of "melting" into a culture of assimilation as once popularly touted, we've learned that the larger ethnic groups retained important aspects of their heritages through succeeding generations.[18] More recently, the notion that "instead of linear progression, immigrants faced a continual dynamic between economy and society, between class and culture,"[19] speaks to the Irish experience with particular relevance. As the cultural theorists increasingly emphasize, and as the chapters here reveal, New York's post-Famine Irish transported a specific heritage and created a unique identity on that basis. Mobilized by what one analyst dubbed the "ethnic pockets" constituting the putative cultural foundation, the amalgam of immigrant and host cultures in Irish New York inaugurated a transatlantic world built on a post-Famine cultural exchange.[20] The occasional theoretical testimonial can assist in our understanding of this kind of development and help document the process, especially as what Meagher describes as "useful language, to help conceptualize and explain the historical evolution of ethnic communities or groups in transition"[21] still remains elusive.

As the cultural theory parameters continue to shift impatiently, recent redirections in immigration theory and the concept of "homogenization" as a functional term can be useful. The notion of "a pluralism following racial lines, one in which class formation took place in separate melting pots,"[22] for example, helps foreground daily life and illuminates previously obscure corners of the expatriate world.[23] New York's Irish past has been rendered most visible from the vantage points of politics, religion, and education; these lenses facilitating direct entry into the settlement world.[24] The decades between the Famine and the 1920s fostered the key associations with culture-shaping cornerstones for the Irish in cities of extensive settlement such as New York and throughout North America,[25] but the recent upsurge of interest in the relationship between settlers and their native cultures, and immigrants and their homelands—the cross-cultural Atlantic currents, as it were[26]—prompts new questions about Irish New York. The nature and extent of *Ireland's* influence over Irish America, generally speaking, and Irish New York, more specifically, arise for consideration within the immigrant experience. America's Irish influx obviously transplanted the foundation stones best representative of its ethnic heritage, but histories dealing with the stock themes and their role within the settlement experience tend to explore the success of Irish institutions in terms of assimilation into their new urban contexts. The rush to pinpoint the moment of assimilation and expose the inner sanctum of American impact on the acculturation process has rendered vague and underrepresented the importance of Ireland's influence over the settlement process.

At the heart of this study, the stock social, political, economic, and religious themes underpinning traditional Irish-American history are all present, but explored as products of Ireland that powered the settlement experience during a highly significant era. The transatlantic nature of settlement underscored the force of ancestral heritage over Americanizing immigrants, a force that exerted tremendous impact during the post-Famine years. In identifying manifestations of this impact and mapping its roots and energies within the New York Irish experience, the following chapters recast the city's Irish settlement process as a dual-culture genesis and the logical outcome of the transatlantic connections that produced it.

Consideration of any dimension of Ireland's influence requires familiarity with a turbulent history dominated since the Middle Ages by a volatile relationship with England. As John Bull's Other Island, the tempestuous union between the neighbors produced Anglocentric cultural markers well entrenched by the nineteenth century and important in the transatlantic context. The 1801 Act of Union conferred new political status on Ireland's government, law and land ownership, and these cross-cultural connections survived Atlantic passage to reemerge within Irish America.[27] Similarly, Britain represented "the dominant focus for the Irish export effort" within pre-Famine economic development, and other dimensions of critical influence rose within the expanding commercial base of Belfast and the administrative locus in Dublin. These emerged in response to population and industrial growth, but more directly as a result of Ireland's new role within Great Britain to subsequently resurface in Irish New York.[28] Chief Secretary during the formative years of the Union, Robert Peel worked to transform a complex set of social, political, and economic conditions into as strong a foundation for British administration in Ireland as could be expected in the post-Penal era.[29]

The Anglo-Irish cultural fusion produced the "association of ideas," in the words of Patrick O'Sullivan, operating between British and Irish cultures that co-existed uneasily alongside the set of deep-rooted political traditions commonly called "nationalist."[30] The conflicting elements within this diverse and diffuse heritage played a key role in the creation of the New York Irish identity, as we shall see.[31] Over the centuries, the variety of subaffiliations bedeviling Irish identity directed the course of her evolution, most prominently Native Irish (or fior-Gaelic), Anglo-Irish, English, and Scots-Irish, to subsequently affect the formation of the new urban identity in the world's most cosmopolitan city. Given such a backdrop, the application of "homogenization" theories within the New York Irish context should be carefully broached.[32] Within the city characterized as a place "of turbulence and venality" in the post-Famine decades, rather than a specious and misplaced notion of Irish "homogenization," the following chapters explore a complex settlement process deriving from a multifaceted heritage.[33]

The creation of a hybrid culture distinct to New York also raises the issue of the omnipresent "Irish-American" character. As Meagher and others point out, a precise definition still awaits us. In the meantime, recognition that one all-encompassing phrase may not suffice to cover the multifaceted Irish-American profile seems more pertinent. The formation of the hyphenated identity included such a large range of Ireland's influences typically overshadowed by the Catholic/Democratic umbrella, for example, that one definition or even one study cannot hope to address all of them. As a cog in that larger wheel, the hybrid New York Irish culture offers valuable insight into that panorama. For example, the argument that class distinction affected the settlement experience is not new, but the extent to which Ireland's class structure affected the New York settlement process remains vague.[34] We may be familiar with integration of domestic servants into American culture on the strength of urban labor shortages, to take another example, but we're less well acquainted with the role of domestic servants themselves in the preservation of their native heritage. Likewise, the skilled workers, enterprising merchants, and shopkeepers that ascended the lower rungs of city commercial life and helped forge a new middle class in the process suffused another dimension of Ireland's cultural baggage into the new settlement experience. More generally, what we might call Irish "intellectual capital" generated in New York reflected much about its origins, transporters, and the connections with the new urban American context. As the various representations of Ireland's heritage materializing in New York are examined here, the understanding of a new post-Famine Irish-American identity emerges as a product of a transatlantic process highly visible between the 1840s and 1921.

Illuminating obscure layers and uncovering less visible strands accomplishes more than just mapping a settlement process. Understanding the development of a culture that was not fully American but no longer Irish, intrinsically bound up with the city culture that produced it but a product of and continually fed by the well-spring of Ireland, empowers our understanding of a vital stage in the creation of a unique identity, and establishes Ireland's history and culture as perhaps *the* key force behind post-Famine New York settlement.[35] A quarter million Catholic and Protestant immigrants transported a wide variety of cultural affinities and identifications across the Atlantic, some more influential than others.[36] To this end, the themes of gender, religion, the arts and politics have been chosen as lenses through which to explore the influence of the ancestral homeland over the formation of the Irish-New York character. The role of immigrant women, for example, has been buried under generalized treatments of male settlement for years, and scholarly treatment of women's experience rarely transcends stereotypical depictions of impoverished colleens flocking into domestic service or education. Evidence for New York in the second chapter demonstrates that Ireland's female contingent maintained traditional sociocultural practices during settlement. They wrote publicly and privately, politicized toward the goal of Irish independence, and played a vital role in amalgamating their heritage within the city culture they settled into.

The very notion of Irish-American Protestant settlement summons up images of excavations in lost civilizations! To date, our understanding of this immigrant tradition rests on reasonable success on the topic of Colonial Scots-Irish and Presbyterian frontier culture. Historians have only recently engaged in a conscious effort to raise Protestant consciousness, as it were, highlighting the issue of Irish Protestant underrepresentation within the American experience.[37] Urban Protestant America remains largely undocumented, despite the uncomfortable awareness that upwards of one-third of the total influx from Ireland subscribed to this religious affiliation. Addressing the underrepresentation of this grouping in the record, the third chapter sheds light on a major component of Irish city settlement. As in Ireland, a vibrant Protestant New York culture harbored both conflict and community, often under the strangest of circumstances, reflected traditional alignments particular to Ireland's past, played its own role in the road to Ireland's independence, and merits full inclusion within the acculturation process.

Irish writing showcasing the day-to-day business of establishing in a new city stubbornly fixated on the land the authors left behind. The rhetoric of a motley assortment of politicians, journalists, and poets exposed an extraordinary degree of identification with and remembrance of its place of origin, providing the fourth chapter's focus and another vital mechanism of contribution to the new identity.[38] This material is useful as a means of mirror-imaging Ireland's culture in the post-Famine, pre-Independence decades. In tandem with specific organizations examined in the final chapter, politically charged "texts" reveal so much about the Irish mentality during these years they deserve special attention as a major fount of transatlantic connection. That same connection spawned a variety of terms describing the process of leaving home to establish a new life in a new land. Consideration of sometimes congruent but often disparate meanings behind the commonly cited "emigration" and "exile" arises perhaps most directly in the fourth and sixth chapters. As we ascribe these terms variously to classes of people, individuals, time-specific incidences and organizations, to aim for what Patrick Ward characterized a "critical method" centering on "the context out of which the text is produced" makes sense. His insistence on "relating authorship to time, place, prevalent discourses, available forms, codes, conventions, audiences, omissions and representations" aids in the creation of historical representation inclusive of the myriad attitudes, perspectives, inflexions; the broad panoply that made up Irish culture and what we might call its New York branch.[39]

Within that panoply, the theme of religion and its cultural foundation surely merits our attention. The sudden Catholic upsurge into a Protestant-dominated nation during the Famine years altered not only Irish visibility within that milieu, but challenged notions of hegemony, mainstream, and assimilation within American society in fundamental ways.[40] Notwithstanding the significance of the influx and its repercussions, sizable issues overshadow the field for chroniclers of Irish-American Catholicism. Lamenting the lack of intellectual focus, to take an example, Colleen McDannell summarized:

> If the Irish are to American Catholicism what the Puritans are to American Protestantism, why the paucity of historical studies? Why is there no tradition of studies on Irish American Catholicism that can be challenged and revised by new scholarship? One of the reasons is that, unlike the Puritans, the Irish did not feel compelled to write down their spiritual trials and triumphs. While the Irish went to mass, sodality meetings, and parish schools, they did not put pen to paper and detail their feelings about Catholic life. Little is known about how they felt going to confession or challenging the authority of the parish priest. If such reflections were written down, they have not been preserved in libraries and archives.[41]

Despite such problems, the development of parishes, hierarchy, and Catholic-sponsored social welfare and educational institutions has been well documented,[42] but claims that American Catholicism "was nowhere wholly Irish" challenges long-held equations of "Irish" with "Catholic." Likewise, the view that "enormous Irish aggregates, as in New York City and Boston, seem to have promoted religious complacency, diminished Mass-going rates, and led a majority to identify with public rather than parochial schools" incorporates a new conceptualization of the relationship. Warnings such as David Doyle's conclusion that "those . . . who see catholicism as the collective manifestation of Irish ethnicity are wide of the mark,"[43] and Hugh McLeod's opinion that immigrants did not subscribe to a uniform brand of institutionalized Catholicism in New York build a case for the argument that the "equation . . . Irish-Catholic-Democrat" did not play out nearly as neatly as popularly thought.[44]

Despite these caveats, most would concede that clerical influence remained important in the creation of Irish-Catholic urban identification and served to empower the faithful in a number of respects. "In 1842 the Irish-born John Hughes had become Bishop of New York, and in 1850 he became the first Archbishop," McLeod confirms, continuing that "every one of his successors, down to O'Connor at the present day, has been Irish by birth or descent."[45] Decades ago, Glazer and Moynihan posited that Irish influence over the American Catholic church remained "incomparably the most important thing they have done in America," but at a cost, as they affirmed. Revenue that might have established the trappings of an Irish middle-class culture instead poured directly into Church coffers. Increasing Church influence effectively compromised socioeconomic development and "the celibacy of the Catholic clergy . . . deprived the Irish of the class of ministers' sons which has contributed notably to the prosperity and distinction of the Protestant world."[46] Many contemporary Catholics of Irish birth in New York enjoyed a significant degree of success by secular standards, however. The influence of traditional religious affiliation over their expanding immigrant culture comprises an absorbing dimension of the emerging Irish city identity, as we see in the fifth chapter.

The bewildering array of political affiliations under the "nationalist" umbrella transplanted directly from the home country commanded elevated attention for contemporaries. The more prominent organizations under the spotlight in the sixth chapter ascended within a fragmented political world, drawing sustenance and gaining ground from the tumultuous course of events across the Atlantic that led to the creation of the new independent Ireland. The Fenians, Clan na Gael, the Land League, Cumann na mBan, the United Irish League, and other high-profile groupings professing righteous independence-minded agendas of one kind or another illuminate a tremendously variegated political culture. Rising out of the politicizations identified in the fourth chapter, the parade of organizations active during the late nineteenth and early twentieth centuries framed an American-based representation of Ireland's volatile progress to independence. As the sixth chapter illustrates, this representation contributed enormously to the New York Irish identity under construction during these years.[47]

In essence, the chapters that follow do not constitute local history. Notwithstanding occasional forays into the daily grind of the ambitious laborer or the lavish style of the successful professional, the aim here is not to produce a street-level window into post-Famine Irish city life. Nor can this work be dubbed narrative history in the usual sense of the term. But what has been described as Irish "compulsive narrativity" connects the focus points and the themes of the chapters and reinforces an overarching component of settlement. Candice Ward's emphasis on a "compulsive narrativity, whether in ballad or story but always to lunatic proportions—a drive not just to narrativize, but to allegorize, thematize, mythologize" played out in distinct patterns in post-Famine settlement.[48] Within the sphere of intellectual history, for the most part, the following chapters map an Irish "narrativity" built on a native heritage, the forces at work in the new urban context, and the role of Ireland's independence in New York through the post-Famine decades.

Rather than tracing the lives of individuals from dockside to lace-curtained affluence, or concentrating merely on the opportunities greeting immigrant sons and daughters of Erin, the themes explored here act as lenses through which to view the vital social, cultural, and political transplantations empowering the New York Irish to sustain their heritage. Peter Quinn's re-creation of the smells and sounds and the push and jostle of the mid-century metropolis and Terry Golway's reconstruction of the emotions and passions echoing through the offices of Devoy and O'Mahony bring the textures of the contemporary experience to life, not to mention recent interest in the bloody machinations of Lower Manhattan's antebellum gangs.[49] Kevin Kenny has made real progress in merging the immigrant narrative into *its own* historical context; mapping the narrative onto the contemporary history of Ireland, and reconfiguring some of the older history in so doing. Reference to "episode[s] in Irish transatlantic history" and the linking of influential progressions between the old home and the adopted one such that they can be understood more fully has resulted in a comprehensive and nuanced re-reading of the Irish-American experience.[50] More recently, emphasizing the recovery of Ireland's Protestant settlement within the Irish-American experience, Kenny continues to view the relationship with Ireland as a vital context within which to explore the history of Irish arrival and settlement in the United States. As he points out, much has been accomplished to date, but much is yet outstanding in an area that continues to generate questions of significance for the broader history of America in general.[51]

The building blocks accumulate, then, for the multilayered narrative of Irish-America that took root in cities like New York. But in this particular urban context, revealing aspects of the immigrant world often obscured by the hubbub of streets and tenements and by the expansive personalities that rose to the fore—the less tangible dimensions of the experience, as it were—expands our understanding of a complex process beyond the more obvious landmarks and parameters. Within the realm of the less physical and the less corporeal we find the ideologies and creeds underpinning the daily lives of settlers. Literature and rhetoric articulated publicly and privately, organizational missions and informal expressions, the strident pages of the daily and weekly press, and the arguments emanating from popular pamphleteering and weightier output collectively reveal the essence of the new culture. In effect, the intellectual history of Irish New York invites us into the settlement process and its less visible aspects. As the focus of this study, the transatlantic connections encompassed the more obvious acculturation landmarks set against their points of origin at home.

Access to this realm demands crossing historiographical boundaries, delving into the cultural and intellectual history of our immigrant community to reveal Ireland's patterns of influence and the key points of transition along the road to the new identity. As such, this study is synthetic in nature, utilizing primary material to support the solid foundation of the Irish-American canon. Familiarity with the scholarship and close acquaintance with Ireland's history from the battle of the Boyne to the Treaty (and before and after those sacrosanct milestones) constitute prerequisites for identifying and assessing Ireland's influence in New York, such that much in the way of prior knowledge in these fields is assumed throughout the chapters that follow. Data on the Irish-American and New York Irish experience, most prominently settlement statistics, employment opportunities, political affiliations, and religious practices that are available in existing scholarship are cited as such throughout to avoid unnecessary repetition. The broad settlement patterns and major turning points are treated prominently enough in the existing scholarship that brief introductions and references will suffice, notwithstanding the occasional foray to include inflections and nuances that affected the experience in significant ways. The achievements of Daniel O'Connell, the intensity of the Land War, the convolutions of Home Rule and 1916; such allusions form the bedrock of Ireland's historical progression that traveled beyond the native shores to exert a major impact in Irish New York.

Reliance on what may be termed *settlement axioms* informs this work. First, the strong Irish city press readership that sustained through the nineteenth century certainly played a vital role in the creation of Irish New York. Second, the influence of prominent politicians and contemporary commentators, together with the impact of the popular political organizations, affected the construction of the city's Irish political culture to a visible and important degree. Thirdly, the course of general Irish arrival and struggle against a multitude of socioeconomic and socio-political forces has been well recovered within the Irish-American canon, and this study builds on that foundation to explore the less public spaces within the post-Famine decades. Finally, although Patrick Ward's concern for specificity in usage of such terms as emigrant, exile, and expatriate within the host-nation is well founded, and suggests a number of options for the chapters that follow, the opportunity to allow the "texts" to elucidate the context serves to maximize sensitivity to the more shadowy aspects of the settlement. While a heavily theoretically based approach may hold value, a one-theory-fits-all model risks losing contemporary meaning and shades of reference. While the term "emigrant" applied more or less universally to those leaving Ireland, "exile" imposes a political agenda while inviting artistic and inventive associations sometimes relevant, sometimes not. Thus, the chapters that follow do not so much "take the term at its face value," as Ward fears in the case of expressions like "exile," as use contemporary evidence as the jumping-off point for a variety of different idioms.[52]

Amounting to a history exploring the intellectual and cultural capital reflective of origins in Ireland, this approach views post-Famine Irish-American immigration within a methodological framework both inclusive of and appropriate to the history, while engaging with the ubiquitous narrativity throughout. R. F. Foster has recognized the omnipresence of the national storyline in what he terms "the compelling notion of a Story of Ireland, with plot, narrative logic and desired outcome," calculating that such a conception "reached its apogee in the later nineteenth century."[53] By the same token, the study here is not the Story of Irish New York, replete with "plot, narrative logic and desired outcome," but the chapters that follow do invoke some of the requisite components of such a Story. The intellectual proclivities of the post-Famine immigrants may have included a tidy, romanticized vision of a contemporary world, but the forces exerted by two of the most tumultuous historical progressions imaginable; riotous nineteenth-century Ireland and the expansion of the most cosmopolitan city in the world rendered that vision ambitious, at best. The confluence of these progressions as expressed by the New York Irish created not the Story of the New York Irish but a fragmented, disjoint world that directly reflected the one they left behind.

Lastly, the pressures exerted by Ireland's history both illuminate and complicate the rich new identity generated out of the ashes of centuries of struggle, and to search merely for Irish "community" in New York obscures the complexity of a culture sustaining as much from the old as it co-opted from the new. On the topic of the Brian Friel play "*Making History*," Declan Kiberd wrote "there can be no single History, only a plurality of self-interested histories, each composed at the mercy of its own moment of creation and at the mercy also of the literary form in which it is encased."[54] Through the intellectual world transported by "the Irish plurality" and the forces that affected it, we can map the course of the new representative identity. The discourse mapped here contains enough of Ireland's "literary form" and New York's "moment of creation" to render it worthy of attention.

Shaping the Presence

THE TRANSATLANTIC WORLD
OF POST-FAMINE IRISH NEW YORK

Dreams of prosperity tempered with shadows of apprehension beckoned daily to shiploads of mid–nineteenth-century arrivals, lending the grand metropolis of New York an exciting and speculative air. But not every hopeful encountered the city in the same way. The view from under the peaks of Irish tweed caps presented a different prospect to that greeting English or German immigrants confronting the clamor of the dockside scene for the first time. Even as Ireland's newcomers landed into the harbor side frenzy intent on deploying either basic laboring or more sophisticated artisan skills, some were comforted by the thought of a small capital sum tucked safely away while others could plan no further than escape the specter of famine, half deadened as they were by the anguish left behind and the misery of a journey barely survived. The opportunities greeting the sons and daughters of Mayo, Galway, Clare, and Kerry along the thronging thoroughfares of Lower Manhattan spanned as broad a spectrum as the range of individuals preparing to avail of them. The variety of educational and labor proficiencies facilitating competition with assorted Northern Europeans and the sprinkling of other nationalities exerting ethnic-based influence within the greater New York area also spanned a diverse spectrum. As the specter of nativism loomed about them, Ireland's men and women transported a dynamic culture across the Atlantic to set the scene for the evolution of a unique city identity. This chapter maps out the parameters of mid-century settlement and highlights some of the more significant social, cultural, and political transplantations as the foundation of the New York Irish immigrant movement and the basis of a new nineteenth-century Atlantic World.

The origins of Famine-era Irish identity may be traced back to the colonial foundations of the city; the New Amsterdam that hosted immigrant influxes dating from the late seventeenth century. At the forefront of the movement, Ulster Presbyterians successfully ingrained what came to be characterized as their Scots-Irish culture throughout the Colonial world, exerting an enduring impact in the process. Descendants of those Scots making the northernmost Irish counties their home during the 1600s, the steady stream of Ulster migrants settled reasonably well into the rapidly Anglicizing region; more readily than the much smaller contingents of Catholic compatriots taking advantage of similar opportunities to move to the Colonies. As networks of Anglican and Dutch Reformed congregations expanded into rising Colonial powers, English merchants profiteering from trading partnerships made their presence felt. Extending out from Western Europe into the Caribbean within an earlier Atlantic World context, mercantile-driven advancement through the northern colonies gave rise to tensions over control of land and church property among assorted Dutch, German, and English neighbors. Such episodes did not, however, threaten the Northern European Protestant foundation or prevent English-speaking, non-Catholic Scots-Irish from prospering within New York's expanding commercial realm, but rather strengthened WASPish culture as the cornerstone of the Colonial world.[1] Successful acclimatization within a secure milieu established the Ulster Presbyterian tradition as the most obvious Irish cultural representation during the eighteenth century and even into the nineteenth.[2] Slight confusion may have set in during the annual Saint Patrick's Day parade on the streets of old New York, as the saint credited with the Emerald Isle's Catholic tradition was ecumenically feted by groups of cheery Presbyterians![3]

But the faded names on the tombstones outside Trinity and Saint Paul's churches of Lower Broadway in Manhattan authenticate a noteworthy degree of diversity in the makeup of early Irish arrival. Although Trinity had been founded in 1696 as an Episcopalian house of worship, Protestants of different denominational affiliations and even a smattering of Catholics buried side by side testify to a multidimensional Irish presence by the post-Revolution decade. Cross-referencing names with early commercial and trading records tells us that a large percentage of those buried left Ireland for the long voyage to the still-New World in the 1790s just prior to the 1798 Rebellion and the atmosphere of oppression permeating the Penal-era decades.[4] Including struggling smallholders and prosperous entrepreneurs, these individuals rarely fled destitution. On the contrary, according to the ever-optimistic Michael O'Brien, "while it is probable that most of the Irish who came to New York in the eighteenth century were of the laboring and artisan class, yet . . . it is seen that many of them rose above their original status and ranked with the substantial business men of the City."[5] Streets on the verge of degenerating into the teeming slums of later decades provided shelter for less skilled emigrants. As was the case in London, Liverpool and the major European ports, waterfront areas attracting contingents of men and women seeking fortunes in opportunities ranging from the legal and legitimate to the questionable and dangerous grew increasingly accustomed to the soft lilt of the more southern counties mixed in with the distinct inflections of arrivals from Ulster and western Connaught. Locating precariously in the soon-to-be notorious Bowery, Tombs, and Five Points districts, poorer Irish sporting a variety of accents and denominational persuasions poured into the area subsequently developed as Central Park. Those that so desired did not have to venture too far to earn a steady wage, as the shortage of skilled and unskilled labor accompanying the ending of the Revolution facilitated employment needs in a timely manner.[6]

The expansion of the early Republic proved fruitful for the motley assortment seeking to improve prospects beyond their old lives across the Atlantic.[7] By now exuding the atmosphere of a thriving port, New York attracted upwards of 25,000 (or around 25% of the city population) to inaugurate a solid Irish presence during the decades prior to the Famine. The steady increase in the numbers of Catholics arriving during the Era of Good Feelings and Jacksonian years did not go unnoticed within the communities of Presbyterians and Anglicans generally comfortably engaged in industrious enterprise. As the newcomers sought out and established points of contact, competing religious and political traditions generated friction from time to time, with outbreaks occurring more visibly and more regularly as the decades passed. Parades and church activities tended to pass off cordially, for the most part, but occasional outbursts of violence in Greenwich Village and on the Lower East Side streets between Ulster Orangemen and Catholics made for florid headlines in the city press.[8] The potential for more serious sectarian-based confrontation, in many respects reminiscent of home, lay dormant as the denominationally based traditions settled into their new environment; too fragile yet to generate much intensity and caught up in the vitality of early national Jacksonian expansion. The probability of direct conflict would lock in rapidly during the years of the Famine and through the Civil War—instigated Draft Riots, but in the meantime, anti-Whig affiliations flowering into Tammany connections by the early 1840s prepared the ground for the intensification of strains between cultural traditions entrenched within a historically adversarial relationship.

Arguably, the settlement process might have continued along the lines of steady expansion and relatively harmonious relations were it not for the dramatic events of the later 1840s. Up to that point, the cosmopolitan city environment facilitated rising prosperity levels, regardless of religious affiliation. The 1830s brought the rise of New York as the principal gateway to the nation, rivaling Canadian ports and superseding them over the next decade. Escalation in immigrant traffic resulted in cheaper fares too, further expanding New York's potential as the ideal port of entry.[9] For the Irish, early inroads into education and welfare and the imprint of ward heeling had already begun to take effect, especially for the poorer elements, but the cataclysmic turn of the late 1840s imposed a new urgency on the expanded settlement. Prior complacency faded as attitudes of fear and evidence of condemnation of Catholicism rose to the fore.[10] As the stream of men and women escaping the earliest outbreak of famine in later 1845 increased to an alarming floodtide within the year, the city struggled against the force which changed forever the character of Irish New York.

Through the late 1840s and into the next decade, the cobbled streets and swarming tenements threw a lifeline to the lucky ones. Literally landing into the melee of the dockside, a decade before formalized immigrant regulation was introduced, tenants and cottiers from Achill, Connemara, Beara, and the host of hardest-hit townlands reduced to utter devastation by Black '47 arrived by the thousand, fleeing the hunger wrought by failure of their sole source of nutrition. Escaping the disease-ridden cabins, avoiding England's feverish industrial cities, and hoping to survive the prolonged horror of the coffin ships ranked as the only priorities for these arrivals. They docked into a haven of sorts, a landfall that foisted a miserable struggle on them as the floodtide overwhelmed native New Yorkers striving to cope with the onslaught.[11] From 1847 through the next decade, the peak years of starvation drove some 848,000 Irish men and women onto the death-carrying armada bound for the harbor. Of this number, between 133,000 to upward of a quarter million remained in Manhattan and Brooklyn to struggle with the next stage of survival. As Kevin Kenny made the comparison, "one in every four residents of Manhattan in 1860 had been born in Ireland, one in every six in Germany."[12] As the starkness of mass death imbued the 1840s and 1850s with imagery that would overshadow Irish New York well into the next century, ideas of exile fused with the reality of emigration within what Patrick Ward described as "a circular, transatlantic justification, rationale and explanation for migration." Cemented by a political agenda accruing from that rationale and strong enough to influence settlement well into the next century, Famine memory locked Irish New York and Irish America in general into the kind of entrenched mindset difficult to challenge and all but impossible to avoid within the Irish-American worldview.[13]

Unable to foresee the course of events ahead, and witnessing but the start of a powerful episode underscored with the kind of Malthusian reverberations their readers avidly consumed, city editors vied to update readers during the summer and autumn of 1845. As reports of a puzzling potato failure intensified from a faraway curiosity into a strident outcry, the indicators of national disaster became more apparent every day.[14] That the publicity stoked tremors of already latent nativist hostility is hardly surprising. WASPish ill feeling escalated daily with the spectacle of what looked like a plague of emaciated foreigners descending into the lower recesses of the city. If Catholicism had posed a theoretical threat to American freedoms in the eyes of English and Dutch colonial descendants safely ensconced beyond the wretched Lower Manhattan warrens, then the springtide of Famine escapees seemed to logically confirm the evils of Roman authority for subsequent generations of city dwellers. "The shrill anti-Catholicism"[15] of the Great Hunger years obliterated the relatively harmonious nature of early national settlement and rendered the newcomers particularly vulnerable to the kind of hostility exacerbated by the Know Nothings during the 1850s. Although the Famine is traditionally cited as the fountainhead of the nineteenth-century emigration tide, the tense political climate in 1850's Ireland drove thousands more smallholders and landless laborers onto ships bound for New York. Political measures designed to maximize agricultural development effectively devastated the class of people subsisting most precariously in the worst-hit provinces of Connaught and Munster, and immigration rates soared even during periods of relative prosperity for other sectors of the population in the more stable Ulster and Leinster provinces. Not unexpectedly, these conditions received a great deal of attention stateside as the flood appeared destined to continue through yet another decade.[16] As the Famine inundation worked to extinguish the memory of relatively compliant Scots-Irish and low-profile Catholic strains in earlier times, an unwelcome upheaval in a once tolerant city created a foundation for a new and more problematic Irish identity.

The New York reaction included a comprehensive response to Famine conditions across the Atlantic. American relief efforts have been described as "erratic," but the private donations, city- and state-sponsored fundraising and corporate collecting that outfitted ships with badly needed provisions and donations undoubtedly alleviated much distress.[17] Assistance continued to pour in up through the later decades of the century. As news from Ireland in the years after the cataclysmic events told of crop devastation recurring with depressing regularity, influential benefactors paid attention. Sufficiently moved by word of economic hardship during the 1870s, for example, Gilded Age Vice-President Levi Parsons Morton became involved in a series of charitable enterprises as he publicized broader concerns with foreign immigration issues.[18] In March 1880, a *New York Herald* report on Ireland's condition characterized the provisioning of a ship for the mitigation of persistent crop failure as the work of "a distinguished citizen of New York." The philanthropist undertook to supply one quarter of the cargo of flour, seed potatoes, and oatmeal on the ship *The Constellation* if the balance could be collected from other city sources, and the anonymous patron wished to transport the goods in time for seasonal planting in late Spring 1880 with a view toward more than a temporary remedy. Levi Morton's contribution eventually amounted to more than 800 barrels of meal loaded onto the brig *The Constellation* berthed at the Brooklyn Navy yard.[19] "The perishing Irish poor" received these foodstuffs in the timeliest manner possible, thanks to the benevolence of Morton and the *New York Herald* in putting up another one-quarter of the cargo. In soliciting contributions, the paper reminded readers of the wretched conditions prevailing in Ireland over previous decades, lest they forget the extraordinary levels of misery wrought by the Great Famine. These reports elicited the anticipated response; business proprietors on Sixth Avenue and others including, unsurprisingly, Mayor William R. Grace, offering substantial sums. Various dry goods purveyors allocated such large consignments of seed potatoes, "barrels of pork and beef, and hogsheads of molasses" that a second ship needed to be immediately outfitted. A view of the loading process conveyed the dockside atmosphere prior to *The Constellation*'s departure. Barrels bearing the label "Potatoes For The Irish Sufferers" found their way on board without the customary receipts changing hands, as the *Herald* observed:

> A bystander remarked it showed how much faith some good man had in the integrity of the ship's officers, that he did not even want a receipt for his gift. He must have been an Irishman, for on the bottom head of each barrel he had written "for the County Cavan" . . . it was considered a singular fact that the first "mite" of the cargo to be put on the great ship should be from an unknown source . . . even the Italian and Spanish sailors who ornamented the foreign vessels of the neighborhood gazed on the barge-loading spectacle with friendly interest.

The Duke of Edinburgh and the Duchess of Marlborough presided over the allocation of these consignments following disembarkation in Dublin, later celebrating the charitable efforts with a ball in the official residence of the Lord Mayor.[20]

The press reports and eyewitness accounts that kept Ireland's horrific conditions in the news sustained city interest in the terrible course of the Famine and its aftermath. The reports also foregrounded a negative reception toward survivors' intent on eking out a new subsistence in New York. That many escapees arrived unskilled with little or no prior experience in paid service or labor made for dramatic reading during the Famine years and beyond. The impression of immigrants moving in tandem from a "context of enforced idleness"[21] in Ireland to paid employment in domestic servitude and laboring in American cities holds a degree of truth, but the transition was neither automatic nor uniform. A large percentage did gravitate toward domestic servitude and paid labor, but alternative patterns of employment existed for those who could take advantage of them. Information on the opportunities available in cities like New York may have peppered the pages of Ireland's provincial newspapers during the Famine decade and thereafter, and did, by all accounts, but the personal testimonies received directly into thousands of hearth-sides in the form of emigrants' letters mobilized more men and women to emigrate than other forms of enticement or endorsement. But this is not to say that the letters home painted a glittering picture of life across the Atlantic. Many, if not the majority, described an experience less paved with gold than very often challenging and occasionally miserable. As Kerby Miller and Bruce Boling documented, the unusual situation developed whereby a mythology surrounding the move to America that co-existed alongside a more realistic vision of what lay ahead steadily entrenched as time went on. As economic conditions at home worsened, and the people looked in vain for a new incarnation of Daniel O'Connell to deliver them from the constrictions of the Act of Union and the ills of landlordism, the lure of the United States took on enhanced significance.[22]

That the city offered tangible opportunities for Irish men and women hailing from a class-stratified background, prepared to leave behind much of the mythology and face the reality of struggle, there is little doubt.[23] For immigrants such as Jerry McAuley, the streets of New York promised a heady mix of education and opportunity, in many respects resembling those he left behind in an expanding mid-century Dublin. Arriving in the 1850s, McAuley hailed from a family background in Dublin most likely Protestant, despite the efforts of his grandmother, a "devout Romanist," to influence his spiritual upbringing. Jerry remarked, "many's the time when she was tellin' her beads an' kissing the floor for penance." Instead of following her lead, he would "shy things at her just to hear her curse an' swear at me, an' then she'd back to her knees." The illiterate son of a convicted counterfeiter had abandoned his less than salubrious home life for a new start abroad by the time he reached thirteen.[24]

Soon after arriving in New York, McAuley's move from the modest home of his sister on the Lower West Side to a den on Water Street bore the hallmark of the itinerant adventurer. Failure as a prizefighter while languishing in the Fourth Ward quickly collapsed him further into his dockside underworld of petty crime. With the aid of a boat, his time as a portside dealer in stolen property and smuggled goods halted at the age of nineteen with a spell in Sing Sing prison, sentenced to fifteen years for a crime he denied committing. Time spent reading novels and carpet-weaving failed to reform him, but five years' incarceration wrought success in the shape of a religious revival that eventually turned him around. The advice of a fellow inmate named Orville Gardner, rather than the influence of any particular version of the bible, finally stirred McAuley. Gardner had been a notorious Five Points thug, but religious ardor empowered him to set a positive example to fellow inmates. The Jerry McAuley released after serving a total of seven years and six months at first bore little resemblance to the man originally jailed. Returning to Manhattan in the early 1860s and avoiding the Fourth Ward in an effort to reconstitute his life, he embarked on a series of moneymaking enterprises, including the following:

> I got work in a hat-shop, an' had good wages, but a strike come, an' I led it an' lost the place. It was war time, an' I went into the bounty business—a rascally business too. Then I had a boat on the river again. I'd buy stolen goods off the sailors, an' then make 'em enlist for fear o' bein' arrested, an' I took the bounty. The end o' the war stopped this, an' then I stuck to the river, buyin' and sellin' smuggled goods an' payin' all I could in counterfeit money.

With the help of a member of the Howard Street Mission, McAuley finally broke with the life of crime and left the docks to establish the Water Street Mission inspired by his vision of a refuge for the Fourth Ward homeless. He and his wife took over "an old rookery of a house, in one room, an' a little sign hung out" for the saving of souls. With the provision of a bath, the process of salvation commenced as he "washed 'em outside, an' the Lord washed 'em inside . . . [and] from that day to this . . . there's been a meetin' every night in the year, an' now it's hundreds—yes, thousands—that can say the Water Street Mission was their help to a new life." Many more reaped the benefit of his next project, a new Mission at Cremorne Garden on Thirty-Second Street. Dwellers here did not subsist in such dire need as residents of the Five Points or the Bowery, but McAuley's experience allowed him heightened awareness of levels of extreme poverty his fellow missionaries lacked and he feared the dangers ahead for those subsisting dangerously close to degeneracy. Known by this time as "the apostle to the drunkard and the outcast," he opened the Cremorne Mission and ran it until his death at the age of forty-five. His funeral at the Broadway Tabernacle was "thronged" with "hundreds . . . unable to obtain entrance" to the ceremony. Following his death, a "Tablet to the Memory of Jerry McAuley" erected on the Water Street Mission wall read: "In Loving Memory of Jerry McAuley, Founder of this Mission. He Rests from his Labors and his Works Follow Him. 'Where I am, there shall also my servant be.' John XII.26."[25]

Jerry McAuley's colorful life story incorporates stock themes associated with mid-century urban Irish settlement. Poor, unschooled, involved in varieties of illegal ventures, his localized entrepreneurship and attempts at labor leadership sound a familiar ring.[26] However, his detachment from three cornerstones in the history of America's Irish, namely Catholicism, Famine immigration, and rural upbringing reconfigures traditional depictions to include aspects of Ireland's culture previously overshadowed within the American settlement experience. His case introduces the type of emigrant who did not conform to the stock characteristics commonly attributed to Irish settlers. As McAuley's history in New York played out as a virtual continuation of his life in Dublin; a man born into the lower echelons of society, excluded from privilege and power and easy prey to a life of crime in New York in the same manner his father experienced at home, his story illuminates connectors between host and native cultures. Dublin's class parameters operated along similar lines to New York's during the mid-century decades. In a time of socioeconomic flux on both sides of the Atlantic, class boundaries experienced limited degrees of flexibility in response to changing economic circumstances, with the emerging middling class standing to gain most ground. As a new element rising to compete with the established and generally prosperous Protestant business classes in mid-century Dublin, Belfast, and Cork, increasing numbers of Catholic commercial proprietors and professionals achieved prominence within a few short decades. Such advancement had germinated in the later 1700s with the relaxation of some of the harsher Penal Laws that restricted a class of Catholics once prosperous and propertied. Allegiance to the monarchy in return for freedom to practice their religion proved acceptable to collectives Maureen Wall described as "the rising catholic middle class of the towns."[27] Relict of the old Gaelic families retaining the memory of provincial affluence and influence, their descendants mobilized through the late 1700s and early 1800s toward the goal of a Catholic emancipation that withdrew many of the strictures barring their progress. A few decades later, the "Catholic urban middle class" achieved prominence as a political constituency with powerful potential.[28] Irish towns and cities such as Limerick, Waterford, and Cork showcased middle-class progress within new neighborhoods beyond the teeming slums but as yet distanced from the stately streetscapes of the privileged.[29]

Logically, the more prosperous middling immigrants found New York much easier to navigate than unaffiliated individuals like McAuley. But even for those yet to attain the trappings of prosperity, economic advancement occurred in what may be described as steady fashion on the lower rungs of the commercial ladder for the Irish creating loosely configured communities in Lower Manhattan. As thousands of Irish women entered the much-vaunted halls and corridors of household service,[30] others took advantage of commercial opportunities emerging in the downtown neighborhoods. The lower thoroughfare's mid-century jumble of stalls and small markets provided a useful stopgap for unaffiliated men and women in the initial stages of entry into the business world, selling every type of household goods, groceries, and apparel.[31] Neither vastly impoverished nor thriving sufficiently to establish in more reputable streets and neighborhoods, many of them unencumbered by trading licenses and operating illegally, these proprietors conducted steady business despite regular (and unscheduled) visits from city authorities. In 1851, for instance, Police Constable William Bell discovered what he described as a number of "junk shops" in Greene Street, Stanton Street, and Ridge Street owned and operated by both male and female proprietors. His warnings of Corporation Attorney attention to Patrick Boyle at 65 Greene Street, Bryan Rogers at No. 63 on the same street, Edward Duffy at No. 23, Catherine Lavelle at 239 Stanton Street, and Mrs. Brady at No. 102 a few doors up led Police Constable Bell to remark that "the above persons exposes their Goods for sale and offered to sell some of them to me." As he "notified them to get out Licenses," the Constable continued in the area, meeting proprietors named Roache, Haggerty, Howard, Waters, McGloin, and a proliferation of entrepreneurially minded Irish who had created a precarious but visible commercial presence through the variety of items they traded.[32]

Those establishing in business, possibly hoarding small capital sums or availing of past experience, mirrored parallel opportunities in provincial towns and villages back home. Even as Dublin experienced a mercantile expansion from the 1830s onward, New York had expanded north from the Battery to Fourth Street during the same time period, a distance of about two miles. With the construction of stagelines, the boundaries were marked by "the Yorkville on the Boston Road, and the Bloomingdale on the Bloomingdale Road," according to John Sturdevant, an Irishman who lived to see the end of horse-drawn transport and the birth of electrically propelled streetcars in New York.[33] References throughout his reminiscences highlight the probability that he hailed from a Protestant background; in the course of his observances he exhibited familiarity with such points of affiliation as city Quaker establishments and Sunday schools and with the Orange Riots of 1871 involving his Protestant and Catholic compatriots. Witnessing the expansion of the port from an anchorage for slow sailing ships that took weeks to cross the Atlantic to a waterway crammed with the new "side-wheel steamers," he wondered at the proliferation of streets like Broadway as they were transformed from rough cobbles to smooth "Belgium blocks." The flagging of the pavements reminded him of how boys from the old neighborhoods would remove the massive stone slabs to create new construction jobs for laborers.[34] A milestone for city householders, the arrival of piped water from Croton led to the construction of wells for select houses in State Street and Bowling Green. People had grown accustomed to the incessant building around them, Sturdevant noted, with new hotels, stores, and dwelling houses springing up constantly. Their house lights operated on gas power, but more commonly used were cheap tallow candles and whale oil to burn in the new street lamps. Busy markets flourished at Washington Street, Tompkins Bowery, and Jefferson Street, with the precursor to the Fulton Fish Market of Dutch origin.[35]

As particular trades and manufactures began to associate with specific areas of Lower Manhattan, mirroring the practice in Belfast and Dublin and the smaller provincial cities over the previous century, men and women from Ireland congregated with the jewelers on Maiden Lane, the leather goods retailers favoring The swamp, and the financiers gravitating together in the vicinity of Wall and Broad Streets. Likewise, city entertainment developed commercially by the 1850s in parallel fashion on both sides of the Atlantic; although Dublin's public entertainment tradition stretched back a couple of centuries. The first Dublin theater had established in 1637, catering largely to the well-to-do,[36] but a range of popular options propagated the notion of mass entertainment for all by the nineteenth century. Assisted by the rise of what R. V. Comerford characterized "the exhibition movement," incorporating a host of well-attended showings in such venues as the Royal Dublin Society, the Museum of Irish Industry (later the Royal College of Science), the National Gallery of Painting and Sculpture, and the Dublin Exhibition Palace and Winter Garden, popular entertainment attracted all classes of patrons by century's end.[37] In Manhattan too, the extraordinary range of theatrical and musical options catered to all sectors, including acts of international renown alongside more localized contributions of particular interest to the city Irish. During the mid-century years, by all accounts, the entertainment was not limited to the stage. Notorious outbreaks such as the MacCready Riots in Astor Place generated fodder for exciting headlines, and riotous behavior within the halls and theaters also kept the evenings lively.[38] Lavish performances in the Opera House contrasted with the more earthy style of Christy's Minstrels in Alhambra Hall on Lower Broadway, while the hugely successful P. T. Barnum "reached his peak when he presented Jenny Lind to audiences of 10,000 at Castle Garden in 1850."[39] Irish performers and promoters achieved much success within the entertainment world rapidly taking over the upper reaches of the expanding city. The histrionic images of the old country conjured up by crowned heads of melodrama Dion Boucicault and Ned Harrigan—the latter "one of the founding fathers of American musical theater"—provided immigrants with alternative evocations of home to those institutionalized by dancers and vocalists of the caliber of Kathleen O'Neil, a variety performer during the Gilded Age years.[40]

Within earshot of the Lower Broadway music halls, Irish innkeepers, hotel proprietors, and tavern-style restaurateurs strove to cater to the theater audiences nightly pouring into the hundreds of stage shows, music performances, circuses, and all manner of low-brow entertainments proliferating up Broadway from the downtown jumble of streets and alleyways. Overlaid with a dash of New World style, the ale and oyster houses identified by red and white striped globes on poles and the premises described as "Club-Houses" contrasted with less prestigious establishments such as Tom Riley's Fifth Ward Hotel and Tom K's Museum Hotel on West Broadway and Franklin Street. "Surrounded by residences of men of noted financial, commercial and moral standing," no less, the latter accommodation aspired to host a more exclusive class of customer. Notwithstanding the commendable character of Tom K's customers, this kind of enterprise brokered a good living for men of the caliber of George Conlon in his famous hostelry. The shutters came down on Conlon's Oyster House every year on the last day of April at 12 P.M. sharp and reopened without fail at the same hour on the first day of September. In those intervening months lacking the traditional "R," Conlon would disappear from the local scene for parts unknown, only to arrive back faithfully each September. Those intervening months provided John Brady with the bulk of his business in the same neighborhood, however. Renowned as the owner of the best "Ice-Cream Saloon" on Canal Street, Brady received his customers in "a gorgeous place, marble floors, marble top tables, a glass for the cream with plated spoon and a glass of cold water ... luxury," according to Sturdevant.[41] But if the pinnacle of luxury city dining did not carry the name of an Irish proprietor, then the splendid fare at Delmonico's attracted those Irish affluent enough to take advantage of a world-class establishment. Well-heeled politicians, successful professionals, old-guard fraternal society members, and the occasional buoyant nationalist temporarily enjoying a full coffer frequented Delmonico's as a matter of course throughout the Gilded Age years. Proffering French cuisine including "eleven soups ... forty hors d'oeuvres ... such items as lamb's kidneys in champagne sauce, Westphalian ham, mayonnaise of lobster, artichokes a la poivrade, oysters scalloped in their shells, chipolata sausage, and fried ham and eggs; twenty-nine variations on beef ... twenty-seven veal dishes (breaded with truffles, fricasseed with gravy, 'spinage,' or sorrel, sealed in oiled paper, and a carbonade with green peas or herbs) ... twenty roasts ... forty-eight fish specialties" and a host of magnificent desserts washed down by selections from the "coffee and punches, twenty-four liqueurs, and fifty-eight wines," Delmonico's afforded moneyed Irish a rarefied vantage point from which to indulge with the city's elite.[42]

As the case in contemporary Ireland, not everyone could afford the higher-end libations and entertainments fraternized by the more affluent classes. For the tens of thousands trying to acclimatize to the teeming Lower Manhattan streets, a makeshift dockside base constituted the new reality for some of the most pitiable emigrants. Those at the lowest end of the scale arriving off the New York–bound ships huddled within the debilitating confines of the tenements and crude dwellings, many too weak to seize whatever small-time opportunities arose around them. It is fair to say that despite an impoverished status at home, and even as victims of the Famine, very little about their past experience could have prepared these men and women for what lay ahead. The British and American commentators touring the western and southern seaboard counties during the pre-Famine years referenced the predominant misery of rural subsistence almost universally, as did the authors of various Parliamentary inquiries into the condition of the population. The adjectives rearing up time and again in descriptions of the sheer brutality of life as a landless laborer or cottier painted a dismal picture of people caught in an economic maelstrom from which escape was really only possible through emigration. As Ireland's post-Union population skyrocketed toward the Malthusian specter lying in wait, the vicious potato blight destroyed the most vulnerable classes within a few short years. The Famine impact hit hardest through the west and south, where tenantry on small mountainous plots euphemistically listed as "grazing land" braced for a disaster too strong for their weak economic structure.[43]

Conditions stretched abysmally from Donegal to Cork, but contemporary commentators occasionally found instances of improvement and even cheerfulness among west coast peasantry such that impassioned descriptions of misery ended up tempered with brighter prospects than the chapter titles or headlines first suggested. American observer Asenath Nicholson, for example, heralded the "tidy and industrious . . . cabiners" she found in remote areas of the western island of Achill. Amidst extreme impoverishment, the turf fires lent a warm and welcome air to the crude rooms. Potatoes and buttermilk nourished, helped along by periodic helpings of shellfish and even occasional meat. Sidelines brought in much-needed income on an intermittent basis through the year, Nicholson meeting one old Achill woman who entrepreneurially "sold whiskey, and by this got her wealth."[44] For the majority of tenants and peasants operating within the confines of life on holdings too small to support any kind of reasonable living standard, implementing such improvements as could be facilitated regularly paved the way toward escape to cities such as New York.[45]

There is little danger of romanticizing Ireland's pre-Famine peasant class. The rush to leave behind the dark chaos of the late 1840s transported hundreds of thousands of smallholders and the landless into the frenetic slums of England and North America to embark on a struggle often just slightly less traumatic than the conditions recently evacuated. Even as contemporary commentators witnessed scenes of basic contentment and even frugal comfort amidst the overarching harshness, the experience of the survivors in cities such as New York occasionally turned up a similar pattern. Ex-tenants of the marquis of Lansdowne, including the family of future Tammany operative "Big Tim" Sullivan, moved en masse into the Five Points and made good to a surprising degree within a few years. In settling into perhaps the worst of New York's spectacularly filthy and dangerous ghettos, this peasant grouping initially personified the popular stereotypes surrounding mid-century Irish arrival. But, as Nicholson and others found in Ireland, such preconceived notions did not bear out quite as concretely as popularly thought. Notably, Tyler Anbinder found, "the Lansdowne immigrants had undergone a remarkable transformation in a few short years from destitute Irish peasants to moderately successful New Yorkers."[46]

The same teeming Sixth Ward housed elements tapped into by Tweed during the Famine era; Five Points Irishmen who built a local reputation within the rough-cut streets of the worst slums. By the time the stream of immigrating Irish infiltrated the poorer wards most visibly, these men had scaled the lower rungs of city administration to institutionalize a Tammany system serviceable for decades to come. As Anbinder recovered their story, men of the caliber of Con Donoho,

Matthew T. Brennan, and John Clancy marshaled a support base wide enough to exert influence not only over their own ramshackle world but, within the decade, over the entire city.[47] Through the 1850s and 1860s, Irish newcomers living in the Shantytown squalor that cleared out to make way for Central Park witnessed the same patterns; contingents of Irish initially surviving as ragpickers and engaging in the most menial of occupations latching onto political opportunities calculated to elevate them from the worst excesses of poverty.

Even as this kind of evidence advocates a more varied range of standards—both social and economic—prevailing amongst these Irish than many contemporaries allowed, hardship proved all too real for thousands caught in the deadly cycle of lower-class immobility. John Sturdevant commented on those unlikely to overcome such pressures, noting that these newcomers all too rapidly melded into the New York streetscape, their carts pulled through the streets by women, children, and dogs. Characterization of "a drunken good for nothing set" represented a common attitude towards them, shared by this commentator as he distanced himself from his ill-begotten compatriots.[48] He might have been cheered to learn that the cottiers and landless laborers who left Ireland's hardest-hit counties established close familial relationships within their makeshift new neighborhoods and sought to avoid the trauma of broken families and vagrant children.[49] Further, men and women forced to settle between the overrun Sixty-Second and Seventy-Second streets in the 1860s succeeded in relocating to more improved areas in a relatively short period of time. Typically entering the workforce at the bottom of the socioeconomic scale, the intention of escaping a locale which "had a life and picturesqueness unknown and undreamed of by the reputable regions farther down" could hardly be begrudged. As the case with more fortunate fellow countrymen and -women finding their feet in small businesses in the proximity of Wall Street, the "Shantytown" dwellers first operated commercially within the confines of neighborhoods often drawing together people from the same townland or county in Ireland. Taking advantage of opportunities scarce in Ireland, where family association with specific trades stood the test of time and would-be entrepreneurs found it difficult to compete with long-standing businesses, the poorer elements could anticipate achieving higher degrees of prosperity within a relatively short time span in New York, as one contemporary noted:

> The dweller in Shantytown is a natural politician. Aldermen and city officials have often come from ragpickers, truckmen, and the various orders of labor that make up the population of this district. It is from just this region that some of the present City Fathers have come. They had little groceries, such as are still standing, and furnished sugar and tea and tobacco to the neighborhood. One of them had a ball-room where occasional festivities were held; a ball-room rejoicing in wealth of pink and blue fly-paper, wooden benches in long rows against the wooden walls, on which kerosene lamps in iron brackets were screwed. There they

are still, and at night one may hear the sound of fiddle and jingling piano, and the thud of feet dancing merrily as if the day held no work.[50]

Removed from the sights and smells of the ghettos, a different class of immigrant rose to exert a presence during mid-century. Embracing a more glamorous facet of urban life, those with the wherewithal to avail of elegant accommodations and artistic outlets attracted Irish of means to the proliferation of fashionable leisure-based pursuits opening up by the later nineteenth century. While Dublin, Belfast, Cork, and Galway, not to mention towns like Westport, County Mayo, provided an increasing range of spare-time activities for the newly emerging middling element, the options patronized by the upper classes continued to remain virtually off-limits to other sectors of the population well through the nineteenth century. "The disparities of wealth" dominating provincial Ireland facilitated enormous class-based gaps reflected in limited access to social amenities and leisure-time pursuits.[51] Despite the encroachment of new land ownership legislation easing the grip of the aristocracy on the upper end of the spectrum, the continued association of richer gentry with the round of elitist sporting and social activities marked class boundaries as they had done for generations past.[52] The same pattern emerged in Colonial New York as the older Dutch and Anglo families dug a social foundation that survived the pressures of Gilded Age excess.

By the 1870s, new outlets showcased the city as a haven for the privileged and fashionable. Central Park, for example, transformed into one of the principal social amenities in New York, and one that displayed the golden lifestyle at its most glamorous.[53] The landscape played host to fashionable carriage drives and promenades, according to Mrs. George W. Hall, and attracted the well-to-do and their aspirants on a daily basis. A frequent visitor to New York, and affluent enough to partake of the high life, Irishwoman Sophie Hall's commentaries on the enjoyment of the city's parks, galleries, and fine stores contrasted sharply with the limited perspective available to compatriots distanced from her vantage point. Frequenting the art exhibitions, the opera, and elegant theaters, her set of cultural parameters operated worlds away from the abysmal conditions endured by poorer men and women elsewhere throughout the lower reaches of the city. Her observation that "500,000 inhabitants of this city reside in Tenement Houses" constituted her sole pronouncement on life outside her relatively narrow confines. [54]

Hall's enthusiastic reaction to a special day in New York reflected the cheerful atmosphere surrounding the annual landmark. Absorbing the sense of self-confidence and general good feeling parlaying on the midtown streets, the March 17th festivities brightened her stay and engendered feelings of national pride. Calling the annual Saint Patrick's Day parade "one of *the* days of New York," Hall took in the enormity of the 1879 extravaganza that wound its way past multitudes of rain-soaked onlookers for hours. The energy of the music and the marchers infused the streets with an infectious air in a colorful tribute to her native culture.[55] Presided over by resplendently decked dignitaries, Sophie Hall judged the celebration of ethnic identity the predominant image of Irish New York life. To her mind, the joyous atmosphere conjured up sentimental memories of national holidays across the Atlantic. Dignified by an officially sanctioned Catholic commemoration, the interest in honoring the national saint and the immigrant culture responsible for transplanting a by-now ubiquitous symbol represented a successful assimilation process.

Privately cheering on one of the more popular transatlantic connections, Sophie Hall identified different aspects of the New York Irish world, including her peers, the rising commercial element, and the poorer sectors struggling at the lower end of the scale, even if she assiduously avoided contact with the latter grouping. Her experience paralleled that of a more familiar name during the same decades, that of William Smith O'Brien. Embodying a similar class identification but sustaining infamous political connections that kept him in the public eye during the post-Famine decades, the occasion of Smith O'Brien's death in July 1864 accorded all manner of city Irish an opportunity to reflect on an individual whose experience served to reinforce connections between the city and their native home. A man who imbued Irish-American political issues with new measures of sophistication and complexity, Smith O'Brien's place in the nationalist pantheon was assured by the time of his death. Born in 1803 into one of the oldest county seats in Ireland, Dromoland Castle in West Clare, his stints at Harrow and Cambridge and subsequent election to the House of Commons by the 1820s set his future on a predictable course. But instead of the natural progression into the Conservative ranks, he joined and later led an organization representing the other end of the political spectrum, the populist Catholic Association.[56]

Protestant son of an Irish baronet, Smith O'Brien the O'Connellite Member of Parliament attracted considerable notoriety as one of the rebels of '48, subsequently exiled to Tasmania. Pardoned after a few years, the insurgent-turned-gentleman author and lecturer ended up inducted into the select group of "household names, men who in their day had fought against incredible odds to establish the peasant on his land and themselves as his respected and skilful representatives in the greatest imperial parliament in the world," according to Tim Pat Coogan.[57] News of his revolutionary involvements reached Irish New York via extensive press coverage, pamphleteering, and later on, in the form of personal lectures. Speeches delivered during a visit to New York in 1859 publicized the constitutional-nationalist alliance Smith O'Brien latterly subscribed to, the agenda that would generate increasing attention on both sides of the Atlantic with the Fenian decline and the buildup of the Home Rule campaign in subsequent years.[58] Compatriots seeking to avoid the more turbulent Fenian waters found his moderate freedom formula appealing.

As Hall surrounded herself with the well-heeled and the "quality," in contemporary parlance, and Smith O'Brien infused the notoriety of rebellion with personal privilege and the popular appeal of the O'Connellite tradition, other individuals similarly found their niche and rose to prominence in a variety of city spheres. The chapters that follow shed light on a number of the most influential, but identification of those prosperous Irish living their lives away from the spotlight merit attention as an important sector of the immigrant population. Upon his arrival in the 1830s, for example, Dubliner John Burke's intent to secure employment through the influence of established compatriots proved successful. His first act on docking into the city was to join with a countryman in locating a well-to-do relative of the latter in the Bowery. The relative connected the two young men with a contact in Kimball and Rogers financiers on Wall Street, and John Burke was hired immediately for the reasonable wage of $9 per week. Following his marriage in 1849—the ceremony at the old Saint Patrick's Cathedral in Lower Manhattan performed by Reverend Loughlin, a curate of Bishop John Hughes and later Bishop of Brooklyn—Burke negotiated a wage increase to $12 per week. He began to save toward his own business and eventually opened a shoe store at 83 Nassau Street in 1852. A "courage born of desperation" strengthened him through initial shaky years, but his involvement with a network of familiar contacts gave him the foothold he needed to succeed. He dealt extensively with fellow countryman James French who ran a wholesale shoe business on Wallace Street, but maintained his influence at Kimball, his first place of employment. Over the course of the 1850s and 1860s, John Burke remained in contact with his old homeland and expanded his network of success by assisting his six brothers to settle into American life. John alone remained in New York, the rest of his family ranging as far afield as San Francisco.[59]

As though reinforcing traditional practices across the Atlantic, Burke's property dealings throughout Lower Manhattan usually included contracts with Irish proprietors. For example, his move to 504 Broadway undertaking the lease of a Mrs. Powell at $300 in cash was followed by a deal with Assemblyman Thomas Ward, owner of a candy store on Broadway below Broom Street. Burke concluded his tenure in business without opening his own brokerage house or dealing exclusively with the larger financial establishments on Wall Street as per his earlier aspirations, but his wholesaling partnership with a compatriot named E. Kelly proved lucrative enough to satisfy him. Pleased with his profitable liaison, Burke remarked that this man "acted the most heartily of all the landlords" he had come in contact with. As thousands of Italians, Poles, and assorted Eastern Europeans began to arrive in New York, Burke contrasted their achievements with his own, and not always in favorable terms. Exhibiting pride in his own good fortune and in that of his countrymen, he contrasted what he styled an Irish aptitude for enterprise with a similar deficiency in other immigrant groups. His view that "the Hebrew Class" accelerated the pace of business to a frenetic degree and exerted an ultimately negative influence over the economy matched his unwavering confidence in the more measured approach of his own nationality. Jewish business acumen did not include concern for the greater good of the American people, Burke maintained, leading him to remark that:

> While on Emigration it must engage the study and attention of the thinkers to compose the different attributes of the races who come to dominate in the New World ... here we have the stalwart Irish race who develop to a greater degree muscle and adaptability than any other nationality we import. You find it in the Metropolitan Police Force—a finer body of men not to be found in any country or from any other nationality.

"The soft and sanguine German" characterized as "of a fair hair and a type easy to govern," met with marginally greater approval. As he surveyed a list of significant ethnic groups, his conclusion that most of them could never influence city commerce to benefit either themselves or the United States exalted Irish contributions, in his mind, by comparison. Italians lacked the competitive edge and the basic building blocks of a strong economic foundation: "The Sons of Sunny Italy" would "glut the labour market, bring down wages, degrade labour." Beyond the Europeans, he seemed heartened that "other nationalities ... come in such limited numbers as to make no influence on the general growth of our institutions."[60]

A less xenophobic voice, and one with a higher public profile than John Burke's, turned to similar themes through the course of his writings and contrasted with that of his compatriot's. Jeremiah O'Donovan's celebratory and often entertaining perspective on his adopted home received wide attention in post-Famine New York. The Philadelphia-based author turned out a history almost guaranteed to generate receptive Irish-American (and even American) audiences. The title of his work articulated O'Donovan's intent to engage personally with his compatriots in the United States, promising: *A Brief Account of the Author's Interview with his Countrymen, and of the Parts of the Emerald Isle Whence they Emigrated. Together with a Direct Reference to Their Present Location in the Land of Their Adoption, During his Travels Through Various States of the Union in 1854 and 1855.* As he remarked in pointed fashion:

> Millions, not thousands, of my countrymen were either starved, hanged, or decapitated by remorseless villains who were sent across the channel by the most repacious, unfeeling, ungodly, and cruel government that has been established in any civilized or savage country under the canopy of Heaven, and such of my countrymen as escaped from the meshes of their ferocious enemies were driven like wolves from science and society, until they thought them beyond the reach of future improvement, and irrecoverably plunged in barbarity and unspeakable ignorance. . . . [61]

The reference to "science and society" contains the germ of O'Donovan's dream for his immigrant compatriots. He fervently hoped that his countrymen and -women would redress the limited educational opportunities they were used to and make good in their new communities across the Atlantic. Overall, he judged that immigrants had adapted very well to their new environment. Meeting with accountants, shoe and boot wholesalers, plumbers, lawyers, booksellers, and a long list of prosperous and educated Irish, he happily encountered many that were more than willing to equip him with introductions to others of their standing.

Beneath the high-blown romanticism, the author's enthusiasm for Irish success seemed to have rubbed off on the hundreds purchasing multiple copies of his writings. His encounter with a Mr. James Dillon, for example, keeper of a bookselling business at 417 Ninth Avenue, presented a fine chance to do business with "a distinguished Irishman." In fact, he surmised, "to see him is to detect his greatness." As Mr. Dillon was renowned for selling religious works, he would therefore be in a good position to recommend potential buyers to O'Donovan. "With kindness and patience and perseverance," the author noted, "every time I would call at his store he had a list prepared, and the name of every one on whom I would call with a probability of success, and did this with a cheerfulness beyond the reach of illustration." The merchant tailors, "boss carpenters," mechanics, innkeepers, grocers, and host of other traders and professionals he met with led the writer to visualize an environment where "classically bred" gentlemen and ladies from "the Isle of Saints" could move beyond the constrictions of their land of origin (notwithstanding burgeoning opportunities for Catholics previously excluded from the land-owning and professional classes). A Mr. Daniel Draddy exemplified this new persona, to O'Donovan's mind amounting to "a mechanic of the highest grade . . . a well-cultivated mind . . . a great historian, and writes the Irish language druidically." What more could anyone wish for in a mechanic! The scribe did not ignore similarly enfranchised women on his travels, encountering quite a number of successful female proprietors. Mrs. Brady from Edgartown, Co. Longford, "lives at present in 32 West Street, where she keeps an extensive dry good store, and is one of the most amiable ladies in New York." The women specializing in dry goods, groceries, and fabric sales seemed to satisfy O'Donovan's aspirations for his compatriots, as did the litany of prosperous artisans and businesspeople he was proud to introduce and include in his publications.[62]

Considered collectively, the testimonies of O'Donovan and his contemporaries over the mid-century decades throw light on an Irish world in a new city context in many respects reflective of class structures and expanding social and commercial interests across the Atlantic. The commentaries reveal a multidimensional settlement character in the formative stages of evolution toward what would soon constitute a distinct identity. Resting on a greater degree of diversity than the images of famine horror and oppression popularly suggest, the varied socio-economic affinities originating within Ireland's society and economy fostered distinctive patterns of settlement and employment that rose to the fore in New York. For the Sophie Halls and the John Sturdevants, New York fostered similar standards to those prevailing in Dublin or Belfast during the same era. For others, New York presented the opportunity for degrees of improvement more difficult to achieve in the same decades in Ireland. The landless laborer from rural Clare or Tipperary emigrating as a viable alternative to impoverishment and potential devastation transported a different perspective on city opportunities than skilled craftsmen from Dublin or Kildare. Likewise, the female from Donegal or Leitrim with the advantage of even the most rudimentary education would fare better than illiterate women unable to envision much beyond the most basic forms of domestic service.[63]

Diversity within the immigrant community is also identified and connections with home reinforced through the operations of Irish-associated financial organizations offering material assistance to thousands of arrivals since the early years of the century. Immigrant aid under the auspices of charitable bodies such as the Shamrock Friendly Association (1816–1826), the Irish Emigrant Association (1817–1818), the Emigrant Assistance Society (1826–1829), and the Union Emigrant Society (1829), incorporated a world-within-a-world for city Irish. Within this milieu, some of the more affluent professionals exerted influence over their less privileged countrymen and -women. A series of famines in Ireland in the 1830s motivated members of the Friendly Sons of Saint Patrick, for example, to appoint board member Dr. Robert Hogan to instigate a plan of action. In 1841, just prior to the radically greater impact inflicted by the Great Famine, the board of the Friendly Sons and local Catholic clergy assisted Dr. Hogan in crafting proposals for a committee with a full complement of vice-presidents, secretaries, and executive members drawn from the city's Irish elite. Prominent professionals such as John Quinn, Felix Ingoldsby, Dr. Hugh Sweeney, Dr. William Macnevan, and Cornelius Shehan staffed the executive positions in the new Irish Emigrant Aid Society.[64] Established at addresses on Wall Street, Nassau Street, Maiden Lane, Merchants' Exchange, and Fulton Street, the new board members operated in close proximity to Manhattan's commercial nerve center.[65]

Subscriptions of $5 per annum, members' donations, and activities such as the annual ball kept the Society afloat over the years, with sponsorship of an employment exchange probably constituting its most valuable resource to those Irish lacking immediate employment. The Society policy of patrolling the Battery to instigate immediate contact with disembarking immigrants paid off handsomely in terms of numbers assisted. On the basis of the New York model, sister organizations established in Philadelphia and New Orleans operated similarly. Encouragement from Archbishop John Hughes during his long tenure in office helped empower the

Society's chartering of the Emigrant Industrial Savings Bank in 1850. The bank prospered on the support of professionals who combined philanthropic interest with the potential for profitable investment in recently established Irish nationals. The Society's annual Ball Ticket in 1845 reminded patrons of its munificent goals:

> To assist the friendless Emigrants with advice and information; to find immediate employ-
> ment for those who need it; to protect them from the cruel and daring frauds so frequent-
> ly practised upon them; these are the objects the Society has in view, and for which it seeks
> your support. To have effected these objects, even to a moderate extent, is no small subject
> of congratulation. Each succeeding year, as the Society becomes better known, its field of
> usefulness is enlarged, and the records of the five years it has been in existence make evident
> the still increasing benefits conferred upon the Emigrant.[66]

Decades later, the Annual Report for 1899–1900 demonstrated that the need for such an organization remained strong, and that professionals of means still involved themselves in charitable enterprise. A total of 23,095 new immigrants arrived from Ireland during 1899, for example, over 4,000 more than during the previous year. Of this total, 12,515 females and 10,580 males officially registered; the Society calculating that the vast majority remained in New York. One of the primary duties undertaken by this organization concerned men and women held by the Immigration Authority on the grounds of insufficient means of support. Society President James Rorke organized deputies in 1899 to procure affidavits from relatives or acquaintances of the immigrants guaranteeing support of the individuals in question. In that year, 546 cases merited the attention of the Emigrant Society and, of this number, 531 received direct assistance. Through the Labor Bureau on Pearl Street in Lower Manhattan, which the Society ran jointly with The German Society of the City of New York, a total of 3,013 Irish natives secured employment in this year alone.[67]

The success of charitable organizations and the observations of contemporary commentators collectively generate useful impressions of the Irish presence in the mid-century city. Preliminary judgments yield a multilayered collective within a new urban context of enterprise and entrepreneurship, a city placing a fount of opportunity before its immigrant population. Extending from the abysmal conditions of the Swamp to the lofty mansions of Washington Square and Gramercy Park, New York exhibited nothing if not vicissitude. In the throes of transformation by modern technology, propelled by trams, electricity, and shipping connections toward a new mass-produced Gilded Age and Progressive era, the rapidly moving world greeted classes of immigrants transporting microcosms of the smaller world left behind them.

As we have seen, not all newcomers conformed to the stereotype of the Great Famine's "huddled masses." During the 1840s, there is no doubt that a large percentage of those fleeing the Famine and smaller agricultural crises arrived in various stages of destitution. In the years following the calamity of Famine and up through the following decades, however, thousands arrived skilled in particular professions or trades, educated to varying standards or possessing the means to establish within a particular facet of the burgeoning commercial world. Even as city authorities endeavored to clear the poorest elements from the public spaces, Ireland's entrepreneurs established retail emporia and small markets in goods and services, involved themselves in the developing world of leisure and entertainment, and witnessed and participated in an across-the-board rise in Irish city prominence. As we will see, Irish women exerted a vital influence over their new transatlantic world, and Protestants comprised a much more significant dimension of the experience than the Irish-American canon has traditionally reflected.

The executive boards of such bodies as the Friendly Sons, the Emigrant Savings Bank, and the Emigrant Association reflected strands of Irish culture often overshadowed by the wealth of attention accorded the more cataclysmic aspects of the immigrant influx. Affluent lawyers, physicians, politicians, and other professionals progressed distinctly and often publicly, often distancing themselves from working-class compatriots. Middling elements settling into the proprietorship of public venues epitomized similar opportunities to those developing in contemporary Ireland. In sum, the strata of class and occupation transported over from Ireland and sustained in New York ploughed the furrows and planted the seeds of a new hybrid culture. By the end of the nineteenth century, that culture would entrench an Irish-American identity shaped as much by what was imported as by the forces confronted in New York.

C H A P T E R   T W O

The Silent Majority?

IRISH WOMEN AND NEW YORK IRISH IDENTITY

I rish women in America have received scant historical attention until relatively recently, and their experience has still not been recovered to the degree mandated by such a populous and influential immigrant sector. Traditionally, histories buried gender distinction under an entrenched male agenda centering on the rapid adaptation of manpower to manual labor in urban environments, and a strong affinity for public houses, pugilism, and politics. George Potter's statement that "once the Irish immigrant entered into the mass life of a city, unless he was a man of great ambition, unusual talents or the beneficiary of fortunate circumstances, he became a captive of its poverty through his lack of education and skills" typifies traditional attitudes toward the Irish-American immigrant experience that focused intermittently, at best, on one of its most vital contingents.[1] The view that female newcomers hailed exclusively from Ireland's lower classes, entered into domestic service immediately, and avoided sinking into total obscurity by a characteristically headstrong nature has proliferated within the canon. To scapegoat Potter again, his observation that "an Irish woman remained a 'girl' until she married; and the Irish 'girl' in the U.S. meant specifically to her own race, as she came to mean to her American employer, a domestic servant or, as the Irish described her, 'a living out girl,' who might be almost any age," bristles with long-held perceptions.[2]

But the parameters shift definitively for Famine and post-Famine New York as class structures and politicizations originating in Ireland are explored from the female perspective. As a vital contributor to the city's Irish identity, the diverse population of women operating within charitable organizations, social clubs, nationalist groupings, and the major avenues of employment utilized a variety of means of influence within the immigrant enclaves and beyond. Evidence from women-centered city experience reveals important connections between Ireland and New York while underscoring the significance of women in the creation of the New York Irish identity between 1845 and 1921.

Two points emerge at the outset. First, the numbers of women and men emigrating from Ireland and settling in the United States from the mid-nineteenth century to 1921 remained relatively equal. Second, in contrast to other European groups, women from Ireland tended to travel singly, did not typically establish patterns of family-group migration, and were not usually constrained by family ties on arrival. Despite these facts, however, their experience has remained marginal in comparison to their numbers.[3] The view that "seen through the prism of their roles as wives or daughters within patriarchal families . . . these women have had little independent voice in the historical record" has certainly dominated,[4] with scholarly attention most usually directed toward the sphere of domestic servitude. Over time, the domestic service stereotypes appeared to extinguish alternative perceptions of immigrant women.[5] Patrick O'Sullivan's reference to "this ignoring of women" as "extraordinary,"[6] some years ago is finally becoming increasingly outdated, thanks in part to recent emphasis on a more diverse array of focus points and interest in the influence of Ireland over immigrant progress in the United States.[7]

Engaging with a more diverse set of socioeconomic cultural markers for Irish women, even within a specific context such as New York, raises some initial questions. The idea that Irish women exchanged one form of domestic labor for another on arrival in America is supported through reference to female-centered education as perhaps the only viable employment source other than servitude.[8] These generalized and typically well-documented assertions should not be discounted; arguments suggesting that economic opportunity constituted a primary motive for emigration and that women married later than the norm for immigrant females but earlier than Ireland's female population merit continued attention.[9] But caution is advisable. Kerby Miller emphasized that:

> . . . no single model or interpretation can apply to all female emigrants from Ireland, either before or after the Great Famine. Arguably, the ultimate determinants of gender roles and relationships are sexual divisions of labor, which in turn vary greatly among different socioeconomic classes and cultures . . . women from different class, regional and cultural backgrounds in Ireland had significantly different work and marital experiences in different regions of the new world. Lacking such evidence, historians have inadvertently homogenized the lives and attitudes of the daughters of commercial farmers in south Leinster, landless laborers in north Munster, mill workers in east Ulster, and Irish-speaking peasants in west

Connaught—thereby obscuring these and other crucial distinctions which governed relationships and shaped outlooks in a highly localistic, family-centered and status-conscious
society.[10]

So what of the situation in New York? In exploring connections between Irish
women, the city, and their land of origin across the Atlantic, the very extent of female
representation in New York provides a strong foundation on which to build.[11] In
terms of sheer numerical significance, the 1:1.08 ratio of female to male settlement
enforces the centrality of women within Famine-era and post-Famine city history.
As the Irish-born population of New York reached more than 260,000 by 1860, we
are dealing with a conservative approximation of well over 100,000 as the number
of women located there by the 1860s.[12] Of this number, a sizable percentage hailed
from middling or lower-middle class backgrounds. Those dispossessed by the
dowry system, for example, the "non-dowried daughters of small farmers and the
daughters of agricultural laborers," made up a significant proportion of the immigrants. In uncovering linkages with home, the view that "emigration enabled young
Irish women to reconcile traditional family obligations with new individual moti-
vations"[13] should be borne in mind, remembering that although increased economic opportunities may have encouraged many to settle in America, motivation
to relocate spanned a broad spectrum underpinning a wide range of stimuli.[14]

If contemporaries in the post-Famine decades could not help but notice a
generally expanding Irish city presence, certainly the magnitude of women's settlement ought to have been quite visible to New Yorkers. But contemporary references
often reflected an attitude of marginalization toward them, despite their numbers.
Such attitudes are not unexpected in the later nineteenth-century context, but
when considered in light of women's substantial presence within (and noteworthy
contribution to) the expanding Irish city culture, they project a discordant air. In
1873, for example, Reverend Stephen Byrne issued a series he summarized as *Irish
Emigration to the United States: What It Has Been, and What It Is. Facts and Reflections
Especially Addressed to Irish People Intending to Emigrate From Their Native Land; and
to Those Living in the Large Cities of Great Britain and of the United States.* The
Reverend's musings on the topic of migration typified widely held attitudes toward
women who left their native land. Reverend Byrne speculated that between four and
five million nationals moved from Ireland and the cities of Britain to America over
the previous century, but his testimony made scant reference to the high percentage of women included in the migration. Speaking generally, he claimed that
"much of the unprecedented development and prosperity of the United States is due
to the hardy energy and remarkable perseverance of our race." Many of the Irish
"race" failed to capitalize on America's resources, though. Despite critical contribution to American economic and social development, a high percentage of immigrants seemed indifferent to advancement, in his judgment. The cleric recommended

that the newly arrived move to the West and South where land was available in abundance and the prospect of a permanent home lay within reach. The scale of American cities would never be conducive to the easy acquisition of the home that represented the cornerstone of security, he recommended.[15]

Reverend Byrne made no mention of the city as a female employment stronghold, nor did he refer to women's potential in rural areas of the country or encourage females to travel to the United States. Published by the New York Catholic Publication Society in Devotional times, his *Facts and Reflections* fits the mold of mild propaganda against the dangers inherent in the suspect moral climate of the New World. Although such writings suggest fears for the flower of Ireland's womanhood, this type of observation made little impact judging by the large numbers undertaking the Atlantic crossing.[16] The tide of female movement continued unabated into the twentieth century, women still landing in almost equal numbers to males. Occasionally, immigrant ships docking in transported a female majority,[17] a trend that accelerated toward the end of the century as news of expanded female-centered employment opportunities found a ready reception in Ireland. "Amusing and Pathetic Scenes at the Landing," announced *The New York Times* in April 1897, at the sight of a "large importation of Kathleens, Eileens, Delias and Norahs" that "reached this port yesterday on the steamships *Majestic* and *Servia*." A total of 1,100 emigrants disembarked, the majority young women between the ages of 15 and 30 who undertook removal across the Atlantic after the by-then traditional "American Wake." Embarking on a new life and facing the prospect of never returning to Ireland, each of these women arrived dutifully equipped with health certificates from accredited physicians![18]

The frenetic dockside scene featured relatives, friends, reporters, agents of charitable organizations such as the Rosary Mission or The Mission of Our Lady of the Rosary for the Protection of Irish Immigrant Girls,[19] and prospective employers all mingling around the newly arrived contingent. Accompanying Mr. Patrick McCool of the Rosary Mission, New York Harbor Commissioner Senner declared the "sudden rush . . . unusual" for the particular time of year, but not at all unwelcome. He commented: "we want more of these people, particularly the women. There are husbands here for every one of them." Unconcerned about the prospect of acquiring husbands, at least in the near future, the women had undertaken the rigors of the Atlantic crossing unescorted. The expectation of continuing on the path of self-reliance and establishing an autonomous livelihood in their new place of settlement perplexed the reporter, who seemed incredulous that the women journeyed to face these prospects unaccompanied. He appeared relieved that most of them had at least organized parties of relatives or friends to meet them at the docks. Those few left alone were taken into temporary accommodations by Rosary Mission personnel and representatives from other aid agencies. The journalist estimated that a large percentage would remain in New York, with the rest continuing on to other East Coast and Midwestern destinations.[20]

Unlike women of other ethnic backgrounds who arrived replete with husband or father and often extended family, the new-found reality of independence in New York placed immediate employment at a premium for the less skilled and un-educated Irish. Sustaining transatlantic connections from the start, they sought the assistance of relatives and contacts from home parishes to facilitate immediate entry into the workforce.[21] Those obliged to seek charitable assistance maintained the links through organizations with strong Gaelic connections,[22] ranging from the prominent endeavors of the Rosary Mission to the less overt benevolence of societies such as the Friendly Sons of Saint Patrick that nonetheless expedited mid-century settlement for many needy women. Mapping an interesting confluence of cultural affiliations in relation to women, this fraternal grouping wound up assisting large numbers of impoverished Irish during the post-Famine years. Established by 1783, the Sons attracted physicians, lawyers, engineers, businessmen, and clergymen into a social milieu with an eye to comfortable fraternity and a commitment toward benevolence. A central board assessed cases seeking assistance, and solicitations for aid normally sent directly to members known by name or reputation resulted in the receipt of thousands of requests. A majority of applicants appear to have received some degree of assistance, but solicitations from women typically outnumbered male applications by as many as one-third. Newly docked younger women seeking entry-level employment competed with middle-aged mothers whose circumstances had deteriorated to the point where charity constituted the sole available option. A typical request from a female applicant read as follows:

76 West 36th Street,
3d Floor, Back Room,
November 20 1873.

Dear Friend, I hope you will pardon me for addressing you, as it is now some time since I had the pleasure of seeing you. A few days ago I wrote to Mr. Stuart, but not having had a reply, I fear he did not get my letter. Some seven years ago you were so very kind as to give us a Sewing Machine with which my Daughter and I have supported ourselves respectably. My son always assisted us, but being unemployed at present and I being an Invalid since last January, and confined entirely to the house, has placed me in very straightened circumstances. If your Society will be so kind as to assist me a little over the present difficulties we will consider ourselves your debtors, and will cheerfully repay you as soon as possible. Sincerely,

Catherine Furey.[23]

A donation of $5 from the Central Fund was earmarked for Catherine Furey, the transaction enforcing the kind of ethnic connection that motivated many such applicants to the same end. Board members gave careful consideration to each case, in some instances corresponding over a number of days and even weeks on the merits of individual solicitations. From January 1873 to January 1874, for example, Sons' officers dealt with 71 requests for assistance from a pool of applicants representative of Ireland's most common surnames.[24] Of this total, 48, or approximately 68 percent, of these requests came from women recently settled in New York. Occasionally, letters of recommendation from high-profile benefactors such as self-made immigrant and city Supreme Court Judge John R. Brady merited lengthy responses; others merely a line. In clear-cut cases the procedure was simple, particularly when an applicant had previously received Society aid. In January 1874, to take one instance, Judge Brady wrote from his home on West Thirty-Third Street to Sons' colleague and businessman William Whiteside: "My dear Sir, Mrs. Kelly is worthy, I think. She has been aided before. Truly, J. R. Brady."[25]

The descriptions penned in the applications suggest that many of these women hailed from backgrounds in Ireland facilitating at least a basic education level. Engagement in genteel occupations, generally as governesses or seamstresses, indicated varying degrees of association with the middle classes. By their own admission, standards of living familiar to them proved difficult to maintain in New York due to deteriorated economic circumstances. In July 1888, an Auditor in the Collectors Office of the Custom House and Friendly Sons' member mailed a recommendation for Dublin woman Sarah McCarthy. Providing particulars on her personal history, Thomas Kelly circulated the following for consideration:

> To whom it may concern—This is to certify that I have known Mrs. Sarah J. McCarthy (nee Butler) for twenty-two years—more intimately when she lived with her mother in the City of Dublin and where she sheltered for months James Stephens after his escape from Richmond Bridewell and until he left the country. I know no man or woman who deserves better of the patriotic Irish people for her own sake as well as because she has been deprived of that most estimable gentleman, her husband, Thomas McCarthy, principal editor of the *Dublin Irishman*. Any aid in procuring employment for Mrs. McCarthy cannot fail to be a source of pride to her benefactor and a timely deed well done.[26]

Sarah McCarthy received Society assistance two days later, with the promise of further help in procuring a position of employment. The profile here is that of a gentlewoman experiencing a downturn in both means and status. Associated with levels of literacy, employability, and skills not typically discernible among working-class women, applicants such as Sarah McCarthy constituted the majority of Friendly Sons—assisted women. Expanding the familiar unskilled "Bridget" profile, the women's refined and courteous writing style suggests interest in recouping a measure of gentility lost through altered status. The fifty to one-hundred women that received aid annually certainly comprised a small grouping within the general immigrant influx into New York each year. Yet representative of a class of females often largely invisible within the Irish-American immigrant experience, their efforts to sustain middle-class standards and practices familiar to them from home underscore a set of transatlantic connections often marginalized in the historical narrative.

Advertisements in New York's daily and weekly Irish-run publications further spotlighted Irish cultural affinities pertaining to middle-class female identification. The notices reveal a collective of literate, genteel women seeking city employment beyond the realm of domestic servitude. Between notices for the latest shoe and boot styles and sundry items such as oilcloths or carpets, short inserts offered readers opportunities to engage women as governesses, tutors, or salespersons in stores. Typical advertisements ran as follows:

> A young lady wishes a situation as Governess in a respectable family. She is competent to teach all branches of English; also, plain sewing and fancy work, and has a knowledge of music: or, is fully capable of taking a situation as Saleswoman in a store. Salary not so much an object as employment. Can produce best city references. Address 198 West Twentieth Street, New York.[27]

In such notices, references such as "lady" and "respectable" reflect a worldview similar to the women seeking assistance from the Friendly Sons. While literacy, sewing skills, and music empowered these women to explore options beyond unskilled domestic work, their willingness to take store positions highlights the intention to avoid servitude. Although household wage levels often exceeded wages in the retail sphere, the fact that this coterie preferred lower-paying but higher-status situations suggests the kind of upward mobility often difficult to achieve in class-bound Ireland. Women seeking "situations" as governesses or salespeople were obliged to combine the characteristics of gentility with the pressing need for work; a precarious balance to maintain during the mid- and late-nineteenth century. Excluded from the ranks of the affluent, yet distanced from the laboring classes, the movement toward respectability accorded them a distinct status despite the onset of economic deterioration. Bound by contemporary convention limiting influence and visibility in the public sphere; not affluent enough to generate social or political power, or sufficiently invested in working-class culture to engage in labor activism, these women subscribed to an inherited class structure that placed a premium on the maintenance of strict standards of respectability. In an era when prevailing wisdom decreed that "coeducational schooling was especially dangerous to girls because it was 'injurious to the delicacy of feeling, reserve, and modesty of demeanour which should characterise young girls,'" aspirant women tended to confine themselves within the bounds of their sphere as a mark of class distinction.[28] In general, social mores operated against more visible female representation within the ranks of the paid labor force reflective of largely negative attitudes to women therein. It was not until the turn of the twentieth century that women accelerated their entry into either middle-range, white-collar work or the professions, while traditional engagement with textiles, apparel, education, and nursing persisted well beyond the achievement of milestones such as suffrage and more general access to higher education.[29]

As Famine-stricken escapees flocked to New York, Boston, Philadelphia, Chicago, and the other major urban centers, heightened demand for charitable assistance not only motivated communities of Irish women to respond, but worked to expand public-sphere opportunities, sustain strong connections with sister-communities in Ireland, and play a key role in the transplantation of cultural practices from across the Atlantic within their institutions. Akin to a private benevolence system of sorts, Irish orders of nuns and sisters transferred thousands of women into the United States over the course of the nineteenth century.[30] On the national level, Honora (Nano) Nagle's Sisters of the Presentation of the Blessed Virgin Mary and Catherine McAuley's foundation of the Sisters of Mercy proved particularly influential.[31] During the Famine era, particularly, ministering to large numbers of their more impoverished compatriots occupied much of the Sisters' time in cities such as New York, regardless of foundational affiliation.[32] Among the predominantly Irish-staffed orders establishing early in America, the Ursulines, Carmelites, and Visitation Nuns arrived in the 1700s to locations as far afield as New Orleans and Port Tobacco, Maryland.[33] Communities had proliferated throughout the South and Midwest during the early nineteenth-century decades as Mother Agnes O'Connor headed up the first delegation of the Sisters of Mercy of the Union in New York during the Famine years, but the primarily Irish-born Sisters of Charity of St. Vincent de Paul of New York had foregrounded cultural affinities in keeping with the norms of their heritage since the early nineteenth century. In so doing, the Sisters established a female-based presence within the settlement process based on practices and values honed over previous decades in Ireland. As perhaps an obvious manifestation of this cultural background, the women religious worked almost exclusively with mothers and their offspring, retaining Devotional Ireland's norm of entrusting adult male care to orders of priests and Brothers.[34]

Two years after the establishment of the Academy of Mount Saint Vincent on the Hudson, Ireland's "Apostle of Temperance," Father Theobald Matthew offered a congratulatory message to the Sisters on a commemorative day in 1847[35]:

> The progress you have made is highly creditable to your alma Mater from whom you have also imbibed the pure milk of virtue. I congratulate the Sisters of the community; their labors are abundantly evident in the exercises of this day. Their best reward is in the glorious consciousness of training up future mothers and matrons, their present safeguard of honor and virtue.[36]

Whether or not the "training up of future mothers and matrons" amounted to the greatest reward for their work, the nuns' involvement with needy daughters of Erin certainly dominated their charitable agenda. The Sisters' establishment of Saint Patrick's Orphan Asylum since 1817 catered largely to Irish boys under the age of ten, with approximately eight hundred spending time in the institution during the period 1860–1900. The Asylum Register included a listing of temporary guardians for boys in the care of the Sisters, typically drawn from farming families located outside New York City.[37] The large number of children committed to temporary care by immigrant mothers reflected the harsh and unremitting conditions overshadowing their lives. Although after a time almost forty percent of the institutionalized boys returned to the care of their natural mothers, in most cases between one and five years, approximately sixty percent of the mothers failed to regain custody of their children. Thus, the operation of this facility accorded the nuns a definitive role as charitable providers and educators within the city's Irish community. Other orders with strong affinities to the homeland's Catholic tradition followed suit during the same years. Arriving initially in 1846, the Mercy Order established their House of Mercy at East Houston Street in 1849, a Home for Homeless Children on Second Avenue in 1860, Saint Joseph's Home, East Eighty-First Street, Balmville Boarding School (destroyed by fire in 1891), numerous educational establishments, and the Institution of Mercy in Tarrytown in 1894. The orders operated alongside Protestant denominations in New York running similar establishments; for example, The Wilson Industrial School for Girls founded in 1857 maintained that "there are still from 30 to 40,000 children in this city, with the exception of about 2,000 in the Industrial schools, habitually truant or vagrant."[38]

The sustained interaction of two groupings of immigrant women within the context of the orphanage and the operations of the other Catholic women's institutions point to elements of a transplanted culture operating successfully, yet largely invisibly, outside the narrow parameters they established. As the case in Ireland, with very few exceptions, neither the nuns nor the women they assisted rose to prominence socially or politically, not to mention materially. But the orders attracted increasing numbers to the convents and institutions through the Famine and post-Famine era. The upsurge in women religious vocations during the first half of the nineteenth century resulted in at least 1,500 women from Ireland taking orders by the 1850s, more than 2,600 by 1860, and at least 8,000 by 1900.[39] Despite the successful expansion, what has been described as a "tendency to defer to established authority and the low tolerance for individual deviation"[40] colored the country's Catholic purview and motivated the Sisters' subscription to the type of conservative agenda that institutionalized relatively smoothly in New York, despite the best efforts of prominent nativist elements.

That professional benevolence agencies such as Saint Patrick's empowered the nuns to maintain the work practices and operations developed in parallel fashion across the Atlantic constitutes a compelling issue in a city where antipathy to Catholic institutions took on increasing significance during the 1850s. The New York Sisters adhered to the foundation of privacy and seclusion traditionally associated with Catholic religious, and did not typically utilize the new cosmopolitan center as a platform for accelerated change in the same manner as pioneering nuns in the more rough-and-ready westward localities.[41] As in Ireland, the Sisters' worldview operated within the hierarchical Church organization and did not shift too far beyond its parameters. Further, class structures across the Atlantic informed the process of recruitment of Sisters to the various orders. The Mercies, for example, maintained a traditional affinity "in the popular and ecclesiastical minds with the upper classes," unlike the more democratized Sisters of Charity, whose American base of operations proved less restricting. In fact, the Sisters of Mercy virtually excluded working-class women from their order in keeping with contemporary views doubting whether the less privileged and less well educated could uphold the more refined social and cultural mores of the day.[42] Nonetheless, on both sides of the Atlantic, those same parameters accorded the Sisters the freedom to operate more independently than other middling (or upper-class) women within the bounds of societal practice decreed in large measure by contemporary Catholic standards.[43] By the latter decades of the twentieth century, nuns did move toward instituting a greater degree of autonomy, ironically at a point when their efforts were hampered by dwindling vocations. But as a strand within Irish New York since the early nineteenth century, and particularly during the post-Famine decades, the Sisters and nuns occupied a distinct space that played a role within the creation of the new ethnic identity under construction. In many respects invisible outside their home parishes and beyond the purview of those who benefited by their charitable and educational initiatives, they nonetheless established Irish women in a distinct city sphere—a base of operations sufficiently reflective of the same work in Ireland as to constitute a persistent tradition of post-Famine transatlantic influence.

Other benevolent activities entrenching similar connections similarly illuminate previously shadowy aspects of Irish women's role in the settlement process. The work of the Hibernian Ladies Prison Association, the Belfast Ladies Temperance Association, and the Women's Temperance Association established branches throughout the country and pioneered the efforts of clerically run organizations with evangelical origins.[44] The work of one organization in particular encapsulated private charitable endeavors in the style of the Sisters while cultivating a more comprehensive public profile. After some years of planning, the Ladies of Charity of the Catholic Charities of the Archdiocese of New York finally commenced operations in 1902 at the De La Salle Institute, under the watchful eye of Archbishop Corrigan.

Including new arrivals and descendants of earlier immigrants, approximately twenty women drew up a campaign and inaugurated an association "effected for the purpose of uniting Catholic ladies in works of Charity. They appointed committees on Prison Work, Settlements, Girls' Clubs, Daily Nurseries, Auxiliaries to Institutions, to Conferences of Saint Vincent de Paul, Hospitals, Sewing Circles, etc." Under the direction of President Mrs. Joseph O'Donohue, Vice-President Mrs. Robert McGinnis, Recording Secretary Miss Georgine Slevin, and Corresponding Secretary Miss Teresa R. O'Donohue, the "Union of Catholic Ladies" implemented a range of charitable operations, supplementing the work of the nuns and the male-dominated operations.[45] By 1905, the Ladies of Charity Executive Committee met every two months and directed eighteen subcommittees supervising all branches of operations. Chaired by a group of affluent, well-connected doyennes with prominent social profiles in the city, the committees developed programs of interaction with the impoverished and with thousands of prisoners crowding the city system. Working in tandem with the Saint Vincent de Paul Society, the Ladies organized an extensive schedule of visitations and charitable assistance, as the listing for November 1903–February 1904 demonstrates[46]:

Prison Visits: 500
Homes of Prisoners: 362
Letters Written for Prisoners: 293
Articles of Clothing Distributed: 962
Books, Magazines, Leaflets, Pictures: 3000
Prayer Books: 12 dozen
Marriages Arranged: 1
Wedding Ring: 1
Baptism: 1

In addition to prison visitation, the plight of homeless children generated concern within the Ladies' ranks. Mrs. John O'Keefe chaired the Children's Court Committee in 1903–04 and reported to the Annual General Meeting that petty crime among the youth appeared to have decreased considerably in comparison with earlier decades. Mrs. O'Keefe singled out children of nationalities other than Irish as requiring specific attention from the group. Her January 1904 pronouncement that Italian and Jewish children operating as pickpockets, "child wagon thieves," and petty criminals posed a danger to New Yorkers led her to emphasize the positive influence of Catholic teaching toward child gang reduction.[47] Irish aid recipients did make occasional appearances in the records. "Patients of every nationality—American, English, Irish, Scotch, French, Italian, German and Swedish—have been treated," according to reports on hospital visitations. The Hospital for Consumptives and the New York Incurables Hospital, or the House of Calvary, received a great deal of attention from the Association.[48]

As the post-Famine decades gave way to a new century, an expanding city population and a strident Progressive social reform agenda combined to motivate the Ladies to venture beyond the walls of hospitals and prisons. In 1904–05, officials Geraldyn Redmond and Delancey Kane's program of social activities included dancing and classes in Italian, for example, at Saint Anthony's Club for the Working Girls of Saint Lucy's Church on the Lower East Side. Miss A. C. Riley and Miss H. N. Murphy's Saint Ann's Nursery operated on East Twenty-First Street, while Mrs. B. E. Burke chaired the "Work Among the Syrians Committee." Calculating that approximately 2,000 Syrians merited charitable assistance in turn-of-the-century New York, Mrs. Burke estimated with pride that "a greater number of pupils (Syrian) come to us than are attending all the Protestant classes put together." Impoverished Irish women could take advantage of a "quasi-settlement for the working Girls and Women of the East Side between Fiftieth and Seventieth Streets," although this effort focused more on music and the promotion of the arts than the more usual forms of aid. Occasional entertainments enlivened things, a "Sleight-of-Hand Performer," a "Talk on the Customs of Mexico," and an evening of "Irish Ballads" providing respite from the daily routines for both benefactors and beneficiaries.[49]

Reflecting Devotional attitudes across the Atlantic during the same decades, competition with Protestant welfare organizations encouraged the Ladies to strengthen the Catholic profile of New York benevolence. Emphasizing that the "non-Sectarian Municipal Hospitals must . . . receive the visits of Catholic ladies in order that the backward or negligent may be brought in touch with the priest, and the downspirited may be buoyed up, either in hope or resignation," they called on the Sisters of Mercy to share the labor in the field. Hospitals such as Bellevue, Lenox, Fordham, Blackwell's Island, and a number of Settlement Houses received visits on a regular basis. Activities ranging from instruction in the theological foundations of Catholicism to the distribution of "823 packages of tea and sugar" on one occasion in 1908 in Blackwell's Island Hospital attracted private funding from members. In fact, so successful were the Ladies that it was not until 1916 that public donations were sought. They appealed to active members to donate $1 annually, with $5 for Honorary Members and in excess of $5 for Benefactors. By 1918, the Association registered over 3,000 members, with the vast majority Irish, evidencing of a dramatic expansion from small-scale beginnings in 1902 to the point where the Association and the vision of its Executive constituted a thriving benevolent city enterprise. On the occasion of the death of Mrs. Joseph O'Donohue in January 1918, a founding director who held her rank as President for sixteen years, the Ladies could reflect on a very successful era assisting New York's needy. Mrs. O'Donohue's succession by Countess Georgine Iselin maintained the Irish profile of the organization's leadership. Formerly Georgine (or Georgiana) Slevin, the

Countess held the position of Secretary with the Association since 1902, and her patronage connected the Ladies with some of the most prominent New Yorkers of the day. As the daughter of banker and art patron Adrien Iselin and Eleanora O'Donnell Iselin (commemorated in the 1888 oil by John Singer Sargent), Georgine utilized her title and her extensive family connections to maintain the sphere of influence cultivated by the Ladies to that point. Adrien Iselin, banker at 56 Wall Street, resided at 23 East 26th Street and enjoyed an annual income of over $88,000. His daughter's personal assistance with city charitable causes earned her the Papal title of Countess; particularly her support of St. Eleanora's Convalescent Home in Yonkers Park (now Crestwood), built by her father in memory of his wife. Operated by the Sisters of Charity, the Home provided charitable assistance to needy mothers until 1961.[50]

As with the Sisters of Charity, the women coordinating and staffing the Executive of the Ladies of Charity and their compatriot members up to and beyond 1921 created their own niche within the city's Irish world through which to satisfy a number of objectives. Operating within a distinct social sphere, as the case with other groupings such as the Mission of Our Lady of the Rosary or the Women's Auxiliary of the Ancient Order of Hibernians, and generating as distinct an impact within the settlement experience as the Sisters of Charity, the Ladies' downplayed national visibility among those assisted while institutionalizing connections and allegiances with their native home within the fabric of their operations. Avoiding the type of publicity generated by other formalized collectives of Irish women (that receive attention later in the chapter), and opting to preserve the elitist character synonymous with altruistic practices in Ireland against the more democratic and secularized opportunities available in the United States, the Ladies transplanted a solid, native-born connection involving Catholic tradition, subscription to class sensibilities, and maintenance of the home-based leadership profile in their New York organization.

This type of endeavor raises the visibility of a class of women often obscured within the historical record. For the affluent, usually unencumbered by employment priorities and active within the more exclusive social circuits, the organization of balls, work sales and fundraisers satisfied aspirations of noblesse oblige within the expanding coterie of moneyed Gaels in the city during the Famine era and subsequent decades. Press reports on glittering high-profile events testified to the prominence of women hailing from the provincial towns and county seats in the company of influential professional and commercial families. During the 1860s, for example, the series of extravagant balls to raise money in support of "the Destitute Poor of Ireland" propelled the members of the "Irish Ladies Patriotic Fund" into prominence. Billed as the "Irish Ladies Patriotic Fund Ball in Aid of the Destitute Poor of Ireland, at the Academy of Music, New York, Tuesday Evening April 14, 1863.

Ticket, Admitting a Gentleman and Ladies, Five Dollars," the announcement highlighted the "Gentlemen's" contribution in a most direct fashion. On this occasion, the "noble Irish lady who made, and so efficiently supported, the suggestion of a Patriotic Fund Ball for the benefit of our unfortunate motherland" remained anonymous throughout the process, as did all other participating "Ladies." Male patrons, including the one hundred and sixty "Gentlemen" on the General Committee basked in the glow of favorable press coverage, while the female contingent remained confidential. But the Fund generated more than $10,000 in 1863 alone for the relief of conditions across the Atlantic thanks to "the preeminence due to the fair sex, under whose special auspices it was commenced."[51]

Notwithstanding the rather circumspect attitude toward activist women in these circles, fundraising by means of spectacular social events provided a growing constituency of affluent females with a public platform. By the turn of the twentieth century, a clique of approximately one hundred families featured regularly on the pages of local society columns, associated with such events as the landmark February 1914 "Kerry Ball." Organized by a women's core committee, the Ball attracted an enormous crowd of revelers numbering more than 10,000, bringing together prominent legal, financial, and political grandees, with the display of dress, decoration, and general "impressiveness" almost overpowering all present. Besides the annual festivities surrounding Saint Patrick's Day, the Kerry Gaels, the Raftery Social and Literary Club, the Munster Social Club, the Monaghan Ladies Association, and the Irish County associations afforded women organizers and members' high prominence within the rarefied echelons of the New York Irish community. By 1910, one such body put the final touches to its twentieth annual event. Accorded extensive publicity, the Tipperary Ladies Association's sponsorship of an annual benefit under the capable direction of the (wonderfully named) Mrs. S. Lavender and an all-female committee happily guaranteed both the success of the event and the celebrated status of the organizers.[52]

In addition to high-flying balls and dances, Irish women of means cultivated public association with the arts, usually in the spheres of music and literature. Traditional practices within the arts at home flourished anew during the latter decades of the nineteenth century with the mobilization of the Gaelic Revival initiatives. Concerts, festivals, and poetry readings subscribing to a Revival ethos promoted the arts and their patrons as society pages devoted considerable attention to events such as the series of concerts in the New York Academy of Music and the Brooklyn Academy of Music throughout the 1880s. The actions of a number of influential women in the city not only institutionalized what came to be dubbed the "Gaelic Revival," but the collective efforts inculcated a foundational piece of the developing Irish-American identity.[53] Organizing women worked toward the same objectives as their counterparts in Ireland (including Lady Gregory and Countess

Markievicz)—promoting the Irish arts. A campaign to establish an Irish "opera house" in New York failed to materialize, but a series of "Celtic" musical tributes as project fund-raisers proved an enormous social success for the organizers.[54] A slew of organizations drew like-minded *Gaelgoirs* together in Manhattan and Brooklyn, most obviously, during the Gilded Age era and early 1900s. For example, the Brooklyn Philo-Celtic Society, the New York Society for the Preservation of the Irish Language, the Brooklyn Gaelic Society and New York body of the same name each contrived to promote the language, the culture, and most predominantly, the identity.[55] Although a number of these associations ran aground, members' clear devotion to, and sponsorship of, Ireland's culture and heritage amounted to a visible, if regrettably uncoordinated New York Gaelic Revival. The efforts extended a good deal of social cachet to women while enabling Revivalists on both sides of the Atlantic to draw from the deep well of Gaelic music, song, and story. Besides mounting the variety of artistic productions within the larger urban centers, their efforts raised the female profile within Irish New York and beyond. Alongside the public performances, the establishment in Manhattan in 1907 of An Cumann Comhradh, or the Irish Conversation Society, offered women the chance to interact socially while improving their knowledge of the language. Meetings of the Cumann held at various locations at two-week intervals provided women a new social outlet within the Irish milieu.[56] Physician and nationalist Dr. Gertrude B. Kelly, for example, championed both her culture and her gender on the committee of a Carnegie Hall music festival entitled "Gathering of the Gael" that brought together Archbishop Farley, William Bourke Cockran, Charles Murphy, Thomas Addis Emmet, and the cream of Irish city society in April 1910. The sopranos, harpists, violinists, and accompanists showcased Gaelic culture as a stylish pursuit that could not only "be acquired even in New York" but had become increasingly fashionable.[57]

Even as the wives and daughters of Ireland's prominent politicians and journalists gravitated toward the new culture-based groups and later toward the women's organizations mobilizing in tandem with the Home Rule agenda, what has been described as the "stultifying respectability" of the middling classes continued to restrict them. But the Ladies Land League and Inghinidhe na hEireann, to take two stellar examples receiving attention later on in the chapter, mobilized thousands of women to move beyond traditional gender boundaries and politicize to an extraordinary degree given the prevailing contemporary constraints in public life.[58] The steady female influx into the city during the years 1890 to 1921, in particular, proved significant for the expansion of these types of activities, but not all could hope to achieve the success of the more exclusive elite groupings. In the Annual Report of the Irish Emigration Society in January 1898, President James Rorke reported that 9,000 new arrivals made New York their home during that year alone, with males and females landing in relatively equal numbers. Although the majority could at least read and write, an average of $14 constituted the sum total of their reserves. More than a decade later, the 1914 report continued to warn prospective settlers of the risks involved in relocating to the city. Secretary of the United Irish League of America, Michael J. Jordan cautioned prospective emigrants against moving to America on the basis that they could not hope to compete with native-born citizens in the large urban centers.[59] As the numbers evidence, many of Ireland's poorest did not heed these warnings; indeed the majority of them simply could not afford to heed them. Those subsisting at opposing ends of the social scale from the patrons of charity and culture existed in a radically different world, many barely surviving beyond the boundaries of contemporary civil administration.

Neither Italian classes nor music lessons constituted priorities for these unfortunates. If orders of nuns and organizations of elite women sequestered in different corners of the private spheres in Irish New York, then the worst-off women remained even less perceptible outside the narrow confines of their enclaves, hidden within the dark recesses of the worst slums. Few managed to escape the confines of the underworld. The family of Manhattan politico Timothy D., or "Big Tim" Sullivan, to take a prominent example, should be counted as among the lucky, breaking from the worst excesses of this way of life. During the 1870s, "the Sullivans moved frequently from tenement to tenement within the neighborhood near the lower Hudson River Docks. For this family, as for the vast majority of the half-million people packed into the roughly two-mile square area south of Fourteenth Street, housing and health conditions were abominable."[60] Some of the women who found themselves struggling for survival had availed of one specific means of escaping poverty in nineteenth-century Ireland. Assisted emigration schemes under the care of Poor Law Guardians developed out of what has been described as "a context newly sensitized to the dangers of Malthusian overpopulation." The programs did not relieve Ireland of enormous numbers of female paupers, but the promotion of a specifically female emigration program suited those women lacking alternative opportunities.[61] However, those populating the filthy dock-houses and horrendously crowded tenements seemed to have gained little in their move. Lacking the means to better their station in life and relegated to the most wretched portside streets of Dublin, Cork, and Galway, New York offered at least the prospect of advancement, but for typically lower-class, uneducated women, neither home base facilitated easy access to cleaner housing and improved wage levels.

In January 1866, a policeman accompanying a journalist from *The New York Times* on a nocturnal visit to some of the most notorious streets unearthed women inhabiting some of the city's darkest corners. Heading their report "a glimpse into the very depths of Human Misery," they wandered the narrow streets of Lower Manhattan, on a par with the equally notorious slums of Dublin during the same decade. Knocking on the door of a dilapidated lodging house, the men faced a woman who opened the door after striking a light. The two callers confronted a scene of shocking grimness in the room behind her. Another woman sitting with a ragged youth, and an "elderly Irish laborer" sitting naked in a bed appeared to exist in abject misery in a tiny hovel not more than eight feet from floor to ceiling, and extremely squalid. The women did not speak, but stared with unyielding expressions. The former owner of the building had been incarcerated in either Island or Sing Sing prison, and the house previously operated as a hotel of sorts, the visitors learned. Compared with other underground dwellings visited later that night, the journalist considered this example as among the best ventilated and most spacious. The next port of call in a narrow alley, a type of saloon or "gin mill" known as "John Lane's rum shop" was full of "white boys and prostitutes of both races—Celtic and Negro . . . in the closest fraternity . . . nearly all these whites are Irish." The appearance of the *Times* journalist and the policeman patrolling the area did not in any way disturb the rum shop patrons. Claiming that most of the men and women hailed from the southern county of Kerry, harboring as they did the distinct accent of that region, the officer remarked: "Hanged if you could dig a hole in them with a crow bar deep enough to get any sense into them." Advancing that they appeared to be unkempt to a much greater degree than folks from other areas of Ireland, he became especially apprehensive and melancholic with regard to the women present, describing them as follows:

> There seems to be no hope for them in this life; and hopelessness is written on every line of their faces. And yet there are hardly any traces of *vital* wretchedness. It is negative mainly, it is the utter absence of happiness rather than the presence of misery that impresses one. These women, so lost, so fallen, are called Lofters in the police vocabulary . . . There are men who are as low in character as these women; but *they* can come out of these alleys and dens and redeem themselves. But once there, a woman can escape in one way only—a coffin.[62]

These scenes survived well into the 1900s in some of the older downtown neighborhoods. A Rotary Club of New York found the area surrounding Parnell Street still inhabited almost exclusively by Irish immigrants and their descendants almost a century later, for example.[63] The ghastly conditions evocative of the worst excesses of the mid-1800s still prevailed, with an average of between five and eight people living in two-room tenements in the most wretched streets and alleys. Workers in possession of any marketable skills or prospects aimed to leave the Lower West Side as soon as they could gather the means to establish elsewhere, with the majority of women subsisting on the most menial of jobs, hardly qualifying as wage labor. The "chronic illness" devastating the unfortunates of Parnell Street afflicted women in particular, further exacerbated by the fact that "a large proportion of the mothers and a small proportion of the fathers admitted total illiteracy."[64]

As the case in Ireland, city newspapers and popular literature shed light on the lives of the most pitiable women otherwise unnoticed and rejected within the public sphere. Without a doubt, large numbers of these women turned to prostitution as a means of survival in the post-Famine years. Difficult to trace, not only by sources of authority but also in the eyes of their more prosperous compatriots, by virtue of their oblique lives, the rising percentage of women imprisoned on prostitution charges during the mid-century and Gilded Age years testifies to their existence. The point that many of them made efforts to make low-paying domestic situations their mainstay prior to turning to prostitution suggests the latter option as the last resort for many of their number. New York Irish involvement in prostitution remained most conspicuous among the poorest of the working class, paralleling societal norms in post-Famine Ireland.[65] In a similar vein, other practices overshot with contemporary moral parameters adhered to similar patterns for women on both sides of the Atlantic. In 1869, *The Women of New York, or the Underworld of the Great City, Illustrating the Life of Women of Fashion, Women of Pleasure, Actresses and Ballet Girls, Saloon Girls, Pickpockets and Shoplifters, Artists' Female Models, Women-of-the-Town,* put forward the judgment that Irish women resorted least among the different ethnic groups observed to the practice of abortion, but the opinion was ascribed not so much to religious strictures as to disregard for fashion. "The practice of producing abortions is indulged in by women of nearly all classes of society," the writer declared. "The women of fashion, however, are most guilty in this respect, while it is said that the poor Irish seldom, if ever, resort to the practice." George Ellington explained this statement by stating that "it is not considered fashionable to have children. It interferes with the round of dissipation of the stylish woman, and compels her, for a time at least, to live a life somewhat secluded."[66] Whatever about the fashions of the day, the twin pillars of religion and society operated effectively to relinquish the practice of abortion to the inner sanctum of the female world.[67]

As literary characters such as Stephen Crane's *Maggie* typified the lives of young women who realized early in life that tenement factory work would remain their lot, contemporaries contrasted idyllic theater imagery with the sordid everyday world of the Irish poor:

> Maggie always departed with raised spirits from these melodramas. She rejoiced at the way in which the poor and virtuous eventually overcame the wealthy and wicked. The theatre made her think. She wondered if the culture and refinement she had seen imitated, perhaps grotesquely, by the heroine on the stage, could be acquired by a girl who lived in a tenement house and worked in a shirt factory.[68]

Maggie sought inspiration in local theatricals, as did many of the women who opted for domestic servitude as a pragmatic means of betterment. Entering the employment situation most popularly associated with their profile in America,

Irish women had good reason to place a premium on this type of work. Servants were obliged to adapt to households often dreary and exploitative, but the prospect of earning $4 to $7 a month proved more attractive than suffering the hazardous conditions of factory labor. In an era when immigrants, and particularly females, felt dual pressure from ethnic *and* economic burdens, opportunities for increased earning potential held fundamental value. As Ruth-Ann Harris judged for a number of later nineteenth-century domestics, "The Margaret McCarthys and Mary Harlons of Ireland were expected to display a forelock-tugging humility in the presence of their 'betters,' not because they were Irish or even because they were female but simply because they were poor."[69] In a city where poverty could condemn, and where labor shortages constituted the norm, Irish women soon learned to "bargain for their value."[70] Contemporary commentary and popular literature on the topic of servitude during the post-Famine decades recognized the extensive impact of Irish involvement. Immigrant novelist Mary Anne Sadlier (1820–1903) popularized domestic life as a background for her novels while educating her readership on the nature of the work, for example. Publishing over sixty books and presiding over a literary salon in Manhattan in the 1860s, Sadlier's most famous work, *Bessy Conway; or, The Irish Girl in America*, detailed the life of a newly arrived servant. *Bessy* richly recounted the everyday tasks, the sources of discrimination experienced by Catholic immigrants and women's redeployment of wages to ameliorate conditions at home for friends and relatives.[71]

In contemporary parlance, the "Swarming hives" of "patient Coolies" and "long-tailed children of the sun" from China, and the "millions of Negroes" cited as "prolific children of Ham" yielded traditional labor resources until the Famine decade brought increasing numbers of Irish into the workforce. In New York, where demand outstripped supply, the opportunity for a steady wage and lodgings under the same roof proved welcome. The transportation of "ignorance, her uncouth manners, her varying caprices, and her rude tongue" into her new place of employment constituted necessary evils to be tolerated by her employers for the sake of their value as cheap, efficient workers, according to prevailing attitudes. Lacking formal skills, thousands of working-class women transported the household labor practices best known to them. The parameters rose at home over generations past, with the poorer elements obliged to seek out a form of employment that would house, keep, and accord them some measure of dignity in the process. In the more circumspect environs of New York, "Bridget" tended to live a morally uplifting life, and could be considered "as pious as a nun" and as good a character as servants of other religious backgrounds! The necessity of ecclesiastical obligations in the form of attendance at Catholic church services was generally grudgingly tolerated, while her "strong arm and voluble tongue" enabled domestics to create a particular lifestyle suited to both their requirements and those of their employer's household.[72]

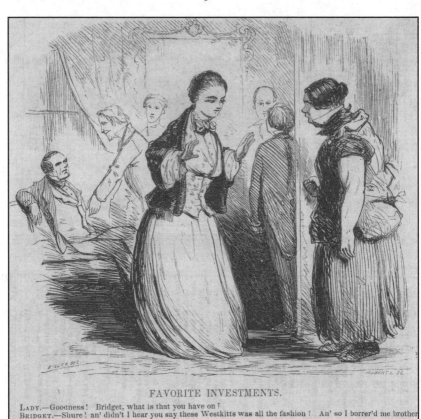

FAVORITE INVESTMENTS.

LADY.—Goodness! Bridget, what is that you have on!
BRIDGET.—Shure! an' didn't I hear you say these Westkitts was all the fashion! An' so I borrer'd me brother Pathrick's to wait at the table in.

Figure 2.1: "Favorite Investments," *Harper's New Monthly Magazine* (June 1852); courtesy of Picture Collection, The Branch Libraries, The New York Public Library, Astor, Lenox and Tilden Foundations.

A contemporary professor of history and statistician at Vassar College apportioned the history of this type of employment into different phases and cited the Great Famine as a primary factor within a shifting mid-century American labor market. The influx of women from Famine shipments altered the course of domestic servitude in cities such as New York, according to Lucy Maynard Salmon, with upwards of 30,000 arriving annually between 1850 and 1880. The work suited a section of the workforce where "physical strength formed a partial compensation for lack of skill and ignorance of American ways," if for no other reason, she surmised. Thus, "the Irish soon came to form a most numerous and important class engaged in domestic employments." Salmon lists the figure of 37.64 percent as the percentage of Irish-born domestics over ten years of age, outstripping the next highest group—the Germans—by over fifteen percentage points. In New York, the ratio of the general population to employers stood at 28:1; a high proportion of employers during the second half of the nineteenth century.[73] An earlier Salmon study entitled *Statistical Inquiry* demonstrated that more skilled household workers generated the highest incomes during the 1880s; cooks and parlor maids commanding approximately $4 per weekly wage and chambermaids and waitresses at the bottom of the scale at $2.50 to $3. Male employees paid $8 as coachmen and $6–$6.50 as butlers and cooks enjoyed an increase of almost $2 over women in equivalent situations.[74]

Despite lower wage levels, women domestics acquired a reputation for good money management. Their income was typically expended in three directions, each reinforcing personal connections with Ireland. Sums donated to relatives and friends back home, to the Catholic Church, and to compatriot-run political organizations in New York accounted for the highest percentages. The "millions of dollars [which] have been sent annually by the servants in America to Ireland to mitigate the miseries of their kindred there, or to relieve them of them forever by bringing them to this paradise of Patrick and his numerous progeny" dwarfed the percentages donated to parish churches.[75] Given the dynamic of the educated employer and the illiterate servant, employers were regularly approached to write letters to families in Ireland, "to them at home in the old country."[76]

By all accounts, significant sums donated to political activities derived "not so much from the well-to-do Irish, as from the servant girls and day laborers." The argument that the relationship between the larger nationalist organizations and domestic servants prospered because these women combined an antipathy toward Britain with a "total ignorance" of the campaign for independence seems spurious, in light of their involvement in the various incarnations of nationalist activity in New York during the post-Famine decades.[77] Even as working-class men and women in Ireland rallied behind various political incarnations during the mid- and late-nineteenth century years, as we will see, New York's Irish servants gravitated toward prominent political activity during the same decades. 1863 reports that women had been dismissed in large numbers from their employments as a result of involvement in the Civil War draft riots, for example, generated raucous attention within the firestorm of the day. "If the draft were not abandoned," a *New York Dispatch* report ran, "the Irish servant girls of New York would set fire to the houses of their employers, and burn the whole city." The Gaelic-based press immediately rallied to its female support-base, *The Irish-American* publishing a harsh indictment against the *Dispatch*, denying any truth in the report, and placing the episode in the context of a nativist attack on the servants. Calling the reports a "mean hypocrisy," *The Irish-American* accused the *Dispatch* of "persecuting an inoffensive and really estimable class of the community" and of mounting "a crusade against the Irish servant girls." Horace Greeley's *Tribune* joined the fray, maintaining that even though this accusation was undoubtedly false the general public might be persuaded to believe it, thus bringing "odium, suspicion, and persecution upon some, at least, of these against whom it was levelled."[78] *The Irish-American* judged the servants blameless and connected them with their male compatriots who fought valiantly as officers in Northern regiments. The women, according to one report, shared the same struggle as male compatriots even though they could not participate directly as soldiers. The contribution of female servants to the war effort must also be acknowledged, moreover, especially as any of the Irish officers and soldiers who were willing to die for the Union "would have as readily died to shield the lowliest of their countrywomen from wrong or insult."[79] In the same week, "The Irish Servant Girls: Their Defence by an American Woman" testified to their integrity and value and implored New Yorkers not to "trample on the already crushed reed." A city dweller who had employed Irish household workers for years cited wretched conditions across the Atlantic as the reason why these women emigrated. In describing the loneliness they experienced and the brave attitudes displayed through the workday, the commendable manner in which they sent hard-earned wages home to support impoverished families, and the way they supported the building of churches and the charities of New York, her concluding view that the recent draft riots constituted a class-based nativist attack on Irish laborers and domestics probably raised some hackles in other enclaves of the city, although the tide of Know-Nothingism had declined to the point of political entropy by this point.[80]

Although the attraction of working-class Irish to servitude remained strong throughout the mid- and late-nineteenth century, some evidence suggests that the job was far from venerated and even actively discouraged as a prospect for lifelong employment among the women themselves.[81] Despite the notion that the headstrong quality marking out Irish servants enabled them to command "none but the highest wages, the greatest privileges, and a minimum of work," the aspiration to move beyond this life remained evident. Although a servant's humble origins belied notions of upward mobility, "Bridget" typically held a "high idea of her own respectability" and demonstrated a consistent degree of "uppishness." By all accounts, educational opportunities constituted a necessary step up the ladder of respectability.[82] City philanthropist Helen Campbell found that although many of the mid-century immigrants took jobs for daily wages, they did not encourage their daughters to follow suit. For working women in the post-Famine years, employment in the commercial world improved on servitude both socially and economically, and "hardships cheerfully endured" in a factory or store "if enforced by a mistress would lead to riot." Campbell found that:

> To be a shop-girl seems the highest ambition. To have dress and hair and expression a frowsy and pitiful copy of the latest Fifth Avenue ridiculousness; to flirt with shop-boys as feeble-minded and brainless as themselves; and to marry as quickly as possible, are the aims of all. Then come more wretched, thriftless, ill-managed homes, and their natural results in drunk-

en husbands and vicious children; and so the round goes on, the circle widening year by year till its circumference touches every class in society, and would make our great cities almost what sober country-folk believe them—seas of iniquity.[83]

The perception of higher status employment in stores remained a steadfast ambition into the twentieth century. As long as "social ill-repute" characterized servitude in a negative fashion, working-class women sought out alternative paths to prosperity. More often than not these were inspired by aspects of their heritage at least generally accessible in New York.[84] One such path involved association with the city's Irish-centered political culture, most usually the various nationalist alliances emerging during the mid-century decades and ranging from the broadly popular to the obscure and outlandish. Regardless of agenda or political affiliation, though, each configuration mobilized in tandem with Ireland's progress toward Home Rule during these years.[85] Women's influence is readily discernible through the Fenian Sisterhood, an associate branch of the widespread Fenian Brotherhood.[86] In 1865, Ellen A. Mahoney succeeded to the title of Head Directress of the newly formed women's auxiliary in New York and commenced a press campaign to raise funds for the expenses of "the glorious work of Ireland's regeneration." Not everyone viewed her agenda in such positive terms! The scathing tone of "The Confidence Woman in the Kitchen Area" berated Mahoney for her connivance in squeezing hard-earned wages from domestic servants. Industrious women had been duped by a clever manipulator, the author expounded, Mahoney clearly taking advantage of their sense of justice, nationalist sympathies, and concern for family members suffering under Ireland's oppressive conditions. But urging working women to rise in support of the Fenian movement at the earliest opportunity, Mahoney expounded on the advantages of purchasing "Irish Revolutionary Bonds," the revenue from which would go to furnish arms for the cause. She encouraged women not only to purchase bonds on credit if money were short, but to act as "bond agents" and advertise the campaign among friends and neighbors. Mahoney met with reasonable success, despite the negative attitudes publicized throughout the organization's heyday. Some of the sharpest criticism encapsulated a variety of agendas, such as the following:

> This attempt to abuse the finest traits of the Irish character with pretexts for levying onerous tribute upon the monthly earnings of the poor and industrious *women*, we have some hope will find a check in the sound sense of the contemplated victims. We have much faith in Bridget: and we sincerely trust that when Mistress MAHONEY or any of these mousing bond agents comes fumbling around her strong-box, or sniffing at her savings-bank book, she will rise in the majesty of her wrath, and turn the trollop out of the kitchen.[87]

But the "new phase in the nefarious game" represented by female Fenian association developed as a visible component of the movement in New York. Consistent attendance at Sunday afternoon social events, regular fund raisers and slews of public meetings facilitated direct participation by thousands of women separated into the camps of organizer and follower. Male leaders undoubtedly manipulated poorly educated women into funding operations and engaging in behind-the-scenes organizing without the privileges of power, but Ellen Mahoney's working women as a "class" aiming to take responsibility for the political status of Ireland in the same manner as men or women of other politically volatile nationalities served to bridge some of the existing gaps. In correspondence with city editors, Mahoney accepted that whereas they plainly loved their country, the women should be motivated to loftier patriotic heights with the obligation to harness as much force as the men toward the dismantling of British authority. In citing the experience of French, Italian, and Polish women, Mahoney knew that arriving in a city like New York and entering the domains of domestic servitude, sales work, or education left little time for nationalist activism. But the pattern of securing employment and remitting wages home worked negatively to strengthen British authority, to her mind, as the bulk of these remittances went toward the payment of exorbitant rents to absentee English landlords. Believing that Ireland's poverty set the seeds for a lifetime of hardship upon emigration, Mahoney publicized the Fenian Sisterhood as a means of establishing a new pride in an ancient heritage, and a vehicle through which Irish Americans might unify. Encouraging women to join, she anticipated that "Speranza's and Mary's may spring up from amongst us," and that "associating together for this holy object cannot but have a beneficial effect upon us as a class." Concluding with the thought that "we can teach Irish women to judge Irish men," she urged female readers to apply for the Sisterhood's Constitution and By-laws and to join as soon as possible.[88]

Organized along the lines of the Brotherhood, New York Fenian Sisterhood branches filled a void for politically minded women seeking to either broaden their horizons and their options in pre-suffrage years or take advantage of this opportunity to assist the long-standing Irish cause. Co-opted from existing groups such as the Daughters of Erin and the women's auxiliary of the Ancient Order of Hibernians, members supported broadly nationalist aims in the 1860s.[89] Groups of predominantly single women organized committees and adopted sets of resolutions from which to proceed with a range of activities. Concerned with what the Sisterhood's General Sweeny Branch considered "a division in the ranks of our countrymen as to which mode should be adopted for the freedom of our down-trodden country," the women sought out the most productive options. Individuals such as "Miss Johanna O'Shea, Directress; Miss Mary O'Halloran, Treasurer; Miss Annie Rogan, Secretary; Committee of Safety, Miss Annie Wilbery, Miss Anne Tyrell, Miss Johanna Buckley" and the non-executive members of the General Sweeny Branch met to support the Ireland they called an "armless slave." The predominant image of British victimization loomed large over Sisterhood meetings and fund-raising efforts as they supported the Brotherhood in the run up to the ill-fated Fenian invasion of Canada in 1868. A time of intense excitement for these female Titons witnessing at once the Brotherhood climax and swan song, the "Invasion" accorded the Fenians massive publicity throughout the United States and Canada. "Having had sufficient talk," Annie Rogan wrote in February 1866, "we now call upon our brothers to prepare for action, as we fully endorse that warrior and the con-stitutional Senate."[90]

The final chapter of the book focuses in more depth on Fenian political cul-ture, but within the female context it is not surprising that an Irish "sisterhood" iden-tified with Fenianism. The movement linked politically minded compatriots with a world otherwise largely closed to them. Beyond social or church clubs, Fenianism facilitated contact with branch and community members, while remittance of money home facilitated the regular exchange of news on the contemporary situa-tion in Ireland. As a forum through which hundreds of women politicized and worked toward the "high ideas" of their "own respectability," the movement had few parallels in post-Famine New York.[91]

Other women's collectives built on the Fenian foundation, expanding New York Irish women's influence and strengthening the burgeoning tradition of North American political activism on behalf of the homeland. In 1880, the Ladies Lecture Bureau mobilized public awareness of conditions in the famine-stricken homeland as a cornerstone of its operations. Within a progressive mission, founders Miss Celia Logan and Mrs. Cynthia Leonard aimed "not alone to do some good for the Irish poor, but to show that women had some executive ability." Benefits ranging from Grand Opera House matinees to lecture series for the Duchess of Marlborough's Ireland fund occupied center stage for some hundreds of members during the early 1880s. Unfortunately for the Ladies, one event at the Grand Opera House took an ugly turn with accusations of missing money between the two founders. Under titles such as "A Tempest in a Tea-Pot" and "Trouble Among the Managers," *The New York Times* covered the affair and the ultimate demise of the Bureau.

But together with what may be described as a proto-feminist sensibility, this type of grassroots politicization established on a loosely configured nationalist foundation proved attractive for hundreds of women.[92] The charitable work under-taken by the Ladies Lecture Bureau and the Ladies Land League exhibited a stronger nationalist edge, but the innocuous-sounding Ladies Irish Aid Society met at No. 61 Union Place to appeal directly to the more militant sympathizers, gath-ering to support the relatives of men "recently executed" in skirmishes with British authorities. The families of those Fenians and Clan na Gaelers assassinated or killed on active service could not be neglected, according to Mrs. Kate Diggs, addressing the proceedings in June 1883. No judgment should be called down on these men, and supportive women in New York ought to do all in their power to assist the suffering families of these patriots. She went so far as to employ her "American" right to free speech to argue that the money England spent on informers should be matched by contributions to aid the unfortunate families. The Central Labor Union endorsed Ladies Irish Aid Society mass-meetings providing for "the families of Irishmen recently hanged." Public support through city Catholic churches for the wife of "Manchester Martyr" Michael Larkin, hanged in England in 1867 following his arrest as a Fenian, could only further such objectives.[93]

Specific incidents involving women further raised the profile of female-driven, Ireland-centered political activism in New York. In March 1872, for example, an elaborate banner arrived at the city docks earmarked for the Saint Patrick's Mutual Alliance Association.[94] A prominent organization under the patronage of Tweed Ring chief Richard Connolly, the fraternal group commissioned a large commemorative banner from Sister Mary Francis Clare Cusack, better known as either the Nun of Kenmare or Margaret Anna Cusack. The influence of this multitalented woman extended far beyond the walls of the Poor Clare convent in Kenmare, County Kerry, where she had originally taken vows. Involvement with a variety of different Catholic ministry roles, eventual alienation from the Church, and flamboyant promotion of a nationalist agenda sparked continual controversy and kept her name in the limelight during her lifetime. Publications on the assistance of immigrant women in *Advice to Irish Girls in America,* the place of women in the mid-nineteenth century in *Woman's Work in Modern Society*, and Irish history in a two-volume biography of Daniel O'Connell, *The Liberator: His Life and Times, Political and Social* and *An Illustrated History of Ireland: From AD 400 to 1800* guaranteed her an enormous fount of publicity for decades, especially in the pages of the city press. Cusack's publishing agent in New York officially received the ornamental standard at the dockside from the steamer *Calabria*. A richly decorated, large-scale tapestry in green and white, the nuns in the Poor Clare convent in Kenmare, County Kerry, had woven an intricate Celtic cross as the centerpiece. The press noted that "the banner, which is about ten feet by seven, displays the mottoes," "Let Erin Hope," "Faith and old Ireland," "God save Ireland," and "God save the Alliance." Surrounded by representations of ancient round towers, wolf dogs, harps, and shamrocks, the inscription read "Presented to the St. Patrick's Mutual Alliance by the Nun of Kenmare," garnering heightened attention for the radical Sister's political agenda.[95]

The tapestry arrived with a presentation of native-grown shamrock from the garden of the Poor Clare convent, and both were formally presented to the Alliance during a ceremony at the Cooper Institute some weeks later following an exhibition of the work by the Cusack's agent. Sister Margaret Anna directed the exhibitions and included instructions to the speaker at the Alliance event to "preface the presentation by a brief sketch of her life and writings" with a view to collecting funds from Alliance members. *The Irish-American* noted that "the Alliance will turn out in its strength upon the occasion, and it is hoped that it will result in placing a very large sum of money at the disposal of the illustrious lady." An accompanying letter from Cusack reinforced her aims to publicize Ireland's cause in New York through the presentation. She and her community had labored intensely over the work, "but if the gentlemen are pleased, and that it does good to Ireland—my dear Ireland— I ask no more." In fact, she asked plenty more, not least that the members of Saint Patrick's Alliance purchase and read her publications, in particular, her forthcoming book on the powerful Daniel O'Connell which promised to be "a grand work."[96]

Cusack's fiction also bolstered the nationalist cause. Her play *Tim Carty's Trial, or Whistling at Landlords*, and her story *From Killarney to New York; or, How Thade Became a Banker*, aimed to amalgamate this agenda within popular literature and appeal to mass audiences in the major Irish-American centers.[97] More on this work as a political message in Chapter Four, but on a similar theme, the appearance of a "Political Meditation" in January 1882 covered much of the same territory the feisty nun publicized in her work. Deriving from one of Ireland's more prominent newspapers, the announcement that "an 'Irish Girl' in the columns of *United Ireland* places the following subjects of political meditation before her sisters in Ireland" cultivated the same type of dramatic appeal the Nun of Kenmare found so useful in her propaganda:

> Remember Irish girl, that thou hast this day, and every day of thy life:
> The suspects to imitate
> The Land League to uphold
> A People to save
> Police to mortify
> Eviction to Expiate
> Disunion to avoid
> Freedom to gain
> Irish-Americans to edify
> Prosperity to prepare for
> Landlordism to exterminate
> Agitation to profit by
> Tories to despise
> Whigs to combat
> The Government to subdue
> Principle to abide by

> Of course, she adds, I don't want to restrict my fellow-country girls to these considerations alone, nor have I any desire to limit their political ardor.[98]

Here, the author expressed familiarity with the course of popular agitation, targeting landlords and highlighting evictions and both Tory and Whig aversion to dealing with the situation. The shibboleths included the ubiquitous imagery of the powerless tenant subsisting at the mercy of unsympathetic landowners, but more unusual is the gender-specific focus of the work. Addressed to her compatriots, the "Meditation" conveyed a specific message to the type of female Fenian or Ladies Aid activist organizing successfully both in New York and Ireland during the same years. The rise of prominent women such as Maud Gonne, Countess Markievicz, and the Parnell sisters during the later 1800s increased the strength and vibrancy of women's participation and reinforced a transatlantic connection with the Home Rule campaign.[99] Their efforts coincided with the work of Irish County and Women's County associations of the 1880s and 1890s that granted women enhanced access to city political channels.[100] Consistently generating wide publicity throughout the city press, efforts to unify the twenty-six factions failed by the early 1900s, despite plans for a building to be owned and operated by a committee drawn from the city's most prominent activist groups. Publicized as the Irish Palace, the building would exemplify a new departure in New York nationalist unity, supported by Clan na Gael and the Land League. Enthusiasm over the Palace peaked in 1897 during a month-long fair to raise funds for its construction.[101] Women came to the fore during the campaign with a "Ladies of the Irish American County Organizations of New York" appeal to *Their Fellow Countrymen and the American Public*. Styling themselves "an Organization of 5000 patriotic daughters of Erin," the women declared their intention of collecting:

> . . . a sufficient sum to form a nucleus of a fund to erect an edifice in this city that will be an honor to our race and a Headquarters for social, political, literary and military functions . . . Parenthetically, it may be remarked that the Irish people are the only race of any promise that are not represented by a hall or Headquarters of their own. The Germans, Bohemians, the Swiss, French, the Scotch, English, each has an institution similar to the one we have in contemplation, with the exception that ours will be on a larger and grander scale.[102]

While the Ladies cannot be faulted for their ambition, the County organizations ultimately failed to come together in any meaningful way. Unfortunately for those aspiring toward some type of energized community, an unwelcome disunity characterized the more expansive Ladies Land League during the 1880s. Founded as an auxiliary to Michael Davitt's Land League by Anna and Fanny Parnell, sisters of Member of Parliament Charles Stewart Parnell, the New York branch held much potential on the basis of the input of Davitt and Parnell, if for no other reason. The organization did expand rapidly through the efforts of the Parnell's and Ellen Ford, sister of the *Irish World*'s Patrick Ford, but never really capitalized on the tremendous impact of Davitt's base of operations.[103] Hosting contingents of male and female speakers and running programs devoted to "the rendition of Irish melodies and airs by some patriotic ladies," in the words of Clan na Gael leader John Devoy, the publicity generated by these women was sure to benefit Ireland's cause, Devoy believed.[104] Sponsoring politicians and journalists of the 1880s well versed in Ireland's land question, the organization vigorously advocated that the "redemption of the whole Irish race and not merely an amelioration of the condition of a class could alone satisfy the righteous claims of the Irish people."[105] But female politicization as distinct as that characterizing the Ladies Land League occasionally resulted in downgrading or ruinous division over the mission of the organization and its relationship to the Land League. Never really able to shake the charges of mismanagement or the perception of the organization as middle-class philanthropy in action, despite the mindset of Anna Parnell and her colleagues who institutionalized a strong political agenda early in the group's formation,[106] members ended up drifting into alternative avenues of activist expression by the turn of the century.

As the Home Rule question reached fever pitch for compatriots on both sides of the Atlantic, perhaps the foremost Irish heart-stopper of modern times saw plans shelved with the outbreak of the World War just as the bill was to become law. Seeking to subvert this disaster, concerned New York women took a stand against what they considered a misguided "parliamentary" path to Home Rule, demanding instead direct military action against British authority and support for the newly formed Irish Volunteers.[107] Countess Markievicz, Hannah Sheehy-Skeffington, Mary Colum, and Dr. Gertrude B. Kelly each tried to build on Fenian and Clan groundwork and rally support for a militant agenda within the muddled politics of the 1910s.[108] Even as contemporary Ireland's rising Catholic middle-class produced female volunteers who joined with Protestant associates to expand male-run organizations and political affiliations, New York played host to a similar development during the same years. Eager for success that would result in improved conditions for lower-class women especially, the impetus for activism combined philanthropic and patriotic interests and a yearning for participation within a longstanding traditionally male sphere.[109] In many ways, Cumann na mBan exemplified this effort. In its English-language configuration, Irish Women's Council branches sprung up in New York in the 1910s and may be considered the pinnacle of the Irish feminist-nationalist effort in the city.[110] Brooklyn resident Rose McDermott examined the establishment of the organization under New York law as per instruction from the parent body in Ireland. She outlined the "Conditions and By-Laws" and the stated purpose as being "to aid the people of Ireland to secure their historical independence" and "to advocate interest in Irish history, language and literature, and improve the conditions of the Irish Race." For the network of women devoted to these objectives, any social function stood secondary to its political role. McDermott's hope for a nonreligiously affiliated grouping placed it ahead of its time in this respect also. Objectives couched in popular language seeking "to advance the Cause of Irish liberty; to encourage a National spirit and love of country in our young" tapped into much the same set of romanticized aspirations as the Fenians decades earlier.[111]

Lecturers and poets enlivened Cumann meetings and often made for interesting press. One December 1914 gathering brought noted linguist and Gaelic scholar Professor Kuno Meyer to the same platform as poets Padraig Colum and his wife Mary Colum, journalist Sydney Gifford who wrote for *Sinn Fein* and *Freedom,* and the founder of the Ulster Literary Theatre, John P. Campbell. As events in Ireland accelerated toward the Easter Rising of 1916,[112] Cumann women organized well-attended and often boisterous meetings. These emulated the United Irish Women of New York's enormous gatherings in Carnegie Hall throughout 1914, 1915, and 1916, organized to protest the ongoing Home Rule negotiations at a critical juncture. On March 28, 1914, United women promoted representation in "every quarter of the globe," no less. In addition to Anna E. McAuliffe, Dr. Gertrude B. Kelly, Miss Eleanor Rogers Cox, and Dr. Madge McGuinness, the presiding Board included representatives from Ireland, Britain, Australia, and Canada in an effort to publicize the Home Rule crisis worldwide. Gathering in midtown as the international headquarters, the women railed against the proposed partition of Ireland. As the prospect that Ulster could be ousted from Home Rule negotiations grew more immediate, veteran speaker Margaret Moore declared that the women would "write our own covenant" which would read: "No surrender. No change of the map of Ireland. No sullying of the Irish flag. Ireland must remain as indivisible as the Shamrock." Moore's slogan "No Surrender" is usually associated with the Ulster Loyalist pledge never to "surrender" to a Catholic Ireland, but in this case the direct opposite is targeted! The week before this meeting, *The Irish American* commented that "it may be assumed that their feminine intuition tells them that the men have done talking enough and that something else should be tried."[113]

Speeches by Mrs. Jerome Rooney portrayed Ireland emotionally and vividly as a "motherland" while Women's Trade Union League's Leonora O'Reilly acknowledged the complexities of the whole issue as the United Irish Women drafted resolutions embodying traditional patriotic themes. Calling themselves "exiled Irishwomen in New York," Dr. Kelly and Anna McAuliffe tendered a set of resolutions to the meeting for approval.[114] The first statement catalogued centuries-long sacrifices made by women on behalf of nationhood, while the second proposed that New York's United Irish Women acknowledge the "right" of Irish men to "differ honestly" on the question of tactics within the broad nationalist spectrum. A third criticized what Dr. Kelly called the "Ascendancy party" in Ireland (individuals identified as Anglo-Irish), and the fourth stressed that the ideal of nationhood must supersede political wrangling as the foremost aspiration. The remaining four articles reinforced the commitment of New York's women to this cause, concluding with another slogan—"No New Pale"![115]

The meeting of the Sons of Free Ireland in Carnegie Hall on May 15, 1916, in the immediate wake of the Dublin executions, provoked a huge reaction as 3,500 Irish men and women adopted a "resolution demanding that there be no settlement of the European war which did not include a plan for the freedom of Ireland." "Fully 4,000" people stood outside due to the massive turnout. Women speakers at the next Cumann meeting held at the Cooper Union on July 11, 1916, galvanized over the news that British newspapers refused to print editorials or letters from the American press, as such publicity would influence public opinion on the issue of independence. The Cumann's "monster mass meeting" of May 31, maintained momentum on this kind of debate through the late spring and into the summer of 1916.[116]

Individuals and groups promoting armed suppression of British authority also made the news.[117] Diarist Rose McDermott published a statement in *The New York Journal* in 1914 testifying to the willingness of women to take their rightful place in the independence effort. She remarked on how happy she was to hear Dr. Gertrude Kelly articulate such a strong feminist-nationalist reaction against what she considered the lame rhetoric of the Irish Parliamentary Party, and drew attention to the Party's support for the inclusion of able Irishmen into Britain's World War recruitment plan. Speaking of the "crawling coward" Party Members, McDermott concluded that "if we Irishwomen sit and weep while the so-called Parliamentary leaders cajole and tempt our countrymen to leave their own shores unprotected and go to fight for our enemy, the robber empire, we too have a share in the great crime and guilt."[118]

Far from sitting and weeping, the design of a Certification of financial assistance to the Irish National Volunteers and the publication of articles chronicling the latest Home Rule developments occupied groups of city women during the crucial pre-Treaty years. Framed by a border of shamrock, a traditional lance-type spear and intertwined with Celtic designs reminiscent of the Book of Kells, the Certification illustrated an armed Irish Volunteer in full uniform on one side and four crests depicting the four provinces on the other. One example dated December 26, 1914, read: "Fianna Duthanach na hEireann, (National Army of Ireland), This is to Certify that on 26th December 1914 Wm. McLoughlin, 631 Fifth Avenue, has Contributed the sum of $0.25 to the Fund to Arm and Equip The Irish National Volunteers to enable them to Defend the Inalienable Rights and the Territorial Integrity of IRELAND. The American Irish Volunteers' Committee." The signatures of three of the foremost names in Irish-American nationalist circles, Joseph McGarrity, Chairman, Denis A. Spellissy, Treasurer, and Patrick J. Griffin, Secretary lent requisite authenticity to the effort.[119]

Women such as Rose McDermott sustained the momentum toward the kind of grassroots movement a city like New York could support. Her single-minded focus was couched in language fraught with emotional appeal:

> The land of Ireland is separated from the land of England, by one of the world's angriest seas. The Irish Sea. There is no reason why the Irish should not be given her independence, note the word "INDEPENDENCE," nothing else and nothing less . . . Poor Ireland, situated as she is situated, must suffer, and has suffered because she had and has no past of interest to other nations in the modern world.[120]

Her recounting of female participation in Ireland's history deployed language reminiscent of epic poetry. Women's traditional willingness to participate in dangerous activities and rise to each challenge armed their New York sisters to support the Women's Council and the Irish Volunteers, McDermott believed.[121] Moral support and practical fundraising for the Volunteers stood at the forefront for women who rose to the defense of their nation, and the amalgamation of different female-led factions through the channel of Cumann na mBan offered the prospect of a strong women-centered political force. Further, the unification of different strands of republican thought could merge Catholic and Protestant women into one visionary organization. A progressive line of reasoning in the early twentieth century, her notion that "we sincerely trust all true Irishwomen of whatever creed or class will join our organization" drew from the philosophy of the United Irishmen and Young Ireland already entrenched as nationalist legend. Affirming a multi-stranded female political culture in New York, the hope that the Cumann would reach out proudly to unaffiliated Irish women in all walks of life sustained her throughout these endeavors.

McDermott's images of young sons sacrificing their lives in the name of freedom retained the typical melodramatic imagery of such appeals. "What is a dollar to you," she proclaimed, "when it may be the means of saving many lives that are very dear to you." Not surprisingly, the end of every request brought an entreaty for financial support. As with Ellen Mahoney's earlier Fenian Auxiliary, women were urged not merely to participate in public activities but to contribute in kind for a comprehensive attack on British authority. Aware that empty rhetoric would be short-lived, McDermott urged women to donate all they could in order that vague aspirations could be rendered real and tangible. Concluding with information on meeting times on the third Tuesday every month at Tuxedo Hall, Fifty-Ninth Street and Madison Avenue, she left her readers with the challenge to "make some sacrifices" for the national cause. Her letters to editors continued recounting women's efforts over past centuries, always with the aim of motivating contemporary women to the same end. A February 1914 address stressed this agenda, deploying some of the more popular individuals as inspiring examples, such as Mary

Doyle, Mary McCracken, and Ann Devlin, most specifically. As with Ann Devlin in Robert Emmet's doomed uprising in 1803, the "unselfish patriotism" of such women would surely prove just as inspirational to the male figureheads! McDermott concluded by signing her letter to prospective insurrectionists not in the Anglicized Rose McDermott but in the Gaelic form "Roisin Nic Diarmuida," emphasizing her commitment to a fundamentalist political tradition. Meanwhile, pamphleteer William Rooney reframed her arguments in more dramatic fashion, with direct focus on female activism:

> In the work towards the restoration of Irish hearths and homes we must have an Irish womanhood—an intelligent, enthusiastic and earnest womanhood who will make Irish wives for the men and Irish mothers for the children of tomorrow . . . we shall need something besides dishevelled hair and tearstained faces. We shall need women like the Mary Dwyers, the Maggie Munroes, and the Betsy Grays, women with the lofty patriotism of "Mary" and "Eva" and "Speranza," women with the quiet firmness and the iron resolution of Ellen O'Leary; women with the fortitude of Mary O'Donovan. They not need be as talented as these latter; let them be as womanly and as resolute and we need not fear, whatever trials the future may bring.[122]

Whereas McDermott might have agreed that the qualities of fortitude and "iron resolution" would prove useful, it is unlikely that she conceived of involvement in terms of "dishevelled hair." Rooney's promotion of women's collaboration alongside spouses and associated males was echoed in another treatise entitled *The Influence of the Irish Woman on the National Movement* originally publicized by journalist and historian James Reidy and delivered to the Brooklyn Gaelic Society on a mid-March Sunday in 1906. Stressing that Ireland's women enjoyed the privileges of equality and the right to a prominent role in the country's history, Reidy spoke to the tradition of female rule exemplified by ancient noblewomen and tribal leaders including Maeve, "the warrior queen," and Granuaile, "the daring and adventurous mistress of the western seaboard."[123] The honor bestowed on a Norman lord on the occasion of his marriage to an Irish noblewoman and verses by Thomas Davis depicting women in a seventeenth-century Limerick battle would have been well received by the women of New York![124] Recounting the actions of the famous Betsy Gray, the County Down maid whose exploits were celebrated in McDermott's writings, Reidy recalled "the blazing turf fires" where "they tell with pride of Betsy Gray, of Granshaw, in the County Down, a heroine whose deeds were worthy of Deborah, the Hebrew prophetess and warrior, or Boadicea, the militant Queen of the Ancient Britons," in fighting with the men of 1798.[125]

His portrayal of militant women included many of the same listed by McDermott, names undoubtedly familiar to readers of New York's Irish press. Remembrance of the roles played by Ann Devlin, Molly Ward, Rose Hope, and Mary Ann McCracken aimed to recover their memory within the historical record and bring them into the contemporary consciousness.[126] Women's participation in Young Ireland and the Fenians, and the names of Miss O'Connell, Lizzie Duggan, Mrs. Boland, Mrs. Butler, Ellen O'Leary, and Catherine Mulcahy promised that nineteenth-century activists did not fail the memory of their illustrious foremothers.[127] With the failure of the 1868 Fenian rebellion, readers learned that "it was a ladies committee that collected funds and arranged for the defense of the men as they were brought to trial." Not only that, but "the government agents sought to intimidate the women in this work, but they refused to give it up. The ladies retaining the most prominent positions on the committee included Mrs. Thomas Clarke Luby, a daughter of J.D. Frazer, one of the Young Ireland poets, Ellen O'Leary, and Mrs. O'Donovan-Rossa."[128]

Reidy's reference to the Gaelic Revival in terms of "the de-Anglicization of Ireland" was designed to strike a chord with nationalists of all stripes.[129] The example here of Mrs. MacManus, known as "Ethna Carbery," whose music "re-awakened the National energies of Ireland" echoed the literary input within the contemporary political agenda. As the fourth chapter here illustrates, the aim of stirring the hearts of sympathizers in New York received a boost in a concluding sequence on the role of women in the current phase of the struggle. In fact, Reidy went as far as to argue that equal participation by women alongside men empowered a successful sociopolitical movement.[130]

The leaders ought to acknowledge the vital role of women, he noted, and those who remained outside the realm of struggle had been misled about the political potential of her gender. Females lacked the experience necessary to act publicly and largely failed to reach their capability as feminist-nationalists. Suggesting that they motivate themselves first from the home by inculcating traditional values in their children, women could perform a noble task for the movement. He cited the "husbands, brothers and sweethearts" who "badly need a lesson, and several lessons, in National duty." From there, women could reach beyond the confines of their homes to wield more general political influence. Concern with the ideal of "race pride" heard decades previously during the height of Fenian agitation again rose to the fore as the rhetoric of race intertwined with the concept of the newly inaugurated feminist consciousness. The Irish woman "can inculcate race pride," and of course, who better than women to inculcate principles as the strongest motives for participation! Reidy followed his own advice, urging emphasis on the Irish language and the highest standards of education for future generations, acknowledging that "there is work for the men and women of the Irish race in America on this question alone to keep them busy for a long time."[131]

Echoing these ideas, the political involvement of women emerged just as strongly from the pamphlet "*Women: Ideals and The Nation.*" The full title ran: *Women: Ideals and The Nation; A Lecture Delivered to the Students' National Literary*

Society, Dublin, by Constance Markievicz (Macha of Inghinide na hEireann). The frontisplate cited members to work for Ireland's independence by inculcating a pro-Ireland mentality in all aspects of life; home, workplace, entertainment, and political affiliation. A treatise reaching the public first in Dublin as a lecture to the National Literary Society appeared in published form in New York in 1910.[132] This work could generate plenty of publicity and reinforce transatlantic connections at a crucial juncture on its merits alone, but the fact of its authorship certainly added to its marketability. Countess Markievicz, or Constance de Markievicz, occupied a unique station in Ireland's society and politics. Born in 1868 into the landed Gore-Booths of Lissadell House in Sligo and subsequently married to a Polish Count, her life bore little resemblance to that anticipated for her. Devoting her adult years to the overthrow of British imperialism, Countess Markievicz ignored the cornerstones of her heritage in her two major conversions, the first to the republican cause, and the second, late in her life, to Catholicism.[133] Active participation as a senior officer in the Irish Citizen Army between 1910 and 1920 amalgamated socialist leanings with fervent republicanism, and duty on the front lines of the 1916 Rising resulted in a court martial and death sentence, the order commuted by virtue of her gender. She combined military activities and politics with an outpouring of literary works, including *A Call to the Women of Ireland* in 1909 and her contributions to *Bean Na hEireann. Bean na hEireann*, or *The Woman of Ireland*, considered "the only Nationalist Woman's Paper" by the Countess, appeared on the first Saturday of each month between 1908 and 1912. Edited by Dubliner Helena Moloney, the paper cost 1s 6d in Ireland per year and 2s in "countries other than Great Britain."[134] Soldier, excellent shot, writer, activist, actress, society beauty, Constance Gore-Booth de Markievicz became a living legend. Her life personified the set of contradictions that elevated her to celebrity status, a woman who spent more time in jails and on the run than in the drawing rooms of her kind, and the first woman elected to the British House of Commons in 1918. Opting not to take her seat, and following a spell as a political prisoner during 1919–21, she held the office of Minister for Labour in the first Dail. During the 1920's Civil War, Countess Markievicz's republican support did not waver. After converting to Catholicism in the 1920s, she ended her life as a Sinn Fein T.D. for South Dublin. On the occasion of her funeral in 1927, almost half a million people lined the streets of Dublin, watching eight large trucks transporting the flowers pass solemnly by.[135]

Her activism inculcates the strong ties between turn-of-the-century Ireland and New York, where in both spheres she led groupings of women into political circles previously considered out of bounds. Inauguration of Inghinidhe na hEireann, or Daughters of Ireland, in 1900, provided the Countess with an outlet for her radicalized agenda. One account has her first contact with the Inghinidhe (Daughters) taking place with Markievicz in a ballgown, en route from Dublin Castle.

Accustomed to a fair measure of pomp and circumstance throughout her early life, the detached reception she received from the assembled Inghinidhe sparked her interest in a women's group more intent on their political agenda than in her personality or heritage.[136] Her reputation preceded her internationally, and the New York press carried extensive accounts of her speeches campaigning for independence alongside details of her social engagements in European cities.[137] Her 1909 *Women: Ideals and the Nation* read as militantly and passionately as any colorful Fenian speech from the pen of a Devoy or a Mitchel, as Markievicz enlightened her readership to Irish women's political potential.

As McDermott and Mahoney before her, Markievicz argued that women in Russia and Poland played a greater role in revolutionary movements than their Irish counterparts, but perceived England as a more dangerous enemy than other European imperialist powers as a result of the British policy of "ultimate good." This idea, in Markievicz's view, was formulated to maintain subservience by ostensibly advocating the general welfare of the Irish people. She raised the "subtle psychological question of why it was that so few women in Ireland have been prominent in the national struggle," lamenting the loss of the "magnificent legacy of Maeve, Fleas, Macha and other great fighting ancestors."[138] Lamenting too the loss of Anglo-Irish elites to the drawing rooms of London where they invested in English ideals even as they abandoned Irish culture, Markievicz intertwined the roles of woman and liberator, emphasizing that:

> For as you are born a woman, so you are born an Irelander, with all the troubles and responsibilities of both. You may shirk or deny them, but they are there, and some day—as a woman and as an Irelander—you will have to face the question of how your life has been spent, and how have you served your sex and your nation?[139]

The statements unify a feminist and a nationalist agenda, Markievicz maximizing both in a strident republican attitude. She urged her readers to believe that "ideas and principles" were the building blocks of a new Ireland where women would constitute equal partners alongside their male counterparts. Commenting personally, she remarked that "lately things seem to be changing," and drew hope from her belief that women would no longer be held to the strictures of an oppressive sociocultural agenda. Concluding with a call to a prospective "Joan of Arc" to liberate Ireland, she challenged women not only to play an active role in the movement, but to "arm your minds with the histories and memories of your country and her martyrs, her language, and a knowledge of her arts and her industries." Not content with that, Markievicz added her final charge: "And if in your day the call should come for your body to arm, do not shirk that either."[140] That she herself never shirked the prospect of physical combat on behalf of her beliefs imbued her writings with a dramatic and yet ultimately serious edge.

On that note, in terms of her legacy and that of others who articulated similar thoughts and arguments on behalf of Ireland by 1921 and the negotiation of the Government of Ireland Act, or "The Treaty," we can be confident that female-centered activism constituted a movement within a movement for New York women participants and spectators. Bearing the hallmarks of what may be described as a feminist-nationalist tradition, women played as authoritative a role in the annals of Irish nationalism in New York as could be expected in pre-suffrage decades. Although sidelined in terms of formalized leadership, Cumann na mBan, the United Irish Women, and the Ladies Irish Aid Society provided platforms for women of all political shades to take initiatives, organize, raise money, and participate in a manner often independent of the dominant male agenda surrounding them. Involved women achieved more than simply reinforcement of connections with Ireland. Instrumental in supporting the homeland's bid for independence in all its expressions and phases, women's support of the male-dominated organizations, their visible role in female-led groups, their contribution to the rhetoric of the day, and their fundraising ability constituted significant dimensions of a dynamic political agenda.

Equally fundamental, in successfully transplanting their beliefs and practices to New York, women forged a key feature of the new Irish-American culture particular to the city. Without their involvement, nationalist politics may well have thrived within specific circles of influence, organizations, political parties, and the like. But the mobilization that occurred in New York owed much to the politicizing female-led force operating at the margins of and also outside the traditional male parameters. Thanks to the movement of a powerful acculturation instrument, Irish women in the immigrant community institutionalized radicalized political agendas during the pre-Treaty years, and played an equally vital role in the establishment of Ireland's independence as an agenda of significance for the New York Irish.

As their experience demonstrates, important conclusions arise to supplement what we know of Irish women's New York settlement, highlighting their role in the creation of a post-Famine transatlantic world that looked back to home as frequently as anticipating an American future. Most basically, that relatively equal numbers of males and females arrived and settled reconfigures traditional immigration depiction. Women's transportation of the values and practices inculcated within their native socioeconomic backgrounds proved significant in the sphere of city welfare, charitable endeavors, and nationalist politics. The variegated character of their experience became visible through the operations of professionals such as the Sisters of Charity and the Ladies of Charity, founders of nationalist organizations such as the Ladies Land League and Cumann na mBan, and the work of women subsisting as domestic servants. Collectively, they created cultural distinctions across the same class and political lines dominating nineteenth-century Ireland. But the image of Irish women as ambitious and politically motivated emerges equally as strong, evidenced by the succession of female-based and female-run organizations that focused four-square on the goal of a free Ireland. That the Fenian Sisterhood, the Cumann, and the Ladies Land League generated so much publicity speaks to female commitment to the cause and to the more generalized political presence in New York.

That they stopped short of unifying all the different feminist-nationalist manifestations in the city should not be viewed as failure. Irish women outside the formal political sphere utilized the advantages within their grasp to a successful degree. Their influence, their energy, and their reaction against traditional gender barriers contributed in no small way to the agenda of improvement and change on both sides of the Atlantic, significantly influencing the nascent New York Irish identity while building a foundation for the components discussed in the following chapters.

C H A P T E R   T H R E E

The Quiet Men
(and Women)

The Irish mind hops back to the Flood when discussing a leaking tap; the Anglo-Irish mind
regards history as an untactful obtrusion on present enjoyment, like a reference to death at
a wedding, a skeleton at the feast.[1]

histories of Irish-American settlement have traditionally referenced Ireland as
agricultural and provincial, with the bulk of the expansive population subsisting fairly miserably on poor land and fleeing en masse to America in times
of particular duress.[2] Most usually, nineteenth-century emigrants gave the impression of being "homeless, nationless, and all but hopeless after a grim sea passage to
an unwelcoming land." While no one doubts, as Dennis Clark summarized, that
the Irish "were trying to survive as individuals, as families, as an ethnic group amid
a deeply disorienting experience of emigration and urban novelty," these character-
izations tended to languish within a historiographic zone where stock themes
overshadowed less visible settlement patterns.[3] The impression that immigrants
hailed universally from the outposts of rural Ireland has just begun to broaden out
to include men and women who had no experience of tenancy or farming and who
merely exchanged one urban context for another on arrival in America, albeit a
much larger one. Although famine affected people living off the land most directly, towns and cities also experienced the pressures of emigration in times of famine-
driven economic duress.[4] For example, Dublin witnessed high emigration levels in
times of particular stress, and the artisans, tradespeople, and unskilled workers that

made the same journey as the West Coast spailpin inculcated measures of social, religious, and political diversity within the settlement process.[5]

The practice whereby older Irish-American historiography circumscribed Catholicism so closely with "Irish" that they seemed virtually interchangeable has also started to abate. The centrality of Catholicism as a religious belief system and mentalite long prevailed, foregrounding the faith as a cultural cornerstone and means of upward mobility for nineteenth-century immigrants,[6] and the perspectives arising from this foundation hold much value within the Irish-American narrative. But the fact remains that not every immigrant was Catholic. A considerable percentage of Protestants subscribing to various denominations joined the transatlantic crossings. Obscured by the "Catholic" character of the movement, and understandably so, given its expansive nature and tragic dimensions, nonetheless, Shea and Casey's note that "some obvious gaps in the literature . . . still wait for a scholar, such as the history of the Protestant Irish community in the city in the late nineteenth and early twentieth centuries"[7] is still pertinent. Kevin Kenny voiced the same concern more recently, calling for attention to this immigrant sector in America and citing incorporation of Irish-American Protestants as one of the more important new directions for the general history of America's Irish.[8] This chapter seeks to uncover the all-but-secret entity, the (predominantly) quieter men and women constituting a virtually hidden strain of Irishness that still played a distinct role in the creation of the city's post-Famine Irish identity. As the chapter illuminates a central strand of Ireland's culture transplanted across the Atlantic, the relationship between Irish Protestants and the exhausting question of Ireland's freedom also comes into play as directly and vexatiously as it did for other sectors of the immigrant population. As Irish women were drawn into a variety of nationalist collectives for a number of reasons, so also would their Protestant compatriots experience similar political mobilizations. The small farmers, artisans and craft workers, and the coterie of affluent merchants and traders hailing from the various Protestant denominations and settling in proximity to their Catholic neighbors represented traditions connected by a turbulent history. Their experience raises key points on the nature of Irish settlement in America, and the transatlantic world converging in New York in particular.

As an umbrella term embracing the most popular denominations of Anglicanism, Presbyterianism, Methodism, and Quakerism,[9] the doctrinal and cultural factors differentiating one denomination from another operate as a minefield of sorts, particularly within the immigrant context.[10] "Even for the coolest heads," Donald Akenson remarked, "Ireland presents a problem, for it contains three distinct ethnic subgroups, which . . . can be identified as the Catholics (of 'Celtic-Irish' descent), the Presbyterians (Scotch-Irish or 'Ulster-Scots'), and the 'Anglo-Irish' (English by descent and mostly Anglican by religion)."[11] Since the seventeenth

years later, this number declined to 5,412,377. Of this total, Protestants numbered 1,293,299 in 1861 and 1,261,510 a decade later in 1871. During the same ten-year period, the Irish-American immigrant total reached 989,835. Following the model, calculating twenty percent of the total Irish-United States immigration for 1861–70 gives us a figure of 138,169 as approximating the number of Protestant immigrants to America in this particular decade. While useful in assessing the general extent of Protestant arrival, this model renders calculation of the proportion of this group settling in New York less fine. However, American census statistics for the Irish-born population of New York since 1860 may be employed to this end. The total Irish-born population of New York in 1860 is accepted as 260,450. A decade later, that total rose to 280,219, a peak for the later nineteenth century. Thereafter, a slow but steady decline resulted in a figure of 203,450 as the total by 1920.[31]

According to our model, if Protestants constituted at least twenty percent of American immigrants from Ireland, we can surmise generally that totals for New York included at least twenty percent from Protestant denominations. From available statistics, we can calculate that at least 50,000 Irish-born Protestants arrived in New York between 1860 and 1870, with the average declining in the proceeding decades as Ireland's emigration totals decreased annually by a few percentage points. These estimations are sharpened by Cormac O'Grada's determination that slightly earlier, from 1835 to 1838, thirty-eight percent of all Ireland's emigrants hailed from Ulster. Kerby Miller's opinion that for much of the post-Famine era "Protestant emigration probably exceed(ed) one-fifth of the total" further supports the probability of twenty per cent as a solid minimum for New York.[32] As rates of population decline remained proportionally similar for both Catholics and Protestants in the period 1861–1926 and, given that sizable contingents of Ulstermen and women had previously settled in New York during the pre-Famine and Colonial decades, we can be confident of an approximation of at least 50,000 Irish Protestants in post-Famine New York by 1860.[33]

In comparison with the larger and more vociferous Catholic element that would dominate mid-century, Ireland's Protestants acclimated more unobtrusively.[34] In the absence of collective public attachment to a single political agenda, intermittent dalliances with abolitionist forces and nativist groups rendered the men and women from Ulster likely to assimilate more smoothly than their Catholic counterparts, even up to the decades immediately preceding the Famine. Convivially, participation in local Saint Patrick's Day parades brought both elements together each March, reinforcing the native-born identification and overcoming traditional antagonism on the part of the celebrants. But perhaps the most public representation of the Protestant-Irish tradition in New York materialized within the lodges and parades of the Loyal Orange Order. As the public face of Ulster Presbyterianism, the Order institutionalized important aspects of the native culture in the nineteenth-century city. Transplanted directly from Belfast and Antrim and the proliferation of prosperous Ulster towns safeguarding the fraternal organization for over a century past, the "powerful instrument of social control," as Patrick Buckland described it, established an early New York presence by the mid-1800s and grew extensive enough to inaugurate the State Grand Lodge of New York in 1874. Akin to Freemasonry, the Order has been described not so much as a secret society as what Tony Gray designated "a society with secrets." Since its formal charter in 1795, the Order spread through Ulster, Scotland, England, and the eastern United States to entrench the system of lodges, elaborate rites, and rich symbolism as a cornerstone Presbyterian institution. The 1869 Application by Orangemen in America to Ireland's Grand Lodge for "National Grand Lodge" status received the following affirmation:

> To all whom these presents shall come. Greeting. Know ye that we, the Grand Master and Members of the Grand Lodge of Ireland, do hereby certify that there is no objection or impediment on the part of the Loyal Orange Institution of Ireland to the formation of an Independent Association of Orangemen in and for the United States of America. Signed on behalf of the Grand Lodge of Ireland. January, 1870, Enniskillen, Grand Master. [35]

Extolling the virtues of Orangeism a century later, William Banks declared the United States an ideal location for the spread of the Order, arguing for preservation of the foundation of loyalty operating so strongly in both contexts:

> The obligation taken in the U.S. is of course unswerving loyalty to that country, and there are no more loyal and law-abiding people within the Union than the Orangemen who, in the dark days of the rebellion and in other times of trouble, fought and died like heroes for the Star-Spangled Banner . . . it is surely time for us to break every political tie and unite to secure the triumph of civil and religious liberty and the downfall of clericalism. [36]

Beneath the colorful emblems and the days of celebration, the transfer of Orangeism across the Atlantic included the shipping over of traditional antagonism toward the perceived threat of Catholicism, or "Romishness," more popularly. The concept of Protestant libertarianism rooted in just authority lay at the foundation of the antagonism. On the nature of what can be described as a siege mentality, Tony Gray remarked that "the plain truth of the matter . . . is that the ignorant Orangeman still has a deadly fear of the Church of Rome." The Order's vision of Catholicism in general and the Papacy specifically generated interesting reading, Louis M. De Cormenin's "The Popes of Rome," for example, leaving readers in no doubt as to his feelings on the subject in 1914:

> Here is seen a frightful picture of monstrous debaucheries, bloody wars, memorable schisms and revolutions. Its recital embraces the long succession of Pontiffs celebrated for their crimes, or illustrious for their exploits . . . The shades of ignorance then obscured the mind; the people, stupefied in a frightful slavery, rent each other like wild beasts, in order to please their tyrants, and subserve their ill-regulated passions—ages of misfortune, massacres, incendi-

arism and famine! . . . The Popes more loose and savage than the tyrants of ancient Rome and Byzantium, seated upon the pontifical chair, crowned with a triple diadem of pride, hypocrisy and fanaticism—surrounded by assassins, poisoners, and courtiers.

De Cormenin did not neglect "the pitiless barbarity of priests" and the damage caused by these "inexorable despots . . . during two thousand years of tyranny and fanaticism."[37] Ireland's Imperial GrandMaster and Member of Parliament Captain L.P.S. Orr reiterated nineteenth-century Orange philosophy in the claim that "it is to this movement that the world owes the establishment of the concept of Civil and Religious Liberty." His definition of the Orange mission lay unchanged over two centuries, essentially that "the principles of this movement . . . were to establish and protect the Protestant Religion (by which general term was understood not any particular sect, but the general concept of freedom of conscience in religion) and to establish Civil and Religious Liberty."[38]

PICTURES OF IRELAND. 499

heroism at Londonderry. I forget the number of casualties on the side of the defendors; but they must have been few, inasmuch as so many survivors seem to have given their time and energy to the benefit of posterity. Derry's situation on a steep hill, not unlike that of Lisbon, is striking and picturesque from the right bank of the river (Foyle), though its abrupt ascents make riding tedious, and walking an exercise too energetic for quiet enjoyment. There, as every where else in Ireland, I heard a great deal of the antiquity of the town, an Augustinian abbey having been founded on the summit of the hill more than twelve centuries ago by a saintly architect called Columba.

In the sixteenth century Derry was made a military station; but a terrific explosion of gunpowder destroyed both the fort and the town, and nearly every body in them, and so filled the vicinity with horror that it was completely abandoned for more than forty years. Derry had just begun to prosper in a rehabilitated state when one of those amiable and apocryphal gentlemen for whom that region has been remarkable—he was of the fertile O'Doherty family—took possession of the fortifications and the town, reduced them to ashes, and butchered both the soldiers and the inhabitants, lest history might do him wrong by charging him with an ungenerous discrimination.

The old walls of Derry still remain, and like those of York have been converted into a promenade. The gates, destroyed at the siege of 1689, have been rebuilt, and that on the site of the one from which the heroic garrison made its first sortie is a triumphal arch in commemoration of the event, and bears the name of the Bishop's Gate. A Doric column, surmounted by a statue of the Rev. George Walker, celebrated for his defense of the town at the time of the siege, was erected in 1828, at a cost of £1200. In the centre of the city is the Diamond, a square from which the principal streets

run at right angles toward the ancient gates. The episcopal palace stands where the old abbey is presumed to have been. The long narrow bridge over the Foyle, on the same plan as the bridges at Waterford and Wexford, is the work of an American architect named Cox, who also constructed the others. The scenery about Derry is pleasant enough, though not impressive. The Vale of Vaughan makes pretensions to pictorial beauty, but the hills that form it are bleak, and the river flowing through it has little to awaken admiration.

Going south you pass through Drogheda, an ancient city with numerous ruins, more interesting to the professional antiquary than to the *poco-curante* traveler. It boasts of the remains of an Augustinian priory—founded by Saint Patrick, of course—a Carmelite convent of the reign of Edward I., a graceful tower of a Dominican abbey, and various ecclesiastic remains covered with ivy, tradition, and superstition.

I was urged to visit what were asserted to be the magnificent ruins at Mellifont and Monasterboise, but I unhesitatingly declined. There are throughout the country so many

WALKER'S PILLAR, LONDONDERRY.

Fig 3.1: "Walker's Pillar, Londonderry," *Harper's New Monthly Magazine* (March 1871); courtesy of Cornell University Library, Making of America Digital Collection.

Far from inspiring him, similar thoughts had prompted Dublin lawyer Thomas Wallace to put pen to paper in an attack on the Order entitled *The Orange System Exposed and The Orange Societies Proved to be Unconstitutional, Illegal, and Seditious*, a pamphlet that appeared in the form of a letter to the Marquess of Wellesley in 1823. Wallace wrote of Orangeism as "the scourge of Ireland" and bemoaned the attachment of the country's Protestants to this organization.[39] In fact, works decrying the connection of Protestantism with Orangeism appeared simultaneously in New York, such as the inflammatory treatise *Orangeism Exposed, with a Refutation of the Charges etc. Brought Against the Irish Nation* in 1824 by another city lawyer, David Graham.[40] Despite the negative publicity (or even perhaps because of it), the Protestant base in post-Famine New York supported an extensive system of Orange Lodges, symbolizing successful acculturation. Although the closed doors of the meetinghouses obscured business from public view, the Order still reached into general city life. The press carried extensive coverage of public activities, *The New York Times* holding a relatively objective line compared with hard-line nationalist-press denigration. *The Irish World*, *The Irish Citizen*, and *The Irish Nation* openly confronted Orange propaganda and the entire Order raison d'etre on a regular basis during the post-Famine decades, but the rhetoric would not translate into real cause for concern until the 1870s.

Order meetings adopted the same format in New York as in Ireland. Members assembled at stated intervals for the traditional ceremonies and rituals, and lodge meetings typically included an opening prayer, the minutes of the previous meeting, proposals for or initiations of new members, items of business, collection of dues, and addresses by invited speakers.[41] By the post-Famine decades, the Order had established sufficiently well to earn prominent city status. A December 1869 exploration into tensions between "the Orange and the Green" invested the Ulstermen with evidence of their achievement. While antagonism had long strained relations between Loyalist Orangemen and nationalists seeking independence from British rule at home, of greater concern was the fact that these pressures had been transplanted almost intact to New York through organizations such as the Order. Following a commentary on the bitterness between the two, *The New York Times* argued that:

> To the wearer of the Green, the Orange recalls centuries of wrong, the English invasion, the atrocities of Strongbow and Cromwell, the inhuman "Catholic laws" which oppressed his race for centuries. The Orangeman sees in the Green the sufferings of every Waldensian and Alligensian martyr—the campaigns of James II, the famine and the siege of Derry—the Catholics wading knee deep in Protestant blood—the glorious rescue under William on the Boyne.

Claiming that sectarianism persevered to afflict the two distinct traditions in New York, the writer exasperatedly pointed out that the history of oppression and bloodshed had survived the Atlantic crossing only too well. Regretful of the degree of "bitterness" and "social estrangement and dissension" in evidence, New Yorkers in general held Irish power struggles in contempt, and wished to see age-old tensions left behind on arrival in America, he held. Calling nationalism "the dream of poets," Ireland could not hope for international support against Britain until it had put its own house in order and dissolved people's hatred of each other. The fact that these antagonisms started to materialize in New York underscored the problem. Advocating that "all these dark and hateful traditions" remain in Ireland, he suggested that the colors of the American flag should fly uppermost in the Irish immigrant mind, irrespective of religious persuasion. The Orange and Green emblems should be relegated to memory as symbols of a bygone age. The challenge to both traditions was clear; the world opted to ignore the Irish Question "because no act of injustice by the servants of England's red banner is one half as brutal as the tyranny of the Green to the Orange, or the Orange to the Green." The author here spotlighted perhaps the heart of the "Irish Question" that would dominate newspaper headlines and political debates through the entire post-Famine era and command the attention of Irish New Yorkers ever more urgently as the century wore on.[42] By 1872, the "two Irish factions" stood ready to test themselves on the new battleground of New York. Notions of "a sort of arbitration between the two high contracting parties of the Orange and the Green as to how they would settle their rival claims to the highways of the City" conveyed the sense of futility surrounding the issue. A barb framed in jest, referring "alike to the Orange and the Green, 'a plague o' both your houses!" seemed to capture popular sentiment on the issue.[43]

On a more positive note, from the Protestant perspective, occasional features on the history of the House of Orange generated a sense of respectability for the Order in the city. References to the genealogical background of the Princes of the House of Nassau and William III's accession to the English throne in the late seventeenth century publicized Orange affiliations in positive tones. In 1885 a *Harper's Magazine* review of the House history ranged from its origins in the French principality of Provence to Orangeism's contemporary status. The triumphal delineation of connections with the monarchies of Europe would reinforce the conclusion that "the House of Orange is inseparably identified with European history in the past three hundred years; to it the independence of the Netherlands is due, and many of the great influences that have affected Continental politics."[44] Meanwhile, the Orange Loyalist presence continued to expand in the city. Meetings, marches, and social engagements surrounding the most famous calendar dates predominated, especially the Glorious Twelfth of July and the Apprentice Boys March anniversary on the sixteenth of August.[45] At the semi-annual gathering of the Loyal Orange Institute of the United States of America in June 1872, held in Manhattan, the Supreme Grand Secretary noted that membership now ran into the thousands.

Surpassing all expectations for that year, the Order had "more than doubled its number of members since last July, particularly in the City of New York, where the increase had exceeded the most sanguine expectations."[46] As expansion increased, Catholic attacks proliferated on a group perceived as existing solely to destroy the faith of their fathers, and the real cornerstone of Irish culture. Incendiary speech-making and hostile exchanges commanded heightened press attention, exacerbating tensions between the traditions even as the Order just as vociferously and just as colorfully denounced Catholic encroachment on liberty and the corruption of just authority. In his 1898 history of the organization, available in each city lodge, William Banks cataloged nationalist incursion through the ages; Brethren enduring long invectives on such incidents as "the hair-brained attempt of Robert Emmet . . . to raise a revolt while Russell was acting the fool elsewhere" and how "the scum of Dublin" failed to exert any pressure on the British government headed by the hapless Russell. Members received a full account of the subsequent execution of Emmet, a story doubtless familiar to every man amongst them.[47]

A speech circulated through city lodges during the same decade by the Provincial Grand Secretary of the Order further illustrates the Ulstermen's sensibility. Nassau G. Gowan deliberated on the power of the small, dedicated fraternity of Protestant standard-bearers to hold the influence of Rome in check, castigating Catholics and describing prominent figures among them as "public jobbers" who corrupted Orangeman's "honest purpose." He reacted directly against the influence of Thomas D'Arcy McGee. McGee the politician, man of letters, and Irish cultural ambassador had risen to such prominence on the North American political scene that Canadian Orangeman Robert McBride published a number of what he described as "satires, directed principally against Thomas McGee," in *The Canadian Orange Minstrel for 1860*.[48] Referring to the Catholic politicians he called McGee's "dupes," Gowan intoned that the time had arrived for change in the public perception of both traditions. He demanded public respect for the Order, even from Catholics. Recent increases in membership seemed to support his argument. "Strange to say," he remarked, "the same Mr. McGee and his minions appear to feel a good share of uneasiness about this dread Orangeism. I would be surprised at the amount of excitement they experience over Orangeism, were it not that I know they belong to the tribe of superstitionists and ghost-seers."[49] The opinions of a cleric of this "tribe" gave further voice to the invective around the turn of the century. Reverend R. M. Ryan's 1900 book ostensibly denounced a revival of Know-Nothingism, but his attempt to highlight Catholic tolerance of nativist movements led him to surmise that "it would require a person to have lived some time in the North of Ireland to enable him to appreciate the forbearance, the long-suffering, and the patient endurance of the Catholics there when the Orange anniversaries came around each year." On the Twelfth of July celebrations, the

Reverend claimed that "every village was covered with flaunting, offensive emblems, which were such an outrage upon good feeling and good taste that they would turn Oscar Wilde green with disgust."[50]

Whatever about the worldly Wilde, the two "traditions" under the New York Irish umbrella exhibited the same characteristics and patterns of behavior as they had engaged in across the Atlantic for centuries past. Perceiving their organization as the last bastion of a political tradition celebrating civil and religious freedom, and a necessary bulwark against the Church of Rome, Loyalist militancy certainly over-shadowed the settlement of other Protestant sects sufficiently well to assume the "Irish Protestant" identity by the immediate post-Famine years. Their transplan-tation to New York of historical episodes symbolic of their political philosophies, the prevalence of their secret society, and their emblems, parades, and insignia publicized their efforts simultaneously on both sides of the Atlantic, and the Glorious Twelfth of July commemoration of William of Orange's 1690 victory over James of Scotland on the banks of the Boyne coordinated the politics and the symbols in the most public Orange activity of the year in both contexts.

New York played host to Twelfth celebrations from the mid-1820s on in the form of organized marches, the first recorded in the United States taking place in the city in 1824 and ending in a short-lived skirmish between participants and unor-ganized Catholic onlookers. Subsequent celebrations turned into more newswor-thy melees involving the use of brick, stone, and bullet.[51] Antagonisms leveled off by mid-century, and it was not until the 1860s that hostilities again arose. In 1868, one reporter made sarcastic reference to the procession of "certain miserable fanat-ics," with the Orangemen converging behind a banner displaying "a truly curious jumble of Masonic emblems" and another bearing a likeness of William of Orange that could have been William the Conqueror for all the onlookers knew. The fol-lowing year a larger group assembled, the Orangemen declining the friendly man-tle of the American Protestant Association that had previously "concealed their identity." Other areas in eastern North America witnessed periodic outbreaks of vio-lence in the same years, with a number of Catholics killed by some "wretched Orangemen" in the winter of 1861–62 over local government disputes in the town of Carbonear, Harbor Grace, Newfoundland, for example.[52] An *Irish-American* prediction in 1868 that "we have 'isms' enough here already; but American soil is not that upon which the persecuting dogmas of Orangeism will take root" expressed nationalist hopes. On the contrary, the next few years saw the city's Lodges orga-nize publicly on the occasion of each Order anniversary. In 1870, Tammany approved the proposed Twelfth march up Eighth Avenue, Governor Hoffman having little reason to anticipate trouble from a parade of middle-aged men decked out in the customary bowlers, dark suits, and regalia.

Reports vary on numbers, ranging from several hundred to upward of two thousand marchers.[53] During the parade, the assorted onlookers probably shuddered at the memory of the Draft Riots a few years previously, women supporters in particular remembering the radicalism and fearing the street violence that took place, but few could really have anticipated trouble from the conservative Ulstermen. On the day, whether a spontaneous rise in nationalist feeling heightened tensions, or some well-placed interlopers managed to alarm the unprotected marchers to the point where things took an ugly turn is uncertain, but the confrontation that took place captured city attention in the days and weeks following. While it is certainly possible that the failed Fenian "Invasion" of Canada in 1866 heightened Catholic-Protestant tensions and sparked a fracas, an estimated 500 Catholics staged a running battle with the sober-suited celebrants and the march ground to a halt as police from several different precincts moved in to disperse the rioters.[54]

These incidents set the scene for 1871. This time, as Michael Gordon has recovered the story, city officials deliberated carefully over whether or not to allow the parade to proceed. Initially, administrators banned the march, concluding that no opportunity for public disorder could arise if it were cancelled. But anti-Tammany lobbies clamored against lame Democratic pandering to Catholics and, to dispel the appearance of weakness, the Democrats reversed the decision and reinstated the march. The unwieldy maneuvering raised the ire of both traditions. Journalist and nationalist John Mitchel—a Protestant, though not an Orangeman—deployed the columns of his *Irish Citizen* to pour scorn on both the Order and the administration. Referring to Hoffman as "Our Orange Governor," Mitchel considered the Democratic-controlled city government's action a "bloody blunder" of enormous proportions, so much so that Hoffman might have succeeded to the office of President of the United States had he not fallen prey to Orange treachery. "If his party now were mad enough to put him in nomination, he could never get one Irish Catholic vote, *not one*; nor the vote of any Protestant, Irish or American, who has any knowledge of the true meaning of that diabolical organization which he has now taken under his protection; and which may now take him under *its* protection," Mitchel thundered.[55]

Approximately 160 stern-faced Ulstermen sallied forth under the protection of 800 police and 2,200 soldiers of the New York State militia amidst verbal assaults from Catholic onlookers that quickly escalated to physical engagement. Unwilling to let the faction fight get out of hand, the police and militia opened fire, killing several assailants. Further violence exploded throughout the Lower Manhattan streets and, unlike previous incidents resulting in a few superficial injuries, the riot of 1871 claimed between 29 and 50 lives, depending on the report cited.[56] Nationalist papers leapt into the fray under massive and dramatic headlines, heatedly declaring old wounds wide open. Conservative opinion pieces bewailed the transportation of old divisions onto American soil. Some expressed sympathy for the Orangemen, acknowledging their right to march and to commemorate past glories on the streets of the great city. The *Christian Advocate* failed to display much Christian charity, railing that "it is well known to everybody that the city of New York is ruled by an overpowering mob of the very worst class of Roman Catholic Irishman—ignorant, bigoted, drunken, bloodthirsty and generally and intensely depraved." The worst excesses of Tammany corruption linked directly to Rome in typical nativist style. Orangemen enjoying a ceremonial cultural exhibition had been denied their basic right, the author decided, continuing:

> Very naturally our Hibernian rulers cherish all the partisan sentiments of their native island, and none more intensely than their enmity toward Protestantism. Of true and genuine Americanism they have not the faintest trace in their mental composition, and the notion that a Protestant, and especially a Protestant Irishman, has any rights that should be respected by them seems never to have entered into their thinking. On St. Patrick's Day—their great national anniversary—they take possession of the city, filling and obstructing the streets with their processions and holding a general carnival of drunkenness and terrorism, and nobody—neither the city government, who are their creatures, nor the respectable Protestant citizens, who dread to offend an enemy so fierce and so powerful—dare utter a word of complaint.

The plight of inoffensive Protestants at the mercy of corrupt Romanists had to be seen to be believed, the writer reiterating that "there is in this city a small body of Irish Protestants, who, wisely or otherwise, choose to commemorate the deliverance of their native island from the rule of the Papists." As enlightened educated civilizers meeting regularly in the convivial atmosphere of the lodge, enjoying blameless social activities such as family picnics and boat trips, Protestants would relinquish a valuable component of their culture and risk decline to the point of extinction in New York without this organization.[57] But the *Catholic World*'s description of the "bloodthirsty party" of Orangemen who attempted to offend Catholics in the most public manner couched the event in terms of "an Irish riot, occasioned by an old Irish feud between two Irish parties, not an American or a Catholic riot."[58]

Conservative publications across the Atlantic viewed the disturbance according to form, a majority agreeing that aggression was inevitable given the political strength of Catholics and the determination of the Ulstermen. Dublin's *Saturday Review* commented that a "great many rabid Orangemen" could expect to organize privately but should not anticipate that public commemoration of an incendiary event would pass unnoticed. Advancing that this incident might open the eyes of Americans to the differences between Protestants and Catholics, the *Review* posited that such a scene was unavoidable and would recur if Orangemen repeated the commemoration. It was obvious, the *Saturday Review* concluded, that the Irish "change the sky rather than their nature" in crossing the Atlantic and that the cultural barriers in New York mirrored those dividing Ireland's population for hundreds of years. Despite the absence in the city of either Irish land law or state religion, her cultural divisions had been well established.[59]

No doubt wary of further trouble, yet intent on preserving the traditional commemoration within their new urban context, smaller processions replete with banners, regalia, and the traditional fife and drum publicly sustained the Orange presence through Lower Manhattan streets in a more peaceable manner over the following years. In 1872, Catholics were warned not to "meddle with the Orange zealots" on the forthcoming day. After the fact, *The Irish American* reported general disregard of the 172 staunch men of Ulster braving July temperatures in Sunday-best serge. Judging by the large police contingent of 750 surrounding them, they looked like a parade of "blue-coated law guardians rather than of Orangemen, and, in that respect, was curious enough to evoke a smile." The following year, 337 of the black-garbed faithful took to the streets accompanied by more than a thousand police, and got through peaceably. After the 1874 procession of just over 500, the pattern of quiet demonstration continued with several hundred Lodge members decking out under the watchful eye of the police. Picnics in some of the parks or boat-trips around Manhattan usually followed the parades. On the bicentennial of the Twelfth in 1890, a sizeable contingent of almost a thousand Orangemen assembled in Jones' Wood to celebrate the milestone. As expected, the nationalist press jeered at the gathering, sniping "a few of the mongrels who keep up the so-called 'lodges' of Orangemen" came together peaceably.[60]

The organization sustained prominence as a cultural badge into the 1900s, occasionally striking association with the nativist revivals of the times. But the group did not take to the streets so publicly thereafter.[61] Headlining in 1894 with allegations of connections with the American Protective Association, *The Irish American* claimed a tight connection between the groupings. "Orangemen Its Leaders: Old Aims (In an American Cloak) of the A.P.A." amounted to a mere repackaging of the Orange platform as American nativism revived through the offices of the Association, it was suggested. Leveled by the pastor of the Unitarian Church of the Messiah, Reverend Robert Collyer lamented the transportation of what he considered the Order's culture of hate to the city. Not surprisingly, *The Irish American* agreed wholeheartedly, quoting publications described as "Orange organs" that championed this new "pure Americanism" and arguing that determination to "preserve the Republic from Papist domination" empowered both Loyalist and A.P.A. agendas. That the president of the A.P.A. in 1894 was a Canadian Orangeman and that "the A.P.A. oaths and declarations and those of the Orangemen are closely identical, showing evidence that they were modeled on the same lines," seemed to support the charge.[62] But unlike Brethren in other cities, New York lodge members associated with nativist groups without resorting to sectarian violence. An outburst on the streets of Montreal in 1877 generated volumes of correspondence in the city press and pamphlets appearing in the late summer of 1877.[63] As Catholic reaction mobilized in July 1877, Father Stafford from Saint Mary's Church, Montreal supported the Orangemen's wish to hold celebrations. They were undoubtedly entitled to do so, Father Stafford reasoned, and Catholic barbs and violence would only entrench existing antagonisms. Extending the hand of forgiveness, he continued: "If we do not agree with Orangemen, and take exception to the offensive airs and tunes they play, and think they are in bad taste and show want of wisdom and civilization, we cannot forget they are fellow-countrymen of our own, that they are generally Irish, that they are Christians." The priest concluded, observing: "Inflict upon Protestants the bitter experience that the Ulster fanatics inflicted upon the Catholics of Ireland! We have not the power; but if we had the power are we to inflict upon Protestants here what in former times was inflicted upon Catholics in Ulster. Out on such language!"[64] In proffering the olive branch, Father Stafford regretted the unfortunate but inevitable transplantation of two Irish cultural traditions to cities such as New York. In the interests of progress and peace, relegating this division to the past could be the only way forward. New York Catholics could not hope to rid the city of the Order or even prevent Orange parades taking place, and public expressions of politically charged heritage would continue to perpetuate traditional antagonisms as long as traditional resentments continued.

Another cleric drew similar conclusions in 1877. A member of the church one Orange historian designated "a moral quagmire . . . a wilderness of error and superstition," Reverend John MacNamara spoke on the same themes.[65] A founder of New York's Saint John's College, Reverend MacNamara boarded a boat on the Hudson in the company of a large group of city Orangemen on the Twelfth of July 1877, where he raised some timely issues.[66] Addressing "Gentlemen and Fellow-Irishmen," MacNamara first appraised the extraordinary relationship between the Irish traditions in New York, proclaiming:

> You are Protestant and I am Catholic. You represent one class of Irishmen; I represent another. You and I have been brought up in political as well as religious ideas that have made us antagonistic to one another, have reddened our nation's soil with the best blood our respected classes could boast, and have made us stand before the world more like savages than enlightened men.

Denouncing the "scoundrelism and hypocrisy" and the "knavish bigots" reviving old antagonisms, the cleric recalled 1870 and 1871 and credited the Order with the wisdom to curtail such inflammatory events. Such grace should have endeared him to his audience! Making reference to their regalia and anthems, the priest cited the right of these Irish to identify themselves through non-incendiary symbols and activities. The assembled lodge members may have even warmed to the priest as he declared that ignorance of the roots of nineteenth-century nationalism ought to be blamed for contemporary atrocities in New York. To illustrate his sincerity, MacNamara reeled off the names of some of Ireland's best-known patriots, among them Protestants Emmet, Grattan, Wolfe Tone, Davis, and John Mitchel. He also declared that he could say "in pride" that he had:

> this very summer mingled in the outdoor gatherings of at least 20,000 Catholic Irishmen who wore the Orange color at their buttonhole, and who floated yellow bunting from every spar of the steamers, and from every point of the barges that bore their tens of thousands of patriotic followers over the waters of the Hudson to all the picnic parks in our vicinity. This was prompted by a spirit of enlightened patriotism, by which they would give you Irish Protestants to understand that they recognize your rights as Irishmen, and that your religion is no bar to their friendship and protection.

The priest concluded with the aspiration that his audience would come to "love the land that bore you," and that they would endeavor to "be patriots and gentlemen." He anticipated the day when the shamrock and the lily would intertwine, and "the strains of whatever music we may individually prefer will sound equally enrapturing by the Shannon, the Lee, the Liffey, or the Boyne."[67]

MacNamara's entreaties would not normally find favor with fired-up nationalist city editors, but Patrick Ford in *The Irish World* occasionally deliberated on the Protestant siege mentality. British rule remained the first obstacle to Ireland's unity, he argued in 1884, and if this block were removed then Protestants could live peaceably with Catholics. During the 1880s, the forthright editor vacillated between degrees of conciliation and barrages of pure invective on the topic of his fellow countrymen. Calling the Orange legacy the "blackest and meanest crime" in 1885, he modified his views to some extent a couple of years earlier, even suggesting that Irish nationals ought to show tolerance toward "our Orange brethren." Considering that Protestant Irishmen would remove to the nationalist camp immediately "if convinced of the error of their ways," Ford suggested that until that point, armed violence would not lead to peace either in New York or Ireland.[68] But such quasi-conciliatory thoughts could not be expected to win over entire enclaves of people who remained convinced of the veracity of long-standing grievances. A favorite intonation of East Coast Irish city militias during the Civil War articulated some of the more radicalized attitudes prevalent thousands of miles from the source of the antagonism. Part of a soldier's prayer petitioning Dublin martyr Lawrence O'Toole for safety, the aspirations ranged beyond both the Civil War and the Saint, invoking as they did the following:

O'Toole Deliver Us
From English civilization, From British law and order
From Anglo-Saxon cant and freedom . . . From the cloven hoof,
From the necessity of annual rebellion, From billeted soldiery,
From anti-Irish Irishmen . . . From a pious Church establishment,

From the slavery of praying for crowned heads . . . From royal anniversaries,
From loyal banquet speeches,
From salvation from the cross of Saint George,
From the curse of Cromwell, From all things purely English.
We beseech thee to hear us, O'Toole,
By the wearing of the Green, By the Grave of Emmett
By our Irish martyrology . . . By the memory of Penal Law,
By the old rebel Pike . . . By the immortal Shamrock.
Grant us victory, O'Toole,
Through O'Neil of the Red Hand, Through the spirit of Lord Edward,
Through Ireland's unwritten history, Through the Celtic tongue,
Through the magic pen of Davis. ..Through the Fenian Brotherhood. . . .[69]

The "memory of Penal Law" and the "pious Church establishment" of Britain, to draw out two examples, resonated heavily with authors such as Jeremiah O'Donovan, who cautioned in 1864 that the "Penal Laws were enacted to compel my countrymen and women to acknowledge the supremacy and divine authority of a new and perverting creed commenced by Henry, amended by Edward, and finished in the Gospel Factory of Elizabeth."[70] Highlights along the nationalist road to independence dominate within the "prayer," but leading Protestant rebels— Emmet, Lord Edward, Davis, et al.—make their appearance in the superficial points of confluence for the two traditions. The lines do not go so far as to suggest a Catholic-Protestant unification against British misrule, and *Irish People* editor Michael O'Leary verified that "sooner will the followers of Mahomet fraternize with Christian pilgrims than will Orange Saxons join with Catholic Celts in a movement for National Independence." Others in New York mused on the same theme.[71] A poem by "Artane" carried in the New York press in 1884 entitled "Song for July The Twelfth" enjoined both elements to lay down their differences for the sake of independence. "Why should hate our ranks discover, Making surer England's way," the first verse concluded. The lines highlighted the advantages of merging the Shamrock and the Orange blossom "Ere they shed their fruitful seed."[72] Such notions of cooperation against unjust British authority also echoed in the writings of a young immigrant in the early 1900s. An appeal to the two traditions to relinquish differences for Ireland's benefit, the verses suggest a misplacement of Protestant trust in England set in the same form and style as "Artane's":

Grasp the hand my Orange brother, Grasp the hand we two are one,
One in race though long divided, Through the deeds our foes have done,
July lilies lose no beauty Though March Shamrocks kindly blow,
We are brothers—Sons of Ireland—England only is our foe![73]

Here is a piece finely tuned to the relationship between the two elements. Symbolized by the Protestant and nationalist emblems of the lily and the shamrock, respectively, the realization that modern Irish history developed out of this relationship included the warning that settlement in a new land would not automatically unify elements at odds prior to emigration. The allusion to England as the ultimate foe and a latent appeal to just authority makes sense in the context of Protestant perspectives enshrined in classic liberalism. The roots of this ideology extended back through Lockean natural-rights philosophy to the initial impulses of the Reformation, Protestant "libertarians" usually "internationalist liberals, anti-government rather than anti-English," who "looked to Hutcheson, to Locke, to America, and most of all to France" for the foundations of their political philosophy.[74] This philosophy centered on the contractual alliance between ruler and ruled, with the right to reject corrupt authority a traditional linchpin.[75] The apparent contradiction of a libertarian outlook rooted alongside religious intolerance became further convoluted as the United Irishmen aimed to redress the grievances in 1798.[76] In his inimitable way, Wolfe Tone aimed to promote a branch of libertarian thought that would reconcile Protestant and Catholic interests in a self-governing republic, but some of his fellow Protestants decried his aspirations as foolhardy. A few years earlier, Tone's admission to Belfast's Northern Whig Club sponsored by parliamentarian and Club Secretary Henry Joy McCracken had mobilized debate over such an alliance.[77] Wolfe Tone's words are worth quoting for their relevance to the New York situation almost a century later. In both contexts, Protestants feared Catholic power on the basis of:

> Danger to true religion, inasmuch as the Roman Catholics would, if emancipated, establish an *inquisition* . . . Danger, generally, of throwing power into their hands, which would make this a Catholic government, incapable of enjoying or extending liberty. . . .[78]

The phrase "true religion" championed freedom over the perceived threat of Catholic influence; an attitude transported almost intact to New York many decades later. In pre-Union Ulster, as in post-Famine New York, the temporary alliances that motivated the United Irishmen could not seem to last long enough to replace hard-line sectarianism.[79]

But we can identify some points of Protestant-Catholic conciliation that sustained the Wolfe Tone legacy. Born in 1815 in Dungiven, County Derry, in the largely Presbyterian north of Ireland, the name John Mitchel directly referenced a particular branch of the nationalist cause.[80] The son of a Unitarian Minister, and a Trinity College graduate in 1836, Mitchel's training in a small Dublin law practice stood him in good stead for later public representation. Succeeding Thomas Davis[81] as editor of *The Nation*, Mitchel admonished Catholics "against driving the Irish Protestants from the patriot cause by needless tests." Following a campaign in his own newspaper *The United Irishman* to mobilize patriotic feeling, Mitchel's arrest on charges of treason in 1848 and sentencing to fourteen years penal servitude in Van Dieman's Land led to his dramatic escape in 1853, following which he arrived in New York via South Africa, Tahiti, and San Francisco.[82] His wife Jane (Jenny) Verner had long overcome the issue of her family's Loyalist heritage to marry John. The daughter of English army officer Captain James Verner and the niece of Colonel Sir William Verner surprised and even angered her family by her choice of husband; particularly an uncle who raised the issue in Parliament on the occasion of Mitchel's transportation to Australia.[83]

Arriving in New York in 1853, John's ill health limited their first stay to four years. Then on to Knoxville, Tennessee, for the next seven years before returning to New York again after the Civil War to settle on Union Street, Brooklyn. Establishing quickly in local Irish-orientated political circles, Jane vividly described their new life in letters to her friend Mary Thompson, in Kingstown, Ireland. Delighted with the fact that her husband was "no longer a bondslave," she remarked that it was for the singular purpose of pursuing the Irish cause that they moved to New York from San Francisco.[84] As an international hub, New York attracted the cream of Irish revolutionaries, but Jane feared that her husband would overwork himself in promoting the cause with exhausting rounds of public dinners, meetings, and fundraisers in the city. They decided that "enough has been done . . . to show England how America treats Irish State prisoners."[85] Her sense of relief at returning to the city conflicted with adjustment to local practices, bemoaning unannounced calling between noon and three in the afternoon, for example. Besides Ireland's future, the immediate concerns of John's health and the demands of her large family of six children burned up time and energy. Both her own and her husband's eyesight had deteriorated significantly since settling in New York due to successive colds, fierce weather, and the effects of reading by gas-powered lamps. But she would always be grateful to the city Fenians that planned her husband's Australian escape from Australia and raised funds to promote his work in their new home base.

Jane enlightened Mary on the secret dimension of the work. "Entre Nous, the Irish Directory here," she wrote, "sent out Mr. P.J. Smythe with a certain large sum to effect the escape of Mr. O'Brien or John, or double that sum for them both," and included details of the break.[86] Alongside arguments over contemporary issues such as the slavery question, and a description of a recent visit by Henry Ward Beecher, Jane struggled with their constant flow of visitors. "We were so annoyed" she wrote, "often by people coming in every evening, that we were obliged to name one for receiving. So we have a large evening party once a week, without the trouble of asking, and the only refreshments are cake and wine." New York's Irish revolutionary contingent did not mind the Mitchel's culinary restrictions, assembling as they did in large numbers and including representatives of both religious-based traditions in the gatherings. The same motives that inspired Wolfe Tone in the 1790s came to the fore in these circles of New York ex-Young Irelanders and fellow sympathizers, including their friend and prominent Fenian John O'Leary. Jane surmised:

> O'Mahony of Limerick is here in New York now, and a very fine fellow he is—about the finest looking of all the men of that town. Many here have still a hope for Ireland, but is it, can it be true, that there is no party in Ireland who cares for freedom? If they be all satisfied with the present state of things, then let them be so, say I.[87]

The Mitchels also forged a friendship with well-to-do and flamboyant character Thomas Francis Meagher. A Waterford-born Catholic established at the New York Bar during the 1850s, Meagher worked closely with Mitchel and O'Mahony on *The Citizen* and *The Irish Nation* cultivating a wellspring of republicanism from the fount of the French and American Revolutions. In a collection of articles published in 1853, Meagher devoted extensive attention to the French case as he described a visit to Paris by some of the 1848 leaders. A full twenty pages on the events of 1789 that led to the proclamation of the French Republic concluded with an aspiration to the same end for Dublin in the near future.[88]

In between references to the "frightful" snow and the birth of a new son to the Meaghers, Jane affirmed another prominent local voice as a valuable addition to their circle. Another well-heeled compatriot practicing at the New York Bar during the same decade, John Blake Dillon occasionally lectured on the same circuit as the Mitchels. Although the Dillons "live a good way off," they normally visited on Saturdays. Also welcomed were the O'Gormans, and a Mrs. O'Reilly "and her dear little child" just arrived in New York. Alive with the passion of true believers, the meetings empowered the Mitchels to extend the republican thrust through their network of local associates and contacts.[89] Jane Mitchel's recognition that Ireland remained locked within the aftershock of the Famine and the bitter memories surrounding 1848 prompted her to view her nationalist circle as a "hope" for "the extensive movement in this land." While her husband constantly mined the city's resources to turn vague aspirations into some kind of realistic agenda, Jane compared promotion work in daily newspapers, public lecturing, pamphleteering, and the never-ending meetings with the potential for similar activism across the Atlantic. She demanded news of progress in Ireland from Mary, but learned that a lull in nationalist activity that set in during the 1850s continued through the Land War in the 1880s, as Famine survivors engaged in the slow process of recovery. As a result, locals had made little progress and issued few of the anticipated directives. "Are they all dead or asleep or mad?" Jane asked of her friend in disbelief, "Have you nothing encouraging to write to us?"[90] Not only was the news—or lack thereof—from Ireland discouraging, the revolutionary spirit seemed too lax for any kind of mobilization, and a sense of futility seemed to dominate. But meanwhile, *The Citizen*,

The Irish Nation, a hard grind of lectures and meetings, and John's account of his transportation in *Jail Journal; or Five Years in British Prisons Commenced On Board The Shearwater Steamer*, won the Mitchels adulation in nationalist city circles. As a widely read invective against imperialism in his polished Trinity style, *Jail Journal* generated the kind of high-profile interest in the cause any incarnation of the movement would have cherished. Journalist and renowned man of letters Sir Shane Leslie called Mitchel an "honest conspirator and brilliant writer, (who) proved that the pen of journalism was sharper than the Irish pike."[91] In well-turned prose, Mitchel's fast-paced account of English-Irish relations quickly took on the mantle of nationalist bible in America. In between accounts of sojourns in Bermuda, South Africa, and Australia, Mitchel articulated some of the emotional baggage permeating Irish New York:

> You address yourself to the public opinion of your countrymen through the newspapers, and for three months your eloquent remarks lie frozen, or if not frozen, at least sodden, in the "region of calms" and the sultry trade winds—it is all the same—your countrymen do not hear a word you say until the whole affair is months old, and when the result of your appeal comes to hand, perhaps you are dead.

But the city's potential to generate a unified force to confront British authority had long motivated him, despite the lack of unity on the Irish cause. Kept up to date while incarcerated in Australia, he referred to the "pitiful quarrels and even riots" over issues, lamenting:

> Ah, we can all meet here, by the margin of the smooth lake, and under the greenwood tree . . . but place us in the very heart of that mean turmoil, even in the refuge city of New York—expose us to the keen, daily torture of conscious helplessness, while so much is to do, to the conversation of sinners, the canonization of nonsense, and the outrages of a triumphant enemy—all together, and then, who knoweth his own heart?[92]

In citing New York as the logical starting point for republican-minded exiles to join forces with Famine refugees and mobilize resolution of Ireland's troubles, the Mitchels both realized that the absence of unity within their city circle was proving all but insurmountable. Not even "of one mind" on the broader perspectives of independence, not to mention the implementation of a plan of campaign, Jane reluctantly admitted that many of their New York friends had "lost all confidence, and ceased to think further on the matter" as time went on, among them Dillon, O'Gorman, and Meagher. By the late 1860s her husband alone kept up his aspirations as others faded in ardor and involvement. Unfortunately, ill health prevented John from developing a concrete plan of campaign. The family's move to Tennessee enabled them to maintain contact with friends in New York, but obliged them to sideline the serious business of revolution.[93]

The years spent in New York disillusioned John in spirit and broke his health. The family returned to Ireland in 1874 and, upon John's death in 1875, Jane returned to the city and remained there until her own passing in 1899. Their departure certainly dulled the potential for broader Protestant nationalist involvement. No pretender to the leadership emerged in the 1880s, and the lively discussions, journalistic output, and gatherings characterizing their tenure as informal leaders disintegrated. Only one name stands out, that of Thomas Addis Emmet, grand nephew of early nineteenth-century orator and martyr Robert Emmet. Converting to Catholicism in later life, Dr. Emmet probably forgoes categorization as a Protestant Irishman![94]

If the end of Mitchel influence stymied Protestant involvement in a broadly pitched nationalist agenda, other voices continued to inform Catholic-Protestant relations for better or for worse. Well-known English historian J. A. Froude came to New York in 1872, primarily to air an incendiary message on historical relations between Ireland and England and rekindle old flames.[95] Ostensibly an apologist for the "justified conquest" of Ireland, James Anthony Froude sought American support for British control of Ireland in a time of upheaval. Froude arrived to deliver lectures really amounting to a diatribe against Ireland, deeming the land suited to colonization and its people sorely in need of civilizing. The "anarchy" existing before the Normans imposed a measure of control in the twelfth century sustained by the English plantations spurred him to reason that if some patriots and priests happened to be martyred along the way, then these measures were warranted for the sake of order. Irish Protestants had carried the earliest torch of independence to Colonial America, but the only way their Catholic compatriots seemed "capable of a perfect discipline, under a good and perfect government" lay in the strength of their involvement with the forces of law and order in New York. Provocative titles such as "Froude's Description of 'The Irish Celts,'" and "Froude's 'Code of Principles,'" as Stated in his Justification of *The English In Ireland*"[96] were bound to incite interest, but how did contemporaries square with the points raised in a timely editorial?

> The reader of Froude's *History of Ireland* must bear in mind the political principles which underlie it, and which are so frankly avowed in the introduction. As these principles are characteristically English, so are the authorities on which the author relies. A document in the Record-Office possesses in his eyes the sanctity which a Protestant attributes to the Bible, or a Romanist to a church tradition. That he has studied his authorities well is evident; that he has made fair and honest report of them there is no good reason to doubt. But a history of Ireland based on English state papers is like a history of the Waldenses based on the manuscripts of the Vatican; it may be painstaking, but it can not be impartial.[97]

The lectures would probably have generated less commotion but for a backlash mobilized by Father Thomas Burke, a Galway-born Dominican friar. During his tenure as "Visitor of his Order," an assignment whereby the appointee visited each

Dominican house in specific countries, Father Burke drew rapt admiration from Froude's detractors in 1872:

> But what kind of preacher is this Dominican Father Burke? What is the power by which he holds hushed and breathless, each one in a crowded congregation; alike the most learned and critical, and the rough men with little either of sentiment or education? A natural gift of oratory no one can mistake in him. He has the richness of voice, and the persuasiveness of accent, that God has lavished so largely on his countrymen. But these are "tricks of the tongue" that the man of trained intellect can arm himself against, even while he admires them. But Father Burke *disarms* this trained intellectual listener, because in him, it is neither *trick* nor *art*—It is the *gift* God has given him, *and that he has consecrated to God!*[98]

As luck would have it, Burke began his local city visitation just as Froude was delivering his onslaught. The Dominican "took up the glove of the English historian" and gallantly rose to the defense of nationalist honor. A packed meeting in the Academy of Music witnessed the Reverend systematically renounce every point raised, counter each allegation, and redefine the historical turning points from the Froudeian theories of history commanding center stage.[99] Covering the episode in November and December of 1872, *The New York Tribune* couched the episode in terms of the relocation of the Irish question across the Atlantic. From the perspective of the British Parliament and its Irish Members, Froude's attempt to defend British imperialism miscalculated, stoking the embers of ancient animosities. *The New York World* judged that the coolness of Burke's redress to Froude deserved special mention as evidence of an unsullied viewpoint against a slew of pathetic outpourings. Froude's thesis that divine right empowered England to accomplish Irish subjugation also gave Burke ammunition to counteract thinly veiled invective. Comparisons between Colonial America and contemporary Ireland also arose, highlighting the similarities between the two colonies and arguing that clear-thinking Americans would support Burke against the antagonistic Froude. The Dominican's tenacity in striding into the enemy's camp won praise from *The New York Herald*, especially for his reluctance to turn the entire proceedings into a mere catalogue of British oppression.[100]

Meanwhile, a conservative weekly that could not easily be accused of Catholic favoritism weighed in, stating that Froude's "political philosophy was not one which the average American could be got to carry home with him and ponder and embrace." The debate continued in *The New York Nation*, highlighting the argument that "the Irish in America are more likely to be exasperated by it than the Irish at home."[101] Illustrating the transatlantic connection, this pronouncement underscored American impact on the New York nationalist contingent. Acclimatizing to a culture built on traditional freedoms, it seems logical that this kind of provocation should inflame nationalist passions in the city. Froude was not lecturing to a select Anglo-Irish audience in Dublin or Wicklow or to a Loyalist congregation in

Ulster. He was publicizing works extolling the divine right of England to rule Ireland in a city of over a quarter million Irish, large contingents of whom subscribed to a broad republican agenda. Even as the Fenians made way for Clan na Gael as the most popular manifestation of that political agenda, Froude's appearance and statements could only have heightened nationalist resolve. *The New York Evening Post* encapsulated the situation, reminding readers of Burke's belief that Ireland could opt either to use force to overthrow the yoke of oppression or "develop[ment of] the natural resources of the island and the building up of a united and strong people by toleration, industry, frugality, temperance and obedience to law." If at all possible, tolerance appeared to be the only way to resolve tensions, Burke reasoned, stating that "Union can be effected by largesse of mind by generosity and urbanity toward your fellow-citizens; by rising above the miserable bigotry that carries religious differences and religious hatreds into relations of life that don't belong to religion."[102]

In retrospect, it is obvious that it would take a new century, a minor revolution and a new departure in Anglo-Irish relations to achieve these goals. In the meantime, the episode exposed a seam within the immigrant mentality marking the development of an Irish-American city identity where aspects of native heritage confronted the host culture in a manner dictated by difficult cultural and political circumstances.[103] Inflammatory reminders that "out of every ten Irishmen in America at the time of the Revolution there must have been nine Protestants" did not help resolve the issues, as Froude's speeches tapped into a dormant political strain among city Protestants.[104] Within the sacrosanct relationship between governor, governed, and the law, Froude clashed with traditional Protestant political values. He did not couch his arguments within the parameters of the contractual alliance as the primary regulator of just authority, but championed England's natural right to superiority underscored by powerful force.

At the end of the episode, John Mitchel's rhetoric soared over the debate in a lecture to the Liberal Club and the public in Plympton Hall on December 20, 1872. In "Froude, From the Standpoint of an Irish Protestant," he reverted to eighteenth-century philosophy to inform the audience of his uniquely positioned perspective on Anglo-Irish relations. The choice candidate for the task, Mitchel possessed the charisma, oratorical skills, and celebrity to publicly counter the eminent Englishman. In "misrepresent[ing]" Irish Protestants, Froude's perspective could not be assumed to reflect their opinion or their grievances. Mitchel found some common ground between the two Irish traditions in New York, declaring that:

> We cannot take his advocacy of establishing our right and title in Ireland on that "superior" ground. We want no superior ground. We want to live in good fellowship and good neighborhood with the Catholic people around us. We want to see some reparation made for the long centuries of rapine and slaughter that have been inflicted upon us.[105]

Mitchel's remarks provide a good example of Protestant advocacy of harmonious relations with Catholic Ireland in the face of unjust authority, but did not inculcate a Protestant nationalist upsurge. Members of the Orange Order would consider his pronouncements latent treachery against their Crown and culture, and would not have appreciated Wendell Phillips's remarks either. Declaring that Froude had never "written anything that deserves the name of history" and pronouncing his work "so discordant; so partisan, so fragmentary, so one-sided," Phillips continued: "if I were an Irishman, I know I should be a Fenian; I should have followed Smith O'Brien . . . to claim of us a verdict that shall be a salve to a conscience that has no rest, haunted by the ghosts of Elisabeths and Henrys that have made the blood of the Saxon race infamous on the records of history."[106]

Other public references during the same years beamed light onto Protestant city culture and politics, the links with home, and an increasingly prevalent Home Rule agenda. A story from October 1875 documented the revival by an ex-priest named MacNamara of the non-sectarian United Irishmen, likely not the same Reverend MacNamara who previously lectured the Orangemen on the boat. "Many years ago there existed a variety of Irishman known as the 'United Irishman,' and so called apparently for the Hibernian reason that he belonged to a society which divided all Ireland into two hostile political camps," MacNamara intoned, anticipating that the Order of United Irishmen Redivivus would expose inductees to stronger anti-British rhetoric than even the Fenians used. A prospective rhetorician, no less, named Thomas J. MacGeoghegan registered with the Order. Inducted with due ceremony, he took his place as a fully-fledged member. But it was not long before MacGeoghegan's parish priest heard about his parishoner's new association and informed him of the seriousness of such a sin. It was not so much the conspiracy against Britain that constituted the sin, but the twin dangers of conspiring in the company of Protestants under the leadership of an ex-priest! MacGeoghegan abandoned the organization soon after.[107]

While the probability of this story as a figment of its author's imagination is high, this kind of reminder maintained the distinction of this facet of Irish city culture, as did the short-lived 1869 serial entitled *The Irish Republic: A Journal of Liberty, Literature and Social Progress.* Broaching the issue of Orange radicalism through the lens of socialism, the February 6 issue appealed for "liberty outside of religion" and for the overthrow of religious-based antagonisms persisting for centuries.[108] Another opinion from a private citizen in December 1876 offered readers a glimpse of the type of Protestant affiliated with neither a specific political agenda nor his Catholic compatriots. Edward Hamilton argued that to lay blame on either England or the Ulster Orangemen for Ireland's divisions was unjust, given that Catholics held as high a stake in the resolution of conflict as other constituencies. Supporting the logic of retaining Britain as a strong protector of Ireland as the only forward path, he judged: "I am an Irish Protestant, and do not wish to be misrepresented in the Irish press. We are often described as 'Orangemen'—which we are not; though, at the same time, I think the Orange institution aims at preserving civil and religious liberty." He concluded: "consequently, it is unjust to speak of Irish Protestants as being false or traitorous to Ireland."[109] Similar thoughts emerged later in the Home Rule campaign in *The Irish American*, where an anonymous "young Ulster Protestant" advanced support for Ireland's independence. Declaring himself an Irishman with a Presbyterian background that should not negatively affect his birthright, he claimed Irish culture and heritage belonged just as much to Protestants as Catholics. He should not become "an alien in my own land in order to follow and be made the dupe of men who have never felt the blood of nationality coursing through their veins." The Ulsterman determined that no band of "narrow-minded soulless materialists" would detract from his status as Irishman and Ulsterman entitled to his share of his nationality.[110]

Ulstermen inducted into the Friendly Sons of Saint Patrick shared an interest in this kind of cross-cultural affinity within the parameters of an easy secularism. Sons' lectures and meetings facilitated an Irish profile that avoided reference to clashes between the two traditions. As we saw in connection with impoverished women, the Sons' High-Church sensibilities with a Catholic flavor managed to preserve a non-affiliated profile within a polarized New York-Irish cultural identity.[111] But a different kind of fraternal grouping hosting a predominance of Ulstermen had established an exclusive Irish Protestant enclave within a citywide network. An international organization by the post-Famine years, Freemasonry extended back to 1725 and the foundation of the first Grand Lodge of Ireland. Pope Clement XII's 1738 Bull *In Eminenti* stemmed Catholic impetus to join the Craft, but northern Ireland's Protestants established a strong tradition easily portable to New York in the later eighteenth century.[112] More precisely, Ireland's four hundred lodges empowered the mobilization of a transatlantic bridge to America by the Gilded Age years.[113] City Freemasonry attracted solid numbers of Protestant Irish, and the organization proffered a haven for those interested in retaining ties with the native home. The official *History* of the Craft in New York City and State directed readers' attention to lodges entitled Saint Patrick's Lodge Nos. 4 and 212 incorporated in 1766 and 1788, respectively. The Grand Lodge named Hibernia in New York since 1821 celebrated early Irish influence. On December 7, 1842, the Grand Lodge of Ireland's Right Worshipful Robert R. Boyd addressed the corresponding Grand Lodge of New York. In full regalia as the official Representative, the Worshipful Boyd remarked that "as a public minister from a sovereign power, which is supported by the most distinguished men of Ireland, it will be your province to pay attention to such as may visit our State with Letters of Introduction."[114]

Such remarks provided ready-made contacts for newly arrived Ulstermen and fellow Protestants hailing from the other provinces. The connection was undoubtedly strengthened by the accession to the status of Grand Master in the Phillips Grand Lodge in 1858 of Dublin-born James Jenkinson. Introduced to Masonry in Dublin, Grand Master Jenkinson carried his enthusiasm to the United States in 1849, where he held the office of Representative of Ireland in the New York Grand Lodge until 1875.[115] The official Dictionary of Masonry in New York testified to the esteem of the Brotherhood within the lives of Irish city Protestants. Freemasonry provided them a meeting place in a strange immigrant world and points of common interest with like-minded compatriots. The significant numbers profiled in the official 1899 directory reveal a sector of the Irish population normally invisible to those outside an immediate circle of friends, local church, or workplace. As the case with William Murphy, an Antrim man from a respectable family of modest means who made the move to America in mid-century, detachment from the usual Irish networked connections accorded many Protestants a different American experience to that of the majority of their compatriots. His journey illustrated that "despite his avowed affection for fellow ex-soldiers, and his subsequent career as a member of sizable, albeit transient, workgroups, close-knit by necessity, William remained remarkably disconnected from the overlapping ethnic and working-class associations . . . that structured the lives of most Irish immigrants."[116] Lacking even the militant edge of Orangeism, the Irish Mason fell into a private, but nonetheless distinct, socioeconomic category.

Typically born in either the northern counties of Ulster or the eastern seaboard counties of Dublin, Longford or Meath, men such as John G. M. Stewart and Claudius F. Beatty personified either solid Presbyterianism or identification with the lower reaches of Anglican stock. Families of prosperous farmers, linen-weavers, and shopkeepers in the small towns dotting the northeastern countryside produced men such as Stewart and Beatty for whom work featured strongly during youth and early adulthood. Unlike Jerry McAuley from a Dublin background hallmarked by trouble with the law, these model citizens attended school and then embarked on small-scale entrepreneurial engagements. Stewart's case appears typical of Protestant involvement with Masonry. Arriving in New York as a boy in the early 1850s, he attended the Ninth Ward public schools and started working almost as soon as he settled in. Early employment in dry goods led him to the position of proprietor of his own store, soon categorized him as a "businessman of affairs." Claudius Beatty's course was almost identical, reaching New York from County Longford at the age of seventeen in 1848, securing an apprenticeship with a manufacturer of hat trimmings, and starting his own business in 1867. Brother Beatty succeeded to Vestryman and Warden in his Episcopalian church, and became well respected through Masonry and church connections.[117]

Of the 135 highest-ranking city Masons in the second half of the nineteenth century, Irish Protestants constituted over one-third. Most of these men had landed into New York during the 1840s and 1850s. Trained from an early age in the advantages of hard work, sobriety, and stability, they established similar patterns in the city. If they arrived as children, as did Anthony Clinchy in 1850 from County Longford, they attended grammar schools and gravitated toward commercial employment, in a feed store on Broadway in Clinchy's case. These Irishmen lived frugal lives, prospering but not ostentatious. Anthony Clinchy changed over to plumbing in 1862 and remained in that trade for many years, eventually rising to the position of Inspector of Gas Meters for the State of New York.

Judging by their close ties with grammar schools and public schools, education played a prominent role for these men and replicated traditional practices in Ireland. Some, like Frederick Barnes from Dublin, attended what his biographer described as "the blue-coat school endowed by King William III, 'of Glorious Memory,' a famous establishment better known perhaps as King's College." His attendance marked Barnes as a "dyed in the wool" Loyalist. From there, his first employment in New York as an apprentice in a "wine-making factory" was followed by his entry in to the real estate business where he prospered. Fellow Mason Adam Huston from Derry followed the lead of Clinchy into plumbing in the 1860s, and Presbyterian Edward Charles Parker from Donegal became a journeyman stonecutter. Parker prospered as a Manhattan truckman with five vehicles on the road by the 1880s. Another entrepreneurially minded Irishman, William Hall from King's County entered the feeding-stuff trade and did well enough to subsequently establish his own business.[118] Rather unusually, Wexford man James Jordan partook of both Freemasonry and Fenianism! Docking into New York in 1852 as a young boy, Jordan became interested in Irish republicanism, so much so that "in 1870 he took part in the Fenian Raid into Canada, being not only a pronounced Irish nationalist, but a believer in a Republican form of government." Such a foray constituted quite an aberration in Masonic circles, judging by the unionist sympathies of his Irish brethren. It is entirely possible that Jordan's republicanism may have stemmed from the same roots as eighteenth-century United Irishman political philosophy.[119]

None of these men appeared to have experienced the horrors of the Great Famine or the trauma of the Atlantic crossing in a coffin-ship. Comprehensively educated, they secured apprenticeships in prominent trades and usually established independently as owners of businesses. A significant number joined army units with the onset of the Civil War; those surviving returning to their previous occupations during the later 1860s. Many joined trade unions and proudly carried the union card long after they had successfully enhanced their own businesses. A large percentage, such as Matthew Arthur from County Tyrone who arrived in 1870 and held "several good positions in many first class establishments" forged strong relationships with city churches. In Arthur's case, joining the West Fifty-First Street United Presbyterian Church to become an active member paralleled the experience of Dubliner John Watson in Saint John's Chapel on Varick Street. Reaching New York in 1857, Watson held the post of sexton for many years. After attendance at night school, Watson earned his living in a variety of trades, after which he joined the police force for the next fifteen years. Happily, he lived to see his son John Fletcher Watson inducted into the Tabernacle Lodge of Masons in 1896.

For the majority of Irish Freemasons, life in New York revolved around the triad of work, worship, and the craft. "Faithful member of the Fifth Avenue Presbyterian Church" Edward Reid from Fermanagh became yet another dry-goods man, while fellow-Presbyterian and Tyrone man Thomas Orr commenced a new life in trunk-making, changing over to a trucking business in 1870. North of Ireland compatriot Andrew Ferguson's thirty-three years as Tyler of his Blue Lodge in New York also included learning the trade of "wine-drawer," to eventually end up running a successful restaurant on Eighth Avenue. His membership of the Reformed Dutch Church occupied much of his time. Fellow Mason William Collins had plenty of spare time, judged by his four trips to Ireland in the 1890s. Arriving in New York from Monaghan in 1856 at the age of ten, his biographer remarked that "the memory and story of his native land are dear to him." Collins's start in a city bakery led him to a lifelong position as a packer in the company of Shepherd Knapp and Co.[120] Communicant at Saint Michael's Episcopal Church in Manhattan, Henry Woods of Tyrone landed in 1880, having left behind a teacher's post in Ireland. Woods turned to the craft of plastering to become an independent contractor. Fellow Mason William Burton settled in the city in 1881 to work at a variety of jobs until establishing as a dancing instructor, a fairly unique occupation among Ulster Protestants! Opening an academy on West Forty-Seventh Street, Burton rapidly rose to prominence and prospered, as he was able to vacation in Ireland on a regular basis. On one occasion he traveled through the thirty-two counties on a bicycle!

"Splendid ritualist" Robert H. Clark also hailed from Ulster and set up in New York in 1865. From employment in a grocery store to the trucking business, Clark maintained nine trucks by the 1890s. His ties to the Episcopalian Church of the Holy Communion on Fifth Avenue constituted the cornerstone of his life. "Piercing the secret and awful mysteries" of the Masonic Temple constituted an important part of life for Thomas Swain, Pyramid Lodge member and Noble Mystic Shrine inductee. Engaged in plumbing since 1868, the Antrim man divided his time between his own business and the Protestant Episcopal Church of the Ascension, where he held the office of Senior Warden. Justifiably proud of their accomplishments, the benefit of a good education at home constituted a recurring theme through the lives of these men. Solid grounding in at least the basics in the classical subjects of literature, mathematics, Greek, Latin, and philosophy cultivated a scholarly aspect in their personalities, often playing out in educational and church-related careers. The experience of John McKinney Parker echoed the typical Ulster Protestant city settlement:

> Born in Londonderry, Ireland, August 21, 1871 . . . [he] came to New York in 1887. Before coming to America he had not only received a good education—some of the finest schools in the world are in the north of Ireland—but had a little experience in business. On settling in New York he went into the drug business, and for some years has been what is known as 'pricer' in the establishment of Merck and Co., Chemical Importers.[121]

Masonic membership showcases an Irish Protestant city culture with distinct patterns. Distinguishable from both Orangemen and nationalists, the grouping constituted a strain of hardworking, sober individuals, attached to the church and trades organizations they belonged to. These Irishmen represented the epitome of the Protestant work ethic. Separate, but not separatist, they enjoyed high standards of education, did not appear to experience much in the way of hardship on arrival (with or without family or business connections), and made few public inroads into the city's expansive social and political public spheres. Opting to remain on the side-lines, they constituted as distinct a sector of the Protestant population in the city as Mitchel's radical nationalists and the politicized Orangemen while sustaining important cultural links with their particular native heritage.

The 1896 publication of the Masonic tale *The Irish Prince and the Hebrew Prophet* further testifies to connections between Ireland and New York in this regard, surviving as a unique Masonic document. Proceeding from the biblical scenes of the Fall of Jerusalem through the prophets, the story substituted biblical references for Masonic imagery and symbolism. For example, Ephraim represented England, that country with "the peculiar characteristic" in "pronouncing the let-ter H." The Irish connection came in when Jeremiah and Baruch the prophets brought the Ark of the Covenant to Ulster, the author attesting that "it is an indis-putable historical fact that in 580 BC there arrived in the North of Ireland a Hebrew princess whose name was Tea Tephi, and she was accompanied by two men, one of whom was a prophet."[122]

Whatever about the Ark's landfall in the north of Ireland, Ulstermen prospered quietly in the trades and in steady business ventures as the 1910s witnessed yet another branch sprung from their cultural foundation. As their name suggested, the Protestant Friends of Ireland represented an interesting contrast with and the fur-thest point on the political spectrum from the Orangemen and the Freemasons. Closer in spirit to the Mitchels and their friends, certainly an anomaly when con-sidered alongside their Orange compatriots, and founded in New York in the 1910s during a Home Rule campaign accelerating on a daily basis, the Friends affiliated more closely with the broad sweep of traditionally Catholic nationalist ideals than any other Protestant organization. Successfully established with membership in the hundreds, by 1919 the Friends had become embroiled in a lengthy controversy. Detractors accused members of unifying to further personal political ambitions, and city editors accused the Friends of acting as a puppet organization in the grip of the similarly named but much more extensive Friends of Irish Freedom (FOIF) led by Judge Daniel J. Cohalan. By all accounts, the FOIF controlled every move the Protestant Friends made. Right Reverend Patrick James Grattan Mythen serving as the National Executive Secretary of the Protestant Friends in the city through the 1910s and into the 1920s replied at some length to the charges in October 1919.[123] He testified that detractors and begrudgers had almost destroyed the organization and the positive relationship it had built up with contacts in Clan na Gael and the FOIF. One of these "begrudgers" turned out to be Dr. Norman Thomas, Presbyterian minister, and socialist libertarian activist.[124] In private correspondence with the Friends' directors during 1919 and 1920, Grattan Mythen wrangled with Dr. Thomas over alleged misuse of Friends' finances. Grattan Mythen may have exaggerated in remarking that Dr. Thomas should remember he "was received with a loving heart by a united Irish race in America," but believed Dr. Thomas "cannot expect to evade [his] share of the blame for bringing about this most unhappy condition."[125] The attacks continued into 1920, when the point that Dr. Thomas "was not of Irish blood and cannot feel as we do" seemed suddenly valid; Grattan Mythen wondering "how does it come that you, who are openly and avowedly a member of the Socialist Party and therefore pledged to opposition to the rule of the bourgeoisie, be so tremendously agitated about the recognition of the Irish Republic and the administration of President DeValera?"[126]

In defense of the Protestant Friends, Grattan Mythen alluded to the extensive membership lists, large donations, and the successful establishment of a headquarters at 409 Fourth Avenue, but his own reluctance to recognize Eamon DeValera as President of the newly formed Free State of Ireland offers further insight on the group.[127] The 1916 leader, President of the first republican government in 1919, and true believer in a united, Catholic Ireland, Eamon DeValera's ideology undoubtedly conflicted with typical Protestant perspectives.[128] As though to entrench the more traditional attitudes, a group representing the opposing point on the political spectrum arrived in New York in 1920. The Delegates of the Protestant Churches of Ireland publicized their unblinking Loyalist agenda under the sponsorship of the International Protestant Alliance headquartered on Madison Avenue. These Delegates first and foremost distinguished their support base from the city's nationalists. Fearing for the status of Ireland's Protestant minority the year before Partition locked in, the Delegates argued that although Ireland had suffered in past centuries under English authority, a new era had now dawned and Protestants were entitled to their place on the new platform. Such a proposal may have found favor with Orangemen, especially the declaration that: "whatever the wrongs Ireland endured and often she was herself greatly to blame, for many years past the story of Britain's dealing with her has been one of a generous endeavor to enfranchise, to benefit, and to bless." The Delegates followed this statement with an appeal to New Yorkers to recognize the status of Protestants within whatever form of independent Ireland might evolve in the near future.[129]

Ultimately, Home Rule obligated Protestants of all political stripes to adapt to changing fortunes in 1921 as the signing of the Government of Ireland Act redrew Ireland's political map. In Famine-era and post-Famine New York, the solemn loyalties of the Orange Order, the activities within organizations ranging from the Freemasons to the Protestant Friends of Ireland, and the unaffiliated voices collectively constituted a culture of significance within Irish immigration. A diversity previously obscured or overshadowed emerged through the Froude debate, the Mitchels' nationalist fervor, the Orange Order's militancy, and the Protestant Friends' unique station to reveal a degree of breadth and depth in the New York Irish experience and in the city's response to Ireland's political issues previously overshadowed by the more expansive Catholic experience.

As the political crusade across the Atlantic consumed the attention of city Protestants, the agenda seemed to reinforce historical barriers between the different denominational traditions. Points of conciliation failed to mobilize Protestants en masse toward a visible community, but notwithstanding, the different elements within that settlement established their native heritage as securely as the much larger Catholic constituency. Incidents such as the 1870 and 1871 riots should not be considered typical of Irish Protestant-Catholic relations between 1845 and 1920, but it is clear that predominant configurations of city Irishness allied either with the Catholic or some branch of Protestant cultural identity, directly reflective of whichever one they left behind.

The relationship between the elements spanned the spectrum between the openly hostile and warmly conciliatory. Dictated by the prevailing political situation between Ireland and Britain and the escalating Home Rule campaign, it was not until the milestone of the Government of Ireland Act that tensions could afford to ease and interest shift to the viability of the Northern Irish statelet and the newborn Free State of Eire. The mayhem of the previous decades was replaced by another stage along a centuries-old culture clash. As history has since revealed, the Treaty did not herald the end of antagonism, but marked a stopgap along the way. But these groups settled into a new era in 1920's New York and Ireland that at least promised much in terms of peace, prosperity, and progress. Irish men and women faced the new decade with renewed hope that continues up to the present day. They left a legacy of a more vibrant, strong, and visible culture than popularly acknowledged.

Language as a Message From History

ere it possible for an essay in literary criticism to inflame political tensions and incite outbreaks of violence, then Matthew Arnold's 1868 "On the Study of Celtic Literature" held that kind of potential. The execution of three Fenian prisoners in Manchester and the Gladstonian plan to disestablish the Anglican Church of Ireland certainly generated a highly charged contemporary political atmosphere within which to explore Celtic literature.[1] The prominent critic's foray into his neighboring literary heritage did not constitute a one-time novelty or eccentricity, but paved the way for an extensive body of work on the topic in the following decades.[2] Arnold's interest in the early stirrings of the Celtic or Gaelic Revival[3] may even have "reaffirmed . . . a neo-Burkian version of cultural nationalism as a philosophy designed to act as an alternative to and even a safeguard against revolutionary republicanism," Seamus Deane has suggested.[4]

Throughout the nineteenth century, the proponents of what came to be popularly characterized "cultural nationalism" articulated a reasonably distinct branch of patriotic ideology, while advocates of the agenda most commonly represented as "revolutionary republicanism" took to the fields and the streets in slightly more militant fashion.[5] Populist, and occasionally subscribing to a militant directive, the Fenians, the Land League, and the Irish Volunteers, among others, planned for and occasionally engaged in rebellious activity. Transported to New York and the other major American urban centers, the broad spectrum of revolutionary republicanism would play a significant role within Irish immigrant political culture. Less militantly, perhaps, but equally passionately, the range of patriotic impulses inspired by Ireland's literary and artistic past wound up transplanting equally well. Occasionally, individuals such as John Mitchel, Margaret Anna Cusack, Countess Markievicz, and Padraig Pearse incorporated both avenues of expression into crowded political agendas. During their well-publicized lives, their writings expressed support for the rebellions that had taken place, and for future plans that never quite came to fruition. But collectively, the assorted Catholic and Protestant men and women converging on New York transported sufficient hoardings of both cultural and revolutionary nationalist affiliation to exert a profound influence on post-Famine settlement.[6] Dominating the world of public and private correspondence generated by the individuals and groupings establishing an imprint on a new home place, the rhetoric underpinning the political platforms referenced contemporary Ireland, charting progress toward the goal of long-awaited independence as a salient dimension of settlement, and institutionalizing the heart of the New York Irish identity.

Rhetoric and writing materializing as "popular literature" emerged early in the process. Often over-sentimental, usually florid, and frequently maudlin, popular writings supported the political doctrines of a people struggling with the formation of a new culture on both sides of the Atlantic. Harboring many of the hallmarks of the displaced, the poetry, drama, and speechmaking contained the "diasporic imagination" of post-Famine New York.[7] Contemporary fiction and all manner of writing crafted within homes, churches, businesses, and schools highlighted political trends and cultural references in patterns reflective of their sources within the immigrant community. Dennis Clark's opinion that "the use of folklore material on family life, work life, and leadership, like the use of oral interviews, may perturb some very traditional historians who focus exclusively on written documents, but the use of such data is especially important in the study of groups lacking extensive written records"[8] is certainly borne out in the case of New York. Famine-decade and post-Famine Irish city culture generated its fair share of such "records"; such sources opening windows onto the inner sanctum of settlement. Pieces of fiction, amateur speechmaking, private diary entries, and the material produced away from the public eye supplemented the operations of the political movements or organizations like the Orange Order to enhance understanding of the Irish city experience. Within the works, the notion of "nationalism" in all its diverse forms surfaced often enough to constitute a pervasive theme through the decades between 1845 and 1921. Men like John Mitchel and Thomas Francis Meagher fixated on different nationalistic connotations than Margaret Anna Cusack or Daniel Cohalan, for example. The "notoriously gelatinous" meaning of "nationalism" had no single fixed association, but subscribed to a variety of meanings.[9] Shades of reference including "ethnic consciousness," "patriotism," "chauvinism," and "issues of state power, domination, liberation and sovereignty"[10] each found purchase, but cultural nationalism as "quite independent of political nationalism" drew on a variety of associations.[11] Incorporating a broad purview, the "notion of kinship" that perpetuated "the myth of common descent and common destiny [as] the most powerful cement holding nations together"[12] found resonance within Irish New York, and is reflected through this chapter.[13] A vital linkage between Irish New York and its point of origin, nationalist expression articulated through popular writing and rhetoric anchored the post-Famine Atlantic world within historical parameters established in Ireland over centuries past.

The array of popular rhetoric imbued with nationalist overtones exerted significant impact over the entire American settlement process, but this kind of deterministic writing distinguished New York's Irish from other ethnic groups, and one element from another within the immigrant community itself.[14] Poet Gerald Dawe's observation that "language becomes a message from History which the poet receives and transcribes through the medium of vowel, consonant and assonance" finds resonance within the New York Irish experience, illuminated within all manner of contextual association.[15] The image of Ireland as female, for example, depicted either as an old crone—the Sean Bhean Bhocht—or Yeats's reincarnation of the nation as a heavenly, supernatural vision, permeated nineteenth-century nationalist literature.[16] As the female figurehead Cathleen Ni Houlihan extended her influence over the Gaelic Revival, the "emotive symbol[s]" that surfaced in New York Irish writings employed building blocks from the older literary tradition. Of course by the post-Famine years, the bardic output had well disappeared into what Declan Kiberd called "a sort of nowhere, waiting for its appropriate images and symbols to be inscribed in it."[17] And men and women moving across the Atlantic had more pressing matters on their minds. In the post-Famine era, "the home rule party and the agrarian agitation were more urgent than early Irish texts of lesson books."[18] But Irish city texts generated a well of identity in a foreign land, broadly evocative of the politicizations inherent in the great old bardic tradition. The columns of the city's Irish press represented a poor substitute for a lost heritage, in many respects, but this outlet served the immediate needs of a developing immigrant community. Fiction, balladry, and selections of poetry enlivening the pages of dailies and weeklies such as *The Irish World*, *The Irish Nation*, and *The Irish Democrat* gave voice to often painful themes of emigration, exile, and oppression, hammered out in the Sixth Ward, the Five Points, the mid-town neighborhoods, the convents and Orange lodges, the front offices of doctors and lawyers, the halls of schools and colleges, and every conceivable venue within Irish New York.[19]

Turning his attention to Irish political culture on both sides of the Atlantic in 1919, ubiquitous man of letters George A. Birmingham singled out some of the more prevalent themes held in common. A member of the Grand Synod of the

Church of Ireland, the Belfast-born author, critic, and social commentator Canon James Owen Hannay (1865–1950) used the pen-name George A. Birmingham throughout his literary career, his urbane style disguising the razor-sharp perceptions characterizing his writings.[20] Party affiliation among the nineteenth- and early–twentieth-century Irish remained generally stable, he believed, the nationalists amongst them occasionally changing tactics but never aspirations. Unionist opposition remained resolutely steadfast, as a rule, and politicians did not try to convert the opposition. The ordinary voter, Birmingham went on, did not read the "important and expensive magazines" carrying political debate, but instead, read local newspapers that delivered little in the way of deliberation, and merely maintained the status quo. He continued that:

> Intimate friends, if they happen to be educated men, will occasionally discuss politics with each other. But the ordinary Irishman does not discuss politics with his neighbour. It is a gross breach of good manners to suggest that a man's political faith is wrong. It would scarcely be more offensive to tell him that his wife's virtue is doubtful. He is bound to believe in his politics and his wife's honour. He would, very naturally, resent an attempt to discuss either.

One factor clouded his political horizon. "In spite of the faithfulness of the people at the polls and in spite of an almost perfect party discipline," nationalists "have never possessed a fundamental unity." He distinguished between "moderate" and "extreme" affiliations, stressing the gap between "constitutional agitators and believers in physical force." Very few adherents to the latter perspective would resort to violence should any other path remain open, in his opinion. The real difference lay in the realm of theoretical abstraction. The moderate branch believed that the Union binding Ireland and Britain should be abandoned because it failed to achieve unity and conciliation. Extremists remained equally convinced that Ireland should constitute a separate nation; to be achieved by overturning the miscarriage of justice wrought by the Act of Union.[21]

As moderates and extremists brought the Home Rule campaign to life, stifling sentimentalism blurred the political boundaries in New York as in Ireland. Poetry, in particular, served as an outlet for raising the emotional stakes high in New York, as exemplified by some of the more prominent practitioners and political pundits. Encapsulating an evocative patriotism of the kind that resonated well with immigrant readers and public audiences, the work of James Clarence Mangan circulated in the city from the 1840s on, although Mangan himself never actually visited the United States.[22] One of his collections earmarked for an American readership veered onto a hard-line perspective with an introduction by John Mitchel, known to the poet since the rebellious atmosphere around 1848. Lending Mangan's 1859 work an authentically radicalized tone and unequivocal sense of political purpose, the imprimatur publicly associated the poet with the much-vaunted author of *Jail*

Journal, published just a few years previously.[23] Poems such as "The Fair Hills of Eire O" articulated a pervasive sense of separation and some of the deeper reaches of exile for his immigrant readership. As one contemporary phrased it, of "the sons of the Gael here in this broad, free land . . . what son of the Gael will not join with the poet, whose feet never strayed from her enchanted shore, in these tender greetings to old Erin in the sea."[24] Mangan's themes explored the same metaphysical territory, imploring "Alas! alas! why pine I a thousand miles away, From the fair hills of Eire, O!"[25]

Patrick Ford's *Irish World* published the poem in December 1882 following its excellent reception as an encore at a downtown Cooper Union literary evening. Galway-born and Boston-schooled Ford could always be counted on to maximize opportunities to expand his readership and promote his politics. A stint with William Lloyd Garrison during his formative years in America only underscored his taste for the high-profile radicalism he would later subscribe to,[26] and this kind of gathering generated the kind of drama he readily identified with. Under a large banner with the legend "God Save Ireland," the extensive crowd assembled at the Union to commemorate the fifteenth anniversary of the executions of the Fenian Manchester Martyrs. Supporters heard Mangan's words amplified by an extravagant appeal to their nationalist sympathies; useful during an event expected to raise funds for the cause. Delivered in an Irish language translation by the crowd-pleasing choice of Mary O'Donovan-Rossa, wife of Fenian Jeremiah O'Donovan-Rossa, the poem provided an ideal finale for the evening.[27]

Mangan's more famous "Dark Rosaleen" evoked the struggle against English domination in the fashion of a lament, and undoubtedly substantiated the feelings of sympathetic Fenians and Clan na Gaelers during the post-Famine decades. Ostensibly a love poem, "Dark Rosaleen"[28] plumbed the depths of a nation struggling against an oppressive power, as did the sentiments publicized by Frances Isabelle Parnell disseminated via the press and in pamphlet form in the 1870s. Conveying the same impassioned patriotism as Mangan's protagonists, Parnell's lines evoked a sense of despair over Ireland's misfortune. Lines overflowing with patriotic affirmation, such as: "I have also loved her in her loneliness and sorrow" anticipated a brighter future for Ireland, but not within the poet's lifetime. The last line, "Then contented I shall go back to the shamrocks, now mine eyes have seen her glory!" intertwines death with the hope of a free nation in the ubiquitous style of the patriotic lament.[29]

The poem is distinguished from the multitude of others of its kind by its author, Frances Isabelle Parnell. For immigrants everywhere, the name Parnell and Ireland's Home Rule agitation remained permanently linked. In the words of Yeats, the "solitary and proud Parnell" represented the best hope for a constitutional upheaval in later nineteenth-century Ireland.[30] Fanny Parnell's immersion in the cause of freedom took the form of militant activism as a founding member of the Ladies Land League, but her ballads and poetry continued to appear at regular intervals through the 1880s and long past her death in 1885.[31] Her overtly patriotic expression and the omnipresent shadow of her iconic brother ensured prominence for her work among those subscribing to her agenda. The same motifs permeated another work by the almost as well known and similarly well-connected Mary O'Donovan-Rossa. The first verse of "To Miss Rita O'Donohoe, The Little Girl From Ireland" enshrined more of the same misty patriotism for Carnegie Hall audiences of the faithful, "a magic wand" evoking "memories bright and fond" left behind in Ireland.[32]

Here, lavish expression wrought a picture-perfect image of another world on the strains of fairy violins. As with the influential Parnell name and the impact of Mitchel's blessing on Mangan's work, the melodramatic overtures took on increased significance by virtue of Mary O'Donovan-Rossa's imprimatur. The piece commemorated a performance in Carnegie Hall by newly arrived soloist Rita O'Donohoe. Applauding O'Donohoe's performance, *The New York Irish American* referred to her as "the star of the evening's entertainers," in association with such a well-known personality as Fenian wife Mary O'Donovan-Rossa, and proffered the opinion that Mrs. O'Donovan-Rossa had not "taken a poetic license in her praise of the young artiste." Another such work extolling "the struggle for self-definition . . . conducted within language"[33] appeared in 1886. Ordinarily, a politically charged play by a female would have generated interest, but the news that a Catholic nun produced a nationalist satire surely broadened the patriotic sphere beyond its usual parameters. Cultivating a prominent niche for herself compared with the private daily life of a Sister of Charity or a Mercy nun, the same Margaret Anna Cusack or "Nun of Kenmare" that wove tapestries and wrote books in support of a free Ireland generated constant publicity for herself and her agenda during the post-Famine years.[34] *Tim Carty's Trial, or Whistling at Landlords: A Play for the Times,* she announced in the Preface, "is especially suited to passing events, and a little Comedy may not lessen the value of the Information which it conveys, on the important subjects which so deeply affect the temporal and spiritual future of the Irish race."[35] In so expressing, the Nun of Kenmare employed a popular medium often resorted to as a political device. Yeats's reference to the rise of "a true literary consciousness"[36] holds relevance for works like *Tim Carty's Trial;* polemics that sought to couch long-standing political grievances within a theatrical rendering. A straight shot at the rack-renting landlords that all but eliminated the class of tenant farmers at the lowest rungs of the scale, the play encapsulated the essence of Davitt's Land League agenda articulated in the same decade.[37]

A glance through the "Dramatis Personae" set the scene. Led by "Lord Drive-em-Out, Irish Landlord who lived in England," and "Mr. Evictem, Lord Drive-em-out's Agent," the stock figures in contemporary rural life comprised the cast. Father O'Sullivan, the Parish Priest, acquainted with "Two Sisters," six-year-old Tim Carty, and a number of justices, accompanied "Mr. Happyrock (Gladstone), Queen's Counsel, solicitors, policemen, and groups of tenants in disseminating a storyline of critical significance to a majority of Ireland's rural-based population in the late nineteenth century. Representations of contemporary landlords, among them "Lord Stopper (the Earl of Cork)," the "Earl of Uplands (the Earl of Lansdowne), and Sir Very Very (Lord de Vere)" completed the cast. Under the list, Cusack's note stating "a child was really tried in Ireland for whistling as a landlord passed by" prefaced a script that raised one pressure point after another. The stock themes of eviction, destruction, forced immigration, death, apathetic politicians, and brutal treatment at the hands of landlords intertwined to provoke an anti-Establishment reaction. In the first act, the agent Mr. Evictem calculated that Lord Drive-em-Out took in 120,000 pounds from his Irish estates and would certainly clear 60,000 pounds profit. But the Lord's displeasure at the state of his financial affairs led him to thunder:

> Do you know, sir, I am master of the hounds in the county in England where my smallest property is, and it costs me 10,000 pounds a year to keep that up. And, if my Irish tenants don't pay for it, who is to pay for it? Just answer me that, sir. The lazy hounds—I mean the lazy Irish. Sir, my hounds must be well fed; and they cannot live on potatoes, sir. And, then, the parson of the parish in England expects me to give coal, and blankets, and soup, and flannels all the winter round, and where is the money to come from for that, sir, if I am only to get Griffith's Valuation from these lazy blackguards. Evict them, sir! evict the whole of them! Clear the country, sir! Do what Cromwell did, sir! He knew how to manage Ireland, sir!38

In this passage, Cusack wrenched open some of the deepest sores in contemporary Ireland. At one point after the Lord extolled the merits of buckshot over bullets (the former ensuring a swifter death), a knock came to the estate office door. "You need not be afraid, my lord," the Agent said, "I assure you the people are very quiet. The priests won't allow them to commit any outrages. We had real difficulty to make up any for the papers."39 Concluding with a final swipe on a judge's pronouncement that the landlord was even obliging enough to tell "his English friends there was no manure for land so good as RAISING THE RENT," Cusack offered her audience a glimmer of hope at the final curtain. The judge's verdict was interrupted by the sound of cheering outside and a voice shouting to the assembled in court: "Cable message just arrived. Ireland Free!!! Mr. Gladstone's Bill to give Ireland a Parliament of her own passed by tremendous majority!"40

The publication and its authorship helped to institutionalize a most prominent political message within the city's Irish community. While formalized meetings and debates sponsored by the main organizations commanded huge public attention, nationalist endorsement by individuals operating outside the more mainstream

PICTURES OF IRELAND. 505

IN THE GALLERY AT THE THEATRE.

nature in a very remarkable way. The mimic show is like a reality to them, and they display as much feeling over the counterfeited passions as if they were burning inspirations.

The Irish drama there is in no manner different from what it is here. It has the same brave, blundering, swaggering, joking, gallant, ultra-patriotic heroes, who love women and the bottle as they detest tyranny and the Saxon, and who always extricate themselves at the end from innumerable difficulties, and declaim about the glory of Ireland as the curtain descends to the music of some national air. There is always, of course, the unvarying British spy whom the Irish are perpetually discovering in their most secret councils, and in all their convocations, wherever their lot may be cast. He turns up as regularly on the Cork, Dublin, and Limerick stage as he does in ward meetings and Fenian circles on this side of the Atlantic. Whenever he appears he is hissed and hooted at as if he were a veritable culprit, and I have seen apples and oranges hurled at him when he happened to play his part with any degree of excellence. I was informed that one of the company of the Cork theatre, usually cast for the character of informer, became so odious to the impetuous and unreasoning public that he was compelled one night to jump into the river to escape from an infuriated mob.

The gallery audience laugh and weep and roar and swear over what they witness on the stage, and go into such ecstasies of sympathy, indignation, and choler as would not be possible to the most excitable throng at the Théâtre Beaumarchais or the Funambules. The fact that the dramas always violate both history and probability adds to their charm for the ingenuous and impassioned people. In spite of the valor and the virtues of the latter they have neither nationality nor independence, and in the strict distribution of poetic justice at the conclusion of the performance they have the compensation through the imagination that stern and stubborn circumstance denies to them in the larger theatre of life.

Of the wit and humor of the Irish no one who sees them on their native soil can doubt. They are the only peasantry in Europe who can lay any claim to qualities that are usually reckoned intellectual. They have more of the mental attributes of Shakspeare's clowns—the least natural of his wonderful creations—than any living mortals unblest of education. The English, Scotch, German, Italian, and even French peasants are the veriest clods in comparison with the Irish, who say bright and sharp things without effort or premeditation. Their ready wit and power of repartee are extraordinary, and improve as one journeys toward the south. I have frequently heard scintillations from "gorsoons" and porters and car-drivers that would have been applauded in the Academy, and have created envy in the most exclusive drawing-rooms. They never lack for a word or a phrase, and have a verbal knack of getting out of a quandary peculiarly their own, as respects both the knack and the quandary. It is

Fig 4.1: "In the Gallery at the Theater," *Harper's New Monthly Magazine* (March 1871); courtesy of Cornell University Library, Making of America Digital Collection.

political process certainly remained limited to smaller spheres of influence. But an extensive New York publication record centering on Ireland's history and culture provided Margaret Anna Cusack a public platform from which to address the more aggravating issues overshadowing the post-Famine Irish on both sides of the Atlantic. Energetic and controversial, and often inconsistent, her views on topics like women's rights and the influence of class often vacillating between the radical and the conservative, Cusack generated a public niche for herself by means of her extraordinary literary output. And her focus on Ireland's oppressed occasionally resulted in improvement. An Appendix to the play included a citation from a "Report of the English Miners Delegation to Kerry" detailing the financial assistance Cusack provided to the starving tenantry in Kerry. In all, the Nun of Kenmare was able to distribute over £15,000 to the needy, thanks to the publicity generated by her work.

The effort to "reinforce[ed] the sense of collective national destiny among these scattered peoples,"[41] in Jacobson's words, found expression in Cusack's play and in the poems of Parnell, O'Donovan-Rossa, and Mangan. Some of the more anonymous works, too, played a role in this reinforcement. Evoking the memory of Ireland while speaking directly to the immigrant mentality, broadsheets circulating in the city advertising reactions to contemporary events occupied a similar niche.[42] Stirring entreaties during the mid-century years anticipating that "McClellan will be President" or articulating homesickness in "Oh! I Vants To Go Home, or Maximillian's Lament,"[43] included plenty of Irish representation. "O'Toole and McFinnigan On the War" depicted the men of the title bemoaning the interruption of business occasioned by the Civil War and debating potential England-United States confrontation over the Fenian invasion of Canada. The notion that America could be drawn into war with Britain (and offer the Irish an opportunity to establish self-government while Britain remained otherwise occupied) forms the basis for a satirical rendering from the two "gintlemin":[44]

> Joost mind what old England's about,
> A sending her troops to Canaday,
> And all her ould ships, on the coast,
> Are ripe for some treachery any day;
> Now, if she should mix in the war . . .
> Be jabers! it makes me head spin again,
> Ould Ireland would have such a chance . . .
> You're right, sir, says Misther McFinnigan.[45]

The lyrics to "Our Own Flag of Green" probably antagonized city Orangemen, but should have appealed to other compatriots harboring thoughts of exile during a time of Fenian-inspired tensions. The "vanquished Lion" England would surely fall against the force of "the Eagle and our Shamrock," in the hope that "the downtrodden Celt shall be Free!" Notwithstanding such high hopes, the ballad cited the disunity impeding nationalist progress.

> We, brave Irish Soldiers, are preparing to march again, proudly, o'er the sea:
> The contest of Races endearing, And the down-trodden Celt shall be Free!
> If we bury divisions for ever, And no more, in our Island, shall be seen:
> Then, our Green Treble Shamrock shall be won; We'll march 'neath our own
> Flag of Green![46]

Received "with immense success" in the city, according to the broadsheet, humor promoted the message of self-reflection broadcast by "No Irish Need Apply," in the tale of "a dacint boy" who was refused a job upon arrival in 1860's New York. Derided as "a dirty spalpeen," the prospective employer alluded to here merited a colorful description stopping just shy of vulgarity:

> I'm a dacint boy, just landed from the town of Ballyfad;
> I want a situation: yis, I want it mighty bad.
> I saw a place advertised. It's the thing for me, says I,

But the dirty spalpeen ended with: No Irish need apply.
Whoo! says I; but that's an insult—though to get the place I'll try.[47]

Know-Nothingism made an occasional appearance in this kind of rhetoric, as in the lyrics by Tom Robinson sung to the air of the older ballad "Rory O'More." Chronicling a ruckus between a group of Irishmen and a party of Know-Nothing supporters, some of the lines ran:

Our party was thirty, all armed wid big sticks,
Sure we'd knock 'em about like a thousand of bricks;
At the villains we went, we 'brave men of the hod,'
An I gav' a big Yankee a belt in the gob.
'Wide Awake' was their war-cry, from near and from far,
We answered their challenge wid' 'Erin-go-bragh,'
On my eye I then got a wee bit of a whack,
Which laid me right out on the broad of my back.

The lesson that the vote would prove mightier than the stick during the coming elections suggested an acceptable consolation prize.[48]

A fount of patriotic evocation showcasing the language and imagery of the battlefield and echoing the Gaelic bardic epics of past centuries also emerged during these same years. As one of the more flamboyant figures associated with this type of output, Lady Wilde, or Speranza, as she styled herself, attracted heightened attention to her unique version. Jane Francesca Elgee Wilde roused a cult of celebrity in Ireland and England during her life as a composer of elegiac poetry embellished with the air of the eccentric and the avant-garde, not to mention her role as the mother of Oscar Wilde. A passionate advocate for republican propaganda, especially during evening salons, Speranza operated in spheres safely removed from grassroots militancy. But her name sold newspapers and filled lecture halls everywhere she went on the strength of her dynamic personality, and she imbued her rhetoric with à la mode appeal. New York's Irish press reported the arrival of Oscar Wilde to the city in December 1881 under the heading "Speranza's Son," for example, establishing his identity in terms of his renowned mother. Fascinated by Speranza and her bohemian idylls in London and Dublin, contemporaries found her anti-British rhetoric just as compelling, rendered especially conspicuous in light of her Anglo-Irish background. Perhaps her best-known collection, *Poems by Speranza*, included the dedication to her sons: "I made them indeed Speak plain the word country. I taught them no doubt That a country's a thing men should die for at need." To the Irishman or woman who turned traitor, Speranza taunted: "Was it the gold of the stranger that tempted him? Ah! we'd have pledged to him body and soul . . . Smiled, tho' our graves were the steps to his goal . . . Hush! tis the Sassenach ally you greet." In these lines, the "stranger" referred to English efforts to quash nationalist sympathies by means of titles, land grants, or business opportunities, and "Sassenach" recalled a Gaelic reference to an English person.[49] The personal appearance of Oscar Fingal O'Flahertie Wills Wilde only heightened the public interest surrounding mother and son, especially in such a fashion-conscious milieu as New York. His dramatic height, his "long brown hair," the "seal ring on one of the fingers of his right hand," and the possibility of "a gold watch chain across his waistcoat," conveyed a different impression of Irish culture than that inculcated by fellow travelers John Mitchel or William Smith O'Brien. About to reach the peak of his celebrity across the Atlantic and years before scandal would beleaguer his last years, no aspect of his appearance escaped attention, particularly "the all-enveloping great-coat [that] also prevented observation being made as to what sort of trousers one has to wear to be aesthetic."[50] The type of publicity tour showcasing Wilde to advantage lent city nationalist support a dash of fashionable levity shot through with the hard-hitting satirical edge that made him famous.

Speranza's rhetoric and her son's celebrity helped publicize nationalistic writing, with the devotion of at least a page per week to poetry, ballads, and short literary pieces in the major Irish-run city newspapers and magazines that propelled the genre onto the front ranks of contemporary New York Irish attention. As a forum for advertising the notion of an Ireland struggling against an oppressive empire, the body of popular literature provided daily reminders of conditions in post-Famine Ireland. The "secular imperatives"[51] mobilizing American-based men and women toward the creation of a new identity found echo in a genre that attracted widespread interest in Irish New York, judging by its predominance in the contemporary press. *The Irish Democrat* in 1872 provided a new outlet catering to this interest, devoting its pages to the "essential qualities" of "Irish Nationality and Democracy in America" in what the editor touted "a first-class, high-toned political, literary" publication. Commercializing its political leanings, the journal would "advocate Republicanism in the Old Land," and spare no expense "to make the *Irish People's Democrat* worthy of their race and history."[52] This kind of forum generated interest in the concept of "race" as time went on. In March 1886 a physician living on the Upper East Side commented on the old idea of Irishness as a more complex notion than the simple homogenization typically represented.[53] Exploring the earliest distribution of Celts and Teutons in Britain and Ireland, Dr. James J. Delany suggested that the notion of a pure, unadulterated race should be abandoned in favor of acknowledgment of the Irish as "a mixed race." The interactions of tribes, sects, and different ethnic groupings from pre-Christian times up to the twelfth century and beyond had created a people of mixed blood. Nothing but the influence of political circumstances distinguished the Irish from the English, to his mind, and the term "Celtic Race" should not be considered as other than a nineteenth-century "political epithet" developed by opportunists. As Dr. Delany affirmed, the ubiquitous

James Anthony Froude provided an abundance of evidence in support of this kind of contention.[54]

Dr. Delany's words proffered a conception of "race" differing from the sentimentalism couched in patriotic rhetoric dominating the post-Famine Irish press. A perspective dismissive of an illusory "Celtic Race" ideal would surely clash with the anti-British invective popularized by the Fenians and successor-organizations, but so as not to completely alienate the traditionalist standpoint, the good doctor expressed sympathy with the plight of Ireland's rural dwellers struggling to survive as impoverished tenants. But he trod on some well-worn Fenian ground. Promotion of the concept of an Irish "race" arose most pointedly, perhaps, from New York Fenian Brotherhood rhetoric.[55] Throughout the 1850s and 1860s, Fenian meetings, demonstrations, and social events commanded much space in the city press, utilizing this outlet to cultivate "race" awareness. In July 1865, Brotherhood Chief-of-Staff Lieutenant-Colonel W. R. Roberts castigated those Irish-born who failed to exhibit the militant degree of patriotic fervor he deemed appropriate. Speaking of "my own race and land," Lt. Colonel Roberts demanded "facts not fancy," "dollars as well as sympathy," "muskets not advice, and bullets in place of words," in language revealing a liberal measure of "fancy" itself! Roberts invited his audience to believe that "the man who holds back now, shrinking and doubtful, is no warm lover of his land, and his patriotism is like the poor Irishman's blanket, too short at one end, and not long enough at the other." Following this, he declared:

> Ah, she little thought when hunting the Irish children from their homes and country, with her cruel and unjust laws, and her brutal and unfeeling execution of them, she was but placing them where they could one day furnish the means of redeeming their country and avenging her martyrs . . . that the wild geese who crossed the Atlantic would one day return with the sinews of war.[56]

Roberts portrayed the Fenian city membership as a potential rejuvenator of the "Wild Geese" tradition, the panoply of soldiers of fortune drawn from the old Gaelic nobility that fled Ireland in the seventeenth century seeking glory on the battlefields of Europe. Envisioning his audience as potential keepers of the flame, Roberts invoked the powerful tradition of exile and resurgence to generate resistance to foreign rule. Scorning the latest breed of "patriot" rushing to exact personal advancement as "pretended friends of Ireland," he highlighted the role of rhetoric as a valuable tool in the move against deceivers and betrayers. That he deployed histrionic language himself to maximum advantage reinforced his commitment to the power of words as a political weapon. Warning of threats posed by the false prophets with their "seemingly sincere language," he drew on the same brand of evocative imagery he condemned in the betrayers. Enlivening his oration with Biblical references, he declared that: "We are tired of shams, we are sick of cant, we stretch forth our arms across the Atlantic and grasping a brother's hand of every creed; Catholic, Episcopalian, Presbyterian, Jews, Turks, if there are such beings in Ireland: aye, even those of repentant Orangemen (for the Son of God forgave his murderers) and swear Ireland shall be free, and we must free her."[57] Portraying the New York Irish as inhabitants of a place apart, removed from the land of oppression but retaining their birthright, they emerge from his hyperbole as creators of a new culture. By encouraging readers to "stretch forth" their hands "across the Atlantic," he minimized the distance back to their old homeland. Immigrants not only retained their connections with the mother country, they entrenched the proud "wild geese" tradition of exile as a linchpin of their new transatlantic world.

Arguments for the validity of Irish race-consciousness and the threat of betrayal by the faux-faithful also wove through the private writings of James Stephens. Echoing some of the same ideas as Roberts, Ex-Young Irelander and Fenian co-founder Stephens divided his time between Ireland, Paris, and New York as he sought to establish the Brotherhood as the pre-eminent revolutionary group. The story of how he capitalized on the mass Famine immigrations to New York to serve as a useful base for his ambitions is well known.[58] From 1858 to 1860, Stephens's commitment to strengthening the American Brotherhood required residence in New York. His distrust of insincere nationalists reflected the opinions of Lieutenant-Colonel Roberts, and in similar terminology, Stephens strengthened his convictions in the face of detractors. Wary of "men . . . who had done me foul wrong," he preached vigilance against the threat of false patriots, stressing the power of language as a formidable weapon. He worried constantly about "carrion knaves" and traitorous activists, greeting each acquaintance with cynicism, scrutinizing expressions, and judging character within minutes of meeting.[59] An extensive media campaign covering the gamut of Fenian maneuverings kept his name to the fore. Seeking to develop activist networks and raise large sums of money for the cause, he became embroiled in sporadic gun-running and arms-dealing while producing heady prose redolent of Speranza and Mangan. Describing fellow Fenian leaders unflatteringly as "puddle-pated or puddle-gizzarded," he held co-founder John O'Mahony in relatively high regard.[60] Calling him the "first patriot" of the nation, Stephens reckoned that few held their native home in such high regard as O'Mahony, and few would go to such lengths to secure her freedom as he. Under the umbrella of propaganda set against a misty backdrop, Stephens's florid affirmation of his comrade displayed all the fervor of the seasoned stump-orator. Surpassing his previous high-blown romanticism, he declared, "compared with me, then, O'M is a cosmopolite against the grain of his nationalism; while I am a nationalist against the grain of my cosmopolitanism."

Satisfied that O'Mahony was the only fit candidate to step into his own much-vaunted shoes, Stephens endeavored to secure Fenian unity on the basis of an acceptable campaign plan. His writings showcased a dream of unity among the different Irish elements, and his aspiration to "establish a democratic Republic in Ireland" suggested quite a radical course of action as he declared "anything short of a thorough *social* revolution can effect but small good for the people."[61] Viewing himself as the last hope to generate enough support and capital to broker the anticipated "revolution," Stephens declared himself the cornerstone of the movement in the metaphors redolent of every elevated patriot before him. In effuse style, he remarked: "how gladly I would go into exile, how firmly and proudly meet death to serve this cause! But will the fools and traitors around me allow me to do so? Accident or design, they seem bent on my ruin, indifferent alike to the salvation or woe of Ireland." Assigning himself the role of messiah, and judging fellow-activists "fools and traitors," he surrounded himself with an entourage in common with the Mitchels in the same time period. Dividing his time among several meeting places, including private Fenian homes, Tammany Hall, Lower Manhattan trade union offices, and the upscale atmosphere of Delmonico's, he wistfully pursued his ideal of Ireland's deliverance. Even John O'Mahony, who merited heartfelt praise and confidence two years previously ultimately proved unworthy. "For I fear," Stephens boldly judged, "that even he lacks many of the essentials of a leader. This fear has been eating into my soul for some time. As to letting him go home in my place, it is out of the question."[62]

Even as he settled into "retirement" from the front lines in the early 1860s, James Stephens fervently anticipated the mobilization of initiatives such as the 1866 Fenian "invasion" of Canada. "England's difficulty will be Ireland's opportunity," he ventured, and depending on the achievement of a unified front, the Irish forces could realize their dream "as the united Jews will return some day and build the waste places of Zion."[63] The familiar propaganda proved useful in times of high drama. In the context of a "national spirit," Fenian "District" captains, local unit commanders, the leadership "Directory," and an assortment of prominent politicos publicized the aspiration within their circles, despite the lack of coordination and basic disagreement as to how such a vision would play out in reality. The rhetoric of the late 1860s represented the last gasps of a dying movement, but with an eye to posterity. The almost crusader-like imagery ascribed an elevated, quite messianic quality even as the organization lost its place in the front ranks of radical nationalist activity. On the occasion of the national Congress of 1867, the words of Fenian chief John Savage in Cleveland, Ohio, drew the attention of the press in New York, including *The Irish Citizen*, *The Daily Star*, *The Irish American*, and *The Irish People*. Arguing that "revolution" against England constituted the only means of separating the two islands politically, Savage expounded forcefully:

> Our cause is a just and holy one; it is the struggle of right against wrong, of freedom against oppression. It is not alone the cause of a nation striving for the thralldom and debasement

of feudal tyranny. The elevation of a down-trodden people is a benefit conferred upon the whole family of nations; and of none might this be said more truly than of Ireland, which, from her position and resources, is capable, if once free, not alone of rendering her own population happy and prosperous, but of diffusing, by example and influence, the spirit of independence throughout the world, wherever her scattered children are to be found.

"Save this," the Fenian President concluded, "we desire nothing for our race or our country."[64] The injection of a moral justification for revolution cropped up equally valiantly in the more comfortable surroundings of the Society of the Friendly Sons of Saint Patrick. For well-to-do gentlemen relaxing in elegant club surroundings on Fifth Avenue, the push and jostle of Fenian invective may have come across as outlandish, were it not for the fact that the Sons' resorted to equally highblown rhetoric. Post-Famine members included Mayors William R. Grace and Hugh Grant, and the Emigrant Savings Bank's Eugene Kelly. Honorary inductees Grover Cleveland and Theodore Roosevelt added an attractive national dimension to the membership.[65] As the high point of the club year, the annual dinner held on Saint Patrick's Day provided a glamorous setting for the Sons to engage in their particular brand of romanticized remembrance.[66] The Eighty-Sixth dinner at the St. James Hotel in 1870, to take a typical example, followed the usual protracted banquet style. An elaborate affair, with salmon, lamb, and beef imported from Ireland interspersing green turtle soup, fresh oysters, and lobster, the carefully selected wines, Champagne and liqueurs accompanying each course made for a grand repast. These evenings brought together a coterie of the city's Irish elite, most of whom came prepared to share laudatory thoughts with the assembled. Scaling extravagant heights with a schedule of traditional toasts honoring favored institutions and national allegiances, the speeches generated the kind of patriotic, convivial atmosphere reflective of the Sons' brand of armchair nationalism. The order in which the toasts were called indicated priorities, one more gallant and distinguished than the next. "The United States and Their Chief Magistrate" led to "The Day and the Name We Celebrate, Our Eighty-Sixth Anniversary: St. Patrick's Day and Its Many Memories," and "New York," accompanied by excerpts from poems and songs "Hail Columbia," "St. Patrick's Day," and "The Red, White and Blue." Next, "The Nationhood of Ireland" framed "Memory of the Dead" and "The Harp That Once, Through Tara's Hall." Composer of the ever-popular "Harp That Once," Young Irelander Thomas Davis also penned the verse intoned in the toast to Ireland, lines from which ran: "She is a rich and a rare land, A fresh and a fair land, A dear and rare land, this old land of mine." On the local level, "the City of New York," with "Mynheer Van Dunk" sung by all raised glasses to "Our Guests the Exiled IRISH PATRIOTS," described by President Charles P. Daly during the 1870 dinner as "Being victims of English tyranny, they are the more entitled to American sympathy." If the identities of these patriots were not made public, then at least the tribute was. The next toasts heralded "France," the New York Bench, the Bar, the press, the Army and Navy, and finally, a lengthy commemoration of "Woman," to the Irish air "The Girl I Left Behind Me."[67]

Once the United States and New York received due homage, the national saint and whichever "exiled Irish Patriots" happened to be in New York on those particular evenings were elevated to exalted heights. In effect, the dinner evoked the kind of token symbolism preserving a superficial but affectionate attitude to Ireland and its status. As a further nod to patriotic aspirations, lengthy speeches by Sons' officers exuded the same tenderhearted quality. In 1888, city lawyer Daniel Dougherty responded to the toast "The Day We Celebrate," at Delmonico's by reminding his audience of his national roots and the centuries of oppression suffered by his forebears. Dougherty's rousing speech might have been delivered by a member of the Fenian Directory but for a twist the majority of the Brotherhood would hesitate to privately contemplate, much less publicly condone. Extending the hand of friendship to the British government, Dougherty declared that in spite of "the direful cruelties of centuries, we are willing to forget and forgive"—a gracious gesture, surely beyond the inclinations of most Fenians and Land Leaguers. In the privacy of her diary, Rose McDermott explored the possibility of a nationalist-Orange alliance but even she stopped short of extending the sentiment to British authority.[68] John Mitchel and James Stephens also advanced conciliatory thoughts toward Orangemen deep within their personal journals, but did not refer to Great Britain publicly in this regard.[69] Dougherty cited William E. Gladstone's leadership as his inspiration for the eventual reconciliation of the two nations, acknowledging the Prime Minister's role in the successful passage of the long-sought Land Acts. Warming to his subject, Dougherty's characterization of Gladstone as "illustrious," "revered," "venerated," and "the foremost man of all the world" did not meld easily with the condemnation of British "oppression" in other speeches, but the Friendly Sons tended to accommodate patriotic rhetoric into a flexible format rendered attractive by forces of time and distance. For the membership, contemporary Ireland had evolved into a nation where the shamrock and the lily should intertwine peaceably and ancient hatreds should fade into oblivion. Citing Protestant revolutionaries, Dougherty declared to the assembled:

> I verily believe that the last Irish Catholic would die before he would desecrate the memory of Henry Grattan, Robert Emmet and Isaac Butt, or do injustice to the religious opinions of their living leader, C.S. Parnell . . . above all, Ireland united, demands her nationality, and she has an inherent right to it![70]

Loyalty to their adoptive country, rosy attachment to Ireland, and acknowledgment of a more benevolent England permitted the Friendly Sons' to sidestep the shrill cant of Fenians, Clan na Gaelers, and Land Leaguers. The honeyed tones of urbane gentlemen contemplating the larger Anglo-Irish political issues of the day in the salubrious surroundings of the Waldorf and Delmonico's generated a different brand of fervor to the tirades unleashed on the meaner city streets, while occupying a distinct niche within Irish New York's nationalist panoply.

In other neighborhoods, the lecture circuit afforded multiple opportunities for oratorical championing of the political cause. Flamboyant styles introduced colorful shades of republicanism to eager audiences. Delving into familiar territory, Very Reverend Thomas N. Burke drew on Ireland's foremost pre-Famine personality at the New York Academy of Music in May 1872. As "The Liberator" who pushed the Emancipation Bill through the House of Commons in 1829 to give Catholic Ireland her most resounding early nineteenth-century success, the name Daniel O'Connell could not fail to generate excitement for the Reverend that would take on Froude in the same year.[71] Available in pamphlet form by 1875, Burke's booklet opened with a frontispiece illustrating a monument at the Irish College in Rome. The monument depicted the visit of an angel to the Holy Family placed over an image of O'Connell recalling his career as a barrister.[72] The title page contained the words reputedly inscribed on The Liberator's grave: "My Soul to Heaven, My Heart to Rome, My Body to Ireland."[73] Two of the most powerful Catholic nationalist images intertwined on the page more eloquently than words could express.

As Burke unleashed the full power of his voice, constructing a picture of a people oppressed for centuries yet rising like the phoenix from the ashes to confront a latent foreign oppression, images of soldiers dispersing O'Connell's splendid Monster Meetings arose in a highly lyrical fashion. Burke intoned that "[on one] day in Clontarf, there were twenty-eight thousand soldiers in and around Dublin ready to pour their murderous fire upon the people."[74] Emotion-filled reference to these meetings led to Burke's trump card, a no-effort-spared evocation of a blood-stained Great Famine and the O'Connellite reaction to it. A blatant appeal to a patriotism entrenched in the tragedy of some twenty years previously was calculated to reawaken past horrors in the minds of his listeners. "Then came the hand of God upon the people," Burke began, dramatically conjuring up images of the "fearful scenes" when "the people cried for bread, and there was none to break it to them." The curse of British oppression raised the stakes even further. "The strong man lay down and died," the priest told the audience, generating the spell of the seanachie and his hair-raising tales on winter nights:

> The tender maiden and the poor and aged matron of Ireland lay down and died; they were found in their shallow graves, scarcely buried; they were found crawling to the chapel door that they might breathe out their souls in wings over the land, and the Liberator, the Emancipator, the father of Ireland was doomed to see his people perish, and he had not the means to save them. O'Connell's heart broke . . . he crawled to London . . . the wreck of all that was once glorious appeared before the astonished eyes of Parliament. The voice that used

to fill the land with the thunder of his eloquence, was lowered to the merest whisper—the language of a broken heart. He arose and pictured before these men the agony of Ireland, and, with streaming eyes, he implored the mercy of England upon a dying people, and a subsidy from the Parliament to save the people . . . That subsidy was denied him. England closed her hand . . . O'Connell set out for Rome. The Irish people started for America . . . O'Connell's heart was broken. . .was broken for love of Ireland![75]

The impassioned recounting of the Great Hunger and The Liberator's death in its midst concluded with the kind of eulogy accorded a small circle of heroes.[76] A decade later, a man personifying the pinnacle of Irish achievement in New York resorted to a more updated version of this type of patriotic fervor. Cork-born William Russell Grace (1831–1904), shipping baron, millionaire, and first Catholic mayor of the city rose to power with the industrialists and professionals reaping the excesses of the Gilded Age.[77] As a two-term mayor serving from 1880 to 1882 and from 1884 to 1886, William Grace's influence stretched into the heart of the Irish city as few prior to him. First delivered in Boston during his last year in office and reissued in pamphlet form for distribution in New York, his speech relied on the same fount of heritage as Burke, but bridged the gap between a dark Ireland of memory and a new breed of pragmatic nationalist. "The Irish in America" used their unique "race feeling" to create "a permanent political value," he advanced. This awareness lay at the heart of the organizations of the major American cities, elevating the status of immigrants in their adoptive land and readying direct assistance for the political struggle across the Atlantic.[78] Like many of his compatriots, Mayor Grace was not averse to overblown rhetoric shot through with a directness calculated to endear and to motivate. The future for the Irish in cities such as New York rested on a couple of important attributes, he believed. "They have shown powers of adaptability to new conditions which have secured to them full recognition," the mayor remarked about the present generation, "while at the same time, they have preserved their race individuality to such an extent as to have profoundly influenced the course of English politics in relation to the home country." The notion that the New York Irish could exert influence over the relationship between Ireland and England may still have seemed innovative in the 1880s, despite the aspirations of Fenian and Clan na Gaelers, but Grace's foregrounding of "an Irish race" connected the broad parameters of nationalist heritage with future advancement in America. "Fenianism. . .miscarried,"

. . . but the seed from which it sprang was not without fruit, and the Land League of these days owed no small part of its existence. Stephens may fairly be said to be the precursor of Parnell . . . Fenianism successfully appealed to the sentimental side of the Irish character and fanned a flame of patriotism which burns strong . . . even to the second and third generations of those who have left their native land forever . . . Clan na Gael and the National League are the heirs of all that it has accomplished.[79]

Fanning the Stephens/Parnell flame played to the radical consciousness yet wisely retained appeal for the moderates, and Irish New Yorkers witnessed these same strands similarly intertwine in the wide array of locally published books and essays referencing the Emerald Isle between 1870 and 1920. If rhetorical flourishes designed to ignite highly charged emotions characterized contemporary lecturers, then the authors writing on the same themes did not stray too far behind. Educators, politicians, military officers, and religious figures of note produced a body of work best described as popular literature. The formulaic patriotism exposed the same impulses as the poetry, broadsheets, speeches, and songs—the expressions of an identity firmly focused on righting the wrongs of centuries past in Ireland.[80] The publications avowed the aspirations for Ireland's independence and molded a vital dimension of the New York Irish identity in so doing. The text of Colonel James E. McGee's 1874 *Lives of Irishmen's Sons and Their Descendants*, for example, documented the "burden" of oppression, the "Dedication" including immigrants and "my young fellow-citizens Born in America of Irish descent or parentage." Celebrating the righteous strains coursing through their blood, the "latent genius of our race" was also broached early on. The politicians and journalists detracting from this "genius" by applying the label of Irish nationality willy-nilly to all claiming "Gaelic nomenclature," the author deplored as "neither correct nor complementary."[81] Four years later, the Jesuit Reverend Augustine J. Thebaud's *The Irish Race in the Past and Present* argued for the quality in the Irish character that aspired to "the secret cause of their final success, which is now all but secured." Not material success but the goal of Ireland's independence was the point, the reader facing long passages on English attitudes with constant reference to attempts at "emptying the island and destroying the race." His conclusion best sums up his thoughts on a nationalist consciousness.

> Let the Irish see what they might effect toward the resurrection of their native country, if they only seriously began at last to organize and associate for that purpose, they would thus turn the immense force of their nation, now scattered over the world, to the real advantage of their birthplace.[82]

English commentator Philip H. D. Bagenal's tone in the 1882 *The American Irish and Their Influence on Irish Politics* took exception to some of the ideas of McGee and Thebaud while tackling the oppressive thrust of nativism. Bagenal's notion that "their distinctiveness of race and religion" articulated through "their bands, their societies, their newspapers and their foreign politics," enabled New York's Irish to construct a barrier against nativist hostilities and elevate themselves commercially and politically. Viewing politics as the best means to achieving this end, he felt that the mushrooming of organizations seemed ill-fated and not designed to affect development across the Atlantic. "The Irish in New York pour forth to attend the demonstrations of Mr. T. P. O'Connor, Mr. Healy, and Fr. Sheehy, and pay out their hard-earned dollars to keep up a political agitation thousands of miles away, in which they can never have actual hand or part, or derive any benefit whatever," he surmised. However, he granted that the growth of the organizations did counteract nativist oppression by foisting a useful political identity on Irish immigrants.[83]

The sense of "political agitation" motivating these writers colored the pages of some of the lengthier manifestoes. *The Cause of Ireland Pleaded Before the Civilized World* by Reverend Bernard O'Reilly came to light in New York in 1886, with metaphor and high sentimentality elevating nationalist rhetoric to new heights. Well qualified to engage in patriotic moralizing, O'Reilly had been born in Ireland in 1803 in the wake of the 1798 Rebellion, just as the Act of Union incorporated Ireland into Great Britain. His service at the old St. Patrick's Church in 1834 led to his consecration as Bishop of Hartford before his death in 1856, but frequent contributions to the city and national press and the appearance of his work in pamphlet form throughout his career continued his impact through later decades. Never one to refrain from the dramatic, a passage from his "Preface" encouraged "fortitude and hopefulness" from the "inspired voice and pen for the heroic temper of the Irish soul," as O'Reilly contrasted the nobility of the aspiration with the magnitude of the struggle. "We have contributed by word and deed," he asserted, "as the trial deepened, and the struggle became ever fiercer, to soothe the suffering whose source we were powerless to remove, and to aid the brave men and true who where battling for the cause of the Martyr-Nation."[84]

Dense evening reading in the Friendly Sons' library or from the bookshelves of scholarly Clan na Gaelers, not to mention the erudite Sisters of Charity or well-read feminist-nationalists; irrespective of lifestyle, Irish readers would have entered familiar territory with chapter titles such as "We Plead that husbandry, handicraft, industry and commerce flourished in Ireland, when not stamped out by England: Testimonies," accompanying sections celebrating the glory of Celtic history before the English plantations. Particularly vitriolic toward Elizabeth I, the "odious duplicity of James I," and "the . . . process whereby Bible and Sword cleared out the land," O'Reilly's five-hundred-page testimony to his "Martyr-Nation" proudly did his subject justice. Images of oppression suffered by his beleaguered countrymen probably held a morbid fascination for readers, even covering those clergy "hunted into bogs, morasses, or the wildest mountain tracts." Charging that Protestants be accorded their due as "the boldest and most eloquent champions of Ireland" and anticipating the day when the denominations would join forces against Britain, he explored a central dilemma for adherents to the traditions of the shamrock and the lily in New York. "Irish Catholics have suffered wrong, instead of inflicting it.

They will be the first," according to O'Reilly, "to forgive, and to forgive generously." However, he concluded:

> The Protestants have, confessedly, been the wrong-doers. Are they going to prove the truth
> of the old pagan saying, that it is the man who has injured his brother, who can never lay
> aside his hate? Beneath all the old hard crust of religious and political bigotry, beneath all
> the prejudices of birth and education—there still beats a warm, generous Irish heart in the
> Orangeman's bosom. It is there that lies the hope of a cordial union in the future. The
> Government still appeals to this antiquated bigotry and these stupid prejudices—the Castle
> Government, that is.[85]

Professors Joseph Dunn and P. J. Lennox drew on similar themes as they
amalgamated famous names on the political, intellectual, literary, and cultural circuit in *The Glories of Ireland.* Such luminaries as Sir Roger Casement, Douglas Hyde,
Reverend Canon D'Alton, Louis Ely O'Carroll, Sir Shane Leslie, and historian
Alice Milligan contributed essays dedicated to "The Irish Race in Every Land,"
ranging from the establishment of early monastic settlements to the promotion of
the "proudest monuments" ruins dotting the countryside.[86] "Irish Precursors of
Dante" and "Irish Influence on English Literature" brought readers to the more
familiar landscape of a short verse from John Boyle O'Reilly, for good measure,
acknowledging the "innumerable inquiries" that prompted the anthology. Dunn and
Lennox claimed that "the performances of the Irish race in many fields of endeav-
or are entirely unknown to most people," and set out to provide "an outline of the
whole range of Irish achievement during the last two thousand years." The ambition to celebrate race pride for posterity seems clear throughout, but particularly
from the conclusion:

> . . . to give to people of Irish birth or descent substantial reason for that pride of race which
> we know is in them, by placing in their hands an authoritative and unassailable array of facts
> as telling as any nation in the world can show. Our second motive was that henceforward
> he who seeks to ignore or belittle the part taken by men and women of Irish birth or blood
> in promoting the spread of religion, civilization, education, culture, and freedom should sin,
> not in ignorance, but against the light, and that from a thousand quarters at once champi-
> ons armed with the panoply of knowledge should be able to spring to his confutation.[87]

Intent on illuminating previously shadowy cultural watersheds, and imbuing
Irish arts with a new energy, Michael J. O'Brien's "The Irish in the United States"
worked well with Joseph I. C. Clarke's colorful recounting of battles involving
Irish soldiers in "The Fighting Race."[88] Casting back to earliest colonization
attempts, O'Brien observed that "the Colonies which now form the United States
may be considered as Europe transplanted." Not constrained by an overly modest
style, he continued:

Ireland, England, Scotland, France, Germany, Holland, Switzerland, Sweden, Poland, and Italy furnished the original stock of the present population, and are generally supposed to have contributed to it in the order named. For the last seventy or eighty years, no nation has contributed so much to the population of America as Ireland.[89]

This kind of high-blown statement struck a familiar note in an era dominated by newspaper headlines featuring descriptions that ran the gamut from "aweful" to "calamity" on a daily basis, so "the flower of the men of Irish blood" could expect to command full attention via the Land League, the Irish National League, and the Knights of Columbus during these years.[90] John O'Dea as National Historian for the Ancient Order of Hibernians examined the Hibernian Societies in New York since the eighteenth century, making reference to powerful Fenian and Clan Na Gael influences. Overcoming the obstacles of impoverishment and nativism by establishing such groups accorded them a clear political identity, O'Dea argued. Mobilizing thus enabled men and women to entrench their nationality as a vital component of their settlement process and reinforce the notion of an Irish "race" in the city.[91]

Bringing the reader up to the minute in terms of contemporary "flower of the men of Irish blood," Michael MacDonagh considered the influence of John Boyle O'Reilly and Patrick Ford as vital in inculcating Ireland's heritage within city journalism and, more broadly, within a developing Irish-American identity. Since founding *The Irish World* in 1870, the charismatic and fractious Ford exerted considerable reach over the range of city activities linked to Ireland.[92] As the right arm of the Land League, with special print runs of 1,650,000 issues distributed throughout the city and as far afield as Ireland to publicize League activities, Ford's newspaper empowered an eminently practical and often solidifying influence over the cause. MacDonagh's estimation that over $600,000 flowed into the offices of *The Irish World* as a direct result of Ford's work further testified to the journalist's ability.[93]

In contrast to Ford's brash character, MacDonagh offered readers a glimpse of Wicklow-born Lawrence Godkin, a journalist, author, and political commentator of note. A series of contradictions characterized Godkin, most notably his status as a Protestant immigrant of English birth editing a nationalist publication; however, such details did not compromise his status for his biographer. "The son of a Presbyterian clergyman," MacDonagh recounted, "Godkin in 1865 established the *Nation* in New York as an organ of independent thought; and for thirty-five years he filled a unique position, standing aside from all parties, sects, and bodies, and yet permeating them all with his sane and restraining philosophy."[94] But if this "sane and restraining philosophy" had not included active promotion of the broad aims of the nationalist cause, Godkin may not have merited even a passing mention. As Dunn and Lennox announced in the Preface, the objective was to strengthen what they envisioned as a nationalist image. "Pride of race" had to be rescued from oblivion and entrenched in every immigrant. "Pride" in achievement would lead to useful solidification of an omnipresent national consciousness. Thus unified, and "armed with the panoply of knowledge" in their achievements, immigrants could influence world opinion in Ireland's favor and break Britain's oppressive hold in a peaceable manner as befitting inheritors of such a rich cultural heritage.[95]

To sum up, the common threads permeating these writings highlight key features of the New York Irish immigrant character. The promotion of a political agenda reflective of centuries of Ireland's history loomed large within the Famine-era and post-Famine city. Hearkening back to the bardic tradition documenting the valor of kings and chieftains, expression of broadly configured nationalistic fervor transported across the Atlantic to materialize in New York Irish popular culture. As we have seen, the idea of an Irish "race" gained purchase within the immigrant consciousness, intertwined under the nationalist umbrella and entrenched by the ideal of freedom for men and women at home and abroad.

That these varieties of nationalist rhetoric did not mobilize into a unified program for Ireland's future does not detract from the significance of what did occur. As Ireland's exiles streamed across the Atlantic, settled in cities like New York and anticipated a successful future, these literary endeavors served a more immediate objective. The transplantation of a cultural bedrock drawn from tales of past glories made portable the basic building blocks of a new identity. In an alien land, the words eased a complex and challenging acculturation process. Reflecting the centuries-old tradition of Gaelic literature and language preserved against Anglocentric replacement, the language operated as a beacon of hope. As literature, it fell short of standards set by the bards of yore. Most of it was overlong, suffocating in its sentimentality, and required fired-up orators to imbue it with life. As material consigned to the higher shelves of libraries, the morocco-bound tomes dusty with age were seldom visited beyond the life of the print run. But in the post-Famine decades they were produced and referenced within the various enclaves of the New York Irish community, and highlighted throughout the pages of the city's Irish press. They provided a well-spring for the O'Donovan-Rossas, Mitchels, Burkes, and Bourke-Cockrans to reach audiences. They accumulated in layers as a living history for all manner of compatriot from the Friendly Sons and the Irish County members to the nuns and the hardened activists. The rhetoric enforced remembrance of where they came from and where they were headed. Through the works ran the lifeblood of immigrants articulating transition to an alien city, and their ideals for the old homeland and its future. Not directly addressed to Ireland's population, in most cases, but rather designed to convince local audiences of an ability to assert influence over the land inspiring the stories, plays, letters, and speeches, the genre espoused the nationalist agendas, supported the goals of the Gaelic Revival, and anticipated the rejuvenation of a nation struck low by horrific famine. The output reflects a search for pride in an independent Ireland, a homeland some of them had never personally experienced. The place of legend and saga and Gaelic lore provided sustenance in the creation of their new immigrant identity.

Bishop John England of Charleston, North Carolina, explored such themes in the 1820s, as though preempting Irish life in New York decades later. He announced in a sermon in 1824 that "the island from which we are sprung is but small upon the surface of our globe," continuing:

> We do not substitute a theory for an history, but we present you with a series of facts differently testified; some having the evidence of history, the others possessing that strong moral evidence to which any reasonable being must give a willing and a ready assent.[96]

Here, Bishop England viewed immigration not merely in terms of the transportation of a solid and immutable history or cultural heritage, but in terms of a further dimension within that experience. What he characterized "strong moral evidence" occupied as central a place in the Irish mentality as did those facts supported by "the evidence of history." The different strands of this consciousness identifiable in New York evidence the Reverend's observation. The poems, ballads, speeches, and lectures gave voice to a heritage transported and expanded, trained on Ireland and both her past and future. The stuff of dreams, their importance as nationalist armaments should not be underestimated within the culture mobilizing in late nineteenth-century New York.

Many-Roomed Mansion

IRELAND'S CATHOLICISM
AND POST-FAMINE NEW YORK

S ir Shane Leslie considered "Ireland's greatest international asset" as "the feeling which Americans have for those who have become Americans without losing their Irish qualities." He joined old reliable John Boyle O'Reilly in avowing that "Irishmen exercising in America the power of their moral force are a leaven to be heeded more by English statesmen than the armed rebellion of the same men or of their fathers in Ireland."[1] An elucidation of this kind from the renowned Sir John Randolphe (Shane) Leslie carried weight in cities such as New York by virtue of his associations with the most prominent literary and political figures of the day. Nominally a literary personality, the baronet's family connections with the Churchills (he was a cousin of Winston Churchill), his nationalist activity (which may have thwarted his election bid to Parliament on the Irish Party ticket), and his collaboration with Bourke Cockran and others in America in seeking a solution to the Irish Question collectively earned him a position of prominence among leading contemporary commentators.[2] His pronouncement finds resonance in many dimensions of New York Irish settlement, but perhaps most pointedly within that of the religious. Elemental, often divisive, ubiquitous; Catholicism's role within the cultural makeup of Ireland affected the course of the nation's history perhaps more directly than any other institution, and the transatlantic settlement process connected the new parishes of the city with the older ones left behind. The process is examined in this chapter; with emphasis on the confluence of Catholicism and Ireland's post-Famine independence movement.

Transported across from the dioceses and parishes of the Four Provinces, Catholicism's expansion as an immigrant linchpin by the mid-century years is a story well known to anyone interested in the Irish-American experience. As we've seen, thousands of prosperous but less vociferous Protestants had arrived earlier and amalgamated into the cultural fabric of the Colonies with relative ease. But the institution examined in this chapter emerged as richly layered and powerful during the post-Famine years, eclipsing the Protestant incarnation of Irishness by dint of sheer numerical strength within a parish system that adapted well to its new environs. While it is not the intention to undertake an exhaustive survey, given the wealth of material available on this topic, consideration of Famine-era and post-Famine Irish settlement without focusing on the religious affiliation of the majority subscribing to the emblem of the shamrock would surely result in an obvious gap. The connections between Irish New York's most prominent religious foundation and home, the nationalist associations, and the ultimate role of Catholicism within the development of the city's Irish-American identity merit direct attention, and are considered throughout this chapter.[3]

The Famine drove tens of thousands of Catholics from the home counties to the city, relocating a cornerstone institution for over three-quarters of the immigrant population in the process. By 1900, 22 percent of the total city population affiliated with a much more expansive Church than the mid-century arrivals confronting shrill nativist voices as a matter of course. Tempered by the decline of Know-Nothingism by the 1860s, hostilities re-energized briefly some decades later during large-scale eastern and southern European immigrations.[4] And it was not always the sensationalist voices that harbored the radicalized attitudes. "A Note of Warning" in 1879 marked Irish-Catholic progress in America with a sobering castigation, cautioning that:

> Owing to their faithful devotion to the Roman Catholic authority and the vigilant care of the Church to keep them in a state of obedience, they have failed to fuse into the mass of citizenship. They stand as distinctly defined in the body politic as though they were separated from the rest of the nation within actual territorial limits. It is equally true that the Romish Church, whose authority over them is stronger than that of any secular authority, is hostile to free institutions . . . While this is true, are we really in danger from Romanism and the multiplication of the race in our population which is its obedient instrument?[5]

As though offsetting such admonitions, the simple logic of community-based belonging motivated many thousands of the Irish faithful to "finance the dramatic growth of American Catholicism," in the words of Kerby Miller and Patricia Mulholland Miller, adding that "for destitute, often bewildered new arrivals, the church was a familiar source of charity, comfort, and guidance, insulating them from nativist scorn."[6] While it seems unreasonable that most New York WASPs went about their lives fearing Papal interference orchestrated by the Irish or anyone else of the faith, doubtless many perceived Irish Catholics as a distinct social and political constituency that ought to be viewed with suspicion, even by the 1870s. But by then, the Irish-Catholic identification had acclimatized sufficiently well that it had actually begun to lose some of its earlier potency, despite a continual Gaelic-dominated hierarchical powerhouse.[7] As Ireland's churchmen flocked into the higher echelons of the New York institution from the early years of the century onward, they transported with them the parish-based administrative structure of their homeland. Their efforts inculcated a strong Irish character within early nineteenth-century parochial life. Colorful characters such as the "brave old priest" who "broke up a Five Points riot by wading into the melee with a stole about his neck and a missal in his hand" on one occasion during the 1820s popularly linked the Irish-Catholic connection for the faithful and on the broader city cultural landscape.[8]

Operating on the grassroots level within a system familiar to them, the founding Fathers cultivated and subsequently benefited from a sizable fount of support through the Famine-era decades.[9] That over half of the city's clergy between the 1840s and the 1880s arrived directly from Ireland, with only the Germans coming close to rivaling this dominance, puts the influence into perspective.[10] Supported in fundamental ways by the orders of Sisters, missionary priests, and Brothers devoting their lives to institution building, "Irish" Catholicism expanded its progress within the new neighborhoods and maintained valiant connections with the home parishes across the Atlantic.[11] As the immigrant church reflected Catholic practice in Ireland during the post-Famine decades, the imprint of 1850's Devotional reform seemed to suit the new urban context quite well. Popularly considered the brainchild of Archbishop Paul Cullen of Dublin, the reform effort ostensibly aimed to replace elements forced out of Catholic practice as a result of Penal Law legislation and ongoing isolation from Continental models of the faith; most notably hierarchical control, a reorganized education system, pioneering efforts in social welfare, and the restoration of lost theological foundations.[12] The "Revolution" to bring Ireland's church into closer affiliation with a more homogenized Church structure had begun prior to Cullen's administration, but his rise to power linked his name with the movement to bring his flock into line with Rome's directives and replace old practices with an updated mission.[13] The movement proved timely for missionary clerics transplanting the faith to New York. Given that "Irish American bishops, like their Irish counterparts, were strong champions of ultramontanism and displayed an aggressive Catholicism in promoting the building of churches and schools,"[14] the influence of mid-century Ireland over the development of the city Church came through strongly and pervasively.

The parish structure transplanted relatively easily during the early nineteenth century, not only in New York, but in Boston, and across the Northeastern United States, to account for initial Irish strength and mark out a solid foundation for post-Famine expansion.[15] By the 1840s, lay organizations had begun to generate a broader profile for the church within the spheres of education and welfare. The sodalities and associations occupied a middle ground between clerics and lay church members, and expressed a measure of Catholic self-confidence in serving diverse agendas.[16] Grassroots proliferation mobilized under the leadership of pioneering clerics within an organization facing persistent challenge. But Archbishops Hughes, McCloskey, Corrigan, and Farley supervised a hierarchy inculcating more than just an Irish flavor. While couching their administrations in strongly articulated American values, they invested the city faith with the character of their nationality that remained steadfast for generations.[17] That Irish influence sustained through decades of diverse immigrant influx testifies to the commitment of clergy and congregations, despite the extent of the institution as the century wore on. Some of the older city parishes did readjust to meet the changing dynamic wrought by new immigrant influence, but as eastern Europeans thronged into the old neighborhoods of Lower Manhattan, most of the older foundations such as Transfiguration Church in the Sixth Ward, Saint Peter's Church on Barclay Street, and the old Saint Patrick's Church on Mott Street retained the Irish profile solidified in the 1810s and 1820s.[18]

By mid-century, the label "Irish Catholic" came to infer a political as well as a religious affiliation, and within the immigrant community itself, nationalist aspirations occasionally intertwined with city Catholicism in quite a forthright manner.[19] The 1860's funeral of Terence Bellew McManus, for example, generated a richly hued church-nationalist association. As the story unfolded, the Ulster-born clerk and shipping agent's exile to the Tasmanian penal colony followed his participation in the ill-fated 1848 rebellion. The tale of his escape to San Francisco in 1851, his welcome into a circle of California-based revolutionaries, and his accidental death ten years later might have gone virtually unnoticed were it not for the group of San Francisco Fenians who designed one of the most blatant political set pieces in Irish-American history. Enlisting the support of counterparts in New York in a joint effort, the West Coast Fenians staged the first act of their political theater around a funeral service in San Francisco. As Louis Bisceglia reconstructed the story, prominent New Yorkers including Thomas Francis Meagher, Michael Doheny, Horace Greeley, and John O'Mahony organized a commemorative requiem for the dead Fenian. The spring of 1861 found the McManus Obsequies Committee overseeing the arrival of the remains to New York on September 13.[20]

With preparations for a large-scale demonstration complete, the volatile relationship between the hierarchy and the movement relaxed as O'Mahony and

Meagher consulted with Archbishop Hughes on funeral details. Fenian propensi-
ty toward violence had alienated the hierarchy, despite pressure from clerics who
openly supported the organization in defiance of official policy. Radically inclined
priests whose names would be enshrined in ballads and poems included Father
Murphy from (Old) Kilcormac, Co. Wexford, a 1798 leader; Archbishop of Tuam
John McHale, champion of the peasantry during the Land War; Father Patrick
Lavelle of Partry, County Mayo, who delivered the oration at the McManus funeral in Dublin and also an 1862 address entitled *The Catholic Doctrine of the Right of
Revolution*; and Archbishop Dr. Thomas William Croke of Cashel, Co. Tipperary,
cautioned by Pope Leo XIII to forego his radical involvements.[21] As Sean Cronin
put it, "the Fenians were Catholics, but Fenianism was not 'a Catholic movement'...
It stood for the ... separation of Church and state, which worked well in America."[22]
That both the Archbishop and McManus were connected with the same Ulster diocese may have positively influenced John Hughes's attitude to the 1861 proposals![23]
No doubt the Archbishop kept himself informed on Fenian activities and the rise
of prospective martyrs such as McManus.[24]

In spite of a formal warning on the matter from Archbishop Cullen in Dublin,
public support from the Archbishop of New York effectively called the Catholic-
nationalist nuptials. The spectacle turned into an Irish city milestone, a landmark
interaction between the Church and the radicalized elements within the flock. As
the remains lay in Saint Patrick's Church in Lower Manhattan, Fenian delegations
accompanied thousands of the faithful, together with the organizing committee and
the Irish Brigade, to pay their last respects. The Solemn High Requiem on
September 16, 1861 brought a multitude of supporters to the church to commemorate one of their own. But it was the October 18th sight of all the Church-related societies and associations joining with Fenian regiments from all over the East
Coast in a huge cortege that captured citywide attention. Led by thirty-two pallbearers from the highest ranks of the Brotherhood, the march through Lower
Manhattan to Pier Forty-Four ended with the casket received aboard the steamer
City of Washington for transportation to Ireland.[25] The vast crowds of "the children
of Ireland" lining Broadway from Twenty-Third Street to Canal Street witnessed
the exciting spectacle of ex-Young Ireland celebrities John O'Mahony, Thomas
Kearns, Patrick Flanagan, Michael Gillen, and William Hogan turning out in the
company of multitudes of onlookers, military detachments, and funeral bands.[26]

Contingents from each county in Ireland strode alongside delegations from the
major East Coast cities and from California, flying banners and flags spanning the
width of the streets. The usual suspects from the New York Irish strongholds
stepped forth in unison. Following the official city Fenian Delegation, Marshal
William Ackeson led the Brooklyn Ancient Order of Hibernians, with Marshal M.
O'Sullivan and the United Benevolent Society of Longshoremen in its wake. Next

came Marshal Edward Duffy with the Fenian Thomas Francis Meagher Club in full regalia, pacing with the New York Hibernian Benevolent Society under the command of Michael Rowarty. The Saint James Roman Catholic Temperance Society followed behind sister-organization the Father Matthew Temperance and Benevolent Society, headed by Edward L. Carey. The United Sons of Erin's sober black garb made a striking contrast against the rich regalia of the marching bands. The aftermath of a rainstorm made the going difficult on Broadway down near Grand Street, the combination of throngs of people mingling with the large contingent of wagons and hacks causing much commotion. The cortege eventually reached the end of Canal Street and Pier Forty-Four, "thousands moving with it in one great, silent army, on either sidewalk, keeping slow step to solemn dirges."[27]

The extravagance of the funeral procession almost paled in comparison with the Requiem of Archbishop Hughes. By all accounts, the sermon "delighted the Fenians and gravely embarrassed Dr. Cullen."[28] No stranger to controversy, John Hughes had been involved in public wrangling of one kind or another throughout his career. A reputation as a deft defender of Catholic values combining old-school erudition with a creative progressivism, his legacy dominated the nineteenth-century church. Born in Ireland in 1797, the prelate made his imprint as first coadjutor Bishop of New York in 1838, fourth Bishop in 1842, and finally first Archbishop of the city from 1850 to 1864. There is no doubt that his keen intellect, powerful personality, and fearless confrontation of seemingly insurmountable obstacles on behalf of the formative Church played a central role in the expansion of city Catholicism. During the 1840s, the then Right Reverend Hughes published a series of letters in the *New York Observer* reflecting on canonical questions with an Irish agenda and collected in *Letters to the Right Reverend John Hughes, Roman Catholic Bishop of New York, Second Series, by Kirwan.*[29] By the time the thorny McManus issue arrived on his desk, the Archbishop had been well used to the spotlight. He resorted to the writings of Thomas Aquinas to rationalize the usage of violence against unjust authority, in defense of his own role and that of the Church in the McManus case. Hughes believed leaders such as McManus should be vindicated for their aspiration to preserve national unity against oppressive authority. The exaltation of what he characterized "love of country" justified behavior normally roundly condemned by the Church. As typical of a style honed throughout his career, Hughes selected his position and met the opposition head-on. Stunned that the highest officer in the city Church would celebrate the life of a violent and ungodly man, the anticipated groundswell decried the prelate's blatant linkage of Catholicism with politics and his manipulation of Church teachings to accommodate nationalist partiality. Clashing with the convictions of moderates comfortable with pacifist Daniel O'Connell as folk-hero, but aligning with supporters thronging the streets to escort the cortege on its journey to Calvary cemetery, Hughes daily walked the narrow line between committed nationalist and absolutist Catholic leader.[30]

Accompanied by the deceased's sister and city Fenians all "dressed in deep mourning," the New York delegation's journey to Dublin ended the episode on a dramatic note. Including Captain Welply of New York's 69th Regiment, Fenian militias dominated the proceedings. No strangers to the power of an emotional appeal, Denis Cromeyn's eulogy on behalf of the Brotherhood promised that "the soil of Ireland, from of old most holy, shall become still more hallowed when it holds his dust." Journalist Underwood O'Connell seemed irritated that Ireland's hierarchy boycotted the proceedings:

> We cannot, however, refrain from some expression of surprise at what has been a source of keen regret to us. The clergy of America gave such willing cooperation that we could not possibly apprehend anything like what we have witnessed. Even now it is hard for us to understand the motives or the influences which could have kept away the clergy of Cork from a solemn procession, in which the whole Catholic population took such willing part.[31]

New York Irish interest was further stoked during the same episode by a pamphlet from the pen of a West of Ireland priest. Infamous by the 1860s, Reverend Patrick Lavelle denounced Ireland's hierarchy for its official attitude toward McManus, arguing that the clergy should direct hostility against England as the real enemy. Condemning what he charged a political bias against Church members associated with radical nationalism, and lamenting what he considered a lack of Christian charity against Fenians, on the part of Ireland's hierarchy, Lavelle argued that McManus "the Catholic and the patriot . . . [was] denied the honors accorded to every Castle slave, time-serving hypocrite, and Whigling sycophant, whose creed is to sell his soul and his country together to the first buyer for prompt payment! Good God!"[32] Lashing out against Dr. Cullen and his associates for betraying a loyal son, Reverend Lavelle bewailed that the Fenian be "denied a momentary resting place in any church of Ireland, though those whose fathers built those churches would shed the last drop of their blood to honor his memory!" He probably appreciated the rosewood and silver-mounted coffin reposing in a vault within what would later become the National Cemetery in Glasnevin. A month later, a New York poem about Lavelle reiterated pro-McManus support. Entitled "Hail, Patriot Priest!" the eight verses celebrated Lavelle's Fenianism in "Soggarth Aroon." A popularized version of the Gaelic "beloved priest," the work concluded dramatically:

> When voice on voice to God arose, against the murderous foe,
> Whose ruffian law, with hierling blows, had laid McManus low.
> When from the weeping host went up a proud defiant vow,
> That "soon the wrath, so long pent up, should light on Britain's brow."

Illustrious Priest! may death ne'er fold thy heart in lifeless clay,
Until thy glowing eyes behold the sunlight of that day.[33]

As time went on, the city hierarchy did not completely relinquish the stance adopted over the McManus opportunity. Successor to John Hughes, Archbishop John McCloskey did little to undermine positive relations between the Church and militant activists in the 1860s, aside from upbraiding the Brotherhood for a seeming violation of Catholic teaching. His condemnation of a Fenian meeting in 1866 focused on the armed-resistance manifesto but also on another point, the scheduling of a meeting on a Sunday in Lent. Even as a speaker at a Brotherhood meeting at City Hall on June 6, 1866 called for an official church blessing on Fenianism and a commitment to Fenian ideals, the Archbishop may have harbored a small degree of sympathy for the radicals in his flock. But he kept the faith, concluding: "as most of those, unfortunately, who are connected with this movement profess themselves Catholic," the Archbishop wrote, "I feel it my duty to beg you to admonish and exhort your people to take no part in what must be regarded as an open profanation of the Lord's day . . . especially in this holy season of Lent."[34]

Hierarchical alliance with less radicalized commemorations centered on perhaps the best-known demonstration, the annual Saint Patrick's Day parade.[35] Occasionally taking three to four hours to wend its way through the streets of Manhattan "from Harlem to the Battery," the gathering of the Church's finest made for a dramatic sight. The participation of more politically neutral entities as the boys of the Temperance Cadets alongside the Fenian or Clan na Gael faithful did not seem to generate too much unease on the part of clergy, given their enthusiastic participation in the day's celebration. As in Ireland, the moderate nationalist tradition benefited from a strong fount of clerical support that glossed over points of controversy on more than one occasion. Even rival interdenominational factions seemed to relinquish their differences on the occasion of the Saint Patrick's parades.[36] For the more mainstream organizations amalgamated in the Irish Confederation and interested in cultivating public association with the Church, the parade presented a wonderful opportunity for a show of strength. Founded in 1882, the Confederation sought to connect Irish County societies with Clan na Gael and the Land League. If the clergy could publicly support the radicalized Clan and Land League parading before them, then efforts to empower those even nearer and dearer seemed eminently logical. From the 1880s onward, Church hierarchy entered into direct contact with New York's nationalist representations. Such a progression was not surprising, in some respects. Many clerics harbored deep sympathy for Ireland's struggle and for those who sought to redress it, especially as the Home Rule campaign had entered its final tension-filled phase. Clan na Gael and Confederation rallies tended to include a visible clerical presence, as on the occasion of a mass meeting on

February 23, 1883, in Lower Manhattan. "The Irish community's gathering at Cooper Union was hardly distinguishable from any other Irish nationalist rally," one reporter judged, "and like them included participants from the Roman Catholic clergy. At least ten Roman Catholic priests occupied seats on the platform." Baptist Doctor H. M. Gallagher as the lone Protestant on the platform had the effect of highlighting Catholic presence in an event overshot with native Irish cultural and religious overtones.[37]

Together with the more informal endorsements, Church-nationalist alliance moved beyond the commemorative and into the sphere of education. An 1882 solicitation for contributions to the coffers of the Christian Brothers teaching order[38] operating through the offices of John Devoy's *Irish Nation* worked well from both nationalist and educational perspectives, and symbolized the connection between the Brothers' and an overtly politicized agenda. Devoy referred to the Ignatius Rice order of Christian Brothers, commonly considered the "Irish" order to distinguish from the French de la Salle order. The de la Salle brothers recruited heavily in Ireland during the nineteenth century, however, thus rendering the distinction between "Irish" and "French" negligible. As befitting the profile of one of the most influential Gaelic city weeklies, *Irish Nation* support of a Christian Brothers' education maximized the political dimension. "The Christian Brothers," one 1882 article claimed, "teach Nationality in their Schools, and therefore should be supported by all Nationalists." Working to instill the heritage of their forefathers in the hearts and minds of their young pupils, the Brothers institutionalized the type of native Irish Catholic indoctrination holding strong appeal for immigrants fearing the corruptions of the foreign city. Parents might do what they could at home but, the article concluded, "*at school* the seed should be sown."[39] That this message influenced the spread of the nationalist gospel there is no doubt, with the educational process well underway by the 1880s.[40]

Rising levels of prosperity by the 1880s accorded publicity to the more prestigious Catholic educational establishments and, by the same token, highlighted Irish impact and connection with home in this field. As the success of Ireland's male teaching orders marked middle-class Irish progress in New York, the Jesuits at St. John's College (Fordham, after 1907), the Manhattan College de la Salle Christian Brothers, and the Franciscans and Vincentians in Brooklyn at St. Francis and St. John's colleges, respectively, enjoyed increasing enrollments and increased public recognition. The major prizewinners at the annual summer examinations in hallowed halls like Washington D.C.'s Georgetown drew attention to honors-level performances at New York's Saint John's (Fordham), Saint Peter's Academy, Saint Francis Xavier College, Saint Patrick's Academy, the Institute of the Holy Angels, and Saint Joseph's Academy, Flushing. The latter two operated as women's colleges under the jurisdiction of the Sisters of Notre Dame and the Sisters of Saint Joseph.

Schools' medal-winners under the headlines: "The Young Idea. Training Our Coming Men and Women; A Splendid Showing for '82" included a majority of Irish students in each category. The Jesuit-run Saint Francis Xavier College counted a high percentage of Delanys, Donnellys, Synnetts, Cullens, and Cunninghams interspersing with an occasional Schnugg or Erlwein. Saint Joseph's Academy celebrated the academic achievements of the Misses Gilligan, Guerin, Clarke, and Quinn as they kept the academic flag flying high.[41] Three years later, predicting "No Hope for British Supremacy in the Catholic Schools of the United States," Patrick Ford assured the faithful that the Franciscans and the Christian Brothers guaranteed a successful future for Irish Catholics by providing more than a standard education. The "learned, pious, and patriotic Franciscan Brothers in Brooklyn" merited lavish praise. "Second to none in the country," he believed, the Brothers' education resulted in "zealous priests, successful lawyers and doctors" by the 1880s, and "bright and honored and successful business men and mechanics." Laudably, the bright new professionals graduating from schools like Saint Francis College would retain their all-important patriotism. "If their parents are Exiles of Erin," Ford noted, "their sympathies are strong for the Liberation of Ireland; they have the lesson of England's cruelty and perfidy by heart." These same encouraging thoughts informed the editor's assessment of Saint Patrick's Academy in Brooklyn, also run by the Franciscans, and most of the educational establishments run by Irish-dominated teaching orders. Following the presentation of gold watches and medals to the St. Patrick's award-winners, he mused:

> No one was in a hurry home though late the hour and we could not help thinking as we went over the whole [ceremony] in our minds on the way home that if Great Britain had any friends there they got small comfort. There is danger to the Robber Empire in the Catholic schools of America, of which St. Patrick's is a model."[42]

Beyond the classroom, city politicians and Catholic interests interconnected in a variety of ways during the post-Famine decades. New-style professional leaders in the later 1840s and 1850s cultivated lucrative connections between the Church, their personal agendas, and the developing New York Irish identity. Two individuals in particular personified this development: *The Irish People* journalist Denis Holland and lawyer and politician John Develin. Associated with a more moderate nationalist agenda than members of the activist organizations, they worked toward a new integration of faith and politics couched in middle-class respectability. From his birth in Cork city "of respectable parentage" and his pride in "being sprung from the old Celtic stock of his native country," Denis Holland preferred the Gaelic version of his name, O'hUallachain, to the more Anglicized "Holland." Following a stint as an editor in Cork, Holland moved to Belfast and the *Ulsterman* newspaper. His work to publicize injustices against Catholics inflicted by Ulster

Protestants resulted in a prominent profile and good reputation. "His services as a defender of the outraged and downtrodden patriots and Catholics of Belfast and its vicinity during his sojourn amongst them," one report ran, "have rendered the name of Denis Holland to be loved and respected in that quarter of Ireland. It is to-day a household word among the patriot Irishmen of Belfast." Holland founded the *Irishman* newspaper in Dublin before moving to London and from there to New York in the mid-1860s. Rapidly settled with *The Irish People*, his pen-pictures of Irish life in the *Emerald*, the *Shamrock*, the *Celtic Weekly*, the *Irish Democrat*, and the *Brooklyn Sunday* won him a wide readership up to his death in December 1872. His obituary documented the lengthy listing of the principal mourners; among them Irish New York's leading lights, including *The Irish Nation*'s John Devoy and Reverend James McKenna, "P.P. of Lurgan, Ireland, an old friend of the deceased."[43] As a force for the amalgamation of important anchors within the city's immigrant culture, Holland articulated the connections between Church and politics in his popular prose style. His writings wove the fabric of Gaelic heritage into the daily lives of his readers, and helped entrench the native culture within the new city context.

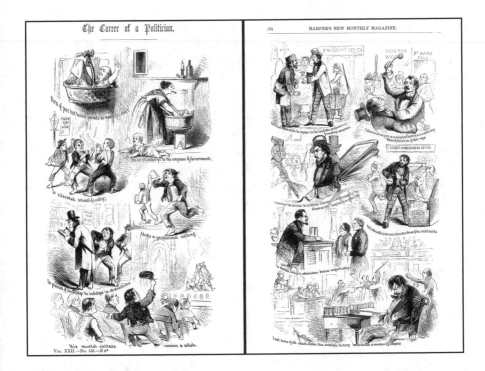

Fig. 5.1: Career of A Politician, *Harper's New Monthly Magazine* (March 1861); courtesy of Cornell University Library, Making of America Digital Collection.

Likewise, John Develin publicly associated Catholicism with the same kind of moderate political agenda favored by his Protestant compatriot William Smith O'Brien. Hailing from Tyrone as one of the "Sons of the Gael Who Have Won Distinction in Foreign Lands," the powerful role of Catholic schooling in John Develin's family life propagated his image as "a gentleman of the old school." His education at Murray Street Grammar School, Georgetown College in Washington and subsequent career at the New York Bar ushered in a stint as counsel to John Jacob Astor. Heading the firm of Develin and Miller, the rising star on the legal circuit developed an interest in city politics that saw him elected Assemblyman in 1845. Develin's first initiative involved moving legislation to establish a Catholic New York university to favorably compare with the best education in the United States. In so doing, he merged personal and professional priorities, and the 1840's sponsorship of a bill establishing Saint John's College (Fordham University after 1907) turned his dream into reality. "Prepared under the auspices of the late Archbishop Hughes, [the bill] was vigorously pushed by Mr. Develin," *The Irish Nation* reported. Membership on the founding board of the Emigration Commission kept him busy, along with charitable operations empowering specific recipients and, more generally, the city's Irish-Catholic foundation. A "Report of the Irish Emigrant Society" in 1882 detailed how the organization provided help and advice for "a large share of the nearly 2,500,000 emigrants from Ireland during the last forty years, coming to America," and how an average of over $9,000 had been raised every year for the assistance of impoverished arrivals to New York. For example, the Institute of Mercy on Houston Street received $22,450 for the education of "poor Irish girls"; Saint Vincent's Hospital on Eleventh Street received $7,050 for care of destitute Irish immigrants; and the Little Sisters of the Poor on East Seventieth Street received donations amounting to $6,150 "for the care of aged and infirm Irish." The Irish Famine Relief Fund Association had to compete for Develin's time with the anti-Tweed agitation that culminated in the fall of the Ring through the 1860s and 1870s, but through it all, public identification with the Catholic Church remained his priority. As *The Irish Nation* observed in 1882:

> For the last twenty years Mr. Develin's name has been closely associated with the charities of the Roman Catholic Church . . . [Through Develin] the Sisters of Charity, the Foundling Hospital, St. Vincent's Hospital, in connection with Msgr. Quinn and the late Dr. L. S. Ives, obtained from the Legislature the charter for the New York Catholic Protectory. He was one of the original managers named in the charter, and still fills that position, as well as being the legal advisor of the Protectory.[44]

While Holland and Develin were busy promoting their Catholic-based agenda, the completion and opening of Saint Patrick's Cathedral on Fifth Avenue marked a key point of nineteenth-century ethnoreligious solidarity in the city.

Symbolizing popular association with a specifically "Irish" city faith, "St. Patrick's was a monument to the spirit and zeal of Irish American Catholicism." The megalith satisfied the ultramontane aspirations of Archbishops Hughes and McCloskey, as an added bonus. As the immigrant population had expanded, so had the number of churches they constructed. "The biggest of them all," without a doubt, "St. Patrick's Cathedral on Fifth Avenue, which opened in 1878, may be said to have symbolized the collective arrival of the Irish as a central and inescapable force in the city's life." Further, "the Irish saw it as a distinctly Irish achievement." The fact that "many non-Irish Catholics felt themselves marginalized by the Hibernian hegemony" must have seemed unavoidable to the mass of the Gaelic faithful.[45]

Replacing the Old Saint Patrick's Cathedral on the corner of Mott and Mulberry in Lower Manhattan, the uptown building seemed to epitomize stability and success for a relatively recent denominational addition to the city. The Mott Street Cathedral had served as the first large-scale Irish parish center in New York in constant use since 1815. Founded as part of Pope Pius VII's Suffragan See, the church catered to approximately 13,000 predominantly Irish worshippers. The Old Saint Patrick's and the neighboring Transfiguration Church near Broadway and the Bowery ministered to concentrations of Ireland's early arrivals to the Sixth Ward, numbering at least 20,000 by 1815.[46] Born in Ireland in 1750, the Dominican who would be consecrated second Bishop of New York in 1815 served as Prior of St. Clement, Rome, before departing for his new appointment in New York. Bishop John Connolly founded a free educational establishment two years later in the Cathedral basement, institutionalizing one of the first schools in the city and hallmarking Saint Patrick's as the key religious presence for decades to come.[47]

Archbishop Hughes presided over the official block-laying for the James Renwick–designed Fifth Avenue St. Patrick's Cathedral in August 1858, marking the occasion with a speech that, by all accounts, surpassed even his usual flamboyant style. The first Mass celebrated on Sunday, May 25, 1879, represented the first large-scale Catholic occasion in the city. The largesse of their contributions points to the high degree of interest by the Gael in the completion of the new Gothic landmark. Cardinal McCloskey had finished what Hughes had started, the duration of the construction exceeding all expectations (although interrupted by the Civil War during 1861–1866). Hughes had collected more than $75,000 in contributions, an impressive sum by contemporary standards when laborers earned between $300 and $500 a year.[48] The 20,000 people that flocked to the massive Cathedral Fair in 1878 generated an average of $6,000 per day for forty-two days toward the completion. The total of more than $500,000 poured into the final stages and finished the splendid structure.[49] The commemorative booklet issued by the Catholic Publication Society detailed the lavish opening ceremony for guests and onlookers. Held on Pope Gregory VII's feast day of May 25th, 1879, the occasion exuded Irish pride through-

out. Naming the huge church for the national apostle surely heaped a large measure of gratification onto the proceedings. The booklet's frontispiece etched out the
imposing lines of the Fifth Avenue facade before drawing the eye toward the more
subtle architectural features. Generously proportioned by nineteenth-century standards, the dimensions of the Cathedral included the main door measuring thirty feet
wide by fifty-one feet high, while the height of the towers, even the length of the
distance between each tower increased the sense of awe and the importance of the
occasion.[50]

Naturally dedicated to Archbishop Hughes as the inspiration behind the Fifth
Avenue presence, in some ways the Cathedral's lofty dimensions personified the
gothic-like Hughes temperament. His "special mission" to Europe in 1861 at the
behest of the American government had taken him to "Paris, Rome, and Ireland,"
with the inclusion of his homeland as a stop on the trip generating a personalized
dimension of publicity! Additional association between the Irish-dominated faith
and Saint Patrick's derived from the building's artistry. Pen-pictures of the stained-
glass windows and depictions of biblical scenes preceded notification of donors'
names in the opening-day program, and it must have been heartening to the immigrant faithful that not a selection, but *every* window bore the name of an Irish bene-
factor. Ascribing a strong foundation of success in New York to Irish backing, the
artistry illuminated the contribution of Ireland's religious, and her working men and
women, and the more affluent sponsors as clearly as stars in the firmament. "John
Kelly, in Memoriam," under a rendering of the Presentation in the Temple, with
Mary and Saints Joachim and Anne, appeared near the "gift of Thomas H.
O'Connor" portraying the Magi at the scene of the Nativity. The "gift of Mrs. Julia
Coleman" provided the Cathedral another image of the Mother of Jesus. Henry L.
Hoguet's sponsorship of an elaborate window in "the southern arm of the transcept"
depicted the presentation of "sacred relics" by Emperor Baldwin of Constantinople
to King Louis and Queen Blanche of France. Henry Hoguet's name does not
invoke immediate association with Ireland; however, the Hoguet brothers Henry
and Robert emigrated from Dublin in mid-century and prospered in a variety of
commercial enterprises. Both belonged to the Friendly Sons of Saint Patrick and
sat on the board of the Emigrant Commission and the Emigrant Industrial Savings
Bank.[51] No doubt some of the less affluent donors and faithful aspired toward the
higher echelons of success achieved by the Hoguets.

Continuing through the northern and southern facings, "Mrs. Eleanora Iselin"
financed the window with the Sacred Heart alongside Blessed Margaret Mary
and an angel. Featuring Dionysius, Saint Paul's window was dedicated "to the
memory of Rev. John Kelly, from his brother Eugene," while portrayals of the
Evangelists donated by Irish sponsors included Saint Matthew by Andrew Clarke,
Saint Mark by Bernard Maguire, and Saint Luke by Denis J. Dwyer who worked

as the "assistant superintendent" of the Cathedral. As the "general superintendent" of Saint Patrick's, William Joyce generously donated the fourth Evangelist image of Saint John. Bernard McKenna's "the Three Baptisms, fire, water and blood," turned out "a strikingly vivid picture." Irish benefactors thus honored the faith of their fathers and mothers with a view to posterity, each name inscribed permanently on a window, a sanctuary, or below a relic of significance. That not a single name other than those of Irish extraction appeared in the Cathedral points to the fount of Irish solidarity encapsulated in the structure. Direct association with the expensive flagship reinforced the judgment that: "whether with regard to church or politics, the Irish were the first to congratulate themselves on their achievements . . . In a highly innovative and often confusing American environment, they seemed the right people at the right time to tackle the job of organizing the American Catholic church."[52]

For those who contributed to the massive monument, the Fifth Avenue edifice presented a more positive image than the faith described as "dreary, pessimistic, guilt-ridden, and not sensual."[53] More compellingly for the Fenians and Clan na Gaelers, the building even appeared to support the broad agenda of the nationalist cause! Irish New Yorkers knew that an edifice on this scale would not arise in Dublin or anywhere in Ireland given the proscriptive nature of British authority. Completion of a splendid cathedral dominating the main thoroughfare and directly associated with Ireland's principal religious tradition represented a dimension of freedom for those associated with it. An 1887 call for the construction of a centralized Protestant symbol of sufficient splendor and stature to rival the "Romish" example seemed to underscore the Catholic achievement. Not intended as the headquarters of "a sect," the construction of a Protestant landmark as a splendid testimony to "the Christian faith which does not accept the Vatican tradition" would require a "stately, impressive, sonorous, ritualistic, and therefore Anglican" structure. Saint Patrick's was judged both "stately" and "impressive" by the majority of contemporaries, but in this case, the *Harper's* editor remained convinced of the Fifth Avenue landmark's "cheap and tawdry air."[54]

Whether "impressive" or "tawdry," the expansive dimensions set in stone a new focus for post-Famine Irish Catholic influence. From the 1870s onward, the dynamism within the New York Church worked within but in some respects facilitated the rise of class consciousness within the settlement community.[55] The emergence of a class of Catholic professionals emulating Protestant philanthropic traditions imposed new solidity on an immigrant Church once pioneering but finally prospering.[56] Organizations such as the Knights of Columbus, the Society of Saint Vincent de Paul, women's Apostolic Workers Unions, and the variety of sodalities and lay organizations mushrooming from the 1860s onward empowered a developing middle-class to align the Church in a progressive direction. The traditional imagery of destitute, ignorant masses clinging to the pillars of an austere institution disintegrated rapidly beneath the rise of a multidimensional, prosperous church structure. The class distinctions reflective of those left behind in Ireland that emerged toward the later nineteenth century among New York Catholic Irish testify to the prosperity levels visible by the 1880s and 1890s. Although such affinities are more strongly associated with the early decades of the twentieth century,[57] the Society of Saint Vincent de Paul and Catholic Club started to facilitate and reflect class differentials and the rise of Irish affluence almost half a century previously.[58]

These benevolent groups fostered the middle-class values often associated with later "lace-curtain" second and third generations, materializing alongside the burgeoning Home Rule agenda. But organized and prospering by mid-century, the Catholic Total Abstinence Union of America (1849), the Irish Catholic Society for the Promotion of Actual Settlements in North America (1856), and the Society of Saint Vincent de Paul were joined a couple of decades later by the Irish Catholic Benevolent Union (1869), Irish Catholic Colonization Association (1879), Catholic Bureau at Castle Garden (1882), Father John Riordan's Mission of Our Lady of the Rosary for the Protection of Irish Immigrant Girls (1883), and United Irish Counties Association of New York (1904), building on the foundations laid during the 1840s and 1850s.[59] The Convention of Irish Societies' amalgamation of some of the more conservative lay bodies under one umbrella during the 1860s imposed a measure of homogenization within this context, and paved the way for new Church professionalization and standardization in a similar progression to the Devotional agenda across the Atlantic.

Convention meetings held in the Hibernian Hall on Prince Street included representatives from neighborhood collectives all over the city. Evening meetings in rough-and-tumble Lower Manhattan must have presented an odd sight, the motley contingents of earnest folk gravitating toward the ramshackle and still crime-bedeviled West Village in hopes of personal fulfillment and civic engagement. The Exiles Club, the Irish National Grenadiers, and the Ancient Order of Hibernians headed up a thriving cohort. The philanthropic agenda drew members to nothing less than a litany of organizations crowding the middle-class Catholic social calendar: the Benevolent Society of Saints Peter and Paul, the County Monaghan Social Club, the Father Matthew Total Abstinence Benevolent Society, the Hibernian Benevolent Society, the Thomas Francis Meagher Club, the Benevolent Society of United Sons of Erin, the Hibernian United Brotherhood Society, Saint James Roman Catholic Total Abstinence Benevolent Society, the Deignan Guard, and others collectively established upwardly aspirant men and women as engaged activists. As with the Ladies of Charity, the entrenchment of a new tradition of American Catholic benevolence served a two-fold purpose for members. First, the agencies

empowered the successful transplantation of a native religious tradition undergoing a modernization process on both sides of the Atlantic, and second, both members and the institution as a whole could be acculturated into the fabric of a
faith-based city and an American cultural context without sacrificing their immigrant identity.[60]

As in the Ancient Order of Hibernians, members of this type of organization
were required "to be Irish by birth or descent and Roman Catholics," and naturally, to be "of good and moral character." The gatherings fulfilled a comfortable
social function for members from the 1860s on. Bringing together men and women
with the drive to organize charitable endeavors and the financial means to see
them through, informal alliances between like-minded compatriots mobilized
rapidly. Promoting the dissemination of useful philanthropic values and furthering
the distinct ethnic quality of the city faith, they expanded the development of a distinct branch of an Irish-American cultural identity. Politically, "anyone who was a
member of a secret society proscribed by the Catholic Church was barred from
membership."[61] For devout Catholics wishing to avoid the nationalist taint rubbed
off by the more radicalized organizations, or even for that rare breed, the apoliti-
cal Irish settler, the Convention provided the perfect forum. Neither too public nor
too private, neither too stodgy nor too activist, the organizations allowed members
to coordinate a multitude of charitable works, interact with like-minded compatriots, maintain links with home through the channels of Catholic charities operating simultaneously in Dublin particularly, and improve both their social status and
their piety in so doing.[62]

Obviously, this type of foundation provided mid- and late-nineteenth century arrivals with a support base in a strange city. These agencies of benevolence assisted immigrants in securing employment and obtaining welfare assistance, provided
benefits to members' families in the event of illness or death, and organized a variety of social activities for members.[63] That groups affiliated with the Convention
offered members the opportunity to socialize while assisting their compatriots
proved a popular incentive to join, judging by the devotion of members to the different activities during the post-Famine decades. Convention meetings usually
consisted of the reading of Minutes, discussion of items of topical interest, and attention to special events. A March 1861 Convention meeting, for example, reviewed
the route for the upcoming Saint Patrick's Day parade and appointed a Grand
Marshall, aides, and a committee of organization for the day's march. The
Convention then "proceeded to draw for the positions of the various Societies in the
line of march."[64] As befitting this gathering, members neutralized the stronger
nationalist influences threatening to overshadow Saint Patrick's Day. With the
exception of the Ancient Order of Hibernians and some of the County Associations,
the groups displayed little or no political identification, preferring instead to focus

on the faith-based aspects of commemorative occasions; namely the protocol of processions, the selection of uniforms, and the choice of music for the marches.[65]

The Society of Saint Vincent de Paul[66] developed from French lay origins to progress toward a strong conservative Irish affiliation. From 1855, the aptly referenced St. Patrick's New York Conference of St. Vincent de Paul mobilized with the blessing of Bishop Loughlin of the predominantly Irish Saint James' Cathedral parish in Brooklyn. The Society's mission, to implement "the large and effectual alleviation of suffering among the deserving poor, by the aid and direction afforded by the benevolence of the charitably disposed . . . zealous members," proved inspirational and timely in terms of membership recruitment. In its 1861 Society report, the Council of Directors stressed that Vincent de Paul success rested on the aim that "this is a religious Society, and . . . it is not the recipient who derives the greatest benefit, but the giver." In a remark acknowledging a burgeoning class differential, the Council called on all, regardless of income, to contribute whatever charitable assistance they could manage even though some members were "removed scarcely one degree above those they are relieving." Many members had not yet attained the ranks of the affluent but could still participate fully in Vincent de Paul operations.[67] As an entity encapsulating the sense of noblesse oblige traditionally associated with Protestant philanthropic efforts, the V. de P., as it was popularly known, performed a role of significance for the post-Famine city Irish.

In similar fashion, the Catholic Club of the City of New York that originated as the Xavier Alumni Sodality on December 8, 1863, expanded as the Xavier Union in the 1870s from a home base at 20 West Twenty-Seventh Street. Strong membership growth through the 1860s and 1870s developed Sodality potential toward its distinct city profile and provided the same kind of philanthropically minded outlet for Irish Catholics in the process. A group facilitating the interests of conservative professionals motivated to serve in the company of like-minded individuals, the Xavier Union embarked on a development course that in many respects paralleled that of the city's Irish Catholic identity. From its formal inauguration in 1881, the October meeting of 1887 amended the Xavier Union's constitution to commission a new name, that of "Catholic Club." Deploying a more colloquial overtone than "Sodality" or "Union," a proposal for a new headquarters uptown at Fifth Avenue and Fifty-Ninth Street would reflect advancement to the heart of Manhattan and locate the Catholic Club alongside some of the more salubrious gentlemen's establishments. The organization succeeded in vacating the downtown premises for the more prestigious address the following year, even as Irish Catholic prospects in general were advancing beyond the memory of darker mid-century decades. With a flagship cathedral open on Fifth Avenue, an Irish mayor in place, and an assortment of by now prestigious faith-based organizations predominating, the Irish Catholic identity had succeeded to a positive representation by the 1880s.[68]

A glance at the board of officers reads in the style of a shipping list from decades earlier, the names McLoughlin, Doherty, Farley, Lalor, McKeon, Gibney, Coleman, Hamilton, Dealy, and Malone constituting a majority presence within a membership approaching 500 by 1890. The Club professed itself in existence "to study the subject of Catholic Interests" in New York, but in reality, this organization served the cultivation of *Irish* "Catholic Interests," given the well-represented ethnic background of its membership. Mirroring the middle-class values and practices extolled by groups, such as the Ladies of Charity, the Emigrant Commission, the total abstinence groups and the Irish county societies, the "interests" reflected most visibly in benevolent activities and generation of a Catholic-based social network. In many respects, the Catholic Club paralleled the workings and the role of the Friendly Sons of Saint Patrick. Financier Robert Hoguet served on the governing boards of both bodies during the 1870s,[69] as the Club aspired to the cultural affiliations of William Smith O'Brien and locally, William Bourke Cockran and Thomas Grady. As we see in the next chapter, these men and their families epitomized the new class of professional publicly driving the emerging Irish city identity.

Following the minutes, reports from various board members, and announcements from the floor, Catholic Club members exchanged philanthropic news and appropriated monies accordingly. Acknowledgment of benefactors' largesse occurred frequently, and even singled out individuals excluded from membership! As a private male domain, the following note of thanks from October 1887 conveyed a sense of the exclusive atmosphere.

> The committee begs to tender its special thanks to a very generous contribution (to the "Jubilee Offering") from a lady who has asked the privilege of uniting her donation to those of the members of the Union. May her noble example be followed by others. When the hand of good fellowship is extended so timely it is doubly appreciated if it comes to us from those to whom we had not presumed to address our appeal.[70]

Ironically, as soon as the organization settled into the safety zone of prosperity within a middle-class milieu, a decline in membership ushered in a less visible profile for the Catholic Club. In one sense, the deceleration evidenced fulfillment of immigrant objectives. This style of organization waned during the 1890s and the turn-of-the-century years throughout New York as improved socioeconomic conditions spread through the ethnic communities, and once-staunch members drifted away from the more formalized religious support networks. The trend continued into the twentieth century with the continued expansion of the Irish middle class.[71]

Their significance lies in the success achieved by these agencies. As the type of collective that underwrote a new stamp on New York City Catholicism between the 1840s and 1890s within an immigrant Church struggling against the onslaught of the Famine's force, the sheer volume of newly arrived faithful expanded the old parishes beyond recognition to eventually generate a broad, citywide presence. As St. Patrick's Cathedral represented a monument to a solidified New York Irish institution, the political affiliations attached to the label "Irish Catholic" still inferred Democratic support and included a range of nationalist connections within the city's Irish community, but by the turn of the century, the ethnoreligious connective encompassed a different institution to the adolescent organization of the Famine decade. The same process that empowered the rise of a strong religious presence in the city also held true for the Irish-Catholic identity that prospered in a similar fashion. Given that the fortunes of the Church were so closely inscribed with the supporting settlement culture, such a parallel is hardly surprising.

In sum, while the contention that those "who see catholicism as the collective manifestation of Irish ethnicity are wide of the mark"[72] certainly provides a useful yardstick for consideration of Irish-American religious affiliation, the intertwining of this particular faith with ethnic Irish affiliation generated a substantial proportion of the emerging New York Irish identity, retaining the structures and parameters of Ireland's largest religious affiliation. As we have seen, the proliferation of Protestant Irish in the post-Famine city alters previously all-encompassing views of the Irish experience as almost exclusively Catholic. But the 200,000 faithful importing their religious tradition directly from home played a definitive role in shaping New York Irish identity; their Catholicism constituting a vehicle through which a particular branch of Irish ethnicity grew increasingly visible by the later nineteenth-century years.

Politicizing intermittently during the 1860s and 1870s and cultivating connections with radical nationalism on a number of occasions, the more conservative agendas of Denis Holland and John Develin occupied a niche within an increasingly sophisticated city church structure that paralleled the rise of Catholic politicians and a Catholic middle class in Ireland during the same years. As we will see in the final chapter, what may be described as Catholic-based political power required affiliation with specific agendas and organizations to become meaningful beyond the occasional political endorsement or the establishment of benevolent lay clubs and societies. Association with the largest church building in Manhattan inculcated Irish prominence and stability, and helped implement Devotional linchpins from across the Atlantic. A faith base considered superstitious and outmoded gradually replaced by a modernized system emulated similar development in New York, although Ireland had a more comprehensive task in hand than American cities in terms of this kind of grassroots change. As the mid-century nativist threat subsided, Irish clergy, hierarchy, and religious orders enjoyed sufficient opportunity in an expanding city to establish the parish pump and the school as cornerstones of ethnoreligious success.[73]

As their lay organizations entered into decline by the turn of the century, the dawn of a new era loomed for the faithful. Much had been accomplished by the early 1900s. Free from the intensity of Ireland's still-authoritarian hierarchy, immigrants carved out new parameters to their relationship with their Church. The absence of a powerful leader in the mold of a Hughes or a McCloskey resulted in a less absolutist institution, and decreasing emphasis on the Church as a means of advancement. Imbued with modernizing influences and energized by increasing affluence and secularization, "Irish" Catholicism continued to anchor a sizable component of a new identity closely circumscribed with the old.

C H A P T E R   S I X

Powerful Partitions

TRANSATLANTIC TENSIONS IN NEW YORK'S
IRISH POLITICAL CULTURE

New York Irish affiliations mobilized from the dynamics of party and population in the city, while enforcing linkages with a heritage born and bred across the Atlantic. Like a wild river with strong undercurrents, whitewater dangers, and plenty of adventurers willing to try their luck, a set of political traditions honed for decades and even centuries past confronted a city system ill-prepared for this kind of onslaught. Incorporating what Ronald P. Formisano called "sensitivity to context and local variation,"[1] the organizational experience fostered in pre-Famine and mid-century Ireland built on New York's formidable voter constituency and opportunist leadership to generate a political presence of significance. This chapter explores the presence and the links with home while integrating the role of post-Famine struggle against the fetters of Union with Britain.

Over these decades, familiarity with and empowerment within the new cultural context developed,[2] even as Ireland remained a powerful influence into the early twentieth century. In terms of sheer voter power, as a reporter noted in 1871 when he remarked that "our political power follows population," Irish success seemed almost inevitable. But the gravitation toward the Democrats by one of the largest ethnic groups generated grudging city interest and not a little distaste that took years to dissipate. As "the ranks of the lowest and most ignorant class of the whole community" used their numerical advantage to win power, "Irish Catholic laborers and [the] tenement-house population of New York led by shrewd native demagogues" slid into the system from a variety of angles other than the front door. Operating under "able and audacious leaders," compatriots speedily shepherded onto the lower rungs of authority utilized tight voting controls and took advantage of corrupt administrators conspiring to sustain the grip. Ironically, nativist prejudice often hampered effective opposition to Irish progress by creating a wider gulf than usual between WASPish natives and the huddled masses.[3]

During the post-Famine decades, personalities like George Birmingham, Sir Shane Leslie, and Countess Markievicz occasionally cast a sardonic eye and rendered a pithy turn of phrase on the state of New York Irish progress. Among them, Timothy M. Healy's transatlantic perspective accorded him evaluative powers of some distinction. A household name in Ireland, and almost as well known in Irish-American political circles, Member of Parliament Healy's observations frequently made the news. His New York compatriots' "political character" held particular interest for him during the 1880s and 1890s.[4] Announcing breezily "American air sharpens Irish wit," Healy determined that although the majority of Famine Irish had vacated the tenements of the Bowery and the Tombs for the tree-lined avenues uptown by the Gilded Age, such advancement did not stem the tide of entry into city government. He remained convinced that, far from altruistically motivated, however, some still sought such positions for purely personal gain.[5]

The journalist, parliamentarian, barrister, and sage pundit cited organizational experience in the O'Connellite and Young Ireland campaigns as the silver lining in the post-Famine Irish political success story. Stormy relations between Ireland and England under the 1801 Act of Union had institutionalized valuable political experience that transplanted well to cities like New York. "Nothing but the persecutions to which their kin at home have been subjected under coercion would have roused them to their present pitch," Healy declared. Further, he went on, leaders connecting their new urban context with the vexatious situation left behind might nobly "be called cold-blooded in their methodical determination by no official act to commit the people at home to any official impudence." As time passed, he reflected, rising prosperity levels and expanding educational opportunities created a political climate where insurgents could conserve energy previously expended on unrealistic dreams. By the Gilded Age, Healy confirmed, the firebrands of mid-century had been replaced by a new generation of professional politicians and administrators.[6]

In connecting contemporary opportunities and prior experience, Healy described an Atlantic World scenario where similar factors mobilized Irish constituencies in the Old World and the New. Numerical strength, coupled with the kind of hardscrabble organizational style employed by O'Connell in Ireland and ward heelers in New York elevated an immigrant culture at once blessed and cursed by its sheer size. "The world moves, and we move with it," declared *The Nation* in

1871. "If anybody had predicted, fifty years ago, that nearly a third of New Yorkers would be Catholic Irishmen, he would have been laughed at for his pains, if not worse; and yet that has come to pass."[7] Not merely that, but those same Catholic Irishmen had carved out a lucrative niche for themselves in the world of city politics. Spurred on by memories of a political culture in Ireland that had effectively ostracized the bulk of the native population as far back as they could remember, enfranchised Irish rallied to the opportunities proffered by the Democrats to expand their ward politics out into the broader city context.[8] *Harper's Magazine* had already satirized Irish progress in the story of a destitute slum dweller rising to become a powerful lawmaker. Revolving around stereotypical references ranging from the pipe-smoking washerwoman to interactions between ward bosses and fresh-off-the-boat new voters, the cartoon charted escalating political influence in the Thomas Nast style popularized in *Harper's* and John Tenniel's *Punch*.[9] Illustrated by John R. Chapman in 1861, readers met a Moses-like baby in a basket with the words "Born of poor but honest parents, he makes his debut." The child grew alongside his laundry-consumed mother; her only comfort the clay pipe and the line: "he is provided for at the expense of Government." Next came youth and adolescence, where the boy was "educated scientifically" as per the depiction of a street fight, and "adopts a professional calling" in the guise of a newspaper delivery boy. His education in pickpocketing and duping innocent gentlemen "receives a polish" through attendance at lowbrow music-hall entertainment, where "Paddy" cheered on a Shakespeare-like performance while fellow audience members either watched agape or fell asleep. Completing his education in the university of the street, our friend took his place in the adult world of politics. First priority was a livelihood. The aspiring politician set out in the style of the professional conman-as-public representative as he assumed his first role since he "arrived at man's Estate." Setting up shop at the docks outside the Emigrant Office facilitated the easy swindling of hapless arrivals as our protagonist eased into his new life. From there, introduction to the wards sees Paddy publicly thrashing an unlucky voter in hopes of influencing the outcome of an election. As his star rises, the new Alderman "dispenses the hospitality of the City" through the neighborhood during his ascension to power. Able to milk his status for the benefit of his compatriots, the "Street Commissioners Office" proved useful as a foothold on the lowest rungs of the machine. He succeeded to the office of judge to "administer[s] Justice impartially," but the bag of gold exchanging hands behind the judge showed the depth of his impartiality. The series concluded with a view of our champion finally elevated to Congress. The "last scene of all which closes this eventful history" left the reader with a picture of the new Congressman fast asleep amid a brawl in the House.[10] See Fig. 5.1.

In an era when the cartoon carried politics to the people as did the broadsheet ballad years before, *The Irish Nation's* view that "art is stronger than statecraft" played out daily in the city press. Commenting in the context of a case between *United Ireland* magazine and *Punch,* remarks to the effect that the "caricaturist . . . [will] outlive dynasties"[11] must have struck a familiar ring with contemporary readers. Thomas Nast in *Harper's* honed the stock caricature of ape-faced shillelagh wielders mobilized by ward-heeling thugs on one hand and a fire-and-brimstone breathing hierarchy on the other to the point of ubiquity. Such images became so popular during the late 1800s that news items rarely ran without some such accompaniment.[12] But exactly what kind of political culture did Nast and *Harper's* satirize? How did the immigrant influx sustain connections with a troubled native land? And, ultimately, how significant was the goal of Irish independence for the sons and daughters of Erin? In broaching these questions, different strands of Irish involvement in city politics are identified in terms of their origins across the Atlantic, toward the aim of a deeper understanding of a critical dimension of Famine-era and post-Famine Irish New York.

The most popular Irish partisan affiliation had originated in the 1820s as the Democratic organization started to take hold as a full-fledged American party. By the 1840s, the bosses in urban wards and boroughs molded new structures that fostered the Irish connection for decades to come[13] through the rise of such stalwarts as Judge James T. Brady, City Administrator Charles O'Conor, Common Councilor Peter B. Sweeney, and Comptroller Richard Connolly. Their accession through the Tammany ranks to form the core of Tweed's Ring by the 1850s empowered aspiring bosses to embrace the Machine as the most direct way to mobilize masses armed with votes and little else. Although just a small percentage of jobbers reached the higher levels of city government, the system generated the best potential for working-class immigrants lacking prospects beyond the most menial levels.[14] For the vast majority, "blue-collar patronage" in the form of low-paying manual labor constituted the significant benefit of Tammany association.[15]

By the immediate post-Famine years, charges of "misgovernment" harried the Irish-Democratic alliance on a regular basis. In a city infamously rife with jobbery opportunities beckoning daily to the poor and powerless, ward heelers strengthened links between the city government and impoverished compatriots seeking the solidity of a regular wage. While certainly distasteful and rampantly illegal, enrollment on the payroll still managed to inculcate a romanticized aura within the burgeoning political culture, and New York City public representatives could not easily avoid the workings of the patronage system; in large measure the foundation of Democratic success.[16] As Scots-born William M. Tweed amalgamated his sprawling voter base, the borough bosses institutionalized Democratic control during the 1840s and 1850s. Tweed enjoyed greater initial success motivating German voters than the more volatile and disunited Irish,[17] but efforts to attract support from the Famine influx paid off. The outfitting of "Elegant" Mayor Oakey Hall in a green suit to review the Saint Patrick's Day parade in the late 1840s represented a detail in an extended courtship. In effect, Tweed "humored the prejudices of the mob when forced to recognize them."[18] Away from the teeming wards, politics operated on a more congenial basis. *Harper's* publicized a dinner at Mayor Fernando Wood's residence in 1855, the guest list including future mayor Oakey Hall, Winfield Scott, Martin Van Buren and "his tall son John," Washington Irving, a couple of "burly and bluff" commodores, and numerous lesser grandees. In between extravagant courses washed down with Champagne, General Scott and Governor Seymour regaled the table with tales of Japanese expeditions, the gardens of landed estates, and the spot near Columbia College where "Peter Stuyvesant used to retire of damp nights . . . to air his wooden leg"![19] Within a decade, frontrunners such as John Develin and William Bourke Cockran would broaden the Anglo-Dutch profile of city leadership to include a prominent Irish constituency.

As heavy involvement in menial but relatively steady employment merged Irish aspirations with Democratic affiliation,[20] willingness to sweep streets and hold down basic construction jobs for lower wages than standard strained at native New Yorkers' sensibilities. But from the Famine-survivor perspective, city jobs reaped higher status and often higher wages than private employment. An 1871 view that "an American is, until he turns loafer, averse to accepting minor service under the government, because it is of uncertain duration, and he counts it no particular honor," contrasted with immigrant entry into an often precarious labor culture that wrought a crude stability through constant interaction with bosses and administrators. "For an Irishman, according to contemporary opinion, the uncertainty has perhaps a charm, and his self-importance is swelled by the character of his paymaster," journalist Charles Nordhoff remarked, musing that willingness to accept official benevolence in the form of illegal city "charity" separated the Gael from more law-abiding New Yorkers and other foreign groups. Cementing the relationship with powerful "patrons" evolved into common practice with the accession of compatriots into positions of authority. There is little doubt that the close-knit world of the boss and his base of support built around the allocation of resources to his clientele suited the impoverished Famine tenement dwellers. In a world where large numbers of propertyless immigrants subsisted from day to day, as the case in Ireland for decades past, the power of those who succeeded in marshaling their voting strength readily increased.[21]

But the golden goose tarnished as Tammany corruption escalated out of control. Reports that Tweed allocated forty-six posts to Germans but many hundreds of jobs on the 1869 city payroll to Irish takers hastened the Ring downfall.[22] Comptroller Richard Connolly's city audits for July 1871 contained enough damning evidence to bring the issue to a head. No surprise here; Richard Barrett "Slippery Dick" Connolly had long epitomized the shady profile of the Tweed Ring, his crooked career showcasing perhaps the highest levels of corruption, even by Ring standards.[23] New York City paid the sum of $275,600 in rent for twenty-four armories in 1869, for example, while the real value should not have exceeded $79,000. Repairs and furnishings for the buildings ran to $941,453.86, including bills for ten unoccupied armories! For 1869–1870, the total came to $5,663,646.83. The bill for carpets alone reached $565,731.34, "money enough to carpet the City Hall Park all over with three thicknesses of carpeting." Bills for plastering netted Tweed and his cronies a grand total of $2,870,464.06! Many of these transactions occurred on Sundays when all offices would have been closed, and documents signed by the fictitious Phillip F. Dummy and Fillippo Donnarumna underscored a wealth of truly remarkable city activity.[24] Despite (and in large measure because of) such rampant corruption, Irish relations with Tammany sustained through mid-century years and up through the Gilded Age. In its heyday, the Ring quite literally directed cash and material necessities toward the needy.[25] Alternative political affiliations failed to generate the same kind of momentum, with the Republican Party's chiefly Protestant profile encouraging the Irish-Democratic connection.[26] The mass appeal worked to advantage, even as Daniel O'Connell had harnessed Monster Meeting strength-in-numbers in pre-Famine Ireland. Tammany Hall on Fourteenth Street, for example, accommodated five or six thousand people comfortably but packed in as many as 30,000 for a speech from a big-name boss of the stature of a George Washington Plunkitt or a "Big Tim" Sullivan. (In 1870, Westside boss Plunkitt concurrently held the posts of Assemblyman, Police Magistrate, and County Supervisor.)[27] "Well-dressed men of the clerk or business class" of an average age of thirty were happy enough to jostle with as many manual laborers and domestics as the venue could hold. On nights when the Tammany Boss appeared, such as the evening in October 1901 when the Hall beside the Academy of Music overflowed with throngs of the faithful to hear Colonel McClennan, a flurry signaled the arrival of Boss Richard Croker to the platform. His speech dropped down on the masses like rain in a desert, celebrating a familiar Tammany anthem holding particular appeal for an Irish audience; "the truth is that Tammany stands for the populace against class rule."[28]

The issue that Irish voters by and large displayed little or no ideological identification with the Democratic Party but developed a political culture around the exchange of votes for favors made for an unsatisfactory long-term relationship for the more visionary and ambitious of their number. But for the teeming masses, "the weakness of the Irish was their strength." Exchanging access to political power for handouts and jobs on the city payroll empowered this element to channel weakness into socioeconomic improvement.[29] Had the Republicans assumed control of city government and all its lucrative opportunities, an Irish-Republican affiliation might very well have materialized. But the voting strength settled more compatibly with the less Establishment-minded Democrats at the helm of the material-benefit exchange.[30] By the time "Honest" John Kelly took the wheel in the 1880s, their support still guaranteed that "wherever Irish-Americans went, Tammany could not afford to be far behind."[31] The Democratic "pro-Irish, pro-immigrant position" of the 1840s laid a solid foundation for a pragmatic loyalty. By all accounts, "as the Democrats splintered among an ever-changing set of factions, the Irish shifted among them, calculating who could give them the best deal and who was most likely to win." Their alignment remained fluid enough that the rewards needed to flow constantly if the support were to remain consistent.[32] Despite John Boyle O'Reilly's warning to John Devoy in 1871 to stay away from "Irish or American political 'rings'" and carve out his own niche, a warning that bore out in the fall of the Ring leaders that same year,[33] the organization struggled onward with John Kelly at the helm and Irish affiliation sustained through the successive Gilded Age Bosses despite increased pressure from German Democrats. According to *The New York Times* in 1869, "They [Germans] are no longer satisfied that the Irish shall control the party and hold all the offices while they content themselves with selling *lager-beer* and voting the 'straight' ticket."[34] After Kelly's demise in 1886, Richard Croker's reduction of jobbery to "reasonable limits" sustained the extensive Irish-Democratic support of past decades.[35]

As the influence of prior experience within a political system designed to exclude the majority of its constituents arose with the same kind of gritty persistence O'Connell's Emancipation and Repeal campaigns had fostered across the Atlantic, Irish grafting within the rough-cut backrooms of the Bowery sustained a process institutionalized even further back during the campaigns of Tone and Emmet. Such a tradition forged political skills for aspiring Assemblymen or City Councilmen, but also for those of greater ambition who sought to serve at the more prestigious grades of the city system. As attractive as the Tammany mantle may have appeared to the more impoverished contingents, other avenues opened up for those in a position to take advantage of them. Spending as little time as possible on the streets or on the stump in the role of ward or borough boss, these men strove for the higher echelons of respectability.

Their rise paralleled a similar occurrence across the Atlantic. Since the seventeenth century, the exclusion of the majority of Ireland's population from representation was anchored by the Penal Laws and the Act of Union. Following Crown installation in Dublin Castle after 1801 and through the middle decades of the century, it is likely that "had an attempt been made early to offer a measure of Catholic participation in the workings of the Castle, the system might have had some chance of popular acceptance."[36] But it was not to be. The O'Connellite Emancipation victory constituted the first step for Irishmen subscribing to the Church of Rome on the road to public representation. Distinct from the upper and gentry classes, members from which were traditionally returned to Parliament, Catholic businessmen and professionals in the expanding towns and cities changed the denominational profile of national representation. Although the confluence of a musty aristocracy and an energized middle class poised to take over parliamentary control played out toward century's end, the complexities of protracted cultural change and the longevity of once-powerful Ascendancy forces did constrain Catholic middle-class progress through the early twentieth-century decades.[37]

A combination of factors empowered expanding groups on both sides of the Atlantic to seek and achieve political success. Solid education, powerful oratorical skills, and the confidence to take advantage of changing social norms and practices enabled growing numbers to avoid the hardscrabble experience of the street-level operator and take advantage of the commercial and industrial opportunities exploding around them. In New York, the names of Michael Norton, Thomas F. Grady, and William Bourke Cockran relegated the cheap whiskey and coalbags to a different class of compatriot, pursuing power traditionally vested in the hands of Colonial elites. If local ward bosses and aldermen personified a blue-collar, working-class political style, then these men may be viewed as the "black-tie" division. Like John Develin and, more particularly, William Smith O'Brien, they cultivated a high-profile, fashionable aura that exuded greater sophistication than previously associated with Irish political involvement. With style and lavish patronage, Michael Norton, Thomas F. Grady, and William Bourke Cockran embodied the kind of celebrity air that elevated the ethnic Irish persona away from the teeming brutality of the wards.[38]

The first of this trio, Michael Norton's birth in Galway on the West coast of Ireland led to early adventure in the move to New York with his parents in the 1840s. Life on the Lower West Side earned him early experience in prizefighting that sharpened his competitive edge. Lucky enough or smart enough to fight, win, and move on, he managed to stay clear of the perils of slum life and set about establishing citywide contacts. Learning the cooper's trade developed into business enterprises netting him a comfortable livelihood, and working as a production assistant in the famous No. 444 Broadway Butler's American Theater in the 1860s stood him in good stead for a future career in politics. As one of the landmark New York social centers, No. 444 or, the American Varieties, attracted affluent theater-goers to flamboyant nightly productions. As one contemporary observed, "there he made friends who led him into politics."[39]

Unfulfilled as yet, Norton joined the Volunteer Service in 1861 and won election as Company D Captain of the Twenty-Fifth Regiment. Enhancing his confidence and honing his leadership skills made feasible the idea of running for election as Alderman for the Third Aldermanic District on the Republican ticket a year later. But it was too big a leap so soon. His nomination in 1864 under the

Tammany banner proved more successful. This switching of party allegiance did not upset Michael Norton too severely in a time when conflicting partisan ideologies generated relatively little trouble among lower-level politicians. Although some of the more senior Democrats and Republicans occasionally reacted negatively against the mavericks, the changeover worked to increase Norton's popularity with the electorate. The same ambition toward political power without the limitations of strict party association would motivate his compatriot William Bourke Cockran a few years later.

As with John Develin, Norton operated within a variety of city committees. As Chair of the Committee on Streets, Lamps and Gas and the Joint Committee on Accounts, his accession to Senator by 1867 on the Tammany ticket empowered him to lead the anti-Tweed Young Democracy. Unhappy with Tweed's political style and uninspired by his own prospects, yet still invested in the dream of public representation, Norton publicly declared against Tweed in 1871, risking his name against the force of the Machine. Unfortunately for him, as it turned out, 1871 brought the Ring collapse, but he had made his move a few months too soon. The turmoil blustered into every corner of the city system and upset both seasoned politicians and rising stars. Out of the melee, Erastus C. Benedict representing the Citizens and Republicans beat Norton soundly in the well-publicized 1871 outing. Had he resisted the bold move of confronting Tweed when he did, the Ring probably would have collapsed without adversely affecting his prospects. But in early 1871 the waters were murky enough that it was impossible to know exactly when Tammany might crash. Some thought the Machine was invincible, stacked on layers of retainers in the pay of the city for years. But topple it did and Norton reverted to his contacts under pressure in hopes of regaining momentum. As befitting his status as an ex-Senator with a record of public service and strong administration experience, his success in Manhattan's First District election for Civil Justice seemed assured. Standing for the County Democracy, Norton won out over Tammany nominee John Callahan in the 1881 election.[40]

Rising to prominence alongside his compatriot William Grace, Norton became known as "The Thunderbolt" in the wake of his "bolting" against Grace's nomination for Mayor in 1884. The move did not unduly upset his prospects. His political star and judicial career rose steadily until 1887 and re-election as Civil Justice on the by-now less-tainted Tammany badge. Reverting back from the County Democracy, he attained considerable status in politics and law before his untimely death in 1889 that ended the career of a successful New York Irishman, by all accounts. A large funeral drew members of the Michael Davitt Club, the Young Men's Lyceum of Saint Anthony's Church, and the Tammany Hall General Committee of the Fifth Assembly District together with a group of mourners representative of every office in city politics.[41] The esteem which Michael Norton enjoyed among his peers radiated vividly from the proceedings of a meeting held about a month after his death to raise money for his family. Leading political and business associates attended at Hoffman House to subscribe to the Norton Fund, among them Richard Croker with $2,500 from Tammany Hall and $250 personally, Mayor Hugh Grant with $250, and similar sums from city judges, precinct captains, sheriffs, and civil justices amounting to almost $6,000 in total.[42] Further donations increased the fund the following Sunday with a program of entertainment at the Academy of Music. Boxes sold for $25 to $100 to prominent friends such as Henry Purroy, Police Captain John J. Ryan, Police Captain John F. Welsh, Congressmen E. J. Dunphy, E. T. Fitzgerald, and William Bourke Cockran, who contributed $100. Even boxer John L. Sullivan sent $50 from his training center. After the speeches, "orchestral selections" and music recitals, attended by "nearly all the prominent politicians of the city, independent of party," the large sum of $11,610 had been raised for the Nortons.[43]

Paralleling the rise of Catholic entry into local and national politics across the Atlantic, an Irishman with the panache of an O'Connell stepped into the spotlight in post-Famine New York. Born into families of sufficient means to access at least the lower reaches of national and city governance, men such as New York State Senator Thomas F. Grady took advantage of the nascent opportunities to scale the heights of city politics. The son of Irish parents recently arrived to the old Fourth Ward in 1853, Thomas Francis Grady's early training in the classroom minimized the pressures of the rough-and-tumble Lower Manhattan streets. Grady's family afforded a comprehensive education for their son at Saint James Parochial School and the de la Salle Christian Brothers Institute, followed by a master's degree from Manhattan College and a law degree from New York University in 1877. Championed by such prominent voices as Patrick Ford, this type of educational pathway became standard for lace-curtain aspirants in the next generation.

From the publishing house D. Appleton and Company and a stint as a stockbroker with Stone, Nichols, and Stone, the engaging, charismatic Grady embarked on a successful legal career with Middlebrook and Phillips. Turning down entry to West Point in 1877 in favor of the law, and already known as "Silver-Tongued Grady" for his speechmaking ability, his infiltration of the lower reaches of city politics during graduate education spurred him to join Tammany in the 1870s. Living up to his reputation as "an oratorical fencer," and certainly equaling the Fenian and Clan noteworthies in the same years; in fact, "one of the very few men to whom nature had imparted the rarest of all gifts—oratory,[44] Grady drew lavish tributes from John Quinn (no mean public speaker himself) who commented in the *New York Tammany Times*:

> To the close observer and analytical student Senator Grady was a source of constant and ever increasing surprise. Flashes of wit, lightning-like retort, bubbling humor and stirring elo-

quence crowded his rostrum performances so full of entertaining illustration and persuasive appeal that the average mind grasped only the result, yet the wonder of it all was in the marvelous mental kaleidoscope which carried the enraptured audience through ever changing scenes and happy surprises to the goal toward which the welfare of the orator's cause impelled him.

As with John Develin and Michael Norton, legal contacts brought Grady within close proximity of the city administration. A developing friendship with soon-to-be Mayor Hugh J. Grant could only foster useful support, as did contact with voting constituencies in the Fourth Ward through Bowery boss Tim Sullivan. Mayor Grant's appointment of Grady as a Police Justice in 1880 cemented these alliances, cloaking them in an aura of respectability in the process.[45]

As his name became associated with Grant's, Grady's reputation escalated. Aside from the Mayor, he courted powerful contacts such as William Grace and Richard Croker. "A man of splendid mental equipment, a fighter for what he wanted, an orator with powers of sarcasm and invective few sought to test"; but "for all his sharp wit, biting sarcasm and grim humor" his colleague Senator Murtaugh surmised, "he was a stickler for punctilious points of honor." Although a battle of wills with New York Governor Grover Cleveland in 1883 removed Grady from the Senate seat he won the previous year (the incident expanding into a public exchange between the two that risked negatively affecting the young politician's prospects), the enmity failed to forestall his ambitions. Serving as Assemblyman from 1877 to 1879, he was returned to the Senate for two further terms, 1889–1890 and 1896 to his death in 1912.[46] Senator Tom Grady's career contained enough of the sparkle of Irish roguery to generate celebrity, many stories about him involving wild sums of money and large living at high-priced sporting events. In 1908, for example, he "gained a lot of undesired notoriety" in the aftermath of a police raid on a gambling den in premises known as "Bob Davis's clearing-house" on Fulton Street. A bank slip detailing the establishment's liability for the sum of $300 was discovered in the safe of the clearinghouse, either having been deposited or made ready for deposit into Assemblyman Grady's Windsor Trust Company account. The Senator reportedly placed $200 with Bob Davis on a horse called Azelina in the fifth outing at a recent race meeting. *The New York Times* noted urbanely that "for months following this, Mr. Grady, when cartooned, was always astride Azelina."[47]

By his death in 1912 Thomas Grady's high profile earned fulsome tributes coordinated by a Senate committee including Robert F. Wagner, James J. Frawley, Timothy D. "Big Tim" Sullivan, Edgar T. Brackett, and Harvey D. Hinman. These prominents choreographed an impressive narrative of his life's work, characterizing the Senator as "a most courteous, polished gentleman," according to Robert Wagner, as he presided over the ceremony on February 15, 1912. The large and representative list of dignitaries joining the cortege to the East Twenty-Eighth Street Saint

Stephen's Church included as pallbearers future presidential candidate Alfred E. Smith and William Bourke Cockran. Tammany top-brass Charles Francis Murphy, Richard Croker, and Colonel Asa Bird Gardiner all turned out in force. "Dissensions that had in the past torn Tammany were forgotten," intoned Senator John F. Murtaugh, "and the chieftains and braves gathered amicably about the bier of one whom they all loved."[48] The Senator's assessment of Grady as "an orator and politician of the Old School," and, in recognition of his Catholic background and constituency, "a man of intense religious feeling" reflected the esteem of those present. Winding up the commemoration, Senator Wagner concluded "few men have ever left so indelible an impression upon the political history of this State."[49]

As the third member of this trio of ambitious Irish politicos, William Burke Cockran represented the class in Irish society usually characterized as "Castle Catholic."[50] The term rose to prominence in eighteenth-century Ireland with the establishment of a "court" of prominent Catholics in Dublin Castle.[51] As James Andrews remarked, Bourke Cockran "was hardly a typical Irish ward heeler . . . a patrician by nature and, soon, by professional and social standing."[52] Family wealth in Ireland afforded William Bourke Cockran the best education available to a Catholic boy during the 1850s; a year with the local Christian Brothers in his hometown of Sligo followed by a stint abroad at the Institut Des Petits Freres de Marie in Lille. On his return, his final years of schooling at Saint Jarlath's College in Tuam, County Galway further cultivated a lifelong appreciation of Catholic classicism.[53] New York in 1871 must have appeared cosmopolitan to the handsome, gentlemanly Bourke Cockran after his years in the small towns of the west of Ireland and France. His path into politics stretched before him as it would have done in Ireland in the same decade, hallmarked by his class affiliation and his education and characterized by his disconnect from the seedier elements of political life. As with Norton and Grady, Bourke Cockran's admittance to the Bar in New York in 1876 (five years after he arrived in the city) provided a useful starting point for a career in public life. From a small-time start on an upper floor at 178 Broadway, he prospered rapidly, his training in classical political thought fostered by Catholic priests and Brothers according him self-confidence and developing a nimble debating style that would stand him in good stead. The Democratic Conventions of 1884, 1892, and 1920 provided him national platforms for the oratorical skills that made him famous. In a manner reminiscent of Daniel O'Connell decades earlier, Bourke Cockran the Congressman presented the public façade of a politician that developed backroom skills without resorting to backroom tactics.[54]

By all accounts, his close associations with the Catholic Church and even personal acquaintance with Pope Leo XIII did not injure his political ambitions. Honorary degrees from leading Catholic Church-run institutions Saint Francis Xavier College, Georgetown, Manhattan College, and Saint John's College,

Brooklyn, would have certainly endeared him to Patrick Ford and the Irish element interested in deploying Catholic education as a means of advancement.[55] Related to Bourke Cockran through his wife, Sir Shane Leslie commented on the Congressman's ability to use his erudition to enthrall an audience. Sir Shane observed that "in the silent spaces of his native Ireland the name lives like a pealing memory for those who heard him, or even as the sound of far-forgotten wars beyond the mountains for those who read and followed his words. At least," Sir Shane concluded, rather dramatically, "his fame stands like a lighthouse of ambitious hope to those of his fellow-countrymen who pass from the Old World into the New." Closely connected with the Churchills, especially Winston Churchill's American mother, Jennie Jerome Churchill, and a friend and mentor of Winston Churchill's for many years, Bourke Cockran's speechmaking influenced many of the latter's famous addresses, including the "Iron Curtain," where Churchill made reference to the "great Irish-American orator, [and] friend of mine."[56]

As with Norton and Grady, Bourke Cockran regarded what he termed the "prostitution" of patronage for political ambition as wrongheaded, and the tawdry wheeling and dealing of machine politics as contemptible. When politics strayed beyond the reaches of the law he adopted an automatic stand of opposition, believing that corruption sullied the privilege of democratic elections.[57] During his years in public office, he grew increasingly concerned over the negative influences still discernible within the system, especially that of nativism. Drawing on his interest in and knowledge of Ireland's volatile political tradition, he frequently highlighted aspects of the transatlantic relationship visible in American politics. Engaging in correspondence with financier and Wall Street executive John Byrne on the subject of Irish "Castle Rule," the two men commented on the case of their friend Judge Daly, an unsuccessful contender for a New York county appointment. A recent immigrant, Daly and his family had been victimized under English authority in Ireland. Fearing nativist-led discrimination against him in New York, Byrne commented, "it is a singular fate that the iron heel of tyranny should pursue him here. A manipulated or controlled judiciary means a manipulated and packed jury, a system from which our ancestors suffered enough"—exactly the type of system Bourke Cockran sought to destroy.[58]

Applying himself to a wide range of issues, many of them of national American interest, Bourke Cockran directed his attention to the United States economy, the Southern race question, protectionism, and the state of agriculture, during campaign rallies and national conventions. But Ireland's struggle toward independence remained an absorbing topic of personal focus for the Congressman. Formally unconnected with nationalist organizations,[59] this political maverick's interest in promoting the homeland cause grew deeper as the years went on. Speeches such as "Why I am a Catholic," "The Cause of Ireland," and "The Call of Ireland,

Unchained" publicized the unsettled path to Home Rule throughout its most tur-
bulent years. The final stages of the Home Rule campaign and the lead up to the
1916 Rebellion created a dramatic background for audiences, including many of the
true believers flocking to Clan na Gael and Land League meetings. As the Home
Rule crisis of the 1890s and early 1900s pitted the conciliations of Prime Ministers
Gladstone and Asquith against the retrenchments of Lord Salisbury and Bonar Law,
Parliamentary machinations influenced patterns of behavior some 3,000 miles as
New York's Irish followed the drama on a daily basis.[60] News stories headlining "The
Irish Protestant Establishment," "Ireland, New York Meetings of Sympathy," and
"Irish Morality in Ireland" dominated the intense progression of events.[61] *The
Times*, in tandem with *The Irish World*, the *Freeman's Journal*, *The New York Daily
Tribune*, *The Irish-American Weekly*, and sister publications reported developments
across the Atlantic as carefully as did their counterparts in Ireland.[62]

For Bourke Cockran, the Home Rule issue seemed to work best when inter-
woven in creative ways with the topics of the day. His addresses differed from typical nationalist gatherings in two main respects. First, his gifts at the podium not
only imbued his nationalist rhetoric with excitement and drama, but repackaged the
message to suit audiences typically uninvested or disinterested in the fate of Ireland.
Second, instead of being restricted to venues such as the Cooper Union or
Manhattan's local neighborhood meeting halls, his addresses on the floor of
Congress and at state banquets reached sectors of the American public not otherwise exposed to this issue. Opposition to Grover Cleveland at the Democratic
National Convention in 1884 (where Cleveland won the Democratic presidential
nomination) and debate with William Jennings Bryan in 1890 (in what became
known as the "Gold Democrat" speech) solidified his national reputation as Bourke
Cockran's interest in Ireland's freedom directed a broad spectrum of American
attention toward Dublin and London.[63] One of his more famous speeches to the
Senate in 1913 encapsulated in clear, yet inescapably patriotic tones his interest in
resolving the national struggle. "The Cause of Ireland" reasoned that:

> Whether the right of this country to interfere—at least so far as to exert its moral influence-
> for deliverance of Ireland from conditions that are a scandal to civilization shall be preserved
> or whether it is to be renounced by ratification of this treaty, is not an Irish question. Nor
> is it a question affecting solely England's domestic politics, as some gentlemen have contend-
> ed. It is an international question, because there can be no peace throughout the world until
> Irish discontent is composed. This is not, as many might say, a mere expression of exagger-
> ated rhetoric. It is the sober, accurate statement of a fact which all history attests. My pur-
> pose is to show that the condition of Ireland has been a constant invitation to every country
> with a grievance against Ireland to strike her at that spot where she was believed to be vul-
> nerable, and where she will continue to be vulnerable just so long as the oppressions against
> which the Irish people have struggled for eight centuries are suffered to exist.[64]

In New York, the centenary commemoration of Ireland's 1798 Rebellion took on heightened symbolic resonance under his direction. The ideal candidate to run the show, his tone of class-bound dignity and integrity permeated a potentially divisive event. The banquet he presided over transformed 1798 remembrance from the realm of the bloody and failed into commemoration of a shining example of courage and initiative against a despotic English force. As evocative of Declaration of Independence ideals as of Irish history, Bourke Cockran's stewardship lent an emotional yet dignified air to the proceedings. Historic yet relevant, and public yet intimate, his speech articulated hope for a lasting peace in Ireland, and underscored his aspiration to play a part in the realization of that goal.[65] Such a role lay within his potential, given his assistance with some of the more challenging political initiatives across the Atlantic. For example, "it was largely through his efforts that the late King Edward signed the Irish Land Act, a great benefit to the people of Ireland . . . twenty years ago."[66] Further, Bourke Cockran had held the office of Treasurer on a committee to raise funds for the Irish Parliamentary Party in 1896. With media attention on Home Rule dividing public opinion, the congressman supported the constitutional-nationalist agenda while his December 1910 personal contribution of $1,000 to the Parliamentary fund encouraged an assortment of judges, physicians, and businessmen to rally up to $4,000 in one evening.[67] Amidst efforts to address "a brilliant audience at the Metropolitan Opera House" to raise money for the relatives of the victims of the *Titanic* and "the sewing-girls of Paris" left destitute by World War I, Bourke Cockran's ongoing friendship with the Churchill family placed him in an interesting position with regard to his patriotic aspirations.

Through his long and successful career, Bourke Cockran benchmarked a new Irish outlook in New York. Together with Norton and Grady, he demonstrated that being Irish in city politics encompassed more than confinement to the harsh underworld of the ward. Reflective of contemporary conditions in Ireland during the same era, these professional politicians attracted the masses with polished rhetoric, political clout, and heavily laden campaign purses. Norton, Grady, and Bourke Cockran empowered Irishmen to seek the higher levels of public representation beyond the shadowy background traditionally requisite. The tributes at his death in 1923 testified to his prestige in American politics and his influence on the other side of the Atlantic. An estimated crowd of 10,000 mourners escorted his remains to the Church of St. Jean Baptiste on East Seventy-Sixth Street. Happily, Bourke Cockran had lived to see his life's dream become reality as the embryonic Irish Free State survived civil war to begin a precarious independence.[68]

Other vantage points open up different windows on the panoply of post-Famine city political culture and its relationship with Ireland. The establishment of an Irish Republican Campaign Club in June 1868 aimed to generate identification with a party other than the Democrats, despite the rather more obvious advantages of the Democratic affiliation. Meeting in the Republican Central Committee building, the Club counted several hundred prominent Irish members intent on propagating the evils of corruption identified with Tammany. From the security of a Republican anti-graft platform, the club called for Irish support on August 19, 1868 in an "Appeal to Irish Citizens" promoting a Republican agenda in the run-up to the presidential election. Emphasizing the negative effects of Democratic support, the Appeal challenged that by voting Democrat, Irish New Yorkers "deprive Ireland of the active sympathy and aid of hundreds of thousands of enlightened and generous-hearted Americans." Incendiary pronouncements that continued Tammany support would "cause their own efforts on behalf of her liberation to be regarded with suspicion and distrust by intelligent men everywhere" ought to have hit home with Vincent de Paul and Catholic Club members, for example, seeking a more conservative political platform. Recommending the Republican Party as the choice of freedom-loving supporters of American liberty, the appeal included a special invocation of Catholic and Protestant martyrs as role models for Irish New Yorkers.[69]

Newly emerging "Grant Clubs" attracted a limited degree of support from the same sources. Declaring for Grant and Colfax in September 1868, *The Irish People's* endorsement of a Gaelic-Republican agenda generated some momentum, while Republican meetings emblazoned with banners proclaiming "Irishmen by Birth, Americans by Adoption" drew respectable crowds to the Cooper Institute. As hopes ran high for the Tweed downfall, Denis F. Burke and Daniel J. Hogan as president and secretary of the Republican Club, respectively, represented the sector of the Irish population that wished to capitalize on the moment and:

> . . . assert its freedom of action, to emancipate itself from the control of the corrupt Democratic leaders who have used it for their own profit, and to act more in accordance with the independent spirit of Republican institutions and more in sympathy with the great body of the liberty-loving people of America. We desire the Irish-born voters in the country should appear, not as Irish, but as American voters. We desire that they should act, not at the bidding of priests and politicians, but according to the dictates of their own judgment and conscience. We desire that they should vote not from bigotry and prejudice, but with intelligence and knowledge.[70]

The businessmen inaugurating the Irish American Republican Club of New York in June 1889 continued on the road to "enhance their political rights," as the Executive Committee statement outlined, but Irish Republicanism never amounted to more than an exclusive club in the late 1880s and early 1900s. The collapse of Liberal Republicanism with the death of Horace Greeley and the reorganization of the shattered Tammany by John Kelly managed to sustain the bulk of Irish support for the Democrats.[71]

The majority interests had risen to the fore in the New York system, whereas Republicanism represented the wealthy and was even charged with supporting a platform of "narrow bigotry and persistent intolerance."[72] As to be expected, the pragmatic appeal of the Democrats to immigrants seeking political agency held out. Across the Atlantic, long-standing efforts to institutionalize native representation had proven slow and frustrating. Building on that experience, the New York Irish mobilized as a constituency within the party structure most receptive to their agenda. In comparison with the relatively minor Republican association, though, Ireland's own nationalist representations arose to span a broad and colorful canvas. As the world's most important center of settlement in terms of population size, political muscle, and financial power, New York constituted the crucial source of support for the elements devoted to the struggle for independence. Delegations from all the major cohorts established New York world headquarters through the post-Famine era, including the Fenians, the Land League, Clan na Gael, and the Friends of Irish Freedom. As the first port of call for campaign leaders, New York rose as a crucial stop during the run-up to 1921 and the Treaty. Apart from the city's resource pool, suggestions to adopt American Revolution ideology as an inspirational foundation for the movement met with some success, as did the idea of requesting American pressure on Parliament to grand independence to Ireland.[73]

On the subject of the ubiquitous organizational affiliations and their relationships with home, prominent pundits such as Thomas D'Arcy McGee regularly issued missives to his city compatriots consisting of advice tempered with baleful warnings that made for interesting headlines. His counsel to immigrants in 1866 included the argument that settlers had created political conditions in the tenement wards of Lower Manhattan not dissimilar to those blotting the landscape of contemporary Ireland. The exchange of one form of socioeconomic oppression for another, he felt, could not be judged an improvement for the men and women living their lives in such deplorable conditions. Immigrants should seek out new "habits of discipline" in their adopted land, the foremost of these "habits" being the condition of "self-government." Lacking primary experience of governing in Ireland, they confined innate political skills to existing political structures and away from the idealization of self-government. In short, D'Arcy McGee judged that immigrant politicians had failed to capitalize on opportunities for autonomous power in New York, and their utilization of Tammany as a medium for their education was proof of inexperience within formal political structures.[74]

Writing in the 1860s, D'Arcy McGee anticipated the rise of purely *Irish* organizations enabling immigrants to access the political ladder. He would have been aware that in New York, the familiar cornerstones segregating Ireland's Catholic and Protestant cultural parameters were absent. Thus, Catholics were surely free to aim for the upward mobility just becoming available back home. There the old disparities between Catholic tenants and Protestant landlords reflected daily in a hundred ways, most graphically in images of the "Big House" dominating the physical and intellectual landscape. Symbolizing authority and power hallmarked by longevity and multi-generational control, even the "Protestant" aura of cypress trees in Anglican graveyards marked the boundaries between denominations.[75] But away from the cypresses of old and in the midst of an ever-expanding sea of commercial and political opportunity, post-Famine Irish organizations rooted their Catholic and Protestant parameters as foundations within which to entrench key traditions in a new urban context.

Most obviously, the Fenians and Clan na Gael represented the strands of radicalized affiliation most commonly identified with Catholics, yet espousing the legacy of the United Irishmen.[76] On the tide of numerical strength, the Brotherhood and Clan deployed a trademark romanticism to appeal to expatriates and generate founts of publicity. The core of journalists, labor activists, and scholars harboring militant plans and acerbic anti-English attitudes produced the John O'Mahonys, James Stephens's, and John Devoys so influential within the New York Irish cultural profile.[77] Devoting themselves to the goal of independence and considering American support and financial assistance critical to their aims, these men built on the foundations of popular agitation cultivated in Ireland in preceding decades. The Fenian story in New York is well told, its appeal couched within a romantic vision and a swashbuckling atmosphere surrounding Devoy and O'Leary. The conglomeration of patriotic elements during the 1850s constituted its bedrock; particularly the Irishmen's Civil and Military Republican Union, the Irish Alliance, and the Emmet Monument Association. The Fenians drew their name and inspiration from mythological Celtic warrior band *Na Fianna*, seeking repeal of the Union and utilizing local subunits or "circles" to imbue a military theme through the chain of command. Fenian "Circles" mushrooming across the East Coast by the early 1860s attracted broad support and rose parallel with the Irish Republican Brotherhood across the Atlantic.[78] A strong support base and effective local leadership made New York the logical Fenian headquarters.[79] As we have seen, while incarcerated in Tasmania during the early 1850s, John Mitchel emphasized his belief in the city as *the* international base of operations for the cause:

> After five or six years brooding in bondage, lying down every night in stifled wrath and shame, rising up each morning with an imprecation—a returning exile is prone to exaggerate the importance of all this to the world, to his country, even to himself. How can I expect to find men in New York, though they be banished Irishmen too; or in Ireland, though they be unhappy in not being banished—so full of these thoughts as I am . . . the very nation I knew in Ireland is broken and destroyed; and the place that knew it shall know it no more. To America has fled the half-starved remnant of it; and the phrase that I have heard of late, 'a new Ireland in America,' conveys no meaning to my mind. Ireland without the Irish—the

Irish out of Ireland—neither of these can be *our country*. Yet who can tell what the chances and changes of the blessed war may bring up?[80]

Despite the protestation, Mitchel would likely have welcomed "a new Ireland in America" at this point; but on arrival in New York he could at least take heart that the ill-fated 1848 riot back home had mobilized leaders for the new initiative.[81] By August 1860, IRB leaders assured their counterparts in New York of unqualified Dublin support.[82] Vague aspirations to topple English rule in Ireland left the 30,000 New York members achieving little consensus on an actual plan of campaign. As the "headquarters" in Moffat's Hotel became known as the "O'Mahony Republic," or alternatively as "Moffat's Pillbox," in the words of Thomas D'Arcy McGee—"so-called from a notorious maker of patent medicines who built it," all told, the mass meetings, rallies, picnics, and fundraising events raised the Fenian profile and, as we've seen earlier, Ellen A. Mahoney's Women's Auxiliary met weekly to join the effort.[83] All the activity moved Mr. Dooley to remark: "Be hivins, if Ireland could be freed by a picnic, it'd not on'y be free today, but an impire, be gorra."[84]

As momentum built toward the climactic "invasion of Canada" in 1866, Parliamentary concern over the prospect of armed rebellion prompted Member of Parliament Sir George Grey to call for "an effective blow at these schemes, which were discountenanced by the American Government." News of the steamer *Cuba* and suspected gun-running led Parliament to decide that the boat would be "considered a pirate by all naval powers, and if captured all her crew should be hanged."[85] The plan to attack Canada and draw England into conflict with the United States never left the starting blocks, and the bungled "invasion" halted momentum and disseminated supporters into a variety of alternative outlets.[86] With the benefit of hindsight in 1913, Rose McDermott argued that although the movement lasted less than two decades, Fenianism must be viewed as the foundation of radical nationalism in Irish-America. Expanding despite the opposition of middle-class constitutional-nationalists, conservative "practical politicians," and the British administration in Ireland, Fenianism cultivated "a triumph of the spirit" that lasted through to the 1910s. She emphasized that "it is due to that spirit that the country, as a country, has remained alive, instead of being swallowed up in Seonianism and loyalty, as she would have been, had the so-called practical politicians been given a free hand . . . if there is any fight still left in Ireland, to Fenianism more than anything else it is due.[87]

The slightly better-coordinated Clan na Gael swelled from Fenian ashes, claiming over 11,000 by 1877 headquartered in New York and overseeing smaller units in Boston, Philadelphia, and Chicago.[88] But again, failure to agree and even to maintain secrecy paralyzed the Clan, notwithstanding sporadic (and headline-generating) episodes along on the road to Home Rule.[89] As relations between

Ireland and Britain more visibly determined the volatile course of New York nationalism, Stephens, O'Mahony, Devoy, and Davitt mobilized thousands, recruited effectively among Civil War veterans attached to Irish units and regiments, raised significant sums, and publicized the city as the headquarters of an international movement. But divisiveness over tactics, funds, and leadership ultimately led to demise. Repeated attempts to merge the "three traditional currents of nineteenth-century Irish protest: the revolutionary republicanism of the Fenians, the efforts of parliamentary leaders like Charles Stewart Parnell to achieve home rule, and the social and economic struggles of the agrarian poor" never really took off. The 1880's accord known as the New Departure unified some of the factions for a short time under Devoy, Ford, and Davitt, but the unification collapsed following arson attacks in Britain and disunity over the nationalization of land in Ireland. Despite input from the Land League, the Knights of Labor, the Industrial Workers of the World, Henry George, and the support of Devoy's *Gaelic American* and Ford's *Irish World*, the New Departure did not venture too far.[90]

Fig 6.1: "The Irish Party," *Harper's New Monthly Magazine* (August 1887); courtesy of Cornell University Library, Making of America Digital Collection.

John Devoy's support often proved more troublesome than it was worth. His grumbling about disunity and disparaging references on the efforts of the Ladies Land League came across as ironic from a man who fueled much of the egocentric squabbling. The "noisy gong-beater" and head of "a crowd of brainless shouters," according to the secretary of the Irish National League of America, stirred up no end of conflict even when struggling against that very problem! Devoy's hardscrabble style also clashed with the polished oration of William Bourke Cockran, but kept the *Nation* frontman to the fore within the movement.[91]

With an eye to Parnellite fractionalization across the Atlantic, larger-than-life politico and old Fenian Jeremiah O'Donovan-Rossa hoped to convince warring leaders of the benefits of a more peaceable coexistence.[92] Corresponding with fellow-activist John Kearney around the turn of the century, O'Donovan-Rossa knew that internal divisions were preventing New York from exerting more direct influence over affairs in Ireland. The man who took Tweed's Senate seat in 1871 spent much of his time feted for his melodramatic poetry and a series of lengthy letters to Louis Napoleon on the state of France, but he was forced to agree with Kearney's assessment of Ireland's situation in 1902. "I have lost all hope for Motherland," Kearney wrote to O'Donovan-Rossa in June of that year. "'Irish societies' in New York,'" he continued, "are controlled for the use and benefit of Irish politicians *only*."[93]

O'Donovan-Rossa and Kearney were not the only ones confused about the main thrust of a most diffuse movement by the early 1900s. Rifts worsened a situation growing increasingly negative, to the point where it was not uncommon to have two branches of one organization unable to agree on the most basic agenda and frequently resorting to the courts as final arbiter. During one such instance, a member of the United Irish League in 1904 remarked: "time was . . . when the great city of New York was regarded as the first in the land in rendering substantial support to Irish political movements." By now, even neighborhood branches failed to hold together well enough to mount much in the way of an effective campaign. Although the aspiration to support the cause of Ireland's freedom remained strong into the early twentieth century, disunity over the gamut of tactics, fundraising, and allocation of funds to different strands within the movement undermined the effort as a whole.[94]

Overly ambitious agendas and frustration over the course of events back home haunted New York operatives through the post-Famine decades. The war over land administration and the scandal involving Member of Parliament Charles Stewart Parnell during the 1880s and 1890s undercut Davitt's Land League and successor the Irish National League.[95] Unable to sustain a viable support base in either New York or Ireland, the Ladies Land League also disintegrated, leaving women interested in the progress of the campaign variously affiliated among the surviving groups. Davitt addressed the negative atmosphere in correspondence with President

Theodore Roosevelt in 1905. Writing from Ireland on his return from the New York lecture circuit, Davitt informed Roosevelt that even hard-line loyalists to the Crown recognized that change was imminent. British authority had crumbled and a rise in emigration to America daily threatened to drain the lifeblood of Ireland when needed most. His plea to Roosevelt and the American government to support Home Rule expressed the fervent hope of leaders determined to pursue every avenue of assistance.[96]

But city activists spent many years from 1910 to 1920 in a quandary, obliged to follow the lead of counterparts in Ireland but in disagreement about how best to do that. In fact, since the demise of the New Departure in the early 1880s, the leadership found no other opportunity to guide the process from New York.[97] As a result, the course of events leading up to the 1921 Treaty entrenched the spotlight on Dublin, while a secondary role as a source of funding retained New York influence during these years. The 1916 effort to overthrow British authority, the establishment of a Dublin government apparatus in 1917, and the General Election in 1918 under Eamon De Valera left the New York contingents contributing support and financial assistance, but little else. By 1918, the city's Irish politicos had expended much time and energy striving to overcome the disappointments casting a dark shadow over the home connection.

As befitting Progressive-era reformist zeal, new groupings touted negotiation between Ireland and Britain as the best chance for full independence. The Irish National Federation of America, for example, mobilized in 1891 with New York physician and man of letters Thomas Addis Emmet at the helm. A grand-nephew of the revered Robert, Thomas Emmet lent name recognition and status to the organization that endorsed the Home Rule campaign but waxed and waned through the 1890s to recharge as the United Irish League of America (UILA) in 1901. With the support of Patrick Ford and the *World*, the rejuvenation spread the message so well that by 1903, 200 branches across America had raised more than $10,000.[98]

But the conflicting interests persisted. In 1901, for example, the UILA became incensed over a New York visit by a high-powered United Irish League delegation from Dublin, to include post-Parnell Irish Party leader John Redmond. Communication between New York and Dublin collapsed over protocol, and an ensuing media circus brought out an array of affiliates clamoring to host the deputation. The result was a counterproductive compromise that did nothing to further progress.[99] One pamphlet even outlined opposition to the new representatives under the title "The Citizens of New York."[100] Some years later, the passage of the Home Rule bill on the eve of the First World War temporarily raised the stock of the UILA, only to plummet again in 1916 after the Rising and the executions of the leaders.[101]

In its place, the stridency of the new Friends of Irish Freedom (FOIF) organization redirected the prow of the nationalist ship one more time in early 1916.
Developing out of one of the popular Irish race conventions held in New York in
March 1916, at which over 2,000 delegates from all over America came together
to discuss future plans, city judge Daniel F. Cohalan joined with John Devoy and
ex-Clan na Gaelers to supplant the UILA and marshal funds toward a new focus
for the cause. The FOIF Declaration of Principles and Policy aimed "to encourage
and assist any movement that will tend to bring about the National Independence
of Ireland," and anticipated formalized American intervention such that "Ireland
may be cut off from England and restored to her rightful place among the nations
of the earth." The organization claimed over 275,000 members between 1916 and
the 1920s throughout America, with at least 30,000 in New York alone.[102] As the
foremost republican organization during De Valera's fundraising drive to broker
independence from 1919 to 1920 and in the manner of each organization since the
1860s, these Friends mobilized tremendous support while dividing both leadership
and sympathizers on the very issue they sought to influence.

Conservative organizations with a less deterministic outlook also emerged,
and prospered by sustaining the same objectives they originated in Ireland. From a
mid-1700's origin as a unit of protection for priests amid Penal legislation, the
Ancient Order of Hibernians (AOH) spread through provincial Ireland, the plight
of the tenantry and the complexities of the land question according the Order a
timely political focus until conditions eased somewhat in the later nineteenth century. Less visionary than the United Irishmen or Young Irelanders, and seeking a
niche within the confluence of Church and politics underscoring the newly
emerging Catholic middle-class, the AOH operated successfully within conservative parameters. The American establishment of the group in 1836 fostered a similar comfort zone in the urban conclaves where the organization thrived.[103]

As we've seen, on the other side of the fence, the Orange Order and Protestant
Friends of Ireland defined their agendas within a non-Catholic yet still distinctly
Irish political culture.[104] For Protestants, involvement in these politicized organizations and also within Freemasonry preserved a heritage otherwise at risk within Irish
New York. The transplantation of Protestant traditions needed to sustain alongside
the more numerous and more visible Catholic-based public activities and, to this
end, Protestant nationalists could not be expected to harmonize with fellow-
Christian Fenians and Clan na Gaelers. That the Orange Order upheld an obligation to counteract "Irish Romanism and foreign Jesuitism united against them"
mobilized them at various junctures,[105] but in New York and in other American
urban centers, Protestants could afford to consider their immigrant experience dif-
ferently to their Catholic fellow countrymen. "Using Ireland as a mirror of America,"

as Ignatiev argued, "the meanest 'Protestant' was granted a status above the most exalted 'Catholic,'" and the notion that "Anglo-America" as "Ulster Writ Large" proved compelling to many activist Protestants.[106] As an expression of a successful strain operating outside the more mainstream Irish settlement parameters, the Order's efforts to delineate a proud heritage from competing notions of Irishness and cultivate a distinct Anglo-American agenda paid off during the post-Famine era.

As the city offered a different perspective to each of Ireland's "cultures," the press and pamphlet literature highlighted some of the key features distinguishing them. Declan Kiberd's reflection that "if England had never existed, the Irish would have been rather lonely," helps elucidate this point. "Each nation," he went on, "badly needed the other, for the purpose of defining itself."[107] A post-Famine case regarding the traditions of the Shamrock and the Lily articulated by a prominent Irish-American voice encompassed a similar understanding. Briefly in New York before moving to Canada in the 1860s to serve as Minister for Agriculture and Emigration, Thomas D'Arcy McGee remarked in 1866 that "in Toronto one extreme [of Irish settlement] is made auxiliary to the other; Orangeism has been made the pretext of Fenianism, and Fenianism is doing its best to justify and magnify Orangeism."[108] This model characterized New York as the ideologies developed side by side, clashing verbally and even physically at various junctures along the way. During the Orange riots, for example, a conservative editorial pulled no punches in addressing such an odd situation. Thundering that the 1871 fracas marked "the formal transfer to American soil of one of the most ferocious, baleful quarrels of the Old World," *The Nation* recognized that the divide persisted because neither entity was prepared to leave its agenda behind in Ireland. Transplantation meant conveyance of a clash borne for centuries in an isolated and economically precarious native land.[109] The Orangemen, the Protestant Friends, the Freemasons, and the radical nationalists transported their political texts in the same way the Fenians, the Clan, the Land League, the Friendly Sons of Saint Patrick, Cumann na mBan, and the other groups worked to resolve the tangled history across the Atlantic.

There is no doubt that the press sustained and even exacerbated partitions within the transplanted agendas. Devoy acknowledged the reality of a culture divided across religious lines umpteen times in his own *Irish People* and *Gaelic American* newspapers. He concluded in 1881 that:

> We print in another column a brief notice of a sermon by Rev. Mr. Jubb, agent for the Irish Evangelical Society. He suggests a deep religious awakening as the panacea for Ireland's woes. We won't quarrel with Mr. Jubb or anyone else about religion, but we would like to remind our readers of the excellent maxim attributed to Cromwell; 'Put your trust in God, my boys, but keep your powder dry.'[110]

The columns of the Devoy-influenced press regularly hearkened back to darker chapters of Ireland's past, in particular the parceling out of Munster and Leinster farms and commonage to English adventurers, courtiers, and favored landlords. Almost incapable of writing on the Irish question without reference to sixteenth-century seeds of destruction sown by English imperialist policy, Patrick Ford devoted a section of his 1915 publication *The Criminal History of the British Empire* to a typical diatribe on the allocation of land to English noblemen. The situation "stands unparalleled in the history of the inhabited world," Ford railed against the Lord Romneys, the Lord Albermarles, and the Lord Athlones who received thousands of acres of prime Irish land either for "services rendered," or "for which no motive is assigned in the letters patent."[111] Ford's diatribes provided grist to the mill of the Congregational Home Missionary Society in reflections such as its 1904 *Foreign Elements in American Civilization.* Missionary superintendent Reverend H. A. Schauffler, D.D. directed his views against Catholics, arguing that the speed with which certain sections of the immigrant population organized to further their own ends constituted a terrifying prospect for New York's "Protestant churches." Reverend Schauffler quoted prominent Presbyterian Dr. Parkhurst in addressing questions of political and social corruption as the legacy of less civilized immigrant groups. The stronger the Catholic Church, the more deplorable the socioeconomic state of the country, Dr. Parkhurst maintained, as he castigated Tammany Hall as "the secular side of the Catholic Church."[112]

From another vantage point, society wordsmith Sir Shane Leslie weighed in with a 1919 take on Ireland's relationship with Britain and the highly charged New York Protestant-Catholic divisions. In a chapter entitled "Carson and Casement," Leslie compared prominent representatives from the two traditions from Ireland (in keeping with nationalist convolutions, Edward Carson as the embodiment of Ulster Unionism hailed not from the northern stronghold of Ulster but from Galway in the "to hell or to Connacht" west of Ireland, whereas Ulsterman Roger Casement would succeed to the title of republican martyr!). Accidents of birth did not prevent each man striving toward opposing ends of the political spectrum. Carson led the Ulster Unionist party before a stint as Lord of the Admiralty and inclusion in the 1916 Lloyd George Cabinet. The well-known tale of Casement's resistance and execution for supplying German arms to the republican cause in 1914 exalted him alongside the Tones and Emmets already glorified in nationalist sainthood. Leslie concluded that:

Though history will probably decide that each lost, they acquired a world-wide notoriety, composed for them equally by the execration and adulation of the press. In America Carson is thought of as the cold, lantern-jawed Junker, whose power and pull enabled him to import arms into Ulster without incurring any more serious consequences than being caged in the Cabinet, while Casement is arrayed as the fervid Celt who followed his example, but was arrested and hung before he could get a single gun into Ireland.

Sir Shane concluded that "each . . . was in his way playing the great game that never ends on Irish soil," transplanted almost intact onto the streets of New York in virtually unavoidable sectarian conglomerations.[113]

All in all, it is clear that politically-based divisions between "the green and orange essentialists"[114] guaranteed separatism and the perpetuation of centuries-old antagonism in Irish New York. Catholic cornerstones of faith, class, and national-ism(s) prospered on the new urban platform even as the smaller-scale Protestant population entrenched less visible and less populist representations. Their religious affiliation accorded them a relatively sanguine introduction into their new world, but their organizations delineated a diverse political culture characterized by the issues and divisions confronted on a daily basis in Ireland. As reflective of the homeland they cast away from, adherence to the old antagonisms constituted a com-mon denominator of sorts between the two faith-based traditions.

By 1921, the Government of Ireland Act that created the Free State and con-solidated six northern counties within the United Kingdom redrew the political map. Now that Home Rule had become a reality, Irish Protestants faced a turning point as British citizens in the North or a minority interest in the largely Catholic Free State. A speech by English literature professor Joseph Dunn to the Friendly Sons of Saint Patrick in 1921 resonated with anticipation for the future at a point in time when men and women of all political stripes witnessed the end of the old order in Ireland and a corresponding end in New York, and the dawn of a new era on both sides of the Atlantic. Dr. Dunn's romanticized address avoided direct engagement with the repercussions of the formal partition. "Out of self-respect, then," he remarked, in a lecture entitled "The Irish Consciousness," "if for no other reason, we ought to be proud of our Celtic stock, jealously guard the distinctive properties of our race and protest against the forgetfulness that threatens to invade them." In order to reap the benefits of such pride, the professor concluded, the Friendly Sons "Celtic stock" in New York ought to cultivate a detailed knowledge of Irish histo-ry. That this body of knowledge would include a study of Protestant-Catholic dif-ference over the centuries is left to another day, as is the notion that the flowery romanticism of "Celtic heritage" reflected any of the hard political realities of Partition.[115]

But Dunn put words on the status of the New York Irish identity at this land-mark juncture. In reminding his audience of "the distinctive properties of our race," he might have been talking about the Irish mosaic created in New York over the post-Famine decades, a condensed replica of a tumultuous history played out in writ-ings, artistic renderings, speechmaking, organizing, and publishing. Dunn knew that the breadth of Irish social and political culture covered a wide spectrum. He might have enjoyed a measure of contentment that almost a century later, the Irish culture in the city still references the small island to the east as it persistently seeks new directions for the history of the Irish in Ireland, the Irish in New York, and Irish-American history in general.

Conclusion

For the men and women either relegating to the past the label "immigrant" but sufficiently connected to the ancestral homeland as second or even third generation New Yorkers to sustain an "Irish" identification, the 1921 turning point is symbolized in the persona of Eamon de Valera.[1] If nothing else, the mathematics professor, 1916 leader, and President of the newly declared "independent republic" since 1919 formalized the city's role within Ireland's crusade for an end to British rule.[2] His personal stamp upon the favored New World center encompassed more than mere fundraising. The signing of the Government of Ireland Act in 1921 marked a simultaneous turning point on both sides of the Atlantic; for Irish New Yorkers, Dev's mission to the city confirmed the final flowering of a long-standing connection at a critical juncture, and back in Ireland, New York's promise as the capstone of international support inculcated valuable material and psychological assurance at a point when it was sorely needed. The city's relevance as an Irish stronghold shifted into high gear, emerging from the clubs and halls and newspapers and neighborhoods into the glare of international publicity with the contingent's arrival.

The leaders of the new Ireland put much store by New York's potential to shore up a fragile new political structure. By the same token, the lengthy visit that stretched from June 1919 to December 1920 conferred a welcome measure of national pride on a culture much assimilated, yet obviously retaining its immigrant quality. In confirming the city's status as the center of operations, de Valera personified both a romanticized nationalist consciousness and the starker realities facing what would become the new Free State in 1922 upon Dail approval. Irish New York came of age as a new independence rose from the tangled web of decades past, 3,000 miles eastward. The years of activism and the constant work toward this point finally paid off.[3] The community still bearing the immigrant stamp could draw a measure of pride that its efforts were being marked in such a forthright manner. In effect, the first phase in the creation of their new urban identity had ended on a positive note. With de Valera came the realization of self-confidence not only as a constituency of value, but in solidification as true Irish Americans. The path to this point had incorporated the entire panoply of settlement; the men and women living and working and expressing themselves within the cultural reminders of home and institutionalizing the linchpins of a new culture: part Ireland, part New York; just like Dev himself.

De Valera's fateful birth in the city marked the beginning of a remarkable life. The details are still in dispute; but by all accounts he entered the world in the Nursery and Children's Hospital on Lexington Avenue at Fifty-First Street on October 14, 1882, born to the young Catherine Coll of Bruree, County Limerick. Less well established is the identity of the boy's father, but a Spanish artist by the name of Juan Vivion de Valera who died two years after his son's birth is widely credited as the man in question. Following Juan Vivion's death, Kate Coll's decision to send her son back to her homeplace in Ireland to be raised by his maternal grandmother and her extended family evokes images of the hand of destiny at work in the young boy's life.[4] The birth details took on real significance as de Valera faced execution by the British authorities for his role in the Dublin rebellion. Four hundred fifty deaths and over 2,000 injuries in April 1916 attracted worldwide attention, but the execution of fifteen leaders focused an international spotlight on Dublin (in an unwelcome fashion, from the Crown's perspective) and turned the tide of public sympathy toward the rebels.

De Valera's battalion command made headlines on both sides of the Atlantic in April and May 1916, as Irish New York daily followed the details of his arrest and subsequent sentencing. His American citizenship forced the British to commute de Valera's sentence to life imprisonment, while his martyred comrades took their places on the nationalist honor roll for posterity.[5] Although Dev's accession to power remained steady, controversy surrounding his leadership accelerated throughout the 1910s. A number of organizations doubted he would succeed in guaranteeing Ireland's independence; notably the Friends of Irish Freedom. But symbolizing the dawn of a new era and embodying the fulfillment of lifelong aspirations for the tens of thousands retaining more than just fond memories of their ancestral homeland, the tall, bespectacled teacher-turned-soldier seemed to present the best hope of implementing the new independence. The old Fenians, Clan na Gaelers, Cumann na mBan members, Land Leaguers, the Vincent de Paul faithful, and the whole gamut of concerned Irish New Yorkers joined with the people of Ireland in marking a milestone anticipated for many a long year. It was never a perfect resolution of an age-old question. Compromised by Partition, with twenty-six counties out of thirty-two constituting the new Eire, the diminished republican dream that ushered in Ireland's most significant redirection since the 1801 Act of Union would spark a tragic civil war and prolonged antagonism in the years to come.[6]

The legacy of freedom had not come easily to Irish New York. Between 1801 and 1921, the Famine watershed constituted perhaps *the* vital connection between New York and Ireland. Had it not occurred in all its ferocity, a healthy representation of Catholic Ireland would doubtless have joined Protestant compatriots in the city during the latter decades of the nineteenth century. But its onslaught exerted such a dramatic impact on both sides of the Atlantic that two cultures restructured in the wake of its force. As Ireland lost upward of three million people, New York gained a quarter million by the 1850s as a direct result. Although this new Irish-American culture failed to organize the strands of discord into a unilateral agenda, much else was accomplished by 1921. Famine survivors, middle-class entrepreneurs, and men and women attracted to different dimensions of the city experience availed of the new windows of opportunity open to them. So many of them sought to escape the dreariness and anonymity at the lower end of the economic scale that they succeeded in illuminating the road to self-identity with social, cultural, and political influences transported with them. Despite a number of significant parallel progressions, the city promised much that Ireland could not or would not for at least another century, and made good on that promise for a significant proportion of women. A measure of independence and a degree of political involvement more immediately available than in Dublin or Belfast or Cork, for example, opened up an exciting world, despite retaining the class-based, political and cultural parameters of contemporary Ireland. Implanting a complex Irishness steeped in the weight of the past into the brash opportunism of New York worked well for many immigrant women, for whom preservation of their ancestral heritage proved possible through a variety of avenues of expression. As different sectors of the population guaranteed the longevity of their imprint on New York's immigrant world, the dual nature of New York Irish identity institutionalized the old heritage within the contemporary milieu.

From the strongholds of Ulster and the prosperous farmland of the Midlands, quieter Protestant settlers entrenched the cultural totems of their communities of origin. Skilled Presbyterian and Methodist craftsmen and enterprising merchants attracted to the uniformity and solidarity of Masonry propagated a steady work ethic, while Loyalists transferring their distinct Orange heritage occasionally displayed a radicalized agenda distanced from their compatriots consorting with the fíor-Gaelic struggle for independence. While the Protestant Friends of Ireland supported the nationalist agenda, other groupings mobilized in favor of maintaining direct rule from London. As such, they exerted influence within the formulation of the city identity, and supported the Protestant Irish at home through organizational and community-based connections. Whether long established in the city or arriving in tandem with their more populous Roman-affiliated compatriots, Irish Protestants occupied specific niches and cultivated distinct cultures of expression within the panoply of Irish New York, and their success in institutionalizing their cornerstones alongside those of their countrymen and women accorded them an automatic role in the creation of the Irish-American character. To imagine an Irish-American character lacking the manifold Protestant influence is to generate a false impression. The new identity developed in New York by 1921 reflected each dimension of the variegated landscaping underpinning it.

Large-scale institutionalization occasionally overshadowed another window into Ireland's new metropolitan identity. As conspicuous as the stonework of churches or the self-inflicted associations with Tammany, the writings and rhetoric of Irish New York expressed rich veins beneath the trumpeting of the party faithful. Both genders resorted to the city press and organizational networks to document their experience in a land not so much foreign as physically distant from the focus of their attention. Empowering writers, speechmakers, politicians, and commentators to give vent to emotions running deeper than popular expressions such as St. Patrick's Day parades or County fairs, the personal nature of this output laid bare the investment in mapping a new identity within the words and forms of the old. The poetry, songs, and stories published and read in New York generated sources of expression for men and women beyond the formalized organizations, prioritizing Ireland's freedom and enshrining the politically tempestuous post-Famine decades for posterity. In particular, the Gaelic-sourced press enabled readers to actively participate in the construction of their own identity. Sharing their words in newspapers, personal memoranda, private correspondence, and archaic works quaint and charming and often long-winded and overwrought, supported the foundation for a new-found Irish-American essence as few other activities could.

For the majority, the best of the Devotional innovations entrenched a traditionally minded community Catholic Church structure. Defined by transatlantic class structures, energized by the arrival of tens of thousands of mid century members, and politicized quite radically at times, the Church adapted sufficiently well to its new surroundings to sponsor a major component of the identity. Likewise, the traditional political affiliations took root as a solid platform from which to stake identity. Filled with aspirations toward the ideal of a free Ireland, and in many cases consumed with a romanticized sense of destiny, New York Irish political support mobilized parallel organizations, disseminated information on developments between Dublin and London, and provided a crucial financial foundation. The influence of high-profile politicians, activist editors, authors, and assorted professionals intent on furthering the independence process also predominated. Collectively, the New York Irish prioritized the fate of their ancestral land and influenced the road to independence in many ways as profoundly as any city in Ireland.

As the dream of independence dominated the different Irish layers evident in post-Famine New York, the question arises as to whether this ever-present agenda stifled some dimensions of immigrant potential even as it mobilized toward a positive end. No doubt it did, but the tradition-bound and progressive, patriarchal and female-centered nationalisms nurtured within the city's political landscape could at least derive satisfaction from their role in brokering the identity and maintaining such a long-standing Atlantic World connection with home.

And they did take pride in their achievement. By 1921, the former immigrants arrived at a watershed of note. Not tragic in the way of the Famine, yet especially troubling to the hardliners, the homeland's new status brought Irish New Yorkers to the end of the first era in their history. In the same manner that Frederick Jackson Turner called the end of the first period in American history with the demise of the Frontier, the New York Irish reached a corresponding milestone in 1921.[7] The stream of Colonial pioneers, including Scotch-Irish, Anglicans, Methodists, and Catholics, left an Ireland in the throes of political upheaval, rebellion, and economic insecurity. Little had changed by the 1840s, as the Famine overturned that steady progression and foisted enormous change within the culture relocating across the ocean. But as the struggle for independence reached its climax, the appearance of a leader and survivor of 1916 personified the qualities of survival, stability, and immense hope for the future for the Irish Americans of New York, even as he purported to lead Ireland into a new era.[8]

The gathering of some of the most influential names in the transatlantic context provided de Valera a suitable mobilization point in 1919, engaging him with Bourke Cockran and Sir Shane Leslie in July of that year as a precursor to the contingent of powerful politicians and public representatives he would encounter over the following months.[9] Openly sparring with the powerful Daniel Cohalan and the Friends of Irish Freedom, but reaping the benefits of Joseph McGarrity's experience in the founding of rival organization the American Association for the Recognition of the Irish Republic, it was not all smooth sailing for de Valera in New York.[10] But the highlights kept him and the imminent sense of new beginnings in the spotlight. As Mayor John Francis Hylan, known as "Red Mike," granted de Valera the Freedom of the City in a ceremony at City Hall on January 17, 1920, the honor seemed to solidify the sense of self-determination for the thousands who followed every step of the visit.[11] Under the heading "Hylan and Sinn Fein in $10,000,000 Drive: Mayor Gives City's Freedom to De Valera and Godspeed to His Financial Ambition," *The New York Times* caught the atmosphere of the day and the point in time:

> Under the stirring influence of the martial lays of nine Irish pipers, made doubly martial perhaps by the old Gaelic dagger sticking out of the green plaid halfhose of one of the pipers, a national drive to obtain 10,000,000 American dollars to set up "the elected Government of the Republic of Ireland" was opened yesterday at the City Hall . . . The campaign, which is to be conducted by the American Commission on Irish Independence and is to be continued until the last cent is obtained, was launched by Eamonn de Valera, who at the call of the Sinn Fein became "President" of Ireland. Professor de Valera got the freedom of the city from Mayor Hylan, and beamed delightedly as the Mayor sanctioned the Sinn Fein movement, in a speech in the Aldermanic chambers, where, it seems only yesterday, the Prince of Wales heard so many nice things said to him. And, as the last words of Dr. de Valera rolled out a booming response to the Mayor's sentiments, 40,000 volunteer workers, like an east wind off Bantry, sprang up throughout the city and set out to sell the bond certificates.[12]

Even as de Valera won hearts and dollars, the hierarchy aligned with the success story unfolding from the momentous visit. In a detailed letter to William Bourke Cockran in January 1920, Archbishop Patrick Hayes did more than merely endorse de Valera. Placing his personal sympathies and financial support behind the Long Fellow and his ideals, he enclosed a private contribution of $1000 to the cause. Pleased with his "very satisfactory conference with Mr. Eamon de Valera, President of the Irish Republic," Hayes came away convinced that his "program for the agricultural, industrial, and commercial development of Ireland is entirely practical and constructive." Dev's stately and pious bearing would have made a favorable impression on the Archbishop as he waxed lyrical to Bourke Cockran on the imminent joy of independence; "Erin's long and unbroken dream of racial emancipation awakens to the dawn of fulfillment." Further, Archbishop Hayes went on, New York and America could not but appreciate how Ireland's "exiled children . . . have figured as material, moral and spiritual builders for good nearly everywhere—hard toilers, patriotic citizens, and zealous missionaries." He could trust that "the dying hope of the Celtic soul for freedom under Ireland's own skies and by her own waters" had finally arrived. Two further pages on Ireland's prospects as one of the great free nations of the earth concluded with a thought sure to gratify de Valera, further antagonize the FOIF, and amuse the liberal-minded Bourke Cockran. "With these world facts before us," Hayes finished, "Ireland should be welcomed as one of the most conservative forces of our distressed times."[13]

On behalf of a group that certainly appreciated the spotlight on New York but raised significant issues regarding de Valera's ability to lead Ireland forward, Edward J. McSweeney noted in January 1920 that de Valera really represented "the Irish in

Ireland," whereas FOIF chief Daniel Cohalan stood as "the leader of Americans of Irish blood in America, and represents the interests, aspirations and loyalty of twenty million citizens of this country."[14] Therein lay the turn. The New York Irish had arrived at the moment where they could finally shift away from the numbing pressures of their ancestral homeland's turbulent history and look to a future where the old divisions could gradually meld into the past. Not settled to the satisfaction of everyone, undoubtedly, but the fact that the new Free State achieved greater autonomy in 1921 than the years and even centuries previously, constituted the point of diversion for the inhabitants of Ireland and the men and women of ethnic Irish New York. Boisterous nationalist adherences could enjoy a degree of respite; diffident Protestants could anticipate continued affiliation with the Crown and Parliament within the Northern Ireland state and the proposed Dominion status, and the less politically invested could envision a time when Ireland would finally progress beyond division and dissent.

Bound by the Famine at one end and the Treaty at the other, the Atlantic World connections had facilitated the propagation of Ireland's culture in America. Within that propagation, the deep-rooted political agenda dominated the unfolding of an identity originating out of two sources. What had emerged by 1921? As a hybrid, the New York Irish identity had evolved under the weight of the old as it absorbed the imprint of the new. A tree with many branches, expansive enough to include the different facets of Irishness, but distinct enough to retain an overall uniqueness in a cosmopolitan American city, the identity materialized as an expression of the Atlantic World that produced it.

De Valera knew well the value of transatlantic support for the fledgling Free State. Appealing to the city as the fount of that support, he recognized an entity that had been in development up to that point but now conferred with a new status and legitimacy. No ceremony marked that point in time, and no formalization would commemorate the achievement of the new status, but the flashbulbs and column inches that accompanied de Valera's work in New York served to establish New York Irish identity as an independent entity in its own right and as a recognizable component within the larger Irish-American constituency. As a participant and survivor of the 1916 Rising, his stature rose among the more militant-minded; as a conservative Catholic professional, he won support among the less radicalized and the hierarchy so that the combined power of his leadership, the strength of FOIF efforts, and the operations of thousands of volunteers collectively raised several million dollars, generated international publicity for the new Free State, and brought the concept of the new identity into the mainstream.[15]

The sale of bond certificates accelerated through 1919 and 1920 to envelop the identity in a cloud of success and the allure of the dynamic. As 1921 and the Treaty empowered the Irish to offload some of the cultural baggage, safe in the knowledge that their efforts provided essential support for the most worthy of causes, de Valera's return to Ireland on a sea of New York affirmation provides a fitting conclusion for an exploration into the world of the city Irish. In one way or another, most of them could identify with one aspect or another of his mission. A poem by Trinity College professor of poetry Brendan Kenneally written six weeks before the end of de Valera's long life in 1975 documented the President's legacy on both sides of the Atlantic in a tone evocative of Dev's sparse, upright style. Entitled "De Valera at Ninety-Two," the lines "Here was a search for harmony, The thrill of difficulty, The possibility of solution,[16]" encapsulates the sense of prospect wrought by 1921.

Had Dev remained in New York, he would probably have risen to the challenge of operating within the competing political visions and observing the class distinctions and the religious differences ebbing and flowing within his own ethnic community. He would have seen the cornerstones of his heritage work in tandem with opportunities for prosperity to produce a broad Irish jurisdiction in the 1920s.[17] Had he watched the lead-up to 1921 from the city skyline, he would probably applaud the end of the long Home Rule campaign, the relegation to the past of the horrors of Famine, and a new beginning as inheritors of a free nation.[18]

In January 1921, as the ink dried on the Government of Ireland Act, *The Sinn Feiner* ran advertisements to promote the new Free State.[19] In between notices for "The Kind of Tea They Use in Ireland," with customers urged to "Refuse Substitutes," notices commanded readers to purchase stickers, buttons, posters, flags, and all manner of paraphernalia to "Show That You Demand the Recognition of the Irish Republic." One notice carried an illustration of a button that could be ordered in bulk from the manufacturer, carrying the legend "Recognize the Republic of Ireland" in "brilliant green, orange and white." The button's purpose was to "force the public and Congress to recognize the fact that Recognition of the Irish Republic is demanded by hundreds of thousands of upright red-blooded men and women of this country." To reassure skeptics, the notice guaranteed that "it is ALL union made, by an Irish firm."

The manufacturer, Bannister Company, informed readers to "WEAR IT," and "have every friend and member of your family wear one, every man and woman in your council or union, every pupil in your school, every parishioner in your church, every member of your lodge or club," etc. The minimum order was fifty buttons for $1 but optimistically, readers could order up to 10,000 for $85, should they so wish![20] Whether on buttons or badges, in stump speeches or the poetry of exile, Catholic or Protestant, affluent or struggling, Irish New Yorkers had given voice to a set of hopes and dreams and aspirations through the post-Famine decades. Most of them were realized in 1921 at the crossroads between the forces that had shaped them for better or for worse in Ireland, and those that continued the process in Irish New York.

Notes

Introduction

1. On John Quinn's friendships with Yeats, Maud Gonne, and Picasso, see Alan Himber, ed., *The Letters of John Quinn to William Butler Yeats* (Ann Arbor, Michigan: University of Michigan Press, 1983) and Janis and Richard Londraville, eds., *The Letters of Maud Gonne and John Quinn: Too Long a Sacrifice* (Selinsgrove, PA: Susquehanna University Press, 1999). Benjamin Reid's biography of Quinn, *The Man From New York: John Quinn and his Friends* (New York: Oxford University Press, 1968) remains useful.

2. Typed letter from John Quinn to Seamas O'Brien from 31 Nassau Street, New York, February 24, 1915; Seamas O'Brien Papers, Box 1, Folder 7, American Irish Historical Society, New York.

3. Immigration history and evocative titles go hand in hand: Oscar Handlin's *The Uprooted: The Epic Story of the Great Migrations That Made the American People* (1951; Philadelphia: University of Pennsylvania Press, 2001); John Higham, *Strangers in the Land, Patterns of American Nativism 1860–1925* (1955; New York: Atheneum, 1963); and John Bodnar, *The Transplanted: A History of Immigrants in Urban America* (Bloomington: Indiana University Press, 1985), constitute examples.

4. The work of Andrew Greeley and John Corry's *Golden Clan: The Murrays, the McDonnells & the Irish American Aristocracy* (Boston: Houghton Mifflin, 1977) provide popular background. See also John Canon O'Hanlon's two-volume *Irish-American History of the United States* (New York: Murphy Publishers, 1907), and Stephen Birmingham's *Real Lace: America's Irish Rich* (New York: Harper & Row, 1973).

5. Lawrence McCaffrey, *The Irish Diaspora in America* (Bloomington: Indiana University Press, 1976); and his essay "Diaspora Comparisons and Irish-American Uniqueness" in *New Perspectives*

on the Irish Diaspora, ed., Charles Fanning (Carbondale and Edwardsville: Southern Illinois University Press, 2000), pp. 15–27. Quotation, p.17. Kerby Miller's work is vital, starting with the commanding *Emigrants and Exiles: Ireland and the Irish Exodus to North America* (New York: Oxford University Press, 1985). Edward T. O'Donnell has written authoritatively on the Irish-American field in "How the Irish Became Urban," *Journal of Urban History* 25, no. 2 (January 1999): pp. 271–286.

6. Arthur Gribben, ed., *The Great Famine and the Irish Diaspora in America* (Amherst: University of Massachusetts Press, 1999), and James S. Donnelly's *The Great Irish Potato Famine* (Stroud, Gloucestershire: Sutton Publishing, 2001–02) provide fresh insight into Famine impact. See Timothy J. Meagher's *Inventing Irish America: Generation, Class and Ethnic Identity in a New England City, 1880–1928* (Indiana: Notre Dame University Press, 2001), especially Introduction, pp. 4–6; also standards such as Dennis Clark, *Hibernia America: The Irish and Regional Cultures* (New York: Greenwood Press, 1986), and William V. Shannon's *The American-Irish* (New York: Macmillan, 1963).

7. Essential reading includes the contributions of Thomas Brown, Steven P. Erie, Florence Gibson, George Reedy, and Francis M. Carroll to the field, cited in the following chapters and Bibliography.

8. See the work of Denis Tilden Lynch, Harold F. Gosnell, and Lothrop Stoddard for interesting background ; also Jerome Mushkat's coverage of city politics and Daniel Czitrom's "Underworlds and Underdogs: Big Tim Sullivan and Metropolitan Politics in New York, 1889–1913," *Journal of American History* 78 (September 1991): pp. 536–558.

9. Marianne Elliott's *Wolfe Tone: Prophet of Irish Independence* (New Haven: Yale University Press, 1989) and similarly related work is required reading.

10. On the centrality of this focus, see John Ridge's entry "New York City," in Michael Glazier, ed., *The Encyclopedia of the Irish in America* (South Bend, Indiana: Notre Dame University Press, 1999), pp. 678–686; and Terry Golway's entry on New York Irish mayors, pp. 686–688.

11. Lawrence McCaffrey, "Irish Textures in American Catholicism," *Catholic Historical Review* LXXVIII (January 1992): pp. 13–14.

12. The literature is copious, but see particularly Jay Dolan, *The Immigrant Church, New York's Irish and German Catholics* (Baltimore: Johns Hopkins University Press, 1975); Timothy Meagher, ed., *Urban American Catholicism, The Culture and Identity of The American Catholic People* (New York: Garland, 1988); and the work of, among others, Colleen McDannell, John Newsinger, Dolores Liptak, and Paul Blanshard on this topic.

13. McCaffrey, "Irish Textures," *Catholic Historical Review* LXXVIII (January 1992), pp. 13–14.

14. Cardinal Paul Cullen's "Devotional Revolution" proposed increased emphasis on education, scripture, and the canons of Catholicism and sought to minimize the influence of folk-based religious practice. Emmet Larkin's "The Devotional Revolution in Ireland, 1850–1875," *American Historical Review* 77 (June 1972): pp. 625–652 remains standard. Linkages between Irish ethnicity and Catholicism and the identification of "Irish" ethnicity with Catholicism permeate the scholarship; see particularly the work of McCaffrey, Dolan, Liptak, and Meagher, cited above.

15. Meagher, *Inventing Irish America*, pp. 14, 16. As an example, see Thomas H. O'Connor, *The Boston Irish: A Political History* (Boston: Little, Brown & Co., 1997).

16. It was not until the mid-1990s and Ronald H. Bayor and Timothy J. Meagher's *The New York Irish: Essays Toward a History* (Baltimore: Johns Hopkins University Press, 1995) that the city achieved deserved prominence within the Irish-American canon.

17. See Robert E. Park and Ernest W. Burgess, *Introduction to the Science of Sociology* (1921; Chicago: University of Chicago Press, 1969); Louis Wirth, "The Problem of Minority Groups," in Ralph

Linton, ed., *The Science of Man in the World Crisis* (New York: Columbia University Press, 1945); the work of Lloyd Warner, Leo Srole, and Milton Gordon, and Marcus Lee Hansen, *The Atlantic Migration* (Cambridge, Mass.: Harvard University Press, 1940). Nathan Glazer and Daniel Patrick Moynihan, *Beyond the Melting Pot: The Negroes, Puerto Ricans, Jews, Italians and Irish of New York City* (Cambridge, Mass.: M.I.T. Press, 1970) still harbors points of interest.

18. See Oscar Handlin's *Children of the Uprooted* (New York: G. Braziller, 1966), and his *Boston's Immigrants: A Study in Acculturation* (Cambridge, Mass.: Harvard University Press, 1941), and John Higham's *Send These To Me: Jews and Other Immigrants in Urban America* (New York: Atheneum, 1975).

19. Bodnar, *The Transplanted*, p. xx.

20. Ewa Morawska posits some interesting ideas on these constructs in "The Sociology and Historiography of Immigration," in Virginia Yans-McLoughlin, ed., *Immigration Reconsidered: History, Sociology and Politics* (New York: Oxford University Press, 1990), pp. 187–238. Quotation, p. 189.

21. Meagher, *Inventing Irish America*, p. 6.

22. Forum, "Race, Religion and Nationality in American Society: A Model of Ethnicity—From Contact to Assimilation," Elliot R. Barkan, in *Journal of American Ethnic Studies* 14, no. 2 (Winter 1995): pp. 38–75, with comments from Rudolph J. Vecoli, Richard D. Alba, and Olivier A. Zunz. See also the idea of "The Past as Present," in T. Alexander Aleinikoff's "A Multicultural Nationalism?" in *The American Prospect* 36 (January/February 1998): pp. 80–86. Russell A. Kazal, Review Article, "Revisiting Assimilation: The Rise, Fall, and Reappraisal of a Concept in American Ethnic History," in *American Historical Review* 100, No. 2 (April 1995): pp. 437–471. Quotation, p. 471.

23. Elliot R. Barkan, Jon Gjerde, and Erike Lee's "Comment: Searching for Perspectives: Race, Law, and the Immigrant Experience," in *Journal of American Ethnic History* 18, no. 4 (Summer 1999): pp. 136–166, contains interesting ideas. O'Connor, *The Boston Irish*; Terry Golway, *Irish Rebel: John Devoy and America's Fight for Ireland's Freedom* (New York: St. Martin's Press, 1998); and Timothy Meagher's *Inventing Irish America* are relevant here.

24. Such works as Michael Gordon's, *The Orange Riots: Irish Political Violence in New York City, 1870 and 1871* (Ithaca: Cornell University Press, 1993) and Eric Foner, "Class, Ethnicity and Radicalism in the Gilded Age: The Land League and Irish America," *Marxist Perspectives* 1, no. 2 (1978): pp. 6–55, allows access to different perspectives within the immigrant world.

25. Monographs on other cities such as Oscar Handlin in *Boston's Immigrants*; Lawrence McCaffrey, ed., *The Irish in Chicago* (Urbana: University of Illinois Press, 1987); Dennis Clark's work on Philadelphia for example; or Earl F. Niehaus, *The Irish in New Orleans 1800–1860* (Baton Rouge: Louisiana State University Press, 1965) highlight New York's potential for further scholarly attention.

26. Nicholas Canny's work has enriched the field in recent years, particularly *Europeans On the Move: Studies on European Migration, 1500–1800* (Oxford: Oxford University Press, 1994), and Volume One of Nicholas Canny, ed., *The Oxford History of the British Empire: The Origins of Empire* (Oxford: Oxford University Press, 1998).

27. On the history of Ireland, R. F. Foster's *Modern Ireland 1600–1972* (London: Allen Lane, Penguin Press, 1988) provides a good overview and bibliographic essay. A very wide literature includes older classics and valuable new revisionist and post-revisionist work, but the work of Edward MacLysaght, R. B. McDowell, A. P. W. Malcolmson, F. S. L. Lyons, and T. W. Moody still constitutes a good starting point.

28. Gearoid O'Tuathaigh, *Ireland Before the Famine 1798–1848* (Dublin: Gill and Macmillan, 1972), pp. 2–5; quotation, p. 2.

29. S. J. Connolly, "Union Government, 1812–23," Chapter III of W. E. Vaughn, ed., *A New History of Ireland, V, Ireland Under the Union, 1, 1801–70* (Oxford: Clarendon Press, 1989), pp. 48–73.

30. Patrick O'Sullivan, Introduction to Volume 2 of *The Irish in the New Communities*, from the series *The Irish World Wide: History, Heritage, Identity* (Leicester and London: Leicester University Press, 1992), p. 3. State institutions in nineteenth-century Ireland showcased the "association of ideas," for example, the Royal Hospital, Kilmainham, the Royal Irish Academy, the Royal College of Surgeons, and Queen's Colleges.

31. Some works engage with this approach, including Edward T O'Donnell's "How the Irish Became Urban," *Journal of Urban History* 25 no.2 (January 1999): pp. 271–286; Robert Ernst's *Immigrant Life in New York City, 1825–1863* (New York: King's Crown Press, 1949), pp. 5–7, reissued by Syracuse University Press in 1994; and Kerby Miller's *Out of Ireland: The Story of Irish Emigration to America* (Washington, D.C.: Elliot and Clark, 1994).

32. For an interesting comparison, see Jonathan D. Sarna and David G. Dalin's *Religion and State in the American Jewish Experience* (South Bend, Indiana: Notre Dame University Press, 1997).

33. Lothrop Stoddard's biography of Tammany leader Richard Croker, *Master of Manhattan: The Life of Richard Croker* (New York: Longmans, 1931), personalizes the Machine. Quotation, p. 36.

34. Aspects of this issue are treated in a study that posits a changeover from "oppressed" to "oppressors" on reaching America; Noel Ignatiev's *How the Irish Became White* (New York: Routledge, 1995). See also Terry Golway's perspective in Michael Coffey, ed., *The Irish in America* (New York: Hyperion Books, 1997).

35. In a review of Thomas H. O'Connor's *The Boston Irish*, Lawrence McCaffrey highlights the centrality of Ireland's history in understanding Irish settlement in America. See McCaffrey, "City of the Beginnings," *The Irish Literary Supplement: A Review of Irish Books* 15, no. 1 (Spring 1996): pp. 8–9.

36. John Francis Maguire addressed some of these affinities in a treatise on emigration and American remittances back home in his 1869 pamphlet *America In Its Relation to Irish Emigration*, in Pamphlets in American History Series, CA 1201, pp. 7–8.

37. See references in his Introduction, in Kevin Kenny, ed., *New Directions in Irish-American History* (Madison: University of Wisconsin Press, 2003), and Kerby Miller and Bruce D. Boling, with Liam Kennedy, "The Famine's Scars: William Murphy's Ulster and American Odyssey," in the same volume, pp. 36–60.

38. Matthew Frye Jacobson's interest in "the various texts of immigrant culture (whether poems, stories, newspaper editorials, or parades) . . . in examining the workings of nationalist ideology" provides an important focus. See Jacobson, *Special Sorrows: The Diasporic Imagination of Irish, Polish, and Jewish Immigrants in the United States* (Cambridge, Mass.: Harvard University Press, 1995), p. 6.

39. Patrick Ward, *Exile, Emigration and Irish Writing* (Dublin and Portland, Oregon: Irish Academic Press, 2002), p. 2.

40. Robert Dunne explores the essence of this argument in *Antebellum Irish Immigration and Emerging Ideologies of "America": A Protestant Backlash* (Lewiston, New York: Edwin Mellen Press, 2002).

41. McDannell, "Going to the Ladies' Fair," Bayor and Meagher, eds., *The New York Irish*, p. 235.

42. McDannell provides a detailed bibliography on "Irish" Catholicism in her notes to "Going to the Ladies' Fair" in *The New York Irish*, pp. 630–634.

43. David Noel Doyle's "The Regional Bibliography of Irish America, 1800–1930: A Review and Addendum," in *Irish Historical Studies* XXIII, no. 9 (May 1983): pp. 254–283; quotation, p. 261.

44. McLeod, "Catholicism and the New York Irish," Jim Obelkevich, Lyndal Roper, and Raphael Samuel, eds., *Disciplines of Faith: Studies in Religion, Politics and Patriarchy* (London: Routledge & Kegan Paul Ltd., 1987), pp. 339, 348.

45. Hugh McLeod, *Piety and Poverty: Working-Class Religion in Berlin, London and New York 1870–1914* (New York: Holmes & Meier, 1996), p. 57. Irish domination continues! See also James D. Hackett's *Bishops of the United States of Irish Birth or Descent* (New York: American Irish Historical Society, 1936).

46. Their point that "the Catholic Church does not measure its success by the standards of secular society" is well taken, and should be noted too. Glazer and Moynihan, *Beyond the Melting Pot*, p. 230.

47. There were, of course, a multitude of political affiliations subscribed to by the New York Irish that merit attention; including Irish attitudes toward the larger political questions of the day, i.e., slavery. Noel Ignatiev has focused on Catholic Irish attitudes to abolitionism. He concluded that although Irish immigrants left Ireland as "the oppressed," they acclimatized to the role of "oppressors," remarking that "the Irish had faded from Green to white, bleached by . . . something in the 'atmosphere' of America." *How the Irish Became White*, p. 31. Recently this kind of argumentation has come in for criticism. See Eric Arnesen, "Whiteness and the Historians' Imagination," *International Labor and Working-Class History* 60 (Fall 2001): pp. 3–32; and synopsis in *Historically Speaking* III, no. 3 (February 2002): pp. 19–22. Kevin Kenny too, has raised issues within this context; see "Editor's Introduction: Politics and Race," *New Directions*, pp. 102–103.

48. Peter Murphy and Candice Ward, "'The Irish Thing': A Conversation on the Australian and American Irish Diaspora, Introduced by Vassilis Lambropoulos," *The South Atlantic Quarterly* 98, no.'s 1/2 (Winter/Spring 1999): pp. 117–134. Quotation, p. 128.

49. Peter Quinn, *Banished Children of Eve: A Novel of Civil War New York* (New York: Penguin Books, 1994); Terry Golway's *Irish Rebel*. Outside the Irish experience, studies such as Robert Orsi's *The Madonna of 115th Street: Faith and Community in Italian Harlem, 1880–1950* (New Haven: Yale University Press, 1988) represent this genre well. Recent Hollywood attention has ignited interest in a previously obscure history.

50. Kevin Kenny, *The American Irish: A History* (New York: Pearson Education Limited, 2000); quotation, p. 179.

51. Kevin Kenny, ed., *New Directions in Irish-American History*, General Introduction, p. 3.

52. Ward, *Exile, Emigration and Irish Writing*, pp. 12, 13.

53. R. F. Foster, *The Irish Story: Telling Tales and Making it up in Ireland* (2001; London: Penguin Books, 2002), p. 3.

54. Declan Kiberd, "The Universal Borders of Brian Friel's Ireland," *The New York Times*, July 4, 1999, Arts and Leisure, p. 14.

Chapter One

1. See R. H. Dickson, *Ulster Emigration to Colonial America 1718–85* (London: Routledge and Kegan Paul, 1966); and the work of Cormac O'Grada for coverage of earliest Irish settlement.

2. See David N. Doyle's "Scotch-Irish" entry and references in Michael Glazier, ed., *The Encyclopedia of the Irish in America* (South Bend, Indiana: Notre Dame University Press, 1999), pp. 842–851, and the relevant entries in Kenneth T. Jackson, ed., *The Encyclopedia of New York City* (New Haven: Yale University Press, 1995). See also my entry on "Scots-Irish" in the forthcoming *Encyclopedia of New York State* (Syracuse: Syracuse University Press, 2004).

3. Mike Cronin and Daryl Adair, *The Wearing of the Green: A History of St. Patrick's Day* (London and New York: Routledge, 2002), pp. 8–17.

4. The 1798 Rebellion pitted Wolfe Tone's non-sectarian United Irishmen against Crown forces.

5. Michael J. O'Brien, *In Old New York: The Irish Dead in Trinity and St. Paul's Churchyards* (New York: American Irish Historical Society, 1928), pp. 1, 3, 8, 119, 125, 143.

6. Joyce Goodfriend, "'Upon a bunch of Straw': The Irish in Colonial New York City," in Ronald H. Bayor and Timothy J. Meagher, eds., *The New York Irish* (Baltimore: Johns Hopkins University Press, 1995), pp. 36–37.

7. For information on this era, see the *Shamrock, or Hibernian Chronicle,* a weekly newspaper edited by E. Gillespie, vols. 1–3 (December 1810–June 1813), continued as the *Shamrock* until August 1817.

8. Paul Gilje, "The Development of an Irish American Community in New York City before the Great Migration" in Bayor and Meagher, eds., *The New York Irish,* pp. 70–83; John Ridge, entry on "New York City," *The Encyclopedia of the Irish in America,* p. 680.

9. Kevin Kenny, *The American Irish: A History* (New York: Pearson Education Limited, 2000), pp. 56–57, 105.

10. Press reports on city government elections during the 1840s and early 1850s provide detailed information on the response to Famine arrival.

11. Edwin G. Burrows and Mike Wallace discuss the impact at varying junctures in *Gotham: A History of New York City to 1898* (New York: Oxford University Press, 1998); as do the essays on settlement in Bayor and Meagher, *The New York Irish.* Kevin Kenny cites the Castle Garden opening in 1855 as the first attempt to regulate immigrant arrival. *The American Irish,* p. 105.

12. Bayor and Meagher, *The New York Irish,* p. 551; Edward K. Spann, *The New Metropolis: New York City, 1840–1860* (New York: Columbia University Press, 1981), p. 430; Kevin Kenny, *The American Irish,* pp. 106–107.

13. Patrick Ward, *Exile, Emigration and Irish Writing* (Dublin: Irish Academic Press, 2002), p. 119.

14. Neil Hogan, "The Famine Beat: American Newspaper Coverage of the Great Hunger," in Arthur Gribben, ed., *The Great Famine and the Irish Diaspora in America* (Amherst: University of Massachusetts Press, 1999), pp. 155–179.

15. Hasia Diner, "'The Most Irish City in the Union': The Era of the Great Migration, 1844–1877," in Bayor and Meagher, eds., *The New York Irish,* pp. 87–106. Quotation, p. 103.

16. See Christine Kinealy's entry "The Great Famine," and David Fitzpatrick's "Emigration, 1801–1921," in *The Encyclopedia of the Irish in America,* pp. 295–305; 254–262. For background, see Owen Dudley Edwards, "The American Image of Ireland: A Study of its Early Phases," in *Perspectives in American History* 4 (1970): pp. 255–272; and the general overview in Cecil Woodham Smith's *The Great Hunger: Ireland 1845–1849* (London: R. Hamilton, 1962).

17. Diane Hotten-Somers, "Famine: American Relief Movement," *The Encyclopedia of the Irish in America,* pp. 305–338. Quotation, p. 306.

18. The Levi Parsons Morton Papers, main file, Box 15, New York Public Library (hereafter NYPL). Morton served as Vice-President in the Benjamin Harrison administration.

19. Copy of a letter to the *New York Herald,* March 9, 1889, and documents relating to the merchant banking interests of Levi Parsons Morton and Pierpont Morgan and family; Morton Papers, NYPL.

20. In total, *The Constellation* set sail with 831 barrels of potatoes, corn meal, flour, and oatmeal donated by Levi Morton, William R. Grace, and the *New York Herald.* The report included names of all firms contributing dry goods and clothing to the enterprise. Documents from the main file,

Box 15. The incongruity of a State banquet celebrating food distribution to the starving is compelling.

21. David Fitzpatrick, *Irish Emigration 1801–1921* (Dublin: Dundalgan Press, 1984), pp. 8–9.

22. Kerby Miller and Bruce D. Boling, "Golden Streets, Bitter Tears: The Irish Image of America during the Era of Mass Migration," *Journal of American Ethnic History* 10, no.'s 1/2 (Fall 1990–Winter 1991): pp. 16–36.

23. Diner, "The Era of the Great Migration," in Bayor and Meagher, eds., *The New York Irish*, pp. 87–106.

24. Testimony of Jerry McAuley, in Helen Campbell, *Darkness and Daylight, or Lights and Shadows of New York Life: A Woman's Pictorial Record of Gospel, Temperance, Mission, and Rescue Work "In His Name," With Thrilling Personal Experiences by Day and Night in the Underworld of the Great Metropolis, and Hundreds of Thrilling Anecdotes, Incidents, Humorous Stories, Touching Home Scenes, and Tales of Tender Pathos, Drawn from the Bright and Shady Sides of Life Among the Lowly, by Helen Campbell, City Missionary and Philanthropist, Thomas W. Knox, Author and Journalist, and Thomas Byrnes, Late Chief of New York Detective Bureau, Including an Account of Detective Byrnes's Thirty Years' Experiences, Written by Himself from his Private Diary, With an Introduction by Rev. Lyman Abbott, D.D.* (Hartford, Conn.: The Hartford Publishing Company, 1899), p. 75. Employment of the adjective "Romanist" in reference to a Catholic often identified a less than ecumenically minded voice.

25. Campbell, *Darkness and Daylight*, pp. 75, 78–81.

26. Writing in 1959, Oscar Handlin remarked on European emigration to the United States: "Some entered upon their exodus under the pressure of a great disaster, as did the Irish after 1846." The reading of Irish immigration as a uniform response to Famine conditions has recently adopted a wider discourse, but the earlier foundation is still evident. Oscar Handlin, ed., *Immigration as a Factor in American History* (Englewood Cliffs, NJ: Prentice-Hall, 1959), p. 20. See Alan M. Kraut, "Illness and Medical Care among Irish Immigrants in Antebellum New York," in Bayor and Meagher, *New York Irish*, p. 153, for a more updated perspective.

27. Maureen Wall, "The Age of the Penal Laws (1691–1778)," in T. W. Moody and F. X. Martin's *The Course of Irish History* (1967; Lanham, Md.: Roberts Rinehart Publishers, 1995), pp. 227–228.

28. Alvin Jackson explores this theme in *Ireland 1798–1998, Politics and War* (Oxford: Blackwell Publishers, 1999), pp. 170–171.

29. Gearoid O'Tuathaigh, *Ireland Before the Famine 1798–1848* (Dublin: Gill and Macmillan, 1972), pp. 154–156.

30. Diane M. Hotten-Somers provides an overview of Irish women in service in "Relinquishing and Reclaiming Independence: Irish Domestic Servants, American Middle-Class Mistresses, and Assimilation, 1850–1920," in Kevin Kenny, ed., *New Directions in Irish-American History* (Madison: University of Wisconsin Press, 2003) pp. 227–242.

31. For an overview, see Gilje and Diner's essays in Bayor and Meagher, *The New York Irish*.

32. William Bell, "Diary of William Bell, Policeman, New York City, 1850–51," Microfilm: "New York," New York Historical Society (hereafter NYHS).

33. John J. Sturdevant, "Recollections of a Resident of New York City From 1835–1905." Typewritten transcript, 76 pages, NYPL.

34. "Recollections," pp. 1–4.

35. The Dutch fish market was usually known as the Blei Fly, according to this commentator.

36. James Lydon, *The Making of Ireland, From Ancient Times to the Present* (London and New York: Routledge, 1998), p. 177.

37. R. V. Comerford, "Ireland 1850–70: Post-Famine and mid-Victorian," in W. E. Vaughn, ed., Chapter XX of *A New History of Ireland, V, Ireland Under the Union, 1, 1801–70* (Oxford: Clarendon Press, 1989), pp. 394–395.

38. Leo Hershkowitz offers a synopsis of the Astor Riots involving MacCready, the English actor who was attacked in May 1849 outside the Astor Place Theater for publicly slandering an American rival. See Hershkowitz's summary in Bayor and Meagher, eds., *The New York Irish*, p. 17.

39. Eric Homberger, *Scenes from the Life of a City: Corruption and Conscience in Old New York* (New Haven: Yale University Press, 1994), p. 116.

40. Edward T. O'Donnell, "How the Irish Became Urban," *Journal of Urban History* 25, no. 2 (January 1999): pp. 277–278; and Don Meade, "Kitty O'Neil and Her 'Champion Jig': An Irish Dancer on the New York Stage," *New Hibernia Review* 6, no. 3 (Autumn 2002): pp. 9–22; quotation, p. 14.

41. Sturdevant, "Recollections," pp. 5–22.

42. Michael and Ariane Batterberry, *On the Town in New York: The Landmark History of Eating, Drinking, and Entertainments from the American Revolution to the Food Revolution* (New York: Routledge, 1999), p. 73.

43. See my M.A. thesis "Aspects of Economy and Society in Pre-Famine Mayo," History Department, National University of Ireland, Galway, 1988, for foreign commentary on pre-Famine conditions.

44. Asenath Nicholson, *The Bible in Ireland ('Ireland's Welcome to the Stranger, or on Excursion through Ireland in 1844 and 1845 for the purpose of Personally Investigating the condition of the Poor') by A. Nicholson* (1847; London: Hodder and Stoughton, 1926), pp. 256, 356. See also her *Lights and Shades of Ireland* (London: Houlston & Stoneman, 1850), and supplementary material in *Annals of the Famine in Ireland/Asenath Nicholson*, edited by Maureen Murphy (Dublin: Lilliput Press, 1998).

45. See Joel Mokyr's *Why Ireland Starved: A Quantitative and Analytical History of the Irish Economy, 1800–1850* (London and Boston: Allen and Unwin, 1983), on these and related issues.

46. Tyler Anbinder, "From Famine to Five Points: Lord Lansdowne's Irish Tenants Encounter North America's Most Notorious Slum," *American Historical Review* 107, no. 2 (April 2002), pp. 351–387. Quotation, p. 385; also his *Five Points: The Nineteenth-Century New York Neighborhood that Invented Tap Dance, Stole Elections, and Became the World's Most Notorious Slum* (2001; New York: Plume, 2002); see also passages in older histories by Thomas A. Janvier and Herbert Asbury.

47. Tyler Anbinder, "'We Will Dirk Every Mother's Son of You': Five Points and the Irish Conquest of New York Politics," in Kevin Kenny, ed., *New Directions*, pp. 105–121.

48. Sturdevant, "Recollections," pp. 20, 26, 52, 74.

49. Carol Groneman, "The 'Bloody Ould Sixth': A Social Analysis of a New York City Working-Class Community in the Mid-Nineteenth Century," unpublished Ph.D. diss., University of Rochester, 1973. Also, Groneman's "Working Class Immigrant Women in Mid-Nineteenth Century New York: The Irish Woman's Perspective," *Journal of Urban History* 4, no. 3 (1978): pp. 255–273. Kevin Kenny also supports this point in *The American Irish*, p. 161.

50. Helen Campbell, *Darkness and Daylight*, pp. 412, 418–419.

51. T. W. Freeman, "Land and People, c. 1841," Chapter XI of *A New History of Ireland, V*, p. 243.

52. H. D. Gribbon, "Economic and Social History, 1850–1921," Chapter XII of *A New History of Ireland, V*, pp. 331–332.

53. See Roy Rosenweig and Elizabeth Blackmar's *The Park and the People: A History of Central Park* (Ithaca: Cornell University Press, 1992), and the work of Eric Homberger.

54. Sophie Hall's record emulated travel writers Mr. and Mrs. S. C. (Samuel Carter) Hall in the 1830s and 1840s. Their three-volume *Ireland: Its Scenery and Character, &c* (London: How & Parsons, 1841–43) remains a classic of its kind. Sophie C, Mrs. George W. Hall, "Diary Kept During a Visit to New York," 1 volume (1879), Diaries, Box 5, NYPL.
55. Hall, "Diary." Emphasis in original. On Saint Patrick's Day Parade, see Mike Cronin and Daryl Adair, *The Wearing of the Green*; and the work of Marie Fitzgerald and John D. Crimmons.
56. Roy Foster looks at how the Catholic Association "harnessed the masses" to this branch of political activism in *Modern Ireland 1600–1972* (London: Allen Lane, Penguin Press, 1988), pp. 298–299. He also provides a biography of Smith O'Brien on p. 314.
57. Tim Pat Coogan, *Eamon De Valera: The Man Who Was Ireland* (London: Hutchinson, 1993), p. 109. William Smith O'Brien's daughter Charlotte Grace O'Brien was instrumental in founding the Mission of Our Lady of the Rosary for the Protection of Irish Immigrant Girls (cited in Chapter Two) in New York in 1883.
58. *The Irish-American*, July 9, 1864, p. 2.
59. John Burke, "Reminiscences 1839–1891," handwritten notebook, NYHS.
60. "Reminiscences," pp. 45–59, 72–75.
61. Jeremiah O'Donovan, *A Brief Account of the Author's Interview with his Countrymen, and of the Parts of the Emerald Isle Whence they Emigrated. Together with a Direct Reference to Their Present Location in the Land of Their Adoption, During his Travels Through Various States of the Union in 1854 and 1855* (Pittsburgh: Published by the Author, 1864). Reprinted by Arno, New York, in 1969 in the American Immigrant Collection; p. 5, Introduction.
62. *A Brief Account . . .*, p. 164, and passim. Hasia Diner confirms that O'Donovan "came to New York in 1854 to sell a history of Ireland that he had written," and he "encountered his countrymen in comfortable positions of all kinds." "The Most Irish City in the Union," *The New York Irish*, p. 94; and Kenneth E. Nilsen makes reference to Corkman Daniel Draddy in his "The Irish Language in New York, 1850–1900." *The New York Irish*, p. 255.
63. The next chapter explores class influences among women.
64. See Benjamin Reid's *The Man From New York: John Quinn and his Friends* (New York: Oxford University Press, 1968) and references here in the Introduction.
65. On the Society, see Michael Funchion, ed., *Irish American Voluntary Organizations* (Connecticut: Greenwood Press, 1983), pp. 171–173, including bibliography. Details here obtained from the *Ticket for the Second Annual Ball of The Irish Emigrant Society*, Ann Street (December 1, 1845), Box Miscellaneous Mss. 9.2H.139, American Irish Historical Society.
66. *Annual Ball Ticket*.
67. This last total lists 1,887 males and 1,126 females. *Report of the President, James Rorke, of the Irish Emigrant Society*, 51 Chambers Street, New York (January 29, 1900); Microfilm ZAN-9019, No. 1–15, NYPL. The Society continued to function into the twentieth century.

Chapter Two

1. George Potter, *To The Golden Door: The Story of the Irish in Ireland and America* (Boston: Little, Brown and Company, 1960), p. 509.
2. *Golden Door*, p. 513. The descriptive labels "Paddy" and "Biddy" occasionally emphasize disparaging attitudes to Irish immigrants. Dale Knoble in *Paddy and The Republic: Ethnicity and Nationality in Ante-bellum America* (Middleton, Connecticut: Wesleyan University Press, 1986) and Timothy

J. Meagher in *From Paddy to Studs: Irish-American Communities in the Turn of the Century Era, 1880 to 1920* (New York; Westport, Conn.: Greenwood Press, 1986), among others, take on the political significance of these terms.

3.   Hasia Diner in *Erin's Daughters in America: Irish Immigrant Women in the Nineteenth Century* (Baltimore: Johns Hopkins University Press, 1983); Janet Nolan in *Ourselves Alone: Female Emmigration From Ireland 1825–1920* (Lexington, Kentucky: University Press of Kentucky, 1989); and Kerby Miller in *Emigrants and Exiles: Ireland and the Irish Exodus to North America* (New York: Oxford University Press, 1985) argue that men and women emigrated in relatively equal numbers. This assessment is borne out by Ira Glazier and Michael Tepper, eds., *Famine Immigrants: Lists of Irish Immigrants Arriving at the Port of New York, 1846–51,* 6 volumes (Baltimore: Genealogical Publishing Co., Inc., 1983). Kerby Miller discussed difficulties in calculating precisely, emphasizing that 40 to 50 percent of immigrants did not arrive in New York, but elsewhere in the U.S. and Canada. "Thus," Miller concluded, "the New York passenger lists present a somewhat incomplete and overly-optimistic portrait of the total Famine exodus to the United States." "Researchers," he warned further, "should be aware that the passenger lists themselves contain information which is not entirely trustworthy." Kerby Miller, "Review of *Famine Immigrants,*" in *Journal of American Ethnic History* (Fall 1985), pp. 83–85.

4.   Janet Nolan, "Introduction: The Catholic Immigrant Woman in Urban America," *Mid-America: An Historical Review* 74, no. 3 (October 1992), pp. 201–204. A useful table, "Sex Ratio of Male to Female Irish Emigrants, 1851–1910" appears in an appendix to *Emigrants and Exiles*, where Kerby Miller demonstrated that the ratio of males to females differed only very slightly, at 1.08:1. *Emigrants*, p. 582.

5.   See Diner and Nolan particularly. For recent insight, especially in the field of women religious, see Kathleen Healy, ed., *Sisters of Mercy, Spirituality in America, 1843–1900* (New York: Paulist Press, 1992); Sister Margaret Walsh, *History of the Sisters of Charity of New York, 1809–1959*, vols. 1–3 (New York: Fordham University Press, 1960); Maureen Fitzgerald's "Irish-Catholic Nuns and the Development of New York City's Welfare System, 1840–1900" (Ph.D. dissertation, University of Wisconsin-Madison, 1992) and "The Perils of 'Passion and Poverty': Women Religious and the Care of Single Women in New York City, 1845–1890," *U.S. Catholic Historian* 10, no.'s 1–2 (1990): pp. 45–58, and the work of Caledonia Kearns and Joan McIver.

6.   Patrick O'Sullivan, ed., *Irish Women and Irish Migration*, Volume Four in the series *The Irish World Wide: History, Heritage, Identity* (London and New York: Leicester University Press, 1995), p. 1. Kerby Miller, David N. Doyle and Patricia Kelleher's "'For Love and Liberty': Irish Women, Migration and Domesticity in Ireland and America, 1815–1920"; and Dympna McLoughlin's "Superfluous and Unwanted Deadweight: the Emigration of Nineteenth Century Irish Pauper Women" constitute valuable contributions here. See also McLoughlin's *Women, Subsistence and Emigration, 1840–1870* (Dublin: Irish Academic Press, 2000).

7.   Kevin Kenny has endorsed these perspectives in *The American Irish: A History* (New York: Pearson Education Limited, 2000), with specific reference to women's background in Ireland, pp. 138–139.

8.   Nolan, *Ourselves Alone*, p. 83.

9.   Nolan, pp. 74–75, and Diner, *Erin's Daughters*, pp. 46–49.

10.   Kerby Miller, with David Doyle and Patricia Kelleher, "For Love and Liberty" in O'Sullivan, ed., *Irish Women and Irish Migration*, pp. 43–44.

11.   Nolan, *Ourselves Alone*, 100; Pauline Jackson, "Women in Nineteenth Century Irish Emigration" in *International Migration Review* XIX (Winter 1984), pp. 1004–1020; Ann Rossiter, "Bringing the Margins into the Centre: A Review of Aspects of Irish Women's Emigration," in Sean Hutton and Paul Stewart, eds., *Ireland's Histories: Aspects of State, Society and Ideology* (London:

Penguin, 1991); and Grace Neville, in "Dark Lady of the Archives: Towards an Analysis of Women and Emigration to North America in Irish Folklore," in Mary O'Dowd and Sabine Wichert, eds., *Chattel, Servant or Citizen: Women's Status in Church, State and Society* (Belfast: The Institute of Irish Studies, 1995), pp. 200–214.

12. Kerby Miller, "Sex Ratio of Male to Female Irish Emigrants, 1851–1910, in *Emigrants and Exiles,* p. 582. Ronald H. Bayor and Timothy J. Meagher in *The New York Irish* (Baltimore, Md.: Johns Hopkins University Press, 1995) estimate similarly as to the population of Irish women in the city, with a number of the essays addressing specific aspects of women's settlement.

13. Miller et al., in O'Sullivan, ed., *Irish Women and Irish Migration,* pp. 51–52.

14. A good introduction and important points on the progress of a sizable grouping of Irish women is provided by Carol Groneman in "Working Class Immigrant Women in Mid-Nineteenth Century New York: The Irish Woman's Perspective," *Journal of Urban History* 4, no. 3 (1978): pp. 255–273.

15. Reverend Stephen Byrne, O.S.D., *Irish Emigration to the United States: What It Has Been, and What It Is. Facts and Reflections Especially Addressed to Irish People Intending to Emigrate From Their Native Land; and to Those Living in the Large Cities of Great Britain and of the United States* (New York: The Catholic Publication Society, 1873); reprinted by Arno Press and *The New York Times* in 1969, pp. 11–14.

16. Directives such as this from Catholic clerics appeared at regular intervals in the nineteenth century. The work of Bishop of Hartford Bernard O'Reilly is cited in later chapters as another such example.

17. The ratio of males to females within Irish immigration in the period 1851–1910 was: Males: 2,175,641; Females: 2,001,802. Miller, *Emigrants and Exiles,* p. 582.

18. *The New York Times,* April 30, 1897, p. 4.

19. The Rosary Mission was established in New York by Charlotte Grace O'Brien in 1884. Daughter of revolutionary William Smith O'Brien, poet, essayist, and philanthropist, Charlotte Grace worked to assist thousands of women from the 1880s until World War I. See Maureen Murphy's "Charlotte Grace O'Brien and the Mission of Our Lady of the Rosary for the Protection of Irish Immigrant Girls," *Mid-America, An Historical Review* 74, no. 3 (October 1992), pp. 253–270.

20. *The New York Times,* April 30, 1897, p. 4. Many such reports appeared in the contemporary press on immigrants arriving in New York.

21. Historians accept that networks of family and friends assisted newly arrived immigrants in America. Miller supports this view, and Diner discusses how women gained entry to positions of paid employment. Problems arise in attempts to piece together a more complex framework using evidence of an ambiguous nature; i.e., assumptions that immigrants from specific areas sharing the same last name were related.

22. See Mary Oates's work cited in the Bibliography.

23. Catherine Furey to the Board of the Society of the Friendly Sons, November 20, 1873. Papers of the Society of the Friendly Sons of Saint Patrick, Box 3/4, American Irish Historical Society (hereafter, AIHS).

24. Each year brought in varying numbers of requests, but I have selected 1873 as reasonably typical of an annual load.

25. Friendly Sons, John R. Brady to William Whiteside, January 19, 1874.

26. Thomas Kelly, from the Custom House, New York, July 3, 1888, to the Board of the Friendly Sons. A large cache of similar letters highlighted the plight of Irish women impoverished to varying degrees and unwilling to forego middle-class standards. Nationalist leader James Stephens maintained close links with New York. Richmond Bridewell refers to a prison in Richmond, England.

27. This example is from *The Irish-American*, March 29, 1862, p. 2. The New York Irish newspapers regularly carried similar notices in their advertisement sections.

28. D. H. Akenson, "Pre-university education, 1870–1921," Chapter XVIII of *A New History of Ireland, VI, Ireland Under the Union, II, 1870–1921* (Oxford: Clarendon Press, 1996), p. 537.

29. See Maria Luddy and Cliona Murphy, eds., *Women Surviving, Studies in Irish Women's History in the 19th and 20th Centuries* (Dublin: Poolbeg, 1990), and L.P. Curtis, Jr., "Ireland in 1914," *A New History of Ireland*, VI, pp. 153–154.

30. Kevin Kenny elucidates the response of Irish orders to conditions in New York and also to their relationship with "the standard Protestant model of charity and relief" in *The American Irish*, pp. 145–147; quotation, p. 146.

31. George C. Stewart, Jr., *Marvels of Charity: History of American Sisters and Nuns* (Huntington, Ind.: Our Sunday Visitor, Inc., 1994), pp. 155–156. Margaret Susan Thompson explores the intersections of ethnicity and class in "Sisterhood and Power: Class, Culture, and Ethnicity in the American Convent," *Colby Library Quarterly* 25, no. 3 (1989): pp. 149–75; and see her "Discovering Foremothers: Sisters, Society, and the American Catholic Experience" in Joseph P. White, ed., *The American Catholic Religious Life* (New York: Garland Press, 1988).

32. An extensive literature exists on welfare in nineteenth-century New York. See Deirdre M. Moloney, *American Catholic Lay Groups and Transatlantic Social Reform in the Progressive Era* (Chapel Hill: University of North Carolina Press, 2002) and the work of Robert Cray, Virginia Oiuiroga, Kenneth Scherzer, and David Ward particularly. George Paul Jacoby's bibliography of city charities in *Catholic Child Care in Nineteenth Century New York, With a Correlated Summary of Public and Protestant Child Welfare* (Washington: The Catholic University of America, 1941) is useful.

33. George Stewart provides a listing of American foundations, including hospital and college foundations, in *Marvels of Charity*, pp. 487–556.

34. Maria Luddy, *Women and Philanthropy in Nineteenth-Century Ireland* (Cambridge. Mass.: Cambridge University Press, 1995), p. 51.

35. Irish Capuchin Father Theobald Matthew commenced his large-scale total abstinence movement in 1838, extending the mission to the United States in 1849.

36. A Sister of Charity, likely Mother Mary Rose Dolan, *A Descriptive and Historical Sketch of the Academy of Mount Saint Vincent on the Hudson, 1847–1884* (New York: D. Appleton and Co., 1884), p. 49.

37. The Original Register of The Roman Catholic Orphan Asylum, Saint Patrick's, Boys Department, listings for the years 1860, 1870, 1880, and 1890, from the Archives of the Sisters of Charity, Mount Saint Vincent on the Hudson, New York.

38. Listings from the Sisters of Mercy of the Americas Archives, Dobbs Ferry, New York, and Wilson Industrial School *Annual Report, 1857–1916* (incomplete), microfilm ZAN-9147, NYPL.

39. Emmet Larkin, *The Historical Dimensions of Irish Catholicism* (1976; Washington, D.C.: Catholic University of America Press, 1984), pp. 58, 84.

40. R. F. Foster, *Modern Ireland 1600–1972* (London: Allen Lane, Penguin Press, 1988), p. 351.

41. John J. Fialka surmises that the United States proffered new opportunities for cloistered Irish and European women in *Sisters: Catholic Nuns and the Making of America* (New York: St. Martin's Press, 2003), p. 2.

42. Mary Ewens, *The Role of the Nun in Nineteenth Century America* (New York: Arno Press, 1978), p. 93.

43. Mother M. R. Dolan's 1884 *History* documents that the majority of the Sisters of Charity arrived in New York from Ireland. The dates of arrival for the Sisters, for example, provide information

on birthplaces in Ireland and each nun's status in the order in New York.

44. Luddy, *Women and Philanthropy*, pp. 158–159, 204–207.

45. Ladies of Charity of the Catholic Charities of The Archdiocese of New York, *Annual Report,* New York (1903/04–1951 incomplete), pp. 3–4. Microform ZAN-8736, NYPL.

46. Ladies of Charity: "Association of Catholic Charities. Reports of Members of Executive Committee for General Meeting of Members of the Association," March 1, 1904, Catholic Club, 120 East Fifty-Ninth Street, p. 11.

47. Ladies of Charity, Annual Report, January 1904, p. 17.

48. Annual Report, Mrs. B. E. Burke.

49. Annual Report, Wednesday April 18, 1906, pp. 25, 39.

50. These women's names appeared on city press society pages regularly. The Ladies' 1925 Report and subsequent issues review the work of an increasingly sophisticated organization, with long listings of Executive Members, patrons, and committee members. Reports continue up to 1951. See an introduction to the Home at <http://www.mycrestwood.org>. Eric Homberger, *Scenes from the Life of a City: Corruption and Conscience in Old New York* (New Haven: Yale University Press, 1994), p. 297. The portrait of Eleanora O'Donnell Iselin by John Singer Sargent may be viewed at the National Gallery of Art, Washington, D.C.

51. *The Irish-American,* April 4, 1863, pp. 1–3.

52. *The Irish-American,* February 21, 1914, p. 7; March 5 1910, p. 3. These club and association programs appeared on a regular basis in the Irish city press, particularly *The Irish-American, The Irish Citizen,* and *The Irish World.*

53. Una Ni Bhroimeil, *Building Irish Identity in America, 1870–1915: The Gaelic Revival* (Dublin: Four Courts Press, 2003). Marion Casey argues substantively for connections through music and dance within the Irish community in "Keeping the Tradition Alive: A History of Irish Music and Dance in New York City," *New York Irish History* 6 (1991–92): pp. 24–30. See also John T. Ridge's "The Gaelic Revival in 19ᵗʰ Century New York," *New York Irish History* 1 (1986): pp. 5–6.

54. *The New York Times,* October 7 1883, p. 2.

55. Una Ni Bhroimeil, "The Creation of an Irish Culture in the United States: The Gaelic Movement, 1870–1915," *New Hibernia Review* 5, no. 3 (Autumn 2001): pp. 87–100. See also her "For Yankeemen and Irishmen, Their Hearts and Hands Should Join: Irish America—The View From Gaelic Ireland, 1900–1915," *The Recorder, The Journal of the American Irish Historical Society* 16, no. 1 (Spring 2003): pp. 114–131, on the transatlantic endeavors of the Gaelic League.

56. Kenneth E. Nilsen's "The Irish Language in New York, 1850–1900," in Bayor and Meagher, *The New York Irish,* pp. 252–274, provides valuable background to this society.

57. *The Irish American,* January 26, 1907, p. 4; March 16, 1907, p. 4; and April 23, 1910, p. 1.

58. Curtis, "Ireland in 1914," *A New History of Ireland,* VI, p. 167.

59. *The New York Times,* January 20, 1898, p. 5, and May 25, 1914, p. 5.

60. Daniel Czitrom, "Underworlds and Underdogs: Big Tim Sullivan and Metropolitan Politics in New York, 1889–1913," *Journal of American History* 78 (September 1991): pp. 536–558.

61. Dympna McLoughlin, "Superfluous and Unwanted Deadweight: the Emigration of Nineteenth-Century Irish Pauper Women," in Patrick O'Sullivan, ed., *Irish Women and Irish Migration,* pp. 83–85. See McLoughlin's other published work for further background.

62. *The New York Times,* under the heading, "The Poor of New York," January 15, 1866, p. 8 (emphasis in original). See also numerous entries of relevance in Kenneth T. Jackson ed., *The Encyclopedia of New York City* (New Haven: Yale University Press, 1995).

63. "Parnell Street" here likely commemorates nineteenth-century Parliamentarian Charles Stuart Parnell.

64. Harry M. Shulman, *The Slums of New York, Rotary Club of New York Study, 1931, 1932* (New York: Albert and Charles Boni, Inc., 1938), pp. 45–46.

65. Maureen Fitzgerald provides evidence for the prevalence of prostitution among the poorer female immigrants in "The Perils of 'Passion and Poverty,'" *U.S. Catholic Historian* 10 (1990): pp. 47–48.

66. George Ellington, *The Women of New York, or the Underworld of the Great City. Illustrating the Life of Women of Fashion, Women of Pleasure, Actresses and Ballet Girls, Saloon Girls, Pickpockets and Shoplifters. Artists' Female Models, Women-of-the-Town, Etc., Etc., Etc.* (1869–70; New York: Arno Press, 1972), p. 410.

67. On the complexities of the issue in mid-century New York, see "'The Heart Sickens at Such a Narrative': Madame Restell," Chapter Two of Eric Homberger's *Scenes from the Life of a City.*

68. Stephen Crane, *Maggie: A Girl of the Streets* (1896; New York: Ballantine Books, 1960), p. 45.

69. Ruth-Ann Harris, "'Come You All Courageously': Irish Women in America Write Home," in Kevin Kenny, ed., *New Directions in Irish-American History* (Madison: University of Wisconsin Press, 2003). Quotation, p. 222.

70. Graham Hodges, "'Desirable Companions and Lovers': Irish and African Americans in the Sixth Ward, 1830–1870," in Bayor and Meagher, *The New York Irish*, pp. 106–124; quotation, p. 121.

71. Mary Anne Sadlier, *Bessy Conway; or, The Irish Girl in America* (New York: Sadlier, 1861). On Sadlier's work, see Henry Boylan's *Dictionary of Irish Biography* (New York: Barnes and Noble Books, 1978); and Charles Fanning, *The Irish Voice in America: Irish-American Fiction from the 1760s to the 1980s* (Lexington, Kentucky: The University Press of Kentucky, 1990).

72. "Your Humble Servant," *Harper's New Monthly Magazine* XXIX (June–November 1864), pp. 53–54.

73. Lucy Maynard Salmon, *Domestic Service* (1897; New York: Macmillan, 1911), pp. 62–63, 79–81.

74. L. M. Salmon, *A Statistical Inquiry Concerning Domestic Service, Reprinted from the Publications of the American Statistical Association, 1892.* Pamphlets in American History series, LZ457, pp. 13–18.

75. "Your Humble Servant," *Harper's Magazine* XXIX (1864), p. 57.

76. "Our Bridget," *Harper's Magazine* XXVIII (December 1863-May 1864), p. 389.

77. "Servant Girls' Warfare," *The New York Times*, May 4, 1870, p. 4.

78. Letter from "An American Woman" to the editor of the *New York Tribune*, July 26, 1863; quoted in *The Irish-American*, August 8, 1863, p. 2.

79. *New York Dispatch*, July 19 1863, p. 4; *The Irish-American*, August 1, 1863, p. 2. See Iver Bernstein's *The New York City Draft Riots: Their Significance for American Society and Politics in the Age of the Civil War* (New York: Oxford University Press, 1997).

80. *The Irish-American*, August 8, 1863, p. 2.

81. Exploring the "interdependent relationship" between mistress and maid in "Relinquishing and Reclaiming Independence: Irish Domestic Servants, American Middle-Class Mistresses, and Assimilation, 1850–1920," Diane M. Hotten-Somers characterized as negligible "the social stigma attached to domestic service" in this context. Kenny, ed., *New Directions*, pp. 227–242. Quotations, pp. 227–228.

82. "Your Humble Servant," *Harper's Magazine* (1864), pp. 53–59.

83. Helen Campbell, *Darkness and Daylight*, pp. 267–268.

84. Salmon, *Domestic Service*, p. 211.

85. Hasia Diner, Janet Nolan, and Kerby Miller offer generalized coverage of prominent women nationalists. Bayor and Meagher in *The New York Irish* cite female participation in city nationalist circles, especially in Doyle's "Striking for Ireland on the New York Docks," pp. 357–374.

86. The Fenian Brotherhood constituted the American branch of the Irish Republican Brotherhood in Ireland. The following chapters make further reference to the organization, especially Chapter 6.

87. *The New York Times*, December 17, 1865, p. 4.

88. *The Irish-American*, August 6, 1864, p. 3. "Speranza" refers to literary figurehead and nationalist Lady Wilde, mother of Oscar Wilde. The reference to "Mary" is probably a generalization, given the popularity of the name in contemporary times.

89. John T. Ridge's *The History of the Ancient Order of Hibernians and Ladies' Auxiliary of Brooklyn* (1973; Brooklyn: Ancient Order of Hibernians, 1985) is the stock treatment on the women's branch of this Irish fraternal organization. Destruction by fire of most Hibernian records for New York notwithstanding, Ridge has documented the less politicized Ladies' Auxiliary. Bayor and Meagher reference women's involvement in the Hibernians as "short-lived." *The New York Irish*, p. 661, note 9.

90. *The Irish-American*, February 24, 1866, p. 3.

91. Quotations from "Your Humble Servant," *Harper's Magazine* (1864), pp. 53–59. Kerby Miller provides evidence on this point throughout *Emigrants and Exiles*.

92. Articles appeared on January 25, p. 6, and January 27, p. 8, 1880.

93. "New York Ladies Society Relief," *The New York Times*, June 22, 1883, p. 3. The three "Manchester Martyrs," Allen, Larkin, and O'Brien transitioned from activists to nationalist "martyrs" upon execution in 1867.

94. This Association declined with the dismantling of the Tweed Ring. John T. Ridge provides a brief introduction to this group in Bayor and Meagher's *The New York Irish*, p. 279.

95. Margaret Anna Cusack lived from 1829 to 1899 and published a lengthy list of titles under the name Mary Francis Cusack. See her *Advice to Irish Girls in America* (New York: McGee, 1872). Irene ffrench Eagar's *Margaret Anna Cusack: One Woman's Campaign for Women's Rights, a Biography* (1970; Dublin: Arlen House, The Women's Press, 1979), contains a full listing of Cusack's publications, pp. 221–222. Cusack's memoir *The Nun of Kenmare: An Autobiography* (Boston: Ticknor and Company, 1889) provides a history of her stormy relationship with the hierarchy, leading to resignation from her order and eventually, leaving the Church.

96. *The Irish American*, March 16, 1872, p. 4.

97. Mary Francis Cusack, *Tim Carty's Trial, or Whistling at Landlords, A Play for the Times* (New York: S. Mearns, 1880), and *From Killarney to New York; or, How Thade Became a Banker* (New York: Pustet, 1886). Killarney is a Kerry market town near Kenmare. Chapter 4 includes coverage of *Tim Carty's Trial*.

98. "Political Meditation," *The Irish Nation*, January 21, 1882, p. 4.

99. On the impact of individual women and the organizations associated with them, see Margaret Ward, *Maud Gonne: A Life* (1990; London and San Francisco: Pandora Press, 1993); Anne Haverty, *Constance Markievicz: An Independent Life* (London and San Francisco: Pandora Press, 1988); and Mary Rose Callaghan, *'Kitty O'Shea,' The Story of Katherine Parnell* (1989; London and San Francisco: Pandora Press, 1994).

100. These County Associations occasionally paralleled Daniel Soyer's "landsmanshaftn," or hometown associations, within New York Jewish culture. In his *Jewish Immigrant Associations and American Identity in New York, 1880–1939* (Cambridge, Harvard University Press, 1997), Soyer discusses how these organizations helped Jews assimilate and yet maintain cultural traditions.

101. John T. Ridge's article on the Irish County Societies in New York maps the effort to unite as a single confederation in "Irish County Societies in New York 1880–1914," Bayor and Meagher, *The New York Irish*, pp. 275–300.

102. Pamphlet, *Address of the Ladies of the Irish American County Organizations of New York to their Fellow Countrymen and the American Public*, from the Headquarters of the Irish Palace Building Fair, 734 Third Avenue, New York, 1897. The Dillon Papers, Ms 6844/145–178, No. 111, Trinity College, Dublin. Internal wrangling and the pressures of Home Rule caused the County societies to decline during the 1910s.

103. Michael Davitt's Land League mobilized support for land reform and Home Rule. On the Ladies Land League, see Dana Hearne's edition of Anna Parnell's *The Tale of a Great Sham* (Dublin: Arlen House, 1986); Jane Cote, *Fanny and Anna Parnell: Ireland's Patriot Sisters* (New York: St. Martin's Press, 1991); also Hasia Diner's coverage in *Erin's Daughters*.

104. Ubiquitous journalist and activist John Devoy led Fenian successor Clan na Gael. Connoting a political "family" or community, the Clan generated solid American support during the post-Famine decades.

105. "The Ladies' Organization," *The Irish Nation*, November 26, 1881, p. 4.

106. Mary Cullen and Maria Luddy, eds., *Women, Power and Consciousness in 19th-Century Ireland: Eight Biographical Studies* (Dublin: Attic Press, 1995), pp. 270–271.

107. The Irish Volunteers mobilized with the expansion of the Ulster Volunteers.

108. Lectures by each of these activists received a great deal of coverage in the city press. The speeches of Hannah Sheehy-Skeffington from Carnegie Hall and similar venues were covered on three occasions in 1917 alone, January 7, April 9, and October 31 in *The New York Times*, as well as enormous coverage in the Irish press. See Joanne Mooney-Eichacker's *Varieties of Irish Republican Womanhood: Lectures During their United States Tours, 1916–1925* (Dublin: Irish Academic Press, 2000).

109. Cullen and Luddy, *Women, Power and Consciousness*, pp. 16–18.

110. Cumann na mBan translates literally from Gaelic as council or organization of women, implying a formal group established for a particular purpose, and is sometimes cited as The Irish Women's Council.

111. Article 2 of the regulations laid out the governing structure, the Central Council, to be elected annually. Rose McDermott, handwritten Diary of 88 pages, 1913, Miscellaneous Box 1, AIHS, pp. 82–83.

112. For accounts see any Irish history text. R. F. Foster's bibliography in *Modern Ireland* highlights the more analytical treatments.

113. "Irish Women of New York Pack Carnegie Hall," *The Irish American*, March 28, 1914, p. 1, and March 21, 1914, p. 4.

114. See Joe Doyle on Dr. Gertrude Kelly in "Striking for Ireland on the New York Docks," in Bayor and Meagher, *The New York Irish*, pp. 357–373.

115. *The New York Irish*. This slogan echoes the medieval conception of "the Pale" as the area immediately surrounding Dublin, considered the only civilized part of Ireland.

116. *The New York Times*, December 13, 1914, section 3, p. 4; May 31, 1916, p. 11; and July 11, 1916, p. 7.

117. Joe Doyle covered the episode whereby women picketed the New York docks in summer 1920, highlighting the hunger strike and death of Cork Mayor Terence McSwiney. See Doyle's essay "Striking for Ireland on the New York Docks," *The New York Irish*, pp. 357–373.

118. Rose McDermott, Diary, two page letter attached, addressed to the Editor of *The New York Journal*, October 7, 1914; AIHS.

119. Notwithstanding the small sums involved, the lavish document conveyed the impression of a large-scale, flourishing organization. This example held by the American Irish Historical Society.

120. Diary, McDermott, p. 6.
121. The Irish Volunteers aimed to raise support for Irish independence from 1908 onward. For a profile, see Foster, *Modern Ireland*, 473–474.
122. Rose McDermott, Diary, pp. 47–49, 80–81. The names here refer to prominent women nationalists. Likely the latter author was a Dublin-born poet and Home Rule activist, much of whose work appeared posthumously.
123. James Reidy, *The Influence of the Irish Woman on the National Movement, Lecture Delivered By James Reidy, Of New York, Before the Brooklyn Gaelic Society, on Sunday Evening, March 18, 1906* (New York: Published by the author, 1906). The pamphlet ran to eight pages. Queen Maeve reputedly reigned in Ireland in pre-Christian times. Grace O'Malley, or Granuaile, controlled the western seaboard as a sea captain and pirate during the sixteenth century, famously conversing in Latin with Queen Elizabeth I. See Eleanor Fairburn's *The White Seahorse* (1964; Dublin: Wolfhound Press, 1995), and the work of Anne Chambers.
124. Reidy, *The Influence of the Irish Woman*, p. 2. The first poem, by Thomas D'Arcy McGee—historian, man of letters and immigrant—conjures up images of Norman chivalry in the 1100s. The second, by Young Irelander Thomas Davis, draws on a seventeenth-century example of female valor in battle.
125. Reidy, p. 4.
126. Household names in Ireland's history, these women are cited by McDermott, Diary, pp. 47–49.
127. These women assisted escaped prisoners, harbored military secrets, and supported the movement generally.
128. Reidy, p. 6. Thomas Clarke Luby later rose to fame as a 1916 hero.
129. Reidy's mention here of the "Irish Revival movement" refers to the literary endeavors of the Gaelic Revival.
130. Reidy, p. 7.
131. The question of the place of the Irish language in the context of nationalism is an important one, and is addressed by Kenneth E. Nilsen in "The Irish Language in New York, 1850–1900, in Bayor and Meagher, *The New York Irish*, pp. 252–275. Reidy, *The Influence of the Irish Woman*, pp. 6–8.
132. The title then called on "Irish Women's Clubs" both at home and abroad to affiliate with the Inghinide, and attend whatever meetings and conventions were organized (Dublin: Inghinide na hEireann at The Tower Press, 4 Shipper's Alley, Merchant's Quay, 1909). This copy is held at AIHS, Misc. Files.
133. Her friend, suffragist and activist Esther Roper, included the following paragraph in a biographical sketch of the Countess, worth quoting for its summation of the contrasts in her extraordinary life. "Born to comfort, and luxury even, she chooses to die in the public ward of an hospital among her truest, dearest and now most bereaved of sorrowing friends. Born in a castle—a stronghold of English landlordism and ascendancy—she lies in an Irish Republican's grave, cared for by loving Irish hands. And the people miss her a little less now that she lies so close to them, than they did in the stormy days of her exile to English jails." Roper, in Amanda Sebestyan, ed., *Prison Letters of Countess Markievicz* (1934; London: Virago Press, 1987), p. 120.
134. Quoted from Markievicz, *Women: Ideals and the Nation*, p. 17. *Bean na hEireann* followed in the tradition of serials such as Maud Gonne's *L'Irlande Libre* produced in Paris from 1896–1898, and radical nationalist historian Alice Milligan's rhetoric in *The Shan Van Vocht*, published in Belfast during the same years.
135. Modern histories and works on 1916 focus on her participation, but see Sean O'Faolain's *Constance Markievicz, or The Average Revolutionary, A Biography* (London: Cresset Library, 1987), and the

work of Alice Acland and Jacqueline Van Voris. More recent works include Margaret Ward, *Unmanageable Revolutionaries: Women and Irish Nationalism* (London: Pluto Press, 1983) and biographies by Anne Haverty and Diana Norman.

136. Mary Cullen and Maria Luddy, *Female Activists, Irish Women and Change 1900–1960* (Dublin: Woodfield Press, 2001), pp. 142–143.

137. For example, *The New York Times* cited Countess Markievicz a total of thirty-three times from 1913 to the 1930s, often devoting long articles to her public appearances and activities, and in many cases quoting her speeches in their entirety.

138. Markievicz, *Women, Ideals and The Nation*, pp. 1–3. The same contingent of "fighting ancestors" was also cited by McDermott.

139. Markievicz, p. 4.

140. Markievicz, pp. 4–6, 14–16.

Chapter Three

1. Terence De Vere White, *The Anglo Irish* (London: Victor Gollancz Ltd., 1972), p. 249.

2. See, for example, Lawrence McCaffrey, *The Irish Diaspora in America* (Bloomington: Indiana University Press, 1976); and the work of Oscar Handlin, Arnold Schrier, George Potter, and William V. Shannon.

3. Dennis Clark, "East Side, West Side-New York," in *Hibernia America: The Irish and Regional Cultures* (New York: Greenwood Press, 1986), p. 53. Clark is the author of significant treatments of the Irish in America; see the Bibliography for reference. For context, see also works such as David H. Bennett's *The Party of Fear: From Nativist Movements to the New Right in American History* (1988; Chapel Hill: University of North Carolina Press, 1995).

4. See Cormac O'Grada, "A Note on Nineteenth Century Emigration Statistics," in *Population Studies* 29 (1975); David Fitzpatrick, *Irish Emigration 1801–1921* (Dublin: Dundalgan Press: 1984); Kerby Miller, *Emigrants and Exiles: Ireland and the Irish Exodus to North America* (New York: Oxford University Press, 1985); and David N. Doyle, The Regional Bibliography of Irish America: A Review and an Addendum," in *Irish Historical Studies* XXIII, no. 9 (May 1983): pp. 254–283.

5. See Miller's *Emigrants and Exiles* on nineteenth-century Dublin, pp. 368–69, and his appendix on emigration statistics by county; and W. E. Vaughn and A. J. Fitzpatrick, eds., *Irish Historical Statistics: Population, 1821–1971* (Dublin: Royal Irish Academy, 1978).

6. See McCaffrey and Clark; also Daniel P. Moynihan and Nathan Glazer, *Beyond the Melting Pot: The Negroes, Puerto Ricans, Jews, Italians and Irish of New York City* (Cambridge, Mass.: M.I.T. Press, 1970).

7. Ann M. Shea and Marion R. Casey, eds., *The Irish Experience in New York City: A Select Bibliography* (New York: New York Irish History Roundtable, 1995), p. 1; a comprehensive guide to material on the New York Irish.

8. Kevin Kenny, General Introduction, p. 3; Editor's Introduction, pp. 14–16, *New Directions in Irish-American History* (Madison: University of Wisconsin Press, 2003).

9. Historian Terence De Vere White quotes Canon James Hannay (novelist George A. Birmingham) as reminiscing: "We pronounced the word ('Protestant') as if its third consonant was a D, thereby giving it an explosiveness and an obstinacy which no religion in England has possessed since the days of Cromwell's Ironsides!" Terence De Vere White, *The Anglo Irish*, p. 237. See R. F. Foster's biography on Canon Hannay in *Modern Ireland 1600–1972* (London: Allen Lane, Penguin Press, 1988), p. 454.

10. Donald Akenson clarified that "in the first half of the nineteenth century 'Protestant'... referred to the Church of Ireland as the Established Episcopalian Church. Other Protestants were 'dissenters' or... 'non-conformists.' This usage gradually died out and from 1870 onwards, when the Church of Ireland was disestablished, 'Protestant' was usually taken to mean all non-Roman Catholic Christians." Donald Akenson, *Small Differences: Irish Catholics and Irish Protestants, 1815–1922, An International Perspective* (Kingston and Montreal: McGill-Queen's University Press, 1988), p. 229.

    Emigration records expert P.A.M. Taylor cautioned against overreliance on seaport statistics, calling most databases "casual." D.V. Glass and P.A.M. Taylor, *Population and Emigration*, Introduction by P. and G. Ford, in the series *Government and Society in Nineteenth Century Britain, Commentaries on British Parliamentary Papers* (Dublin: Irish Academic Press, 1976), p. 89.

11. Donald Akenson, *Being Had: Historians, Evidence and the Irish in North America* (Toronto: P.D. Meany Publishers, 1985), pp. 29–30. Akenson advanced: "The term 'Scotch-Irish' is an Americanism, generally unknown in Scotland and Ireland, and rarely used by British historians." *Being Had*, p. 61.

12. De Vere White's *The Anglo Irish* and A.P.W. Malcolmson's *John Foster: The Politics of the Anglo-Irish Ascendancy* (New York: Oxford University Press, 1978) are useful. Confusion derives from interchanging identity labels such as "Anglo-Irish," "Old English," "Protestant Ascendancy," "landed gentry," etc.

13. The Penal Laws entrenched the Catholic-Protestant divide. On the Penal era, see J. G. Simms, *Jacobite Ireland 1685–91* (London: Routledge and K. Paul, 1969); and Thomas Bartlett and David Hayton, eds., *The Penal Era and the Golden Age: Essays in Irish History 1690–1800* (Belfast: Ulster Historical Foundation, 1979).

14. De Vere White states in *The Anglo Irish* that "Brendan Behan's definition of an Anglo-Irishman is as good as we have—'a Protestant with a horse.'" *The Anglo Irish*, Introduction.

15. The quoted phrase is Kiberd's; the inspiration Burke's. Declan Kiberd, *Inventing Ireland: The Literature of the Modern Nation* (Cambridge, Mass.: Harvard University Press, 1995), p. 17.

16. Vera Kreilkamp, *The Anglo-Irish Novel and the Big House* (Syracuse: Syracuse University Press, 1998), pp. 10–11.

17. Jacqueline Hill argues that the term "defend(s) the retention of privilege in Protestant hands; it represented a selfish, negative and reactionary concept, at odds with the 'liberal' spirit which had entered Irish politics during the two previous decades." Jacqueline Hill, "The Meaning and Significance of 'Protestant Ascendancy,' 1787–1840," in *Ireland After The Union: Proceedings of the Second Joint Meeting of the Royal Irish Academy and the British Academy*, Introduction by Lord Blake (New York: Oxford University Press, 1989), pp. 1–2.

18. Jacqueline Hill, *From Patriots to Unionists: Dublin Civic Politics and Irish Protestant Patriotism, 1660–1840* (New York: Oxford University Press, 1997). "Establishment" here represented what Roy Foster described as "the fountain of privilege in Ireland." *Modern Ireland*, p. 156.

19. For elaboration, see Blake, *Ireland After the Union*; De Vere White, *The Anglo-Irish*; and Michael J. Hurley, S. J.,ed., *Irish Anglicanism 1869–1969* (Dublin: Allen Figgis, 1970).

20. "Planter" here denotes settlers granted land in Ulster from Elizabethan times on, as per the impulse to "plant" Ireland with a civilizing Protestant influence.

21. R. J. Dickson, *Ulster Emigration to Colonial America 1718–1775* (London: Routledge and Kegan Paul, 1966), pp. 1–5. Dickson remarked that "tradition has it that the Scotch-Irishman is noted for keeping the Sabbath and everything else he can lay his hands on." *Ulster Emigration*, p. 6.

22. D.V. Glass and P.A.M. Taylor, *Population and Emigration*, p. 61; also see Foster's background in *Modern Ireland*, pp. 157–159.

23. The 1798 Rebellion under Wolfe Tone aimed to establish a Republic. See Kerby Miller, *Emigrants and Exiles,* pp. 157–159, noting that "throughout the eighteenth and even into the nineteenth century, Presbyterian emigration (to the U.S.) retained the flavor of a communal exodus compelled by religious and political oppression," p. 159; also Roy Foster in *Modern Ireland,* p. 357, and elsewhere throughout.

24. See as an example of recent work, the essay by Kerby Miller, Bruce D. Boling, with Liam Kennedy, "The Famine's Scars: William Murphy's Ulster and American Odyssey," in Kevin Kenny, ed., *New Directions in Irish-American History* (Madison: University of Wisconsin Press, 2003), pp. 36–60.

25. Whitelaw Reid, *The Scot in America and the Ulster Scot; Being the Substance of Addresses Before the Edinburgh Philosophical Institution, First November 1911, and the Presbyterian Historical Society, Belfast, 28 March 1912* (London: Macmillan and Co., 1912), p. 28.

26. Akenson, *Being Had,* pp. 43–44 (author's emphases). Akenson portrays some studies as worthless, i.e., a 1909 Bureau of the Census study by W.S. Rossiter and the 1930's "Report of the Committee on Linguistic and National Stocks in the Population of the United States" by the American Council of Learned Societies, headed by luminaries Max Farrand, Howard Barker, and Marcus Lee Hansen. Akenson likens a 1980 attempt by Forrest and Ellen Shapiro McDonald to highlight discrepancies in these works to rearrangement of furniture on the *Titanic.* Forrest McDonald and Ellen Shapiro McDonald, "The Ethnic Origins of the American People" *William and Mary Quarterly* 37 (1980), pp. 179–199.

27. Kennedy states that "Once again rates of population change must be used because migration rates by religion are not available, and some of the observed differences between Catholics and Protestants could have been due to differences in natural increase rather than migration." For the years 1911–1961, Kennedy maintains that "the magnitude and direction of the trends shown ... strongly suggest that the same general pattern would be presented by emigration rates were they available." Robert E. Kennedy Jr., *The Irish: Emigration, Marriage and Fertility* (Berkeley: University of California Press, 1973), p. 121.

28. Akenson, *Being Had,* pp. 72–73.

29. See the table by Thomas Keane in "Demographic Trends," in Michael J. Hurley S.J., ed., *Irish Anglicanism,* p. 169. Keane amassed Irish Census population figures for the years listed, his table headed "Population classified by religious profession at each census 1861–1961."

30. Miller, *Emigrants and Exiles,* Table 1, Appendix, p. 569. Miller's statistics from "Reports of the Colonial Land and Emigration Commissioners, 1851–72, and on Board of Trade Returns, 1873–1921."

31. Statistics here from Ronald H. Bayor and Timothy J. Meagher, eds., *The New York Irish* (Baltimore, Md.: Johns Hopkins University Press, 1995), p. 551.

32. Cormac O'Grada, "Across the Briny Ocean: Some Thoughts on Irish Emigration to America, 1800–1850," in Ira Glazier and Luigi De Rosa, eds., *Migration Across Time and Nations: Population Mobility in Historical Contexts* (New York and London: Holmes and Meier Publishers, 1986), pp. 87–89. 38.8% of Irish immigrants to New York left Ulster; the figures for the other provinces are: Connaught: 14.6 percent, Munster: 13.5 percent, and Leinster: 33.03 percent. Kerby Miller offers 21% (of total immigration) as his estimation for Irish Protestant arrival to the United States for 1856–1920. Miller, *Emigrants and Exiles,* p. 350.

33. In his examination of distinction between Catholic and Protestant cultures, Akenson found family size and "sexual and marital mores" remarkably similar, concluding that the denominations "did not have divergent family patterns." Akenson, *Small Differences,* pp. 26–37. See Robert E. Kennedy's "Table 42: Estimated Number of, and Intercensal Percentage Changes Among Native-

born Protestants, Ireland, 1861–1961," *The Irish: Emigration, Marriage and Fertility*, p. 120. Also Cormac O'Grada's "Irish Emigration to America," in Glazier and De Rosa, eds., *Migration Across Time and Nations*, p. 80; *The New York World* and *The Nation*, both July 1871, and *Reports of the Immigration Commission* Vol. 3, 61st Congress Document No. 753 (Washington, D.C.: Government Printing Office, 1911), p. 538.

34. Whitelaw Reid quoted a member of the Pennsylvania Legislature referring to "a pack of insignificant Scotch-Irish who, if they were all killed, could well enough be spared." Reid, *The Scot in America*, p. 28.

35. Patrick Buckland, *Irish Unionism 1885–1922* (London: The Historical Association, 1973), p. 16; Tony Gray, *The Orange Order* (London: The Bodley Head, 1972), p. 15; and "U.S.A. Orange History," at <http://www.orangenet.org/ >, p. 1. See also Hereward Senior's *Orangeism in Ireland and Britain, 1795–1836* (London: Routledge and Kegan Paul, 1966); and the Reverends Dewar, Brown and Long's polemical *Orangeism: A New Historical Appreciation* (Belfast: Grand Orange Lodge of Ireland, 1967). On Orangeism in Canada, see Cecil Houston and William Smyth, *The Sash Canada Wore: A Historical Geography of the Orange Order in Canada* (Toronto: University of Toronto Press, 1980).

36. William Banks, addressing the Canadian Government in his *History of the Orange Order, Entered According to Act of the Parliament of Canada, in the Year 1898 by William Banks, at the Department of Agriculture* (Toronto: William Banks, 519 Parliament Street, 1898).

37. Tony Gray, *The Orange Order*, p. 17. Louis M. De Cormenin, "The Popes of Rome," in William Shannon's *The Dominion Orange Harmonist: A Collection of the Best National, Constitutional, and Loyal Orange Songs and Poems, Together With a Chronological Table, Showing the Dates of the Most Remarkable Events Connected with the British Empire, The Protestant Religion, and the Loyal Orange Institution; Also A Brief History of The Popes of Rome, and Other Matters Interesting to Orangemen* (Toronto: Maclear and Co., 1876), pp. 368–369.

38. Captain L.P.S. Orr, M.P., Imperial Grand Master of the Imperial Grand Orange Council of the World, from the 1967 Dewar, Brown and Long Foreword to *Orangeism: A New Historical Appreciation*, p. 9.

39. Joly Collection, 1330–1348, National Library of Ireland, Dublin (hereafter, NLI).

40. Pamphlets, IR 300 P41, NLI.

41. *Forms and Ritual of the Orange Order To Be Observed in Private Lodges of the Orange Association of British America* (Montreal: The Orange Order, 1852); Microfiche CHIM No. 47028, Metropolitan Toronto Reference Library, the main repository for Orange Order material in North America.

42. All quotations from "The Orange and the Green," *The New York Times*, December 16, 1869, pp. 3–4.

43. "The Orange and the Green," *The New York Times*, July 1, 1872, p. 4.

44. "The House of Orange," *Harper's New Monthly Magazine* LXX (March 1885), p. 501.

45. These events received extensive coverage, in particular the Twelfth commemorating the Battle of the Boyne and the Apprentice Boys who defended Derry against Catholic forces. *The New York Times* carried extensive coverage from the 1870s through to the 1910s. For example, see June 13, July 13, and August 15 in 1872, and January 13, July 29 and August 16 in 1874. Coverage of Orange activities in the Irish city press remained extensive throughout July and August during the 1870s.

46. "Orange Lodges New York, Increase in Members," *The New York Times*, June 13, 1872, p. 5.

47. Banks, *History of the Orange Order*, pp. 32–33. The revolt and execution of Robert Emmet proved tragic to revolutionary nationalists but triumphant to Loyalists.

48. *The New York Times* solicited the opinions of ex-Fenian Thomas D'Arcy McGee for an article enti-

tled "Irish Life in America," June 11, 1865. Despairing of the effects of industrialization in New York, Thomas D'Arcy McGee emigrated to Canada. He succeeded to the post of Minister in the Canadian government before assassination by a Fenian. See the Bibliography for reference to his better-known publications, and Robert McBride, *The Canadian Orange Minstrel for 1860* (London: Free Stream Printing Press, 1860); also the work of Josephine Skelton.

49. Nassau G. Gowan, Provincial Grand Secretary of the Loyal Orange Order Institution, "Orangeism: Able and Eloquent," Metropolitan Toronto Library, Microfiche CHIM No. 51296.

50. Reverend R. M. Ryan, *The New Know-Nothingism: A Reply to the Charges of Incivism and Want of American Patriotism made by The APA* (New York: Published by the author, 1900), p. 85.

51. The Honorable Joel Headley, *Pen and Pencil Sketches of the Great Riots, An Illustrated History of the Railroad and Other Riots, Including all The Riots in the Early History of the Country* (1882; New York: Arno Press, 1969), pp. 303–304. See also David A. Wilson's *United Irishmen, United States: Immigrant Radicals in the Early Republic* (Ithaca: Cornell University Press, 1998), p. 157 and passim.

52. *The Irish American*, July 18, 1868, p. 3; July 24, 1869, p. 4; March 22, 1862, p. 2. See reports on Orange "Outrages" in Ireland during the 1860s, in *The Irish American*, September 14, 1867, p. 3; October 19, 1867, p. 4.

53. The best history is Michael Gordon's *The Orange Riots: Irish Political Violence in New York City, 1870 and 1871* (Ithaca: Cornell University Press, 1993).

54. Headley, Great Riots, pp. 303–304, and *The New York Times*, July 12, 13, and 14, 1870.

55. "Our Orange Governor," *The Irish Citizen*, July 12, 1871, p. 4. Emphasis in original.

56. See Gordon, *The Orange Riots*, for full coverage. The American press as far afield as Atlanta, Georgia and Butte, Montana covered the riot, as did the London and Dublin media. See *The New York Times*, July 13, the Irish press during the week of the Twelfth, *The Nation* magazine, July 1871, and *The Independent*, July 30, 1871.

57. "The Riot," Thomas Carlton and John Lanahan, eds., *Christian Advocate* (New York: 805 Broadway, July 20, 1871), p. 1.

58. Some Catholic publications conveyed antipathy toward the marchers, as with the *Advocate*. See "The Riot of the Twelfth" in the *Catholic World* XIV (October 1871): pp. 117–126.

59. "The New York Riots," *The Saturday Review*, Dublin, Ireland, July 15, 1871, pp. 69–70.

60. *The Irish American*, July 13, 1872, p. 4; July 20, 1872, p. 4; July 15, 1873, p. 4; July 18, 1874, p. 4; July 24, 1875, p. 4; July 19, 1890, p. 4.

61. Michael Gordon, "Orange Riots of 1870 and 1871," Michael Glazier, ed., *The Encyclopedia of the Irish in America* (South Bend, Indiana: Notre Dame University Press, 1999), pp. 748–750. David Bennett explores nativist movements and cites Orange links to larger organizations in *The Party of Fear*, pp. 169–171.

62. *The Irish-American*, July 16, 1894, p. 1.

63. The material in the official Orange Order archives in North America includes minutes of Lodge meetings, commemorative items and publications of members, usually histories of individual Lodges or of the origins of the Order in Ireland. Pamphlets reveal the interest generated by the Montreal events in New York and the close links between lodges in different countries.

64. Father Stafford, Pamphlet, *Address of Reverend Father Stafford on the Montreal Disturbances*, July 29, 1877, Metropolitan Toronto Library, CHIM No. 40383, pp. 8, 11, 14.

65. Quotation from R. M. Sibbett, *Orangeism in Ireland and Throughout the Empire* (Belfast: The Orange Order, 1914), Introduction.

66. The pamphlet does not clarify the circumstances whereby a Catholic priest came to speak to a group of Protestant Orangemen on an excursion. The context suggests an effort by Reverend

MacNamara to address the men personally on this particular day.

67. *Address of Father MacNamara To New York Orangemen*, 1877, Pamphlet CHIM No. 40383, Metropolitan Toronto Library, pp. 16, 18, 19. The title reference here highlights the popular nineteenth-century practice of veiling controversial issues in the language of the symbolic.

68. "Orange Ranters," *The Irish World*, July 25, 1885, p. 4; "Orangeism and British Rule," *The Irish World*, June 28, 1884, p. 6; "Orangemen and Anti-Orangemen," *The Irish World*, July 20, 1888, p. 5.

69. Quoted by Philip Henry Dudley Bagenal in *The American-Irish and Their Influence on Irish Politics* (London: K. Paul Trench and Co., 1882), pp. 141–143.

70. Jeremiah O'Donovan, *A Brief Account of the Author's Interview with his Countrymen, and of the Parts of the Emerald Isle Whence they Emigrated. Together with a Direct Reference to Their Present Location in the Land of Their Adoption, During his Travels Through Various States of the Union in 1854 and 1855* (Arno, 1969; Pittsburgh: By the Author, 1864).

71. "Are Orangemen Irishmen?" editorial, *The Irish People*, August 2, 1873, p. 4.

72. "Song for July The Twelfth," by "Artane," *The Irish-American*, August 2, 1884, p. 3. "Artane" here makes reference to a Dublin suburb.

73. Journal of Rose McDermott, p. 21, cited in Chapter Two, "Miscellaneous" Box, American Irish Historical Society (hereafter, AIHS).

74. According to Roy Foster, "The United Irishmen were modernizers: they appealed . . . to posterity, not ancestors. (Given the way that the ancestors of Belfast radicals had treated the Gaelic Irish, this was just as well)." R. F. Foster, *Modern Ireland*, pp. 269–270. The Orange Order stuck to a more conservative agenda.

75. Liberals such as Robert Molesworth and Bishop George Berkeley sought freedom of speech and the promotion of objective government. See Marianne Elliott's *Watchmen in Sion: The Protestant Idea of Liberty* (Derry: A Field Day Pamphlet, Dorman and Sons, 1985), on classic liberal thought from the 1600s to the 1900s. See also I. R. McBride's "'When Ulster joined Ireland': Anti-Popery, Presbyterian radicalism and Irish republicanism in the 1790s," in *Past & Present*, no. 157 (November 1997): pp. 63–93.

76. E. W. McFarland, *Ireland and Scotland in the Age of Revolution: Planting the Green Bough* (Edinburgh: Edinburgh University Press, 1994), pp. 6–12, 24–25.

77. Belfast businessman and cotton processor Henry Joy McCracken played a leading role in 1798. See A.T.Q. Stewart's *The Summer Soldiers: The 1798 Rebellion in Antrim and Down* (Belfast: Blackstaff Press, 1995), pp. 54–59.

78. This extract is from a diary Wolfe Tone kept to inform his wife of plans and operations. Reprinted in Melosina Lenox-Conyngham, ed., *Diaries of Ireland: An Anthology, 1590–1987* (Dublin: Lilliput Press, 1998), pp. 83–84. Emphasis in original.

79. R. F. Foster, *Modern Ireland*, pp. 269–270. See also Kevin Herlihy, ed., *The Politics of Irish Dissent, 1650–1840* (Dublin: Four Courts Press, 1997), and Ian McBride, *The Siege of Derry in Ulster Protestant Mythology* (Dublin: Four Courts Press, 1997), for further exploration. See Gerald Griffin's "Songs of Our Land" in *The Irish American*, July 22, 1911, p. 4. These divisions, including "Protestant self-exclusion and unconscious exclusion of Protestants by Catholics" arise in essays honoring Northern poet John Hewitt. The notion that "in the Republic, as part of the . . . turning of historical tables, the 'Hidden Ireland' has now more claim to be Protestant than Gaelic" offers a fresh glimpse into the historical relationship.
From John Hewitt's *Across a Roaring Hill: The Protestant Imagination in Modern Ireland, Essays in Honour of John Hewitt*, edited by Gerald Dawe and Edna Longley (Belfast: Blackstaff Press, 1985), p. 1.

80. Much has appeared on Mitchel, but see Foster's short biography in *Modern Ireland,* p. 314, and Deegee Lester's entry in *The Encyclopedia of the Irish in America,* pp. 621–622 as starting points.

81. On fellow Protestant nationalist, able editor and composer of popular ballads, Terence De Vere White summed up contemporary opinion and historical consensus in stating "Davis's virtues are agreed on by all." *The Anglo Irish,* p. 144.

82. Death notices for Jane Verner (Jenny) Mitchel from the *New York Sun* and *The Boston Pilot,* widely carried through the New York press, and other unidentified newspaper clippings, December 31, 1899, are held in the Meloney-Mitchel Papers Collection, Correspondence, Mss. and Documents, Box 2A, Butler Mss. and Rare Book Library, Columbia University, hereafter referred to as Meloney-Mitchel Papers. This resource even contains a lock of John Mitchel's hair. See Rebecca O'Conner's *Jenny Mitchel Young Irelander: A Biography* (1985; Tuscon: Trust Publishers, 1988). O'Conner's "Jenny" highlights Mitchel's nickname; but I have remained with "Jane" as per primary material consulted.

83. Meloney-Mitchel Papers, Obituary of Jane Mitchel. Her parents eventually became reconciled to her marriage.

84. The series of letters offers detail on life in mid-century New York for expatriates such as the Mitchels. Jane Mitchel corresponded regularly for years with Mary Thompson who lived at Mellifont View, Kingstown, now Dun Laoghaire.

85. Letter, Jane to Mary Thompson, Kingstown, from Union Street in Brooklyn, December 14, 1853. Meloney-Mitchel Papers.

86. Letter, Jane Verner Mitchel, March 11, 1854. Mr. O'Brien mentioned here was revolutionary, Harrow and Cambridge educated William Smith O'Brien, who received the same transportation sentence as Mitchel; commuted in 1856. For a short biography, see Foster, *Modern Ireland,* p. 314; and Blanche Touhill's *William Smith O'Brien and his Irish Revolutionary Companions in Penal Exile* (Columbia: University of Missouri, 1981).

87. John Mitchel took part in Ireland's 1848 Rebellion, another in a succession of failed revolts. The protagonists had banded together as a Young Ireland crew of poets, journalists, and intellectuals. Letter, Jane Mitchel to Mary Thompson, April 20, 1854, Meloney-Mitchel Papers.

88. See *Speeches on the Legislative Independence of Ireland, with Introductory notes by Thomas Francis Meagher* (New York: Redfield, 1853), and the entry by Timothy Walch in *The Encyclopedia of the Irish in America,* pp. 601–602.

89. "O'Gorman" references Richard O'Gorman, a Dublin-based Catholic participant in the 1848 Rebellion who arrived in New York in the 1850s and attained considerable status within business and political circles; and "O'Reilly" to Thomas Devin O'Reilly, another 1848 veteran and city Fenian. Miller provides notes on these in *Emigrants and Exiles,* p. 310. What is less clear is one of Jane Mitchel's intriguing remarks about Mrs. O'Reilly—"It is a sad pity of her."

90. Letter, Jane Mitchel, December 2, 1854, Meloney-Mitchel Papers.

91. Shane Leslie, "Irish Leaders," in Joseph Dunn and P.J. Lennox, eds., *The Glories of Ireland* (Washington, D.C.: Phoenix Ltd., 1914), p. 159. John Mitchel, *Jail Journal; or Five Years in British Prisons Commenced On Board The Shearwater Steamer* (London: R&T Washbourne, Ltd., 1, 2 and 4 Paternoster Row, Published by the author, 1854). The New York edition was published in the Office of *The Citizen,* also in 1854. Miller described this work as "venomously anti-English . . . a . . . minor masterpiece." *Emigrants and Exiles,* p. 311.

92. Mitchel, *Jail Journal,* pp. 196, 222.

93. Jane Mitchel to Mary Thompson, January 15, 1855, Meloney-Mitchel Papers.

94. Robert Emmet was hanged for treason by the British government in 1802. Thomas Addis Emmett led the Irish National Federation of America, of which more in the last chapter.

95. Regarded by many contemporaries as a historian of eminence, R. F. Foster characterized Froude as "that perverse Victorian." *Modern Ireland*, p. 103.

96. Titles of two lectures delivered by Froude in New York in November 1872, collected in *Froude's Crusade-Both Sides: Lectures by Very Reverend T. N. Burke, O.P., John Mitchel, Wendell Phillips and Mr. James Anthony Froude in Summing Up The Controversy, with the Life and Labors of Fr. Burke by James W. O'Brien, and Editorial Articles of the Leading Journals of the Country Regarding the Debate* (New York: J.W. O'Brien, 1872). Pamphlets in American History, Microfiche CA1002.

97. "Editor's Literary Record," *Harper's New Monthly Magazine* XLIV (December 1872–May 1873), p. 457.

98. James W. O'Brien, *Life and Labors of Father Burke, His Career in Ireland, Rome and America, His Influence on the Irish-American Element, His Characteristics as a Preacher, His Controversy with Froude, The Verdict, etc.*, in *Froude's Crusade*, p. 7 (emphasis in original).

99. O'Brien, *Life and Labors*, pp. 7–8.

100. *The New York Tribune*, the *New York World*, and *The New York Herald*, November and early December, 1872. Excerpts quoted in *Froude's Crusade*, pp. 7–15.

101. *The New York Nation*, November 29, 1872, p. 3.

102. *The New York Evening Post*, November 26, 1872, p. 4.

103. Timothy J. Meagher provides evidence of this kind of development for the case of Worcester in *Inventing Irish America: Generation, Class, and Ethnic Identity in a New England City, 1880–1928* (Indiana: Notre Dame University Press, 2001).

104. Froude, from *Froude's Summing Up Against Father Burke, Lecture in New York by Mr. James Anthony Froude, November 30, 1872, in reply to Fr. Burke's Series*, contained in *Froude's Crusade*, p. 24.

105. Mitchel, *Froude, From the Standpoint of an Irish Protestant*, in *Froude's Crusade*, p. 67.

106. Wendell Phillips, *Review of Mr. Froude*, Lecture at Tremont Temple, Boston, December 3, 1872, pp. 75, 80.

107. "MacGeoghegan's Misery," *The New York Times*, October 29, 1875, p. 4.

108. *The Irish Republic: A Journal of Liberty, Literature and Social Progress*, edited by Michael Scanlon, Vol. II, February 6, 1869, 2. New York Historical Society.

109. "Irish Protestants," *The Irish World*, December 23, 1876, p. 5.

110. "Why I Am A Nationalist," *The Irish-American*, February 21, 1914, p. 8.

111. Papers of the Society of the Friendly Sons of Saint Patrick, AIHS. See also Richard C. Murphy and Lawrence J. Mannion, *The History of the Society of the Friendly Sons of Saint Patrick in the City of New York, 1784–1955* (New York: Fordham University Press, 1960).

112. Brother J. H. Edge, K. C., "The Story of Irish Freemasonry," delivered at the Grand Lodge of Instruction of the Grand Lodge of Ireland, November 1912, and published in the city Masonry magazine *The New Age Magazine*, 1913, p. 18. The article claimed Daniel O'Connell as a life-long Mason.

113. Charles T. McClenachan, Historian of the Grand Lodge, *History of the Most Ancient and Honorable Fraternity of Free and Accepted Masons in New York From the Earliest Date. Embracing the History of the Grand Lodge of the State from its Formation in 1781, and a Sketch of each Lodge under its Jurisdiction: Preceded by a Brief Account of Early Masonry in England, Scotland, Ireland, and Several Continental Nations. Together with an Outline of the origin of the Institution in the Thirteen Colonies of the Union* (New York: The Grand Lodge, 1881), p. 47.

114. *History,* Vol. III, The Grand Lodge of New York, pp. 66–67.

115. *History,* Vol. II, Sketches of Grand Officers, p. 579.

116. Miller et al., "The Famine's Scars," in Kenny, ed., *New Directions,* p. 48.

117. Peter Ross, LLD., *A Standard Dictionary of Freemasonry In the State of New York. Including Lodge Chapter, Council, Commandery and Scottish Rite Bodies* (New York and Chicago: The Lewis Publishing Co., 1899); Vol. 1, p. 689; Vol. 2, p. 44. Livingston Masonic Lodge, Grand Lodge Free and Accepted Masons, State of New York, Archives, New York.

118. *Dictionary,* pp. 74, 94, 177.

119. *Dictionary,* p. 205.

120. *Dictionary,* pp. 300, 307, 359, 382, 389.

121. *Dictionary,* pp. 421, 424, 426, 428, 429, 431, and 519.

122. By the author of "The Jerico Papers," *The Irish Prince and the Hebrew Prophet: A Masonic Tale of the Captive Jews and the Ark of the Covenant* (New York: Masonic Publishing Company, No. 63 Bleecker Street, 1896), Preface, pp. 12–13.

123. Instead of the usual Episcopalian or Presbyterian affiliation, Grattan Mythen served as the Archimandrite minister of Saint Nicholas Cathedral, East Ninety-Seventh Street, a Russian Orthodox Church. Grattan Mythen was also involved at the All-American National Committee's National Coordinating Office, at 409 Fourth Avenue during the 1910s, releasing press statements such as the following: "defend and maintain the Liberty handed on to us from the generations past. We call upon you to act *now* that WE MAY KEEP AMERICA AMERICAN!" Box 11, Folder 19, Judge Daniel J. Cohalan Papers, AIHS. Emphasis in original.

124. Dr. Norman Thomas served as pastor of East Harlem Presbyterian Church from 1911 to 1918. He was familiar with the Irish political question of the 1910s, corresponding with the law firm of Michael Francis Doyle in Philadelphia on conscientious objection to war service—Doyle described cases involving "the leaders in the Irish movement" in America in a letter to Thomas from February 26, 1920; and retaining an advertisement for Jeremiah A. O'Leary's *My Political Trial and Experiences* (New York: Jefferson Publishing Co., 1919). See Norman Thomas Papers 1904–1967, Series 1, General Correspondence, October 1905-October 1933, microfilm, reel 1; also Murray B. Seidler's *Norman Thomas: Respectable Rebel* (Syracuse: Syracuse University Press, 1961).

125. Right Reverend Patrick James Grattan Mythen to the Executive Committee of the Protestant Friends of Ireland, Cohalan Papers, Box 12.

126. Letter, Mythen to the Directors of the Protestant Friends of Ireland, New York, October 28, 1920. Cohalan Papers, Box 11, Folder 19; Fifteen-page typed document from Mythen to the Executive Committee of the Protestant Friends of Ireland, October 27, 1920. Cohalan Papers, Box 14, File 6, AIHS.

127. Incidentally, Reverend Mythen cited President Eamon De Valera's name elsewhere as "the Hon. Aemonn De Valera," a misspelling of the name "Eamon."

128. The scholarship on Eamon De Valera is substantial. In the past, laudatory treatments of the father of a free Gaelic Ireland prevailed, but recent works tend to adopt a less romanticized view, i.e., Tim Pat Coogan's *Eamon De Valera: The Man Who Was Ireland* (London and New York: Hutchinson, 1993). Coogan provides a comprehensive bibliography, and see Foster's short biography in *Modern Ireland,* p. 485. More on Dev in the Conclusion.

129. The Delegates of the Protestant Churches of Ireland, *Facts About Ireland for the Consideration of American Citizens,* published by the delegation, pp. 7–8. William J. Maloney Papers, Box 10, NYPL.

Chapter Four

1. See Matthew Arnold, "On the Study of Celtic Literature," in R. H. Super, ed., *The Complete Prose Works of Matthew Arnold, Vol. 3, Lectures in Essays and Criticism* (Ann Arbor: University of Michigan Press, 1962).

2. Seamus Deane makes reference to Arnold's timing in *A Short History of Irish Literature* (London: Hutchinson and Co., Publishers, 1986), p. 84. Also see R. F. Foster, *Modern Ireland 1600–1972* (London: Allen Lane, Penguin Press, 1988), p. 394.

3. See Foster's perspective in *Modern Ireland*, pp. 446–456.

4. Deane, *Irish Literature*, p. 85.

5. For background, see Art Cosgrove and Donal McCartney, eds., *Studies in Irish History Presented to R. Dudley Edwards* (Dublin: Gill and Macmillan, 1979) and the work of R. B. McDowell.

6. *A New History of Ireland Vol. III; Early Modern Ireland 1534–1691*, eds. T. W. Moody, F. X. Martin, and F. J. Byrne (New York: Oxford University, 1976); and *IV; Eighteenth-Century Ireland 1691–1800*, eds., T.W. Moody and W.E. Vaughan (New York: Oxford University Press, 1986), contain useful material; also the work of Robert Kee.

7. Robert Fortner's "The Culture of Hope and The Culture of Despair: The Print Media and Nineteenth Century Irish Emigration," in *Eire-Ireland* XIII (Fall 1978): pp. 38–48 has much to offer, as do David Lloyd in *Anomalous States: Irish Writing and the Post-Colonial Moment* (Durham: Duke University Press, 1993), and Matthew Frye Jacobson in *Special Sorrows: The Diasporic Imagination of Irish, Polish, and Jewish Immigrants in the United States* (Cambridge, Mass.: Harvard University Press, 1995).

8. Dennis Clark, *Erin's Heirs: Irish Bonds of Community* (Lexington: University Press of Kentucky, 1991), p. 4. More recent works substantiate foundational scholarship, including the contributions of Patricia Monaghan, Blanche Touhill, Michael G. Stephens, Caledonia Kearns, and Dennis Smith.

9. Aviel Rushwald, "Untangling the Knotted Cord: Studies of Nationalism," *Journal of Interdisciplinary History* XXIV, no. 2 (Autumn 1993), p. 294.

10. Jacobson, *Special Sorrows*, p. 16. See also his *Whiteness of a Different Color: European Immigrants and the Alchemy of Race* (Cambridge, Mass.: Harvard University Press, 1998), on these themes. See the work of Beth McKillen and Philip O'Leary; also McCaffrey, Skerrett, Funchion, and Fanning, eds., *The Irish In Chicago* (Urbana and Chicago: University of Illinois Press, 1987), pp. 61–98.

11. John Hutchinson, *The Dynamics of Cultural Nationalism: The Gaelic Revival and the Creation of the Irish Nation State* (London: Allen and Unwin, 1987), p. 9.

12. Rushwald, "Studies of Nationalism," *Interdisciplinary History*, p. 303. See also Kerby Miller, "Class, Culture and Immigrant Group Identity in the United States: The Case of Irish-American Ethnicity," in Virginia Yans-McLoughlin, ed., *Immigration Reconsidered: History, Sociology and Politics* (New York: Oxford University Press, 1990).

13. See Richard Caplan and John Feffer's *Europe's New Nationalism: States and Minorities in Conflict* (New York: Oxford University Press, 1996), also Peter Alter's *Nationalism* (Frankfurt am Main: Suhrkamp Verlag, 1985), pp. 60–69.

14. R.V. Comerford, "Nationalism and The Irish Language," in Thomas Hachey and Lawrence McCaffrey, eds., *Perspectives on Irish Nationalism* (Lexington, Kentucky: University Press of Kentucky, 1989), p. 27. See also Eric Foner's "Class, Ethnicity, and Radicalism in the Gilded Age: The Land League and Irish America," *Marxist Perspectives* 1, no. 2 (Summer 1978): pp. 6–55;

Michael Gordon's "Labor Boycott in New York City, 1880–86," *Labor History* 16, no. 2 (1975): pp. 184–229; and Miller's summation in *Emigrants and Exiles: Ireland and the Irish Exodus to North America* (New York: Oxford University Press, 1985), pp. 548–549. On the poetic traditions that persevered within Gaelic folk culture into the nineteenth century, Michael Kenneally wrote: "For a variety of complex social and historical reasons, Irish literature has traditionally displayed an inordinate concern with questions of cultural identity and nationalistic ideals." The Gaelic poet, or "file," commanded exalted status, as did the storyteller or "seanachie." Michael Kenneally, ed., *Cultural Contexts and Literary Idioms in Contemporary Irish Literature* (New Jersey: Barnes and Noble Books, 1988), p. 3.

15. Gerald Dawe, from his essay "A Question of Imagination—Poetry in Ireland Today," in Kenneally, ed., *Cultural Contexts and Literary Idioms,* p. 187. On nationalism and language, see Daniel Corkery's *The Hidden Ireland* (Cork: Arlen House, 1924). Corkery revealed a rural Ireland almost eclipsed by the twentieth century, and touched a nerve in the national consciousness. See also the contributions to the field of Robert James Scally and Terry Eagleton.

16. C. L. Innes, *Woman and Nation in Irish Literature and Society, 1880–1935* (Athens: University of Georgia Press, 1993), p. 47. "Shean Bhean Bhocht" translates as the "poor old woman," often symbolizing Ireland.

17. Declan Kiberd, *Inventing Ireland: The Literature of the Modern Nation* (Cambridge, Mass.: Harvard University Press, 1995), p. 115; and particularly Chapter 23 entitled "Protholics and Cathestants."

18. D. George Boyce, *Nationalism in Ireland* (1982; London: Routledge, 1995–96), p. 237.

19. Kenneth Nilsen's "The Irish Language in New York, 1850–1900," in Ronald H. Bayor and Timothy J. Meagher, eds., *The New York Irish* (Baltimore, Md.: The Johns Hopkins University Press, 1995), pp. 252–275; and R. F. Foster in *Paddy and Mr. Punch: Connections in Irish and English History* (London: Penguin Books, 1993) provide an essential foundation for this discussion.

20. For biographical data on Canon Hannay, see Foster's summary in *Modern Ireland*, p. 454.

21. George A. Birmingham, *An Irishman Looks At His World* (New York and London: Hodder and Stoughton, 1919), pp. 12–20.

22. James Clarence Mangan, 1803–1849, Dublin-born poet. See *Lyra Celtica, An Anthology of Representative Celtic Poetry, Ancient Irish, Alban, Gaelic, Breton, Cymric and Modern Scottish and Irish Celtic Poetry,* edited by E. A. Sharp and J. Matthay (Edinburgh: John Grant, 1924), p. 420; see also the Mangan anthologies by David Lloyd and Augustine Martin.

23. Patrick Ward, *Exile, Emigration and Irish Writing* (Dublin: Irish Academic Press, 2002), pp. 100–101. See Ward's exploration of the connections between Mitchel and Mangan within Irish-America, as he invokes valuable linkages between text and sociopolitical context.

24. Michael Monahan, *Nova Hibernia: Irish Poets and Dramatists of Today and Yesterday* (1914; New York: Books for Libraries Press Inc., 1968), p. 146.

25. Published in pamphlet form, this poem appeared frequently in the city press and in collections of nineteenth-century poetry such as *Lyra Celtica*, pp. 137–138.

26. Edward T. O'Donnell, "'Though not an Irishman': Henry George and the American Irish," *The American Journal of Economics and Sociology* 56, no. 4 (October 1997): pp. 408–410.

27. *The Irish World and American Industrial Liberator*, December 9, 1882, p. 8.

28. *Lyra Celtica*, pp. 139–141. Often appearing as "Roisin Dubh," the ancient name for Ireland translates as a diminutive of "dark" or "black Rose." See also contributions by Diane Bessai and S. F. Gallagher.

29. Poem entitled "After Death," by Frances Isabelle Parnell. Reprinted in *Lyra Celtica*, p. 165.

30. Yeats, quoted by Roy Foster in "Anglo-Irish Literature, Gaelic Nationalism and Irish Politics in the 1890s," in Lord Blake, ed., *Ireland After the Union: Proceedings of the Second Joint Meeting of*

the Royal Irish Academy and the British Academy, London (London: Oxford University Press, 1986), p. 65. Foster continued. "Faced with the necessary venality of contemporary politics, both Yeatsian and Fenian iconography preferred the image of the dead Parnell as an icy, aristocratic Anglophobe."

31. See Jane Cote's *Fanny and Anna Parnell: Ireland's Patriot Sisters* (New York: St. Martin's Press, 1991) and her "Writing Women Out of History: Fanny and Anna Parnell and the Irish Ladies Land League," *Etudes Irlandaises* 17 (1992): pp. 123–134.

32. Poem entitled "To Miss Rita O'Donohoe, The Little Girl From Ireland," by Mary O'Donovan-Rossa. Printed on a single card, and included in the diary of Rose McDermott, American Irish Historical Society, New York (hereafter AIHS). Immediately following the three verses of the poem, the card reproduced the accolade to Rita O'Donohoe from *The New York Irish American* praising her Carnegie performance. The card and clipping are undated, but likely the late 1880s or early 1890s.

33. Kiberd, *Inventing Ireland*, p. 11.

34. See Cusack's own *The Nun of Kenmare: An Autobiography* (Boston: Ticknor and Company, 1889), and her other work referenced in Chapter Two.

35. *Tim Carty's Trial, or, Whistling at Landlords: A Play for the Times,* by Sister Mary Frances Clare (New York: Stephen Mearns, Printer, 1886). Pamphlets in American History, Microfiche CA 988, Cusack 1830–1899.

36. W. B. Yeats, quoted in "The Irish Literary Revival," by Horatio S. Krans, in *The Glories Of Ireland*, eds., Joseph Dunn and P. J. Lennox, (Washington: Phoenix Ltd., 1914), p. 317.

37. Tenant farmers sought the "Three F's"—Fair rent, Fixity of Tenure, and Free sale. See Paul Bew, *Land and The National Question in Ireland, 1858–82* (Atlantic Heights, N.J.: Humanities Press, 1970).

38. *Tim Carty's Trial,* Mr. Evictem, Act I, p. 10. "Griffith's Valuation" refers to the standard evaluation for rented land set in the 1840s.

39. *Tim Carty's Trial,* p. 11.

40. *Tim Carty's Trial,* p. 46. This pronouncement refers to Gladstone's tenant reform efforts.

41. Jacobson, *Special Sorrows*, p. 3.

42. The broadsheet or broadside ballad constituted an art form of note in past centuries. Akin to folk song in terms of popularity, this form of commentary developed into commonplace urban practice. "The act of printing was, so to speak, merely superimposed on an oral tradition that had already found new directions," Leslie Shepard stated in *The Broadside Ballad: A Study in Origins and Meaning* (London: Herbert Jenkins, 1962), pp. 47–48.

43. Broadsheet Ballads SY 1865, No.'s 380–386, Pamphlet, New York Historical Society (hereafter NYHS).

44. The Fenian plot to invade Canada in 1866 failed to produce the desired effect. See Leon O'Broin, *Fenian Fever: An Anglo-American Dilemma* (New York: New York University Press, 1971); the primary account of John Devoy in *Recollections of an Irish Rebel* (Shannon: Irish University Press, 1969), and Terry Golway's engaging *Irish Rebel: John Devoy and America's Fight for Ireland's Freedom* (New York: St. Martin's Griffin, 1998), and further coverage in Chapter Six.

45. Both verses, "O'Toole and McFinnigan On The War," Broadsheet Ballads SY 1865, No. 380.

46. Broadsheet Ballads SY 1865, No. 372.

47. Written by John F. Poole, and sung "by the great Comic-Vocalist of the age, Tony Pastor." Broadsheet SY 1865, No. 386.

48. Broadside, Edwin Patrick Kilroe Collection, Box 26, File 2, Columbia University. In the verse quoted, the "hod" referred to a device for transporting bricks on construction sites. "Gob" stems from a Gaelic term for mouth and "Erin go bragh" is a reworking of an old war cry translated as

"Ireland, powerful forever!" See the material in Williams, William H.A., *Twas Only an Irishman's Dream: The Image of Ireland and the Irish in American Popular Song Lyrics, 1800–1920* (Urbana: University of Illinois Press, 1996).

49. *Poems by Speranza, (Lady Wilde)* (Dublin: M.H. Gill and Sons, Ltd., 1864), p. 27. Terence De Vere White noted "Lady Wilde in her youth breathed defiance at the British Government in prose and verse no less voluminous and extravagant than herself. And she was tireless in pursuit of a pension from the Government she had urged the Irish to rise and destroy." *The Anglo Irish* (London: Victor Gollancz Ltd., 1972), p. 200.

50. *The Irish Nation*, December 30, 1881. See *Speranza, A Biography of Lady Wilde* (New York: Philosophical Library Inc., 1951), by Horace Wyndham, who had sole access to the Wilde papers. See also her own "The Voice of the Poor, To a Despondent Nationalism" from *Poems by Speranza*, pp. 20–21.

51. Ward, *Exile, Emigration and Irish Writing*, p. 134. See Ward's entire chapter entitled "Holy Ireland: Constructions, Omissions, Evasions, Resistance" for further insight into these connections.

52. *The Irish People*, advertisement for *The Irish Democrat*, March 16, 1872, p. 7.

53. James J. Delany, M.D., 336 East Seventy-Ninth Street, New York, "The 'Celtic' Race," *The New York Times*, March 17, 1886, p. 4.

54. In addition to Froude, Dr. Delany also drew upon the work of English historian W. E. H. Lecky. See Lecky's work cited in the Bibliography in this context.

55. See the final chapter for reference to the bulk of the scholarship on the Fenians.

56. Lieutenant-Colonel W. R. Roberts, *Oration Delivered by L.C. W.R.R. At the Great Fenian Demonstration in Jones' Wood, New York on Tuesday July 25 1865* (New York: Office of the Trades Advocate, 166 William Street, 1865), 10 cents. New York Pamphlets, NYHS. This pamphlet is also held at AIHS.

57. *Oration*, p. 10.

58. Engineer and Young Irelander, James Stephens was born in Kilkenny in 1825. From Paris he toured America and resided in New York to raise money and Fenian awareness. He founded the *Irish People* newspaper but returned to Ireland in the 1880s. For a biography, see Foster, *Modern Ireland*, pp. 390–391.

59. Diary of James Stephens, 1858–1860, 38 pages, handwritten, Diaries, Box 3, p. 3, New York Public Library (hereafter NYPL); once housed in the Public Record Office, Northern Ireland.

60. John O'Mahony, born in 1816 in Limerick, educated at Trinity College; Young Irelander and translator of bardic poetry. He died in New York in 1877, and is buried in Glasnevin, Ireland's National Cemetery. For further details, see Foster, *Modern Ireland*, p. 390.

61. Stephens, Diary, pp. 6, 7, 19.

62. Diary, pp. 19–29, 31.

63. *The New York Times*, June 5, 1866, p. 4.

64. *Declaration of Principles, by the Representatives of the Fenian Brotherhood, in Congress Assembled*, Cleveland, Ohio, September 7, 1867. Publications in American History series, Microfiche CA934.

65. Michael Funchion has a useful summary on the organization in *Irish American Voluntary Organizations* (Westport, Connecticut: Greenwood Press, 1983), pp. 257–259, and see references in the final chapter here.

66. Mike Cronin and Daryl Adair provide insight into Friendly Sons St. Patrick's Day celebrations and banquets, citing these gatherings as "venues for expressions of Irish nationalism" in *The Wearing of the Green: A History of St. Patrick's Day* (London and New York: Routledge, 2002), p. 76.

67. Dinner Program, Friendly Sons of Saint Patrick, March 17th, 1870, St. James Hotel, New York. Material from the Friendly Sons holdings, AIHS.

68. Rose McDermott, Diary, pp. 21–22, AIHS.

69. John Mitchel, *From the Standpoint of an Irish Protestant*, in J. A. Froude, *Froude's Crusade-Both Sides* (New York: J.W. O'Brien, 1872), p. 67; and James Stephens, Diary, 1858–1860, pp. 15–23.

70. Daniel Dougherty, *The Response of Daniel Dougherty to the Toast "The Day we Celebrate" at the Dinner of the Friendly Sons of New York City, at Delmonico's, March 17, 1888.* Pamphlets in American History Series, Microfiche CA 993.

71. *Daniel O'Connell, The Liberator (Born August 6, 1775, Died May 15, 1847, Aged 72), A Lecture, Delivered at the Academy of Music, New York, May 13, 1872, by the Very Reverend Thomas N. Burke, O.P.* Pamphlets in American History series, Microfiche CA 689.

72. The booklet was published in New York by D. and J. Sadlier & Co., 31 Barclay Street, in 1875.

73. O'Connell was described by R. F. Foster as "the greatest leader of Catholic Ireland." See his biography in *Modern Ireland*, p. 291; and the Bibliography for further reading.

74. O'Connell held a series of large-scale meetings throughout Ireland in the 1830s and 1840s, where thousands of people heard his message and engaged in non-violent agitation against British rule. The "Clontarf" reference denotes the 1843 Monster Meeting planned for the site commemorating 1014's battle between Brian Boru and the Vikings. O'Connell canceled the gathering under threat of British invasion.

75. Father Burke, *Daniel O'Connell,* pp. 19–20.

76. *Daniel O'Connell,* p. 20. O'Connell headed the ranks of the celebrated, including Sarsfield, Tone, and Emmet.

77. See Terry Golway's entry on Mayor Grace, "Irish-American Mayors," in Michael Glazier, ed., *The Encyclopedia of the Irish in America* (South Bend, Indiana: Notre Dame University Press, 1999), p. 686.

78. William R. Grace, *The Irish In America: A Lecture,* delivered at The Boston Theater, February 21, 1886, published in Chicago by McDonnell Brothers Publishers, 1886, p. 4. Pamphlets in American History Series, Microfiche CA 655.

79. *The Irish In America,* pp. 23, 29.

80. The large number of works published in the later nineteenth century speaks to the popularity of the genre in New York. For background, see Mary Helen Thuente's useful *The Harp Re-strung: The United Irishmen and the Rise of Irish Literary Nationalism* (Syracuse: Syracuse University Press, 1994).

81. Colonel James E. McGee, *Lives of Irishmen's Sons and Their Descendants* (New York: J.A. McGee Publishers, 7 Barclay Street, 1874), pp. vi, vii.

82. Reverend Augustine J. Thebaud, S.J., *The Irish Race in the Past and Present* (New York: Peter F. Collier, 1878), pp. viii, 412–413, 482.

83. Philip Henry Dudley Bagenal, *The American-Irish and Their Influence on Irish Politics* (London: K. Paul Trench and Co., 1882), pp. 37, 72. Here, Bagenal refers to three prominent agitators on the contemporary Irish political circuit in New York.

84. Bernard F. O'Reilly, D.D., *The Cause of Ireland Pleaded Before the Civilized World* (New York: P.F. Collier, Publisher, 11–15 Vandewater Street, 1886), p. iii.

85. *The Cause,* p. 509. Here, O'Reilly refers to the British administration's Irish headquarters in Dublin Castle.

86. Joseph Dunn and P. J. Lennox, eds., *The Glories Of Ireland.* Casement was shot while imprisoned in London, a nationalist martyr thereafter. Douglas Hyde, first President of Ireland and Gaelic Revivalist, drew the following from Terence De Vere White: "Hyde . . . should have been well beat-

en by his father for going into country cottages and learning to speak Irish from the peasants instead of studying his Greek grammar." *The Anglo Irish*, p. 192. It may be suggested that Dunn and Lennox preempted Thomas Cahill's *How the Irish Saved Civilization* (New York: Nan A. Talese, Doubleday, 1995)!

87. *The Glories Of Ireland*, p. v.

88. O'Brien's role as official Historiographer of the American Irish Historical Society accorded him a special perspective on all things Irish in New York.

89. Michael J. O'Brien, "The Irish in the United States," *Glories Of Ireland*, p. 184.

90. The Land League was succeeded by the Irish National League in the 1880s and 1890s. Conservative Catholic organization the Knights of Columbus originated in Connecticut and made its appearance in New York during the 1880s. Miller refers to each in *Emigrants and Exiles*.

91. John O'Dea, "Famous Irish Societies," *Glories Of Ireland*, pp. 176–183.

92. Ford's *The Criminal History of the British Empire* (New York: *The Irish World*, 1915) introduces the journalist's views on the relationship between Ireland and Britain. Chapter titles such as "Landlord-Made Irish Famine," and "English Christianity Following English Bayonets," speak to Ford's perception of the relationship. *Criminal History*, pp. 24, 45.

93. Michael MacDonagh, "Irish Journalism," *Glories Of Ireland*, pp. 312–313.

94. MacDonagh, *Glories Of Ireland*, pp. 312–313.

95. Dunn and Lennox, *Glories Of Ireland*, p. v.

96. Right Reverend John England, Bishop of Charleston, *Substance of a Discourse Delivered Before the Hibernian Society of the City of Savannah in the Church of St. John the Baptist, in that City, on the Festival of St. Patrick, March 17, 1824*, pp. 10, 47. Document in the special collections, Manuscripts, Graduate Library, University of Illinois, Urbana, Ill.

Chapter Five

1. Shane Leslie, *The Irish Issue in its American Aspect: A Contribution to the Settlement of Anglo-American Relations During and After the Great War* (New York: Charles Scribner's Sons, 1919), pp. 205–206.

2. "Sir Shane Leslie Papers," Georgetown University. Accessible via <http://gulib.lausun. georgetown.edu/dept/speccoll/c1163.htm>, pp. 1–2.

3. See Jay Dolan, *The Immigrant Church: New York's Irish and German Catholics* (Baltimore: Johns Hopkins University Press, 1975), especially pp. 170–172; and Hugh McLeod's "Catholicism and the New York Irish 1880–1910" in Jim Obelkevich, Lyndal Roper, and Raphael Samuel, eds., *Disciplines of Faith: Studies in Religion, Politics and Patriarchy* (London: Routledge & Kegan Paul Ltd., 1987). See Colleen McDannell's "Going to the Ladies' Fair: Irish Catholics in New York City, 1870–1900," in Ronald H. Bayor and Timothy J. Meagher, eds., *The New York Irish* (Baltimore: Johns Hopkins University Press, 1995), pp. 234–251; and the work of Timothy Smith and Leonard R. Riforgiato.

4. The work of David Bennett, John Higham, Robert Hueston, Herbert London, William Cullen Bryant II, Robert Ernst, and Graham Hodges is important here. See the Bibliography for details.

5. *The New York Times*, "A Note of Warning," November 21, 1879, p. 4.

6. Kerby Miller and Patricia Mulholland Miller, *Journey of Hope: The Story of Irish Immigration to America* (San Francisco: Chronicle Books, 2001), p. 19.

7. See Lawrence McCaffrey's essay on Irish Catholicism in America, where he argues that ethnic-

ity gradually replaced religion as a prime source of Irish identity in Michael Glazier and Thomas J. Shelley, eds., *The Encyclopedia of American Catholic History* (New York: The Liturgical Press, 1998).

8. Edward Robb Ellis, *The Epic of New York City: A Narrative History* (New York: Old Town Books, 1966), pp. 232–233.

9. See Jay Dolan's *The American Catholic Experience: A History from Colonial Times to the Present* (New York: Image Books, 1987); and his other work on this topic; Colleen McDannell's *American Catholic Women: A Historical Exploration* (New York: Macmillan Publishing Co., 1989), and the issues raised by Kerby Miller in "Class, Culture and Immigrant Group Identity in the U.S.: The case of Irish-American Ethnicity," in Virginia Yans-McLoughlin ed., *Immigration Reconsidered: History, Sociology and Politics* (New York: Oxford University Press, 1990).

10. Jay Dolan used *U. S. Census (Population)* statistics from the 1850s and 1860s on this point in *The Immigrant Church*, p. 22.

11. See references in Chapter Two on Irish religious in the city. Kevin Kenny provides a useful overview of the contribution of Irish nuns to New York welfare during mid-century in *The American Irish: A History* (New York: Pearson Education Limited, 2000), pp. 145–147.

12. See Timothy J. Meagher's description for Worcester in *Inventing Irish America* (Indiana: Notre Dame University Press, 2001), pp. 79–80. Emmet Larkin's "The Devotional Revolution in Ireland, 1850–1875," in *American Historical Review* 77 (June 1972): pp. 625–652, and his other work remain primary reading.

13. Colleen McDannell provides a useful synopsis of this process in her "'true men as we need them': Catholicism and the Irish-American Male," in *American Studies* 27 (1986): pp. 19–36; R. V. Comerford, "Ireland 1850–70: post-famine and mid-Victorian," Chapter XX in *A New History of Ireland, Vol. V, Ireland Under the Union, I, 1801–70*, ed., W. E. Vaughan (Oxford: Clarendon Press, 1989), pp. 386–387.

14. McDannell, "'true men,'" and Lawrence McCaffrey, "Forging Forward and Looking Back," in Bayor and Meagher, eds., *The New York Irish*, pp. 216–222. Quotation, pp. 218–219.

15. Lawrence McCaffrey, "Irish Textures in American Catholicism," in *The Catholic Historical Review* (January 1992): pp. 13–15. See also the input of Gerald P. Fogarty, John Gilmary Shea, John Talbot Smith, and John Tracy Ellis for an introduction to the literature.

16. "From Sanctuary to Involvement: A History of the Catholic Parish in the Northeast," Jay Dolan, ed., *The American Catholic Parish: A History From 1850 to the Present* (New York: Paulist Press, 1987).

17. See Leslie Woodcock Tentler's "On the Margins: The State of American Catholic History," in *American Quarterly* 45 (1993): pp. 104–127. More generally, *The U.S. Catholic Historian, The Catholic Historical Review, Theological Studies, Spicilegium Historicium*, and *Mid-America* contain a fount of information on this topic. See also contributions from Bruce F. Biever, S.J., Andrew, Greeley, John W. Pratt, and Diane Ravitch.

18. Dolan, *Immigrant Church*, p. 46.

19. Thomas Brown, *Irish-American Nationalism 1870–1890* (Philadelphia and New York: J.B. Lippincott and Company, 1966), pp. 35–37.

20. Louis R. Bisceglia, "The Fenian Funeral of Terence Bellew McManus," *Eire-Ireland* 14, no. 3 (Autumn 1979): pp. 45–64.

21. On these clerics, see R. F. Foster's biographies in *Modern Ireland 1600–1972* (London: Allen Lane, Penguin Press, 1988), pp. 386–387, 418.

22. Sean Cronin, *Irish Nationalism: A History of its Roots and Ideology* (New York: Continuum, 1981), p. 89.

23. Discrepancy exists on the exact origin of both men: Bisceglia lists County Fermanagh; Desmond Ryan lists neighboring County Monaghan in *The Fenian Chief, A Biography of James Stephens* (Dublin: Gill and Son, 1967), p. 174; other materials list County Tyrone.

24. Bisceglia, "Fenian Funeral," p. 54. See also Terry Golway's description in *Irish Rebel: John Devoy and America's Fight for Ireland's Freedom* (New York: Griffin Trade Paperback, 1999), pp. 41–42.

25. *The Irish-American*, September 14, 21, 28, 1861; *The New York Times*, October 19, 1861, p. 4; and Bisceglia, "Fenian Funeral," pp. 56–57. *The Irish-American* even sent a reporter to cover the ceremonies in Dublin.

26. These ranked as high commanders of the Fenian Brotherhood in New York during the 1850s and 1860s.

27. *The New York Times*, "The McManus Obsequies," October 19, 1861, p. 4.

28. Ryan, *The Fenian Chief*, p. 174.

29. *Letters to the Right Reverend John Hughes, Roman Catholic Bishop of New York, Second Series, by Kirwan* (New York: Leavitt, Trow and Co., 1847), reproduced in the Pamphlets in American History Series, CA 426.

30. Articles in *The Irish American* on September 14, 21, and 28, 1861 elaborated on the extensive coverage accorded this episode by leading city publications. On O'Connell's influence, see Fergus O'Ferrall's *Catholic Emancipation: Daniel O'Connell and the Birth of Irish Democracy, 1820–1830* (Dublin: Gill and Macmillan, 1985).

31. *The New York Times*, "The Obsequies of T. B. McManus," November 22, 1861, p. 4; reported simultaneously in Ireland's *Freeman's Journal*, November 8, 1861.

32. *The New York Times*, October 19, 1861, p. 4.

33. "Hail, Patriot Priest, Father Lavelle," by "Soggarth Aroon," *The New York Times*, December 7, 1861, p. 4. Gaelic terms *sagart* signifies "priest," and *aroon* "beloved" or "dear."

34. The quotation is from the *The New York Times*, March 4, p. 8, and the meeting report from June 7, 1866, p. 4.

35. On the parade as a nationalist demonstration, see Mike Cronin and Daryl Adair's *The Wearing of the Green: A History of St. Patrick's Day* (New York: Routledge, 2002), the work of John T. Ridge; and the older overviews of John Crimmins for a contemporary flavor.

36. *The New York Times*, March 19, 1867, pp. 1, 17.

37. John T. Ridge, "Irish County Societies in New York, 1880–1914," Bayor and Meagher, *The New York Irish*, p. 282.

38. See Barry Coldrey's *Faith and Fatherland: The Christian Brothers and the Development of Irish Nationalism, 1838–1921* (Dublin: Gill and Macmillan, 1988); also Jean Baptiste de la Salle's own *The Conduct of the Schools of Jean-Baptiste de la Salle* (New York: McGraw Hill, 1935).

39. *The Irish Nation*, January 28, 1882, p. 5. Emphasis in original.

40. McCaffrey, "Forging Forward and Looking Back," in Bayor and Meagher, eds., *The New York Irish*, p. 231. See also the work of Alfred Isacsson, Austin Mattias, Mary Agnes O'Brien, Philip Dowd, and William J. Carr for further insight.

41. *The Irish World* and *American Industrial Liberator*, July 15, 1882, p. 3.

42. *The Irish World*, July 18, 1885, p. 6.

43. *The Irish People*, December 21, 1872, p. 4.

44. *The Irish Nation*, April 8, 1882, p. 5; January 14, 1882, p. 5.

45. McCaffrey, "Forging Forward," in Bayor and Meagher, eds., *The New York Irish*, p. 219; Dolores Liptak, "The Irish Take Charge," *Immigrants and Their Church* (New York: Macmillan, 1982), pp. 77–78. Liptak cited McCloskey's pride in the fact that the "noblest ecclesiastical building ever erected in this City, or in the United States" was financed "largely out of the pockets of poor Irish

servants." Liptak, *Immigrants*, p. 78; Hugh McLeod, *Piety and Poverty: Working-Class Religion in Berlin, London and New York 1870–1914* (New York: Holmes & Meier, 1996), p. 57.

46. See William Taylor, *A Sermon on the Festival of St. Patrick, the Apostle of Ireland, Delivered in the Roman Catholic Cathedral of New York, on Sunday, the 21st Day of March, 1819* (New York; M. Duffee, 1819).

47. Jay Dolan, *The Immigrant Church*, pp. 11, 19, 50–51. On the Cathedral, see John M. Farley, Leland Cook, Mary Peter McCarthy, and Leo Hershkowitz, "The Irish and the Emerging City: Settlement to 1844," in Bayor and Meagher, *The New York Irish*, pp. 28–29. Edward K. Spann, in "Union Green: The Irish Community and the Civil War," provides an illustration of the Old Saint Patrick's Cathedral and adjoining Hibernian Hall, *The New York Irish*, p. 196.

48. Dolan, *The Immigrant Church*, pp. 27, 159, 166–167. See also Margaret McCarthy, *A Cathedral of Suitable Magnificence: St. Patrick's Cathedral, New York* (Wilmington, DE: Michael Glazier, Inc., 1984).

49. Colleen McDannell, "Going to the Ladies' Fair: Irish Catholics in New York City, 1870–1900," in Bayor and Meagher, *The New York Irish*, p. 241.

50. *The Solemn Blessing and Opening of the New Cathedral of St. Patrick, New York, On the Feast of St. Gregory VII, Pope and Confessor, May 25, 1879, Containing a Full Description of the Cathedral and of all the Ceremonies of the Blessing, The Mass, Vespers, and Benediction of the Blessed Sacrament Etc. Etc., With Approbation* (New York: The Catholic Publication Society, 1879). Pamphlets in American History Series, CA956. See also John Talbot Smith's pamphlet *Cathedral Bells: A Souvenir of St. Patrick's Cathedral* (New York: W.R. Jenkins, 1888).

51. See *The Irish Nation*, April 8, 1882, p. 5, for their AGM report on the Irish Emigrant Society for that year. Henry Hoguet is mentioned by William E. Devlin in "Shrewd Irishmen: Irish Entrepreneurs and Artisans in New York's Clothing Industry, 1830–1880," in Bayor and Meagher, *The New York Irish*, p. 192. Ireland's associations with the name Hoguet may have originated with the Norman influx in the 1100s.

52. Quotation, Liptak, *Immigrants and Their Church*, pp. 81–82, and *The Irish-American*, March 23, 1878, p. 1, which dubbed the cathedral "the greatest ornament of the city."

53. McDannell, "Ladies' Fair," Bayor and Meagher, *The New York Irish*, p. 246. McDannell challenged the "image" of Irish Catholicism and argues that "the vibrant fantasy and good humor" of Irish fundraising fairs in New York defied this stereotype.

54. *Harper's New Monthly Magazine* LXXV (1887): p. 472.

55. Dolan, *The Immigrant Church*, pp. 161–169.

56. The rise of a newly prosperous class of Irish Catholic is accorded attention by Colleen McDannell in "Ladies' Fair," Bayor and Meagher, *The New York Irish*, pp. 234–251. The wealthier parishes were easily identified by more expansive ranges of fair goods on offer compared with less affluent parishes.

57. Marion Casey, "'From the East Side to the Seaside:' Irish Americans on the Move in New York City," Bayor and Meagher, *The New York Irish*, pp. 399; 674, n. 18.

58. Colleen McDannell argues for parish fairs as social organizations promoting middle-class, Victorian values among Irish women in "Ladies' Fair," *The New York Irish*, pp. 247–248.

59. Michael Funchion includes notes on each organization in *Irish-American Voluntary Organizations* (Westport, Conn.: Greenwood Press, 1983), and highlights Irish influence over and within each.

60. *The Irish-American*, March 16, 1861, p. 3.

61. This Ancient Order of Hibernians rule was adopted by each of these Convention organizations. See Michael Funchion, ed., *Irish American Voluntary Organizations*, p. 51. This volume contains material on these Convention organizations that does not require duplication here.

62. The Ladies of Charity organization constituted a later example of this philanthropic effort by prosperous city Irish.

63. "United Irish Counties Association of New York," Funchion, *Voluntary Organizations,* pp. 266–268.

64. *The Irish-American,* March 16, 1861, p. 3.

65. These groups did turn out for the Fenian McManus funeral cited earlier, but the strong support of the Church hierarchy under Archbishop Hughes probably encouraged such atypical action.

66. On its American operations, see the Society's own publication, *Rules of the Society of St. Vincent de Paul, and Indulgences Granted by the Sovereign Pontiffs, both to Members and to the Benefactors of the Society* (New York: Sadlier, 1864); also Daniel T. McColgan, Charles Kavanagh Murphy, and Franklin Fitzpatrick on this topic. References by Lawrence McCaffrey, Colleen McDannell, and Diner occur in Bayor and Meagher, *The New York Irish,* pp. 99, 220, 244, 248.

67. *The Irish-American,* March 16, 1861, p. 1. The city's Irish press, most commonly *The Irish World, The Irish-American,* and *The Gaelic-American* reported on a regular basis on the Society's annual general meetings and fundraising efforts.

68. Records of The Catholic Club of the City of New York, Box 15, Bulletins, publications and correspondence, American Irish Historical Society (hereafter, AIHS).

69. Records of The Catholic Club and Membership lists of the Friendly Sons of St. Patrick, AIHS.

70. Catholic Club records, Box 15, AIHS. In this case, the "Jubilee Offering" referred to a contribution to a Papal charity.

71. Funchion, *Irish American Voluntary Organizations,* Introduction, p. xii.

72. David Doyle, "The Regional Bibliography of Irish America, 1800–1930: A Review and Addendum," in *Irish Historical Studies* XXIII (May 1983): p. 261.

73. Jay Dolan has articulated some of these points in *The Immigrant Church,* pp. 162–163.

Chapter Six

1. Ronald P. Formisano, "The Invention of the Ethnocultural Interpretation," *American Historical Review* 99 (April 1994): pp. 453–477; quotation, p. 475.

2. Florence Gibson, *The Attitudes of the New York Irish Toward State and National Affairs, 1848–1892* (New York: Columbia University Press, 1951), pp. 26–27.

3. *The New York Times,* "How Long Will Protestantism Endure?" February 2, 1871, p. 4. For background see David Brundage, "'In Time of Peace, Prepare for War': Key Themes in the Social Thought of New York's Irish Nationalists, 1890–1916," Ronald H. Bayor and Timothy J. Meagher, eds., *The New York Irish* (Baltimore, Md.: Johns Hopkins University Press, 1995); Steven P. Erie, *Rainbow's End: Irish-Americans and the Dilemmas of Urban Machine Politics, 1840–1985* (Berkeley: University of California Press, 1988), and other political historians cited in earlier chapters.

4. Born in Cork in 1855, Timothy Michael Healy wrote for *The Nation,* served as a Member of Parliament 1880–1910, and became first Governor-General of the Irish Free State in 1922. He died in 1931. For an introduction to Healy, see R. F. Foster, *Modern Ireland 1600–1972* (London: Allen Lane, Penguin Press, 1988), p. 401, and Tim Pat Coogan, *Eamon De Valera: The Man Who Was Ireland* (London: Hutchinson, 1993), p. 109.

5. T. M. Healy, "The Irish in America," from *The Newcastle Chronicle,* reprinted in *The Irish Nation,* April 8, 1882, p. 4.

6. Healy, "The Irish in America."

7. *The Nation,* No. 316, July 20, 1871, p. 36, not to be confused with *The Irish Nation,* published in New York during the same time period.

8. Kevin Kenny, Editor's Introduction, *New Directions in Irish-American History* (Madison: University of Wisconsin Press, 2003), p. 101. In the same volume, see Tyler Anbinder's essay "'We Will Dirk Every Mother's Son of You': Five Points and the Irish Conquest of New York Politics," pp. 105–121.

9. See John Kuo Wei Tchen, "Quimbo Appo's Fear of Fenians: Chinese-Irish-Anglo Relations in New York City," in Bayor and Meagher, *The New York Irish,* pp. 131–133, on this style of satire. On political cartoons see L. P. Curtis and Mary Cowling, cited in the Bibliography. R. F. Foster's approach in *Paddy and Mr. Punch: Connections in Irish and English History* (1993; London: Penguin Books, 1995) is offbeat and original.

10. "Career of a Politician" by John R. Chapin, *Harper's New Monthly Magazine* XXII (March 1861): pp. 573–575.

11. "Coercion and Caricatures," in *The Irish Nation,* December 17, 1881, p. 4.

12. Nast is "acknowledged as the pioneer American political cartoonist," according to John Kuo Wei Tchen in "Quimbo Appo" in Bayor and Meagher, *The New York Irish,* pp. 132–133. See also Lawrence McCaffrey's note on Nast, p. 218, *The New York Irish.* Foster reminds us that Hibernia as the female representation of Ireland featured in political satire as "a model of Grecian purity." *Modern Ireland,* p. 363. On Nast and his work, see Morton Keller and Albert B. Paine. Honore Daumier's works offered French audiences a similar satirical outlet.

13. Much has appeared on Irish-American political culture, but George Reedy's *From the Ward to the White House: The Irish in American Politics* (New York: Charles Scribner's Sons, 1991); Florence Gibson, Steven P. Erie, and the work of Thomas Brown.

14. See William Riordan, *Plunkett of Tammany Hall* (Lexington, Mass.: E.P. Dutton, 1963), Harold Gosnell, *Boss Platt and His New York Machine: A Study of the Political Leadership of Thomas C. Platt, Theodore Roosevelt, & Others* (1924; New York: AMS Press, 1969); and Daniel Czitrom's "Underworlds and Underdogs: Big Tim Sullivan and Metropolitan Politics in New York 1889–1913," *Journal of American History* 78, no. 2 (September 1991): pp. 536–558.

15. "The Story of Tammany," *Harper's New Monthly Magazine* XLIV (December 1871–May 1872): pp. 840–848. Steven Erie, *Rainbow's End,* pp. 6–10.

16. Riordan's *Plunkett of Tammany Hall,* Czitrom's "Underworlds and Underdogs," *Journal of American History* 78 (1991), and Gosnell's *Boss Platt and His New York Machine* all explore this theme.

17. Gibson, *Attitudes of the New York Irish,* and Thomas Brown, "The Political Irish: Politicians and Rebels," in Doyle and Edwards, eds., *America and Ireland, 1776–1976* (Westport, Conn.: Greenwood Press, 1980), provide overviews of this process.

18. Denis Tilden Lynch, *Boss Tweed: The Story of a Grim Generation* (New York: Boni and Liveright, 1927), pp. 25–26.

19. A. Oakey Hall, "A Dinner at the Mayor's," *Harper's New Monthly Magazine* XXI (June–November 1860): pp. 654–655.

20. George Reedy demonstrated how "the Irish were the first heavy migration of non-WASP settlers who seized upon politics as a means of making a living." Reedy, *From the Ward to the White House,* p. 12.

21. Charles Nordhoff, "The Misgovernment of New York: A Remedy Suggested," *The North American Review* 113 (July 1871): pp. 321–322, 336. This argument is echoed by Erie in *Rainbow's End* and by Reedy, where he argues that the Irish "exchanged helpful acts" among themselves, and gained control of the police force and the fire departments "as a means of gaining capital for trading purposes." Reedy, *From the Ward to the White House,* pp. 59–60.

22. *The New York Times,* September 17, 1869, p. 4. Directories such as *Doggett's New York City Directory* and *Trow's General Directory of the Boroughs of Manhattan and the Bronx* for the 1880s and 1890s contain employment statistics from which to identify Ring extravagance.

23. See Chapter Three of Eric Homberger's *Scenes from the Life of a City: Corruption and Conscience in Old New York* (New Haven: Yale University Press, 1994).

24. Statistics from *The Nation,* No. 317, July 27, 1871, p. 4.

25. New York board of Councilmen, *Proceedings* 88 (1862–63): p. 29, and 93 (1864): pp. 117, 166; *The Irish-American,* October 15, 1864, p. 2.

26. John D. Crimmins, *Irish-American Historical Miscellany: Relating Largely to New York City and Vicinity, Together With Much Interesting Material Relative to Other Parts of the Country* (New York: privately published, 1905), p. 419; Edward K. Spann, "Union Green: The Irish Community and the Civil War," in Bayor and Meagher, *The New York Irish,* p. 207; Gibson, *Attitudes of the New York Irish,* p. 58; and Erie, *Rainbow's End,* p. 50.

27. See Riordan, *Plunkitt of Tammany Hall.* For more on Timothy D. or "Big Tim" Sullivan, the Bowery District leader in the turn of the century period, see Czitrom's "Underworlds and Underdogs"; and the work of Alvin Harlow.

28. "A Visit to Tammany and Its Boss," October 15, 1901; 1901 Record Book, "Night With Tammany," Ms 9576, DN 45, October–November 1901, Trinity College, Dublin, p. 7.

29. Reedy, *White House,* p. 54.

30. Erie, *Rainbow's End,* p. 26.

31. Eric Foner, "Class, Ethnicity, and Radicalism in the Gilded Age: The Land League and Irish-America," in *Marxist Perspectives* 1, no.2 (Summer 1978): pp. 6–55; quotation, p. 29.

32. Hasia Diner, "The Most Irish City in the Union: The Era of the Great Migration, 1844–1877," in Bayor and Meagher, *The New York Irish,* p. 102.

33. Letter, John Boyle O'Reilly to John Devoy, Boston, May 26, 1871, reprinted in the two-volume collection of Devoy's correspondence, eds., William O'Brien and Desmond Ryan, *Devoy's Post Bag, 1871–1928* (Dublin: C.J. Fallon Ltd., 1948), p. 41.

34. "The Municipal Ring, A Democratic View of the Machine-Possible Mutiny in the Tammany Camp-The Germans Vs the Irish Element," *The New York Times,* July 16, 1869, p. 4 (emphasis in original).

35. Reedy, *Ward to the White House,* pp. 87–88. See also Lothrop Stoddard, *Master of Manhattan, The Life of Richard Croker* (New York: Longmans, 1931) on this point.

36. Gearoid O'Tuathaigh, *Ireland Before the Famine 1798–1848* (Dublin: Gill and Macmillan, 1972), p. 83.

37. F. S. L. Lyons, *Ireland Since the Famine* (1971; London: Fontana, 1976), Chapter 3 "Government and Society," but pp. 102–103 in particular.

38. Even Richard Croker (Tammany boss 1886–1903) started his political career "as a Tammany street thug," his "shrewd, if ignorant" political skills empowering him sufficiently to rise rapidly through the ranks of the machine. Lawrence McCaffrey, "Forging Forward and Looking Back," Bayor and Meagher, *The New York Irish,* p. 222.

39. *The New York Times,* Obituary, April 24, 1889, p. 4.

40. H.H. Boone, *Life Sketches of Executive Officers and Members of the Legislature of the State of New York,* Vol. III (Albany: Weed Parsons, 1870), pp. 114–115. Obituary of Michael Norton, *The Irish World,* 1899, p. 2. Volume and newspaper clippings contained in the Kilroe Mss. Collection, Butler Special Collections, Columbia University, Box 22.

41. Obituary of Michael Norton, *The Irish World,* 1899, p. 2.

42. *The New York Times*, May 14, 1889, p. 4.

43. *The New York Times*, May 24, p. 4, and May 27, 1889, p. 2.

44. *State of New York In Memoriam: Thomas F. Grady: State Senator. Proceedings of the Legislature of the State of New York on the Life, Character and Public Service of Thomas F. Grady, State Senator, February 5, 1912, Albany, New York* (Albany: J.S. Lyon and Co., 1914), 80 pages. Quotation, p. 14. *The New York Times*, April 11, 1889, p. 2.

45. In *Memoriam*, John Quinn's Tribute, pp. 77–79; Senator Murtaugh's Tribute, pp. 42–44.

46. Senator Murtaugh's Tribute, pp. 42–44.

47. *The New York Times*, April 11, 1910, p. 4.

48. *In Memoriam*, Senator John F. Murtaugh, pp. 42–44.

49. Senator Murtaugh, pp. 57–59.

50. In contrast to Norton and Grady, Bourke Cockran's life has received a good deal of attention. See James McGurrin's *Burke Cockran: A Freelance in American Politics* (New York: Charles Scribner's Sons, 1948); and James H. Andrews's "Winston Churchill's Tammany Hall Mentor," in *New York History* (April 1990): pp. 133–171.

51. See R. F. Foster's analysis of the culture of this class in *Modern Ireland*, pp. 208–211. Terence De Vere White also includes useful (and often amusing) commentaries on "Castle Catholics" in *The Anglo Irish* (London: Victor Gollancz Ltd., 1972).

52. Andrews, "Tammany Hall Mentor," *New York History* (April 1990): pp. 134, 137.

53. McGurrin, *Bourke Cockran*, pp. 6–20.

54. Bourke Cockran was elected for New York in the 50th, 52nd, 53d, 58th, 59th, 60th, and 67th Congresses. Bourke Cockran, from Robert McElroy, ed. *In The Name of Liberty: Selected Addresses* (New York: G. P. Putnam's Sons, Knickerbocker Press, 1925), p. v.

55. *The New York Times*, March 2, 1923, p. 4.

56. Introduction by Sir Shane Leslie, in McGurrin, *Bourke Cockran*, p. xiii; and Winston Churchill's "Iron Curtain" speech, delivered on March 5, 1946, in Fulton, Missouri.

57. Letter, Bourke Cockran to Mr. Doogan, n.d., Bourke Cockran Papers, New York Public Library (hereafter, NYPL), Box 1.

58. Letter, John Byrne to Bourke Cockran, October 20, 1898, Bourke Cockran Papers, NYPL, Box 1. "Castle" rule here refers to British control over the governance of Ireland from the Dublin Castle reference.

59. He diverted from the Democrats to support first McKinley in 1896 and then Roosevelt in 1912. *The New York Times*, March 5, 1923, p. 1.

60. The scholarly literature on Home Rule is vast, but see the work of J. L. Hammond, and A.B. Cooke and J. R. Vincent as good starting points.

61. *The New York Times*, respectively, June 20, 1865, p. 4; February 16, 1869, p. 8; and February 4, 1880, p. 4.

62. The Ford family promoted revolutionary ideals in *The Irish World*; *The Freeman's Journal* cemented the Irish-Catholic bond; Horace Greeley's *New York Tribune* prevailed as the voice of the working American, while *The Irish-American Weekly* anticipated Irish assimilation. See William Joyce, James Rodechko, and James Crouthamel for background.

63. *The New York Times*, March 2, 1923, p. 1.

64. Bourke Cockran, *In The Name of Liberty*, pp. 351–352.

65. Letter, Morgan Johnson, Supreme Court, Appellate Division First Dept., New York, November 18, 1897, to Bourke Cockran. Bourke Cockran Papers, NYPL, Box 1.

66. *The New York Times*, March 2, 1923, p. 1.

67. Irish Parliamentary Fund Committee papers, Bourke Cockran Papers, NYPL, Box 1.

68. *The New York Times*, 1923, March 2, p. 1, and March 5, p. 4.

69. "Irish Republican Campaign Club," *The New York Times*, August 8, 1868, p. 1; and "Appeal to Irish Citizens," August 19, 1868, p. 2.

70. "Irish American Club," *The New York Times*, June 23, 1889, p. 6.

71. See especially those articles on the Grant Clubs and the "Irish Republican Greeley Campaign Club" in *The New York Times* and the Irish press in the city throughout 1869, particularly October.

72. Spann, "Union Green," in Bayor and Meagher, *The New York Irish*, p. 207. Steven Erie demonstrated a Republican trend of anti-Irish legislation and attitude in *Rainbow's End*, pp. 91–92.

73. John Buckley, *The New York Irish: Their View of American Foreign Policy, 1914–1921* (New York: Arno Press, 1976), pp. 4–5.

74. The Honorable Thomas D'Arcy McGee, Minister of Agriculture and Emigration, Canada, *The Irish Position in British and in Republican North America. A Letter to the Editors of the Irish Press, Irrespective of Party* (Montreal: Longmoore and Co., 1866). NYPL, Pamphlets, I. E. C., P.V. pp. 5, 11. In the midst of a successful career in Canada that led him away from his nationalist agenda, D'Arcy McGee was assassinated in 1868 on the streets of Montreal by a Fenian antagonist.

75. See R. F. Foster's *Paddy and Mr. Punch* for treatment of the cultural divides operating in nineteenth-century Ireland.

76. David A. Wilson in *United Irishmen, United States* (Ithaca: Cornell University Press, 1998) ties many of these strands together. See especially the conclusion, pp. 178–179, for a useful summary.

77. See Terry Golway's *Irish Rebel: John Devoy and America's Fight for Ireland's Freedom* (New York: St. Martin's Griffin, 1998) on New York Fenian history.

78. An abundance of material exists, some valuable, much of it hagiographical. Noteworthy are references from Michael Funchion, ed., *Irish American Voluntary Organizations* (Westport, Conn.: Greenwood Press, 1983), pp. 106–114; works in the field by R. V. Comerford, T. W. Moody; and the material highlighted in "The Fenians: A Bibliography," in *Eire-Ireland* 4 (Winter 1969). W. B. Yeats was an I.R.B. member for awhile, as Declan Kiberd notes in *Inventing Ireland: The Literature of the Modern Nation* (Cambridge, Mass.: Harvard University Press, 1995), p. 23.

79. Aside from Dublin, London and Paris constituted important nationalist centers during this time, but New York constituted the quintessential "foreign" base.

80. John Mitchel, *Jail Journal; or Five Years in British Prisons Commenced On Board The Shearwater Steamer* (London: R&T Washbourne, Ltd., By the author, 1854), p. 315 (emphasis in original).

81. For a contemporary account of the Young Ireland efforts in 1848, see Sir Charles Gavan Duffy's *Young Ireland: A Fragment of Ireland's History, 1840–1850* (1880; New York: Da Capo Press, 1973). John Devoy's *Recollections of an Irish Rebel* (1929; Shannon: Irish University Press, 1969) charts Fenian progress and its demise.

82. Letter, Thomas Clarke Luby in Dublin to John O'Mahony in New York, August 25, 1860, entitled "Copy of Document of Confidence." William J. Maloney and Margaret McKim Maloney Collection of Historical Papers, Box 4, File 1, NYPL.

83. D'Arcy McGee, *The Irish Position in British and in Republican North America*. The Irish city press carried detailed Fenian news through the 1850s and 1860s, particularly John Mitchel's *The Irish Citizen*, Patrick Lynch's *The Irish American*, and Patrick Ford's *The Irish World. The New York Times* published lengthy articles on the influence of New York Fenianism in Ireland, April 3, 1864, p. 2; and March 12, 1866, p. 1; and the history of "Molly Mahan, First Fenian Regular, Milwaukee," June 14, 1866, p. 4.

84. The creation of Finley Peter Dunne, Mr. Dooley's vantage point on Chicago's South Side allowed him to "observe" Fenianism and "lace-curtain[ed]" Irish progress. Quotation from Leonard P.

O'Connor Wibberly's *The Coming of the Green* (New York: Henry Holt and Co., 1958), p. 90, a history of the Irish in America best consigned to the category of hagiography. See the work of Finley Peter Dunne and also Doyle and Edwards, eds., *America and Ireland, 1776–1976*. For a broader perspective, see the work of Seamus P. Metress.

85. "News-Great Britain," *Harper's New Monthly Magazine* XXXII (December 1865–May 1866): p. 670. For full coverage of the *Cuba* debacle, see the relevant letters exchanged between the insurgents in William O'Brien and Desmond Ryan, eds., *Devoy's Post Bag* (Dublin: C.J. Fallon Ltd., 1948).

86. On the failure to "invade" Canada, see O'Leary, Doheny and Devoy in their publications cited above; also Desmond Ryan's *The Fenian Chief: A Biography of James Stephens* (Dublin: Gill and Son, 1967).

87. Diary of Miss Rose McDermott, pp. 27–28, American Irish Historical Society (hereafter, AIHS). In this quotation, "Seonianism" refers to an affluent and professional element of Irish society that identified with British cultural cornerstones. "Loyalty" refers to professed attachment to the British Crown.

88. Michael Funchion provides a useful introduction to the Clan in *Voluntary Organizations*, pp. 74–93, including a select bibliography of primary and secondary material.

89. For insight on the case of Worcester, see Timothy J. Meagher, *Inventing Irish America: Generation, Class and Ethnic Identity in a New England City, 1880–1928* (Indiana: Notre Dame University Press, 2001), p. 257.

90. David Brundage, "'In Time of Peace, Prepare for War,' Key Themes in the Social Thought of New York's Irish Nationalists, 1890–1916," in Bayor and Meagher, *The New York Irish*, pp. 321–334. Quotation, pp. 322–323. Kevin Kenny traces the transatlantic connections underpinning this episode in *The American Irish: A History* (New York: Pearson Education Limited, 2000), pp. 172–179. Ford's publication was entitled *Irish World and American Industrial Liberator*, symbolizing the nationalist, working-class alliance Ford promoted. On the association with Henry George, see his papers, and Edward T. O'Donnell's "'Though not an Irishman': Henry George and the American Irish," in *The American Journal of Economics and Sociology* 56, no. 4 (October 1997): pp. 407–419.

91. John Devoy, "The Ladies' Organization," in *The Irish Nation*, December 3, 1881, p. 1; and typed letter from John P. Sutton, Secretary of the Irish National League of America, to Michael Davitt, June 26, 1889, Davitt Papers, TCD Ms 9397/1485.

92. On O'Donovan-Rossa's defeat of Tweed, see *In Senate, Before the Committee on Privileges and Elections, in the matter of Petition of Jeremiah O'Donovan-Rossa for Seat as Senator from Fourth District, State of New York, Petition and Statement of Claimant, December 30, 1871, and February 7, 1872* (New York: W. E. Wells Sackett, 1872), Pamphlet CPV 1248, NYPL. See too Jeremiah O'-Donovan-Rossa's memoirs, including the poem "Jillen Andy."

93. Letter, John Kearney to O'Donovan-Rossa, June 8, 1902, O'Donovan-Rossa Papers, Box 1, AIHS (emphasis in original).

94. Address, *To the National Executive of the United Irish League of America*, 1904, case of the Erin's Hope Branch vs. the New York Municipal Council of the UILA, Pamphlets, IR 94108 P33, No. 11, pp. 1–6, National Library of Ireland (hereafter, NLI).

95. See Eric Foner's article "Class, Ethnicity and Radicalism in the Gilded Age: The Land League and Irish America," in *Marxist Perspectives* 1, no. 2, (Summer 1978): pp. 6–55.

96. Handwritten letter from Michael Davitt to President Roosevelt from Dalkey, a suburb of Dublin, March 4, 1905. Davitt Papers, TCD Ms 9576/7.

97. Kevin Kenny, *The American Irish*, p. 178.

98. David Brundage provides a synopsis of the progress of the INFA and the UILA in "In Time of Peace, Prepare for War," in Bayor and Meagher, *The New York Irish*, pp. 325–328.

99. Typewritten letter from H. G. Bannon, Secretary, UILA, New York, September 20, 1901, to the Chairman and Executive of the UIL, Dublin, Ireland. UIL Collection, Ms 9444/3362, folders 1–4, TCD.

100. Pamphlet, *Statement Explaining its Position in Regard to the Delegation from Ireland*, Ms 6844/158c, Folders 1–6, TCD.

101. The pledge of Irish Parliamentary leader John Redmond for Irish support of the British army in World War I and the British decision to shelve the Home Rule bill for the duration of the war constituted blows to constitutional nationalism in New York. See David Brundage on the reaction to Redmond's political agenda in his "In Time of Peace," in Bayor and Meagher, *The New York Irish*, p. 333. The 1916 Rising turned the tide of popular opinion in England toward some form of home rule. See Foster, *Modern Ireland*, pp. 484–493, on the course of events that led to the Treaty.

102. Friends of Irish Freedom Papers, boxed files of collected pamphlets, correspondence and newspaper clippings, AIHS. See John Devoy and Charles Callan Tansill; Patrick McCartan's *With DeValera in America* (New York: Brentano, 1932); and Francis M. Carroll in Funchion, ed., *Voluntary Organizations*, pp. 119–126.

103. Records for the Ancient Order of Hibernians for the period 1860–1920 are scant due to the destruction of most of the papers by fire, but John T. Ridge's history of the Order in America *Erin's Sons in America: The Ancient Order of Hibernians* (New York: Ancient Order of Hibernians 150th Anniversary Committee, 1986) is thorough.

104. *Harper's New Monthly Magazine* XXXVIII (December 1868–May 1869): p. 858.

105. Anonymous, *The Secret Revealed: or, The Origin and End of Orangeism: a Lecture Delivered Upon the Anniversary of the "Gunpowder Plot"* (Montreal: "Published by the Author," 1872). The gunpowder plot likely refers to Guy Fawkes's attempt to blow up the British House of Commons in the late 1790s.

106. Noel Ignatiev, *How the Irish Became White* (New York: Routledge, 1995), p. 187.

107. Kiberd, *Inventing Ireland*, p. 2.

108. Thomas D'Arcy McGee, *The Irish Position in British and in Republican North America*, pp. 13–14. Pamphlets IEC PV5, NYPL.

109. "The Week," editorial from *The Nation*, July 13, 1871, p. 18.

110. Leader from *The Irish Nation*, December 3, 1881, p. 4.

111. Patrick Ford, *The Criminal History of the British Empire* (New York: The Irish World, 1915), p. 20.

112. *Foreign Elements in American Civilization*, pamphlet by the Reverend H. A. Schauffler, D.D., of the Congregational Home Missionary Society, New York, 1904, Pamphlets, IEC PV5, NYPL.

113. Shane Leslie, *The Irish Issue in its American Aspect: A Contribution to the Settlement of Anglo-American Relations During and After the Great War* (New York: Charles Scribner's Sons, 1919), pp. 106–118, quotation, p. 108. See Foster's introduction to Casement and Carson, *Modern Ireland*, pp. 471–472, 465.

114. Kiberd, *Inventing Ireland*, p. 6.

115. Professor Joseph Dunn, *The Irish Consciousness: Address Before the Quarterly Meeting of the Society of the Friendly Sons of St. Patrick in the City of New York* (New York: The Friendly Sons of Saint Patrick, 1921). From the Friendly Sons of Saint Patrick Papers, AIHS.

Conclusion

1. The historical literature on Eamon de Valera, popularly known as "Dev," or the "Long Fellow" (a reference to his height of approximately 6'5"), is extensive. Tim Pat Coogan's *Eamon De Valera: The Man Who Was Ireland* (London: Hutchinson, 1993), provides a full bibliography.

2. R. F. Foster, *Modern Ireland, 1600–1972* (London: Allen Lane, Penguin Press, 1988) provides a useful chronology of events between 1916 and the signing of the Treaty; pp. 612–614. Quotation, p. 613.

3. Kevin Kenny makes reference to "nationalist movements" as the greatest source of what he terms "transatlantic culture and political interactions" during the nineteenth century. "Editor's Introduction: Representation, Memory, and Return," Kevin Kenny, ed., *New Directions in Irish-American History* (Madison: University of Wisconsin Press, 2003), p. 245.

4. That Eamon de Valera was born in New York in 1882 and that Kate Coll was his mother are possibly the only two undisputed facts surrounding de Valera's birth. Coogan offers a full account of the myths surrounding de Valera's parentage, from the opinion that his father was a native of Limerick to the theory that, as Juan Vivion de Valera was 5'7" or 5'8" in height, and Eamon was over 6'5", it is unlikely they were related. In any event, historians continue to debate de Valera's parentage. Coogan, *Eamon De Valera,* pp. 7–10.

5. See Foster, *Modern Ireland,* pp. 484–493. Foster noted that "not only were the executed leaders prayed for (and even prayed *to*); after the rising, even the moderate Irish Parliamentary Party Mayor of Dublin, arrested briefly and mistakenly by General Maxwell, could use the incident to compare himself to Christ. Pearse's poems and addresses, carefully marketed to secure maximum effect, became a sacred book. On every level, martyrolatry had taken over." *Modern Ireland,* p. 487. Emphasis in original. General Maxwell was a British army leader, and Pearse was the executed soldier-poet Padraig Pearse. The Cohalan Papers contain a letter from Reverend Thomas J. Wheelright, a priest living at Mount Saint Alphonsus, in Ulster County, New York, seeking Reverend Power's intervention (from All Saints' Church, New York City) on behalf of his half-brother Eamon de Valera to support the remission of his sentence by virtue of his American citizenship. This letter verifies that "my brother was born in New York on October 14, 1882, and as far as I know has never relinquished his American citizenship." Wheelright to Power, June 15, 1916, Cohalan Papers, Box 14, File 4, American Irish Historical Society (hereafter, AIHS).

6. There is extensive literature on the signing of the Treaty and the establishment of the new Free State. See R. F. Foster, *Modern Ireland,* pp. 657–659, for an introduction to this work.

7. Frederick Jackson Turner delivered his famous lecture in 1896 marking the turning point of the demise of the Frontier as the end of the first period of American history.

8. Chris McNickle, in "When New York was Irish, and After," in Ronald H. Bayor and Timothy J. Meagher, eds., *The New York Irish* (Baltimore, Md.: Johns Hopkins University Press, 1995), pp. 337–356, provides a summary of de Valera's stay in New York, p. 351. See also John F. Buckley in *The New York Irish: Their View of American Foreign Policy, 1914–1921* (New York: Arno Press, 1976).

9. Short article on Bourke Cockran's original Primer; "Even Rarer," Library Associates Newsletter, <http://gulib.lausun.georgetown.edu/advancement/newsletter/61/rarer61.htm>, Fall 2001.

10. Kevin Kenny, *The American Irish: A History* (New York: Pearson Education Limited, 2000), p. 198.

11. On Hylan's tenure in office, see John F. McClymer's "Of 'Mornin' Glories' and 'Fine Old Oaks,' John Purroy Mitchel, Al Smith and Reform as an Expression of Irish-American Aspiration," in Bayor and Meagher, *The New York Irish*, pp. 374–394.

12. *The New York Times*, "Hylan and Sinn Fein in $10,000,000 Drive," January 18, 1920, p. 2. de Valera is addressed as "professor" here, a reference to his former occupation as instructor of mathematics at a teacher training college in Dublin. Bantry is a coastal town in the southern county of Cork.

13. Letter, Archbishop Patrick Hayes to William Bourke Cockran from the Archbishop's House, 452 Madison Avenue, New York, January 17, 1920. Cohalan Papers, Box 6, Folder 8, AIHS. Dev's "$10 million" took on a life of its own within the city's press.

14. Public release from Edward J. McSweeney to the membership of the FOIF, January 22, 1920, Cohalan Papers, Box 7, Folder 11, AIHS.

15. Typed sheet headed "Pledges Made at Meeting of the Irish Victory Fund Committee, Waldorf Astoria, April 15th, 1919," listing the contributions of individuals and clubs, Cohalan Papers, Box 7, Folder 11.

16. "De Valera at Ninety-Two," by Brendan Kenneally, quoted in Tim Pat Coogan, *Eamon de Valera*, pp. 690–692.

17. See David Montgomery's lecture "The Irish Influence in the American Labor Movement" (Notre Dame: Hibernian Lecture, 1984). The Cohalan Papers contain a folder with material on A.F. of L. support for the Friends of Irish Freedom, and Gompers expressed support for the new Irish Independence in 1918 at the St. Paul A.F. of L. Convention. See Box 1, Correspondence, AIHS.

18. See Maureen Dezell's *Irish America: Coming into Clover* (New York: Doubleday, 2000), and Ray O'Hanlon's *The New Irish Americans* (Boulder, CO: Roberts Rinehart Publishing, 1998).

19. The *Sinn Feiner* issued weekly from an office on Duane Street in Greenwich Village from June 12, 1920 to December 10, 1921. Under the stewardship of Francis P. Jones, the paper followed the lead of *Sinn Fein* established in Dublin in 1906 by Arthur Griffith, founder of the political party of the same name. "Sinn Fein" translates generally as "We Ourselves." The party enjoyed considerable success through the 1910s and 1920s and has experienced a recent resurgence in popularity.

20. *Sinn Feiner*, January 22, 1921, p. 22.

Bibliography

Any attempt to discuss linkages between New York and Ireland from the Famine to the Treaty demands selection from an enormous historical literature. Each source listed is either directly referenced in the text, cited as relevant to points raised, or recommended for further reading.

Primary Sources

Archives

Archives of the Archdiocese of New York, Yonkers, New York.
Archives of the Irish Brigade, Sixty-ninth Regiment Armory, New York City.
Archives of the Livingston Masonic Lodge, Grand Lodge Free and Accepted Masons, State of New York, New York.
Archives of the Sisters of Charity, Mount Saint Vincent, Riverdale, New York.
Archives of the Sisters of Mercy, New York Province, Dobbs Ferry, New York.

Collections of Papers

American Irish Historical Society, New York City
American Irish Historical Society Records.
Catholic Club of New York Records.
Cohalan, Daniel F. Papers.

Friendly Sons of Saint Patrick Society Papers.
Friends of Irish Freedom Records.
Irish Race Convention Papers.
McDermott, Rose. Diary.
Miscellaneous Manuscripts.
O'Brien, Seamus. Papers.
O'Donovan-Rossa, Jeremiah. Papers.

Butler Library Rare Book and Manuscript Collection, Columbia University, New York City
Kilroe, Edwin Patrick. Collection.
Meloney-Mitchel Papers.

Graduate Library, University of Illinois at Urbana-Champaign
England, Bishop John. Papers.

National Library of Ireland, Dublin
Joly Collection of Pamphlets.
United Irish League of America Pamphlet Collection.

New York Historical Society, New York City
Bell, William. Diary.
Broadsheet Ballad Collection.
Burke, John. Papers.
New York City Pamphlet Collection.

Manuscript and Archives Division, New York Public Library, New York City
Bourke Cockran, William. Papers.
Hall, Sophie C. Diary.
Irish Emigrant Society Papers.
Ladies of Charity of the Catholic Charities of The Archdiocese of New York. Annual Reports.
Maloney, William J., and Margaret McKim Maloney. Collection of Historical Papers.
Morton, Levi Parsons. Papers.
Stephens, James. Diary.
Sturdevant, John J. Diary.
Thomas, Norman. Papers.
Wilson Industrial School for Girls. Annual Reports.

Metropolitan Toronto Library
Gowan, Nassau G. Papers.
Loyal Orange Order Collection of Papers.
Stafford, Reverend John. Addresses.

Rare Book and Manuscripts, Trinity College, Dublin
Davitt, Michael. Collection of Papers.
Dillon, John. Collection of Papers.
United Irish League Collection.

Georgetown University
Leslie, Sir Shane. Papers.

Contemporary Published Works

Newspapers, Periodicals and Directories

Brooklyn Standard Union.
Doggett's New York City Directory and *Trow's General Directory of the Boroughs of Manhattan and the Bronx.*
Harper's New Monthly Magazine.
New Age Magazine.
New York Dispatch.
New York Evening Post.
New York Observer.
North American Review.
Proceedings, New York Board of Councilmen.
Shamrock, or Hibernian Chronicle.
Sinn Feiner.
The Brooklyn Daily Eagle.
The Freeman's Journal.
The Gaelic-American.
Irish Democrat.
The Irish Citizen.
The Irish-American.
The Irish Nation.
The Irish People.
The Irish Republic: A Journal of Liberty, Literature and Social Progress.
The Irish World and American Industrial Liberator.
The Nation.
The New York Herald.
The New York Sun.
The New York Times.
The New York Tribune.
The Newcastle Chronicle.
The Saturday Review.

Select Contemporary Published Works

Anonymous. *The Secret Revealed: or, The Origin and End of Orangeism: a Lecture Delivered Upon the Anniversary of the "Gunpowder Plot."* Montreal: Published by the Author, 1872.

Bagenal, Philip Henry Dudley. *The American-Irish and Their Influence on Irish Politics.* London: K. Paul Trench and Company, 1882.

Banks, William. *History of the Orange Order, Entered According to Act of the Parliament of Canada, in the Year 1898 by William Banks, at the Department of Agriculture.* Toronto: William Banks, 1898.

Birmingham, George A. *An Irishman Looks At His World*. New York and London: Hodder and Stoughton, 1919.

Boone, H.H. *Life Sketches of Executive Officers and Members of the Legislature of the State of New York*, Vol. III. Albany, Weed Parsons, 1870.

Burke, Reverend Thomas. *Daniel O'Connell, The Liberator (Born August 6, 1775, Died May 15, 1847, Aged 72), A Lecture, Delivered at the Academy of Music, New York, May 13, 1872, by the Very Reverend Thomas N. Burke, O.P.* New York: Privately published, 1872.

Byrne, Reverend Stephen. *Irish Emigration to the United States: What It Has Been, and What It Is. Facts and Reflections Especially Addressed to Irish People Intending to Emigrate From Their Native Land; and to Those Living in the Large Cities of Great Britain and of the United States*. New York: The Catholic Publication Society, 1873. Repr. New York: Arno Press/*New York Times*, 1969.

Campbell, Helen. *Darkness and Daylight, or Lights and Shadows of New York Life . . . With an Introduction by Rev. Lyman Abbott, D.D.* Hartford, Conn.: The Hartford Publishing Company, 1899.

Carlton, Thomas, and John Lanahan, eds. *Christian Advocate*. New York: *Christian Advocate*, 1871.

Corkery, Daniel. *The Hidden Ireland*. Cork: Arlen House, 1924.

Crane, Stephen. *Maggie: A Girl of the Streets*. New York: D. Appleton, 1896. Repr. New York: Ballantine Books, 1960.

Crimmins, John D. *St. Patrick's Day: Its Celebration in New York and Other American Places, 1737–1845; How the Anniversary was Observed by Representative Irish Organizations, and the Toasts Proposed*. New York: Published by the Author, 1902.

____. *Irish-American Historical Miscellany, Relating Largely to New York City and Vicinity*. New York: Privately printed, 1905.

Cusack, Mary Francis. *An Illustrated History of Ireland: From AD 400 to 1800*. New York: Catholic Publications Society, 1868. Repr. London: Longmans, Green and Company, 1868; Kenmare: Kenmare Publications, 1873; London: Bracken Books, 1995.

____. *The Poems of D'Arcy McGee with Copious Notes*. New York: D. & H. Sadlier, 1869.

____. *Advice to Irish Girls in America*. New York: McGee, 1872.

____. *The Liberator: His Life and Times, Political and Social*. Kenmare, Co. Kerry: Kenmare Publications, 1872.

____. *Woman's Work in Modern Society*. London: Longmans, Green and Company, 1874.

____. *Tim Carty's Trial, or Whistling at Landlords, A Play for the Times*. New York: S. Mearns, 1880.

____. *From Killarney to New York; or, How Thade Became a Banker*. New York: Pustet, 1886.

____. *The Nun of Kenmare: An Autobiography*. Boston: Ticknor and Company, 1889.

D'Arcy McGee, Thomas. *A History of the Irish Settlers in North America, From the Earliest Period to the Census of 1850*. Boston: Office of the American Celt, 1851. Repr. Boston: P. Donahoe, 1852; Boston: J.S. Ozer, 1971.

____. *The Catholic History of America, Five Discourses, to which are added Two Discourses on the Relations of Ireland and America*. Boston: P. Donahoe, 1855.

____. *The Irish Position in British and in Republican North America. A Letter to the Editors of the Irish Press, Irrespective of Party*. Montreal: Longmoore and Company, 1866.

Declaration of Principles, by the Representatives of the Fenian Brotherhood, in Congress Assembled. Cleveland, Ohio: Published by the Author, 1867.

Delegates of the Protestant Churches of Ireland, *Facts About Ireland for the Consideration of American Citizens*. Privately published by the Delegation, n.d.

Denieffe, Joseph. *A Personal Narrative of the Irish Revolutionary Brotherhood*. New York: Privately published, 1879.

Devoy, John. *The Land of Eire. The Irish Land League . . . to the Present Day*. New York: Patterson and Neilson, 1882.

___. *Recollections of an Irish Rebel . . . A Personal Narrative by John Devoy.* New York: Chas. P. Young Company, 1929. Repr. Shannon: Irish University Press, 1969.

Dolan, Mother Mary Rose. *A Descriptive and Historical Sketch of the Academy of Mount Saint Vincent on the Hudson, 1847–1884.* New York: D. Appleton and Company, 1884.

Dougherty, Daniel. *The Response of Daniel Dougherty to the Toast "The Day we Celebrate" at the Dinner of the Friendly Sons of New York City, at Delmonico's, March 17, 1888.* New York: Friendly Sons of Saint Patrick, 1888.

Duffy, Sir Charles Gavan. *Young Ireland: A Fragment of Ireland's History, 1840–1850.* London, New York: Cassell, Petter, Galpin, 1880. Repr. New York: Da Capo Press, 1973.

Dunn, Joseph. *The Irish Consciousness: Address Before the Quarterly Meeting of the Society of the Friendly Sons of St. Patrick in the City of New York.* New York: The Friendly Sons of Saint Patrick, 1921.

___ and P. J. Lennox, eds. *The Glories Of Ireland.* Washington, D.C.: Phoenix Ltd., 1914.

Edge, Brother J. H. "The Story of Irish Freemasonry." *The New Age Magazine* (1913).

Ellington, George. *The Women of New York, or the Underworld of the Great City . . . Etc., Etc.* New York: New York Book Company, 1869–70. Repr. New York: Arno Press, 1972.

Farley, John. *History of St. Patrick's Cathedral.* New York: Privately published, 1908.

Ford, Patrick. *The Criminal History of the British Empire.* New York: The Irish World, 1915.

Forms and Ritual of the Orange Order To Be Observed in Private Lodges of the Orange Association of British America. Montreal: The Orange Order, 1852.

Froude, J.A. *Froude's Crusade–Both Sides: Lectures by Very Reverend T. N. Burke, O.P., John Mitchel, Wendell Phillips and Mr. James Anthony Froude . . . Regarding the Debate.* New York: J.W. O'Brien, 1872.

Gibbons, James, D.D. *Funeral Oration on his Eminence John Cardinal McCloskey, D.D., Archbishop of New York, Delivered October 15, 1885, Saint Patrick's Cathedral, New York.* New York: Benziger Brothers, 1885.

Gosnell, Harold F. *Boss Platt and His New York Machine: A Study of the Political Leadership of Thomas C. Platt, Theodore Roosevelt, & Others.* Chicago: University of Chicago Press, 1924. Repr. New York: AMS Press, 1969.

Grace, William R. T*he Irish In America: A Lecture.* Chicago: McDonnell Brothers Publishers, 1886.

Hall, Mr. and Mrs. Samuel Carter. *Ireland: Its Scenery and Character, &c.* London: How & Parsons, 1841–43.

Harris, N.R. *The Situation of Ireland, Stated from a Protestant Viewpoint, to the Right Honorable William Gladstone, Prime Minister of England.* Philadelphia: Presbyterian Print Company, 1880.

Headley, Joel Tyler. *Pen and Pencil Sketches of the Great Riots, An Illustrated History of the Railroad and Other Riots, Including all The Riots in the Early History of the Country.* New York: E. B. Treat, 1882. Repr. Philadelphia: H. W. Kelley, 1877; New York: Arno Press, 1969.

Hughes, Archbishop John. *Letters to the Right Reverend John Hughes, Roman Catholic Bishop of New York, Second Series, by Kirwan.* New York: Leavitt, Trow and Company, 1847.

The Irish Prince and the Hebrew Prophet: A Masonic Tale of the Captive Jews and the Ark of the Covenant. New York: Masonic Publishing Company, 1896.

Janvier, Thomas A. *In Old New York, A Classic History of New York City.* New York: Harper and Brothers, 1894. Repr. New York: St. Martin's Press, 2000.

Lecky, W. E. H. *Leaders of Public Opinion in Ireland.* New York and London: Longmans, Green and Company, 1862.

___. *A History of England in the Eighteenth Century.* 1892–93; New York: AMS Press, 1968.

___. *A History of Ireland in the Eighteenth Century.* London: Longmans, Green and Company, 1892.

Leslie, Sir Shane. *The Irish Issue in its American Aspect: A Contribution to the Settlement of Anglo-American Relations During and After the Great War.* New York: Charles Scribner's Sons, 1919.

Linn, William A. *Horace Greeley*. New York: Appleton, 1903.

Lynch, Denis Tilden. *Boss Tweed: The Story of a Grim Generation*. New York: Boni and Liveright, 1927.

Maguire, John Francis. *America In Its Relation to Irish Emigration*. Cloyne: Privately published, 1869.

Markievicz, Constance. *Bean na hEireann*, or *The Woman of Ireland*. Dublin: Privately published, 1908–1912.

———. *Women: Ideals and The Nation; A Lecture Delivered to the Students' National Literary Society, Dublin, by Constance Markievicz (Macha of Inghinide na hEireann)*. Dublin: Inghinide na hEireann at The Tower Press, 1909.

McBride, Robert. *The Canadian Orange Minstrel for 1860*. London: Free Stream Printing Press, 1860.

McClenachan, Charles T. *History of the Most Ancient and Honorable Fraternity of Free and Accepted Masons in New York From the Earliest Date . . . in the Thirteen Colonies of the Union*. New York: The Grand Lodge, 1881.

McElroy, Robert, ed. *In The Name of Liberty: Selected Addresses*. New York: G. P. Putnam's Sons, Knickerbocker Press, 1925.

McGee, James E. *Lives of Irishmen's Sons and Their Descendants*. New York: J.A. McGee Publishers, 1874.

Meagher, Thomas Francis. *Speeches on the Legislative Independence of Ireland, with Introductory notes by Thomas Francis Meagher*. New York: Redfield, 1853.

Merwin-Clayton Sales Company. Catalogue of the Library, Correspondence, and Original Cartoons of the late Thomas Nast. New York: s. n., 1906.

Mitchel, John. *Jail Journal; or Five Years in British Prisons Commenced On Board The Shearwater Steamer*. London: R&T Washbourne, Ltd., 1854.

Monahan, Michael. *Nova Hibernia: Irish Poets and Dramatists of Today and Yesterday*. New York: M. Kennerley, 1914. Repr. New York: Books for Libraries Press Inc., 1968.

Nicholson, Asenath. *Ireland's Welcome to the Stranger, or An excursion through Ireland in 1844 and 1845 for the purpose of Personally Investigating the condition of the Poor. By A. Nicholson*. New York: Baker and Scribner, 1847. Repr. London: Hodder and Stoughton, 1926.

———. *Lights and Shades of Ireland*. London: Houlston & Stoneman, 1850.

O'Brien, Michael J. *In Old New York: The Irish Dead in Trinity and St. Paul's Churchyards*. New York: American Irish Historical Society, 1928.

O'Donovan, Jeremiah. *A Brief Account of the Author's Interview with his Countrymen . . . in 1854 and 1855*. Pittsburgh: By the Author, 1864. Repr. New York: Arno, 1969.

O'Donovan-Rossa, Jeremiah. *Rossa's Recollections, 1838–1898. Childhood, Boyhood, and Manhood, Customs, Habits and Manners of the Irish People. Social Life and Prison Life. The Fenian Movement. Travels in Ireland, England, Scotland and America*. New York: Mariner's Harbor, 1898.

O'Hanlon, John, Canon. *Irish-American History of the United States*. New York: Murphy Publishers, 1907.

O'Leary, Jeremiah. *My Political Trial and Experiences*. New York: Jefferson Publishing Company, 1919.

O'Leary, John. *Recollections of Fenians and Fenianism*. London: Downey and Company, 1896. Repr. New York: Barnes and Noble, 1968.

O'Reilly, Bernard F. *The Cause of Ireland Pleaded Before the Civilized World*. New York: P.F. Collier, 1886.

Paine, Albert B. *Thomas Nast, His Period and his Pictures*. New York and London: Harper and Brothers, 1904. Repr., Gloucester, Mass.: P. Smith, 1967; New York: B. Blom, 1971.

Reid, Whitelaw. *The Scot in America and the Ulster Scot; Being the Substance of Addresses Before the Edinburgh Philosophical Institution, First November 1911, and the Presbyterian Historical Society, Belfast, 28 March 1912*. London: Macmillan and Company, 1912.

Reidy, James. *The Influence of the Irish Woman on the National Movement, Lecture Delivered By James Reidy, Of New York, Before the Brooklyn Gaelic Society, on Sunday Evening, March 18, 1906*. New York: Published by the author, 1906.

Reports of the Immigration Commission. Vol. 3, 61st Congress Document No.753. Washington DC.: Government Printing Office, 1911.

Riis, Jacob. *How The Other Half Lives: Studies Among the Tenements of New York*. New York: Charles Scribner's Sons, 1907.

Roberts, Lieutenant-Colonel W. R. *Oration Delivered by L.C. W.R.R. At the Great Fenian Demonstration in Jones' Wood, New York on Tuesday July 25 1865*. New York: Office of the Trades Advocate, 1865.

Roche, James Jeffrey. *Life of John Boyle O'Reilly, Together with his Complete Poems and Speeches, Edited by Mrs. John Boyle O'Reilly; Introduction by James Cardinal Gibbons, Archbishop of Baltimore*. Philadelphia: John J. McVey, 1891.

Rorke, James. *Report of the President, James Rorke, of the Irish Emigrant Society*. New York: Emigrant Society, 1890–1915.

Ross, Peter. *A Standard Dictionary of Freemasonry In the State of New York. Including Lodge Chapter, Council, Commandery and Scottish Rite Bodies*. New York: The Lewis Publishing Company, 1899.

Rules of the Society of St. Vincent de Paul, and Indulgences Granted by the Sovereign Pontiffs, both to Members and to the Benefactors of the Society. New York: Sadlier, 1864.

Ryan, R.M. *The New Know-Nothingism: A Reply to the Charges of Incivism and Want of American Patriotism made by The APA*. New York: Published by the author, 1900.

Sadlier, Mary Anne. *Bessy Conway; or, The Irish Girl in America*. New York: Sadlier, 1861.

Salmon, Lucy Maynard. *A Statistical Inquiry Concerning Domestic Service, Reprinted from the Publications of the American Statistical Association, 1892*. New York: Privately printed, 1892.

____. *Domestic Service*. London and New York: Macmillan, 1897–1911.

Shannon, William. *The Dominion Orange Harmonist . . . and Other Matters Interesting to Orangemen*. Toronto: Maclear and Company, 1876.

Sharp, E.A., and J. Matthay. *Lyra Celtica, An Anthology of Representative Celtic Poetry, Ancient Irish, Alban, Gaelic, Breton, Cymric and Modern Scottish and Irish Celtic Poetry*. Edinburgh: John Grant, 1924.

Shauffler, Reverend H. A. *Foreign Elements in American Civilization*. Congregational Home Missionary Society, New York, 1904.

Shea, John Gilmary. *The Catholic Churches of New York City*. New York: J.G. Shea, 1878.

____. *The History of the Catholic Church in the United States*. New York: J.G. Shea, 1886–1892.

Sibbett, R.M. *Orangeism in Ireland and Throughout the Empire*. Belfast: The Orange Order, 1914.

Skelton, I. *Life of Thomas D'Arcy McGee*. Ontario: Gardenville, 1925.

Smith, John Talbot. *Cathedral Bells: A Souvenir of St. Patrick's Cathedral*. New York: W.R. Jenkins, 1888.

____. *The Catholic Church in New York*. New York: Privately published, 1908.

The Solemn Blessing and Opening of the New Cathedral of St. Patrick, New York, On the Feast of St. Gregory VII, Pope and Confessor, May 25, 1879 . . . With Approbation. New York: The Catholic Publication Society, 1879.

Speranza, *Poems by Speranza, (Lady Wilde)*. Dublin: M.H. Gill and Sons, Ltd., 1864.

State of New York In Memoriam: Thomas F. Grady: State Senator. Proceedings of the Legislature of the State of New York on the Life, Character and Public Service of Thomas F. Grady, State Senator, February 5, 1912, Albany, New York. Albany: J.S. Lyon and Company, 1914.

Stoddard, Lothrop. *Master of Manhattan: The Life of Richard Croker*. New York: Longmans, 1931.

Taylor, William. *A Sermon on the Festival of St. Patrick, the Apostle of Ireland, Delivered in the Roman Catholic Cathedral of New York, on Sunday, the 21st Day of March, 1819*. New York: M. Duffee, 1819.

Thebaud, Reverend Augustine J. *The Irish Race in the Past and Present*. New York: Peter F. Collier, 1878.

Ticket for the Second Annual Ball of The Irish Emigrant Society. New York: Emigrant Society, 1845.

St. Vincent de Paul. *Rules of the Society of St. Vincent de Paul, and Indulgences Granted by the Sovereign Pontiffs, both to Members and to the Benefactors of the Society*. New York: Sadlier, 1864.

Secondary Works

Journal Articles

Aleinikoff, T. Alexander. "A Multicultural Nationalism?" *The American Prospect* 36 (January/February 1998): pp. 80–86.

Anbinder, Tyler. "From Famine to Five Points: Lord Lansdowne's Irish Tenants Encounter North America's Most Notorious Slum." *American Historical Review* 107, no. 2 (April 2002): pp. 351–387.

Andrews, James H. "Winston Churchill's Tammany Hall Mentor." *New York History* (April 1990): pp. 133–171.

Arnesen, Eric. "Whiteness and the Historians' Imagination." *International Labor and Working-Class History* 60 (Fall 2001): pp. 3–32.

___. "Whiteness and the Historians' Imagination." *Historically Speaking* III, no. 3 (February 2002): pp. 19–22.

Barkan, Elliott R. "Race, Religion and Nationality in American Society: A Model of Ethnicity—From Contact to Assimilation." *Journal of American Ethnic Studies* 14, no. 2 (Winter 1995): pp. 38–75.

___, Jon Gjerde, and Erike Lee. "Comment: Searching for Perspectives: Race, Law, and the Immigrant Experience." *Journal of American Ethnic History* 18, no. 4 (Summer 1999): pp. 136–166.

Bessai, Diane. "'Dark Rosaleen' as Image of Ireland. *Eire-Ireland* 10, no. 4 (1975): pp. 62–84.

Bisceglia, Louis R. "The Fenian Funeral of Terence Bellew McManus." *Eire-Ireland* 14, no. 3 (Autumn 1979): pp. 45–64.

Casey, Marion R. "Keeping the Tradition Alive: A History of Irish Music and Dance in New York City." *New York Irish History* 6 (1991–92): pp. 24–30.

Comerford, R.V. "Patriotism as Pastime: The Appeal of Fenianism in the mid-1860s." *Irish Historical Studies* XXII (Summer 1980): pp. 241–264.

Cote, Jane. "Writing Women Out of History: Fanny and Anna Parnell and the Irish Ladies Land League." *Etudes Irlandaises* 17 (1992): pp. 123–134.

Cullen Bryant II, William. "No Irish Need Apply: William Cullen Bryant Fights Nativism, 1836–1845." *New York History* 74, no.1 (1993): pp. 29–48.

Czitrom, Daniel. "Underworlds and Underdogs: Big Tim Sullivan and Metropolitan Politics in New York, 1889–1913." *Journal of American History* , no. 2 (September 1991): pp. 536–558.

Dowd, Philip. "The De La Salle Christian Brothers in New York, 1848–1914." *New York Irish History* 7 (1992–93): pp. 29–32.

Doyle, David N. "The Regional Bibliography of Irish America, 1800–1930: A Review and an Addendum." *Irish Historical Studies* XXIII, no. 9 (May 1983): pp. 254–283.

___. "The Irish as Urban Pioneers in the United States, 1850–1870." *Journal of American Ethnic History* 10 (1990): pp. 36–59.

Dudley Edwards, Owen. "The American Image of Ireland: A Study of its Early Phases." *Perspectives in American History* 4 (1970): pp. 255–272.

Ernst, Robert. "Economic Nativism in New York City During the 1840s." *New York History* 29, no. 2 (1948): pp. 170–186.

Fitzgerald, Maureen. "The Perils of 'Passion and Poverty': Women Religious and the Care of Single Women in New York City, 1845–1890." *U.S. Catholic Historian* 10, no.'s 1–2 (1990): pp. 45–58.

Foner, Eric. "Class, Ethnicity and Radicalism in the Gilded Age: The Land League and Irish America." *Marxist Perspectives* 1, no. 2 (Summer 1978): pp. 6–55.

Formisano, Ronald P. "The Invention of the Ethnocultural Interpretation." *American Historical Review* 99 (April 1994): pp. 453–477.

Fortner, Robert. "The Culture of Hope and The Culture of Despair: The Print Media and Nineteenth Century Irish Emigration." *Eire-Ireland* XIII (Fall 1978): pp. 38–48.

Gordon, Michael. "Labor Boycott in New York City, 1880–86." *Labor History* 16, no. 2 (1975): pp. 184–229.

Groneman, Carol. "Working Class Immigrant Women in Mid-Nineteenth Century New York: The Irish Woman's Perspective." *Journal of Urban History* 4, no. 3 (1978): pp. 255–273.

Isaacsson, Alfred. "The Irish Carmelites Come to the Bronx." *Bronx County Historical Society Journal* 25, no. 1 (1988): pp. 21–26.

Jackson, Pauline. "Women in Nineteenth Century Irish Emigration." *International Migration Review* XIX (Winter 1984): pp. 1004–1020.

Kazal, Russel A. "Revisiting Assimilation: The Rise, Fall, and Reappraisal of a Concept in American Ethnic History." *American Historical Review* 100, no. 2 (April 1995): pp. 437–471.

Larkin, Emmet. "The Devotional Revolution in Ireland, 1850–1875." *American Historical Review* 77 (June 1972): pp. 625–652.

London, Herbert. "The Irish and American Nativism in New York City, 1843–47." *Dublin Review* 510 (Winter 1966–67): pp. 378–394.

Mattias, Austin. "Origin of Teaching Brotherhoods in the Archdiocese of New York." *Catholic Educational Review* 60, no. 6 (September 1962): pp. 377–385.

McBride, I.R. "'When Ulster joined Ireland': Anti-Popery, Presbyterian radicalism and Irish Republicanism in the 1790s." *Past & Present*, no. 157 (November 1997): pp. 63–93.

McCaffrey, Lawrence. "Irish Textures in American Catholicism." *The Catholic Historical Review* LXXVIII (January 1992): pp. 13–29.

___. "City of the Beginnings." *The Irish Literary Supplement: A Review of Irish Books* 15, no. 1 (Spring 1996): pp. 8–9.

McDannell, Colleen. "'true men as we need them': Catholicism and the Irish-American Male." *American Studies* 27 (1986): pp. 19–36.

McDonald, Forrest, and Ellen Shapiro McDonald. "The Ethnic Origins of the American People." *William and Mary Quarterly* 37 (1980): pp. 179–199.

Meade, Don. "Kitty O'Neil and Her 'Champion Jig': An Irish Dancer on the New York Stage." *New Hibernia Review* 6, no. 3 (Autumn 2002): pp. 9–22.

Miller, Kerby. "Review of *Famine Immigrants*." *Journal of American Ethnic History* (Fall 1985): pp. 83–85.

___. "Review of *The Irish in Chicago; From Paddy to Studs; Paddy and the Republic; The Paddy Camps; Hibernia America*, and *The Butte Irish*." *Journal of Urban History* 16, no. 4 (1990): pp. 428–442.

___ and Bruce D. Boling. "Golden Streets, Bitter Tears: The Irish Image of America during the Era of Mass Migration." *Journal of American Ethnic History* 10, no.'s 1–2 (Fall 1990–Winter 1991): pp. 16–36.

Murphy, Maureen. "Charlotte Grace O'Brien and the Mission of Our Lady of the Rosary for the Protection of Irish Immigrant Girls." *Mid-America, An Historical Review* 74, no. 3 (October 1992): pp. 253–270.

Murphy, Peter, and Candice Ward. "'The Irish Thing': A Conversation on the Australian and American Irish Diaspora, Introduced by Vassilis Lambropoulos." *The South Atlantic Quarterly* 98, no.'s 1/2 (Winter/Spring 1999): pp. 117–134.

Newsinger, John. "Historical Materialism and the Catholic Church, Irish Example." *Monthly Review* 37 (January 1986): pp. 12–22

Ni Bhroimeil, Una. "For Yankeemen and Irishmen, Their Hearts and Hands Should Join: Irish America—The View From Gaelic Ireland, 1900–1915." *The Recorder, The Journal of the American Irish Historical Society* 16, no. 1 (Spring 2003): pp. 114–131.

___. "The Creation of an Irish Culture in the United States: The Gaelic Movement, 1870–1915." *New Hibernia Review* 5, no. 3 (Autumn 2001): pp. 87–100.

Nolan, Janet. "Introduction: The Catholic Immigrant Woman in Urban America." *Mid-America: An Historical Review* 74, no. 3 (October 1992): pp. 201–204.

O'Donnell, Edward T. "'Though not an Irishman': Henry George and the American Irish." *The American Journal of Economics and Sociology* 56, no. 4 (October 1997): pp. 407–419.

___. "How the Irish Became Urban." *Journal of Urban History* 25, no. 2 (January 1999): pp. 271–286.

Ridge, John T. "The Gaelic Revival in 19ᵗʰ Century New York." *New York Irish History* 1 (1986): pp. 5–6.

Rushwald, Aviel. "Untangling the Knotted Cord: Studies of Nationalism." *Journal of Interdisciplinary History* XXIV, no. 2 (Autumn 1993): pp. 294–360.

Scally, Robert. "Review of *Emigrants and Exiles: Ireland and the Irish Exodus to North America*, by Kerby Miller." *Journal of Social History* 20, no. 3 (Spring 1987): pp. 601–605.

Shanahan, Suzanne, and Olzak, Susan, "The Effects of Immigrant Diversity and Ethnic Competition on Collective Conflict in Urban America: An Assessment of Two Moments of Mass Migration, 1869–1924 and 1965–1993." *Journal of American Ethnic History* 18, no. 3 (Spring 1999): pp. 40–64.

Smith, Timothy. "Religion and Ethnicity in America." *American Historical Review* 83 (1978): pp. 1155–1185.

Thompson, Margaret Susan. "To Serve the People of God: Nineteenth-Century Sisters and the Creation of an American Religious Life." Working Paper Series, Cushwa Center, University of Notre Dame, Series 18, no. 2, Spring 1987.

___. "Sisterhood and Power: Class, Culture, and Ethnicity in the American Convent." *Colby Library Quarterly* 25, no. 3 (1989): pp. 149–175.

Woodcock Tentler, Leslie. "On the Margins: The State of American Catholic History." *American Quarterly* 45 (1993): pp. 104–127.

Secondary Works

Acland, Alice. *The Rebel Countess: The Life and Times of Constance Markievicz*. London: Weidenfeld and Nicholson, 1967.

Akenson, Donald. *Being Had: Historians, Evidence and the Irish in North America*. Toronto: P.D. Meany Publishers, 1985.

___. *Small Differences: Irish Catholics and Irish Protestants, 1815–1922, An International Perspective*. Kingston and Montreal: McGill-Queen's University Press, 1988.

Allen, Theodore. *The Invention of the White Race, Volume One: Racial Oppression and Social Control*. New York: Verso, 1994.

Alter, Peter. *Nationalism*. Frankfurt am Main: Suhrkamp Verlag, 1985.

Anbinder, Tyler. *Five Points: The Nineteenth Century New York City Neighborhood that Invented Tap Dance, Stole Elections, and Became the World's Most Notorious Slum*. New York: The Free Press, 2001. Repr. New York: Plume, 2002.

Asbury, Herbert. *The Gangs of New York: An Informal History of the Underworld*. New York: Alfred A. Knopf, Inc., 1927.

Bartlett, Thomas. *The Fall and Rise of the Irish Nation: The Catholic Question 1690–1830*. Savage, MD: Barnes and Noble Books, 1992.

___, and David Hayton, eds. *The Penal Era and the Golden Age: Essays in Irish History 1690–1800*. Belfast: Ulster Historical Foundation, 1979.

Batterberry, Michael and Ariane. *On the Town in New York: The Landmark History of Eating, Drinking, and Entertainments from the American Revolution to the Food Revolution*. New York: Routledge, 1999.

Battersby, William John. *De La Salle, A Pioneer of Modern Education*. London and New York: Longmans, 1949.

___. *History of the Institute of the Brothers of the Christian Schools of the Eighteenth Century, 1719–1798*. London: Waldegrave, 1960.

Bayor, Ronald H., and Timothy J. Meagher, eds. *The New York Irish, Essays Toward a History*. Baltimore: The Johns Hopkins University Press, 1995.

Beckett, J.C. *The Making of Modern Ireland, 1603–1923*. New York: Knopf, 1966.

Bender, Thomas. *New York Intellect: A History of Intellectual Life in New York City from 1750 to the Beginnings of Our Own Time*. New York: Knopf, 1987.

Bennett, David H. *The Party of Fear: The American Far Right From Nativism to the Militia Movement*. New York: Vintage Books, 1995.

___. *The Party of Fear: From Nativist Movements to the New Right in American History*. Chapel Hill: University of North Carolina Press, 1988. Repr. New York: Vintage Books, 1990.

Bernstein, Iver. *The New York City Draft Riots: Their Significance for American Society and Politics in the Age of the Civil War*. Oxford and New York: Oxford University Press, 1997.

Bew, Paul. *Land and The National Question in Ireland, 1858–82*. Atlantic Heights, N.J.: Humanities Press, 1970.

Biever, Bruce F. *Religion, Culture and Values: A Cross-Cultural Analysis of Motivational Factors in Native Irish and American Irish Catholicism*. New York: Arno Press, 1965.

Binder, Frederick, and David Reimers. *All the Nations Under Heaven: An Ethnic and Racial History of New York City*. New York: Columbia University Press, 1995.

Birmingham, Stephen. *Real Lace: American's Irish Rich*. New York: Harper & Row, 1973. Repr. Syracuse: Syracuse University Press, 1997.

Blanshard, Paul. *Irish and Catholic Power: An American Interpretation*. New York: The Beacon, 1953.

Bodnar, John. *The Transplanted: A History of Immigrants in Urban America*. Bloomington: Indiana University Press, 1985.

Boyce, D. George. *Nationalism in Ireland*. Baltimore: Johns Hopkins University Press, 1982. Repr. London: Routledge, 1995–96.

Boylan, Henry. *Dictionary of Irish Biography*. New York: Barnes and Noble Books, 1978.

Bridges, Amy. *A City in the Republic: Antebellum New York and the Origins of Machine Politics*. New York: Cambridge University Press, 1984. Repr. Ithaca: Cornell University Press, 1987.

Brown, Thomas. *Irish-American Nationalism 1870–1890*. Philadelphia and New York: J.B. Lippincott and Company, 1966.

Buckland, Patrick. *Irish Unionism 1885–1922*. London: The Historical Association, 1973.

Buckley, John F. *The New York Irish: Their View of American Foreign Policy, 1914–1921*. New York: Arno Press, 1976.

Burrows, Edwin G. and Mike Wallace. *Gotham: A History of New York City to 1898*. Oxford and New York: Oxford University Press, 1998.

Byron, Reginald. *Irish America*. Oxford and New York: Oxford University Press, 1999.

Cahill, Thomas. *How the Irish Saved Civilization: The Untold Story of Ireland's Heroic Role from the Fall of Rome to the Rise of Medieval Europe*. New York: Nan A. Talese, Doubleday, 1995.

Callaghan, Mary Rose. *'Kitty O'Shea,' The Story of Katherine Parnell*. London and San Francisco: Pandora Press, 1989.

Canny, Nicholas. *Europeans On the Move: Studies on European Migration, 1500–1800*. Oxford and New York: Oxford University Press, 1994.

___, ed. *The Oxford History of the British Empire: The Origins of Empire*. Oxford and New York: Oxford University Press, 1998.

Caplan, Richard, and John Feffer. *Europe's New Nationalism: States and Minorities in Conflict*. Oxford and New York: Oxford University Press, 1996.

Carr, William J. *The Irish Carmelites of New York City and the Fight for Irish Independence, 1916–1919.* Middletown, New York: Vestigium Press, 1973.

Carroll, Francis M. *American Opinion and the Irish Question 1910–23: A Study in Opinion and Policy.* Dublin and New York: Gill and Macmillan and St. Martin's Press, 1978.

Cash, Johnny. "Forty Shades of Green." *All the Best From Ireland, Vol. 2.* St. Laurent, Quebec, Canada: Distributions Madacy Inc., 1991.

Charity, Sisters of. *Sisters of Charity of Saint Vincent de Paul of New York, 1960–1996.* New York: Privately published by the Sisters of Charity, 1997.

Clark, Dennis. *The Irish Relations: Trials of an Immigrant Tradition.* Rutherford, N.J.: Fairleigh Dickinson University Press, 1982.

___. *Hibernia America: The Irish and Regional Cultures.* Westport, Conn.: Greenwood Press, 1986.

___. *Erin's Heirs: Irish Bonds of Community.* Lexington: University Press of Kentucky, 1991.

Coburn, Carol K. and Martha Smith. *Spirited Lives: How Nuns Shaped Catholic Culture And American Life, 1836–1920.* Chapel Hill: University of North Carolina Press, 1999.

Coffey, Michael, ed. *The Irish in America.* New York: Hyperion Books, 1997.

Coldrey, Barry. *Faith and Fatherland: The Christian Brothers and the Development of Irish Nationalism, 1838–1921.* Dublin: Gill and Macmillan, 1988.

Coogan, Tim Pat. *Eamon De Valera: The Man Who Was Ireland.* London and New York: Hutchinson, 1993.

___. *Wherever Green is Worn: The Story of the Irish Diaspora.* London: Hutchinson, 2000.

Cook, Leland. *St. Patrick's Cathedral: A Centennial History.* New York: Quick Fox, 1979.

Cooke, A.B., and J. R. Vincent. *The Governing Passion: Cabinet Government and Party Politics in Britain 1885–86.* New York: Barnes and Noble, 1974.

Corry, John. *Golden Clan: The Murrays, the McDonnells & the Irish American Aristocracy.* Boston: Houghton Mifflin, 1977.

Cosgrove, Art, and Donal McCartney, eds. *Studies in Irish History Presented to R. Dudley Edwards.* Dublin: Gill and Macmillan, 1979.

Cote, Jane. *Fanny and Anna Parnell: Ireland's Patriot Sisters.* New York: St. Martin's Press, 1991.

Cowling, Mary. *The Artists As Anthropologists.* Cambridge: Cambridge University Press, 1989.

Craig, Maurice. *Dublin 1660–1860: A Social and Architectural History.* Dublin: Hodges Figgis, 1969.

Cray, Robert. *Paupers and Poor Relief in New York City and Its Rural Environs, 1700–1830.* Philadelphia: Temple University Press, 1988.

Cronin, Mike and Daryl Adair. *The Wearing of the Green: A History of St. Patrick's Day.* London and New York: Routledge, 2002.

Cronin, Sean. *Irish Nationalism: A History of its Roots and Ideology.* New York: Continuum, 1981.

Crouthamel, James. *Bennett's New York Herald and The Rise of the Popular Press.* Syracuse: Syracuse University Press, 1989.

Cullen, Mary, and Maria Luddy, eds. *Women, Power and Consciousness in 19th-Century Ireland: Eight Biographical Studies.* Dublin: Attic Press, 1995.

___. *Female Activists, Irish Women and Change 1900–1960.* Dublin: Woodfield Press, 2001.

Curtis, L.P. *Apes and Angels: The Irishman in Victorian Caricature.* Washington, D.C.: Smithsonian Institute Press, 1971.

Dawe, Gerald, and Edna Longley. *Across a Roaring Hill: The Protestant Imagination in Modern Ireland, Essays in Honour of John Hewitt.* Belfast: Blackstaff Press, 1985.

De Vere White, Terence. *The Anglo Irish.* London: Victor Gollancz Ltd., 1972.

De la Salle, Jean Baptiste. *The Conduct of the Schools of Jean-Baptiste de la Salle.* New York: McGraw Hill, 1935.

Deane, Seamus. *A Short History of Irish Literature.* London: Hutchinson and Company, 1986.

Dewar, Brown and Long, Reverends. *Orangeism: A New Historical Appreciation*. Belfast: Grand Orange Lodge of Ireland, 1967.

Dezell, Maureen. *Irish America: Coming into Clover*. New York: Doubleday, 2000.

Dickson, R. J. *Ulster Emigration to Colonial America 1718–1775*. London: Routledge and Kegan Paul, 1966.

Diner, Hasia. *Erin's Daughters in America: Irish Immigrant Women in the Nineteenth Century*. Baltimore: Johns Hopkins University Press, 1983.

Dolan, Jay. *The Immigrant Church, New York's Irish and German Catholics*. Baltimore: Johns Hopkins University Press, 1975.

___. *Catholic Revivalism: The American Experience, 1830–1900*. Notre Dame: University of Notre Dame Press, 1978.

___. *The American Catholic Experience: A History from Colonial Times to the Present*. New York: Image Books, 1987.

___, ed., *The American Catholic Parish: A History From 1850 to the Present*. New York: Paulist Press, 1987.

Donnelly, James S. *The Great Irish Potato Famine*. Stroud, Gloucestershire: Sutton Publishing, 2001–02.

Doyle, David N. *Irish Americans: Native Rights and National Empires: The Struggles, Divisions, and Attitudes of the Catholic Minority in the Decade of Expansion, 1890–1901*. New York: Arno Press, 1976.

___ and Owen Dudley Edwards, eds. *America and Ireland, 1776–1976*. Westport, Conn.: Greenwood Press, 1980.

Drudy, P. J., ed. *Irish Studies 4. The Irish in America: Emigration, Assimilation, and Impact*. Cambridge: Cambridge University Press, 1985.

Dudley Edwards, Ruth. *Patrick Pearse: The Triumph of Failure*. London: Victor Gollancz, 1977. Repr. Dublin: Poolbeg Press, 1990.

Dunne, Robert. *Antebellum Irish Immigration and Emerging Ideologies of "America": A Protestant Backlash*. Lewiston, New York: Edwin Mellen Press, 2002.

Eagleton, Terry. *Heathcliff and the Great Hunger: Studies in Irish Culture*. London: Verso, 1995.

Ehrlich, Richard L., ed. *Immigrants in Industrial America, 1850–1920*. Charlottesville: University Press of Virginia, 1977.

Elliott, Marianne. *Partners in Revolution: The United Irishmen and France*. New Haven: Yale University Press, 1982.

___. *Watchmen in Sion: The Protestant Idea of Liberty*. Derry: Dorman and Sons, 1985.

___. *Wolfe Tone: Prophet of Irish Independence*. New Haven: Yale University Press, 1989.

Ellis, Edward Robb. *The Epic of New York City: A Narrative History*. New York: Old Town Books, 1966.

Ellis, John Tracy, and Robert Trisco, eds. *A Guide to American Catholic History*. Santa Barbara and Oxford: ABC Clio, Inc., 1982.

Erie, Steven P. *Rainbow's End: Irish-Americans and the Dilemmas of Urban Machine Politics, 1840–1985*. Berkeley: University of California Press, 1988.

Ernst, Robert. *Immigrant Life in New York City, 1825–1863*. New York: King's Crown Press, 1949. Repr. Syracuse: Syracuse University Press, 1994.

"Even Rarer." Library Associates Newsletter. Georgetown University. <http://gulib.lausun. georgetown.edu/advancement/newsletter/61/rarer61.htm> Fall 2001.

Ewens, Mary. *The Role of the Nun in Nineteenth Century America*. New York: Arno Press, 1978.

Fairburn, Eleanor. *The White Seahorse*. London: Heinemann, 1964.

Fanning, Charles. *The Irish Voice in America: Irish-American Fiction from the 1760s to the 1980s*. Lexington, Kentucky: The University Press of Kentucky, 1990.

___. *New Perspectives on the Irish Diaspora*. Carbondale and Edwardsville: Southern Illinois University Press, 2000.

ffrench Eagar, Irene. *Margaret Anna Cusack: One Woman's Campaign for Women's Rights, a Biography.* Cork: Mercier Press, 1970.

Fialka, John J. *Sisters: Catholic Nuns and the Making of America.* New York: St. Martin's Press, 2003.

Fitzgerald, Marie. "The St. Patrick's Day Parade: The Conflict of Irish-American Identity in New York City 1840–1900." Unpubl. Ph.D. diss., SUNY Stonybrook, 1993.

Fitzgerald, Maureen. "Irish-Catholic Nuns and the Development of New York City's Welfare System, 1840–1900." Ph.D. diss., University of Wisconsin-Madison, 1992.

Fitzpatrick, David. *Irish Emigration 1801–1921.* Dublin: Dundalgan Press, 1984.

Fitzpatrick, Franklin. *Vincentians in Brooklyn, 1855–1955: the Story of the St. Vincent de Paul Society in the Diocese of Brooklyn.* New York: Brooklyn Eagle Press, 1955.

Fogarty, Gerald P. *The Vatican and the American Hierarchy From 1870 to 1965.* Stuttgart: Hiersemann, 1982.

___. *American Catholic Biblical Scholarship: A History From the Early Republic to Vatican II.* New York: Harper and Row, 1989.

Foster, R. F. *Modern Ireland 1600–1972.* London: Allen Lane, Penguin Press, 1988.

___. *Paddy and Mr. Punch: Connections in Irish and English History.* London: Penguin Books, 1993.

___. *The Irish Story: Telling Tales and Making it up in Ireland.* London: Allen Lane, Penguin Press, 2001.

Funchion, Michael, ed., *Irish American Voluntary Organizations.* Westport, Conn.: Greenwood Press, 1983.

Gailey, Andrew. *Ireland and the Death of Kindness: The Experience of Constructive Unionism 1890–1905.* Cork: Cork University Press, 1987.

Gallagher, S.F., ed. *Woman in Irish Legend, Life and Literature.* Buckinghamshire: Colin Smythe, 1983.

Gibson, Florence. *The Attitudes of the New York Irish Toward State and National Affairs 1848–1892.* New York: Columbia University Press, 1951.

Glasgow, Maude. *Scotch-Irish in Northern Ireland and in the American Colonies.* Baltimore, MD: Heritage Books, 1998.

Glass, D.V., and P.A.M. Taylor. *Population and Emigration,* in the series *Government and Society in Nineteenth Century Britain, Commentaries on British Parliamentary Papers.* Dublin: Irish Academic Press, 1976.

Glazer, Nathan, and Daniel Patrick Moynihan. *Beyond the Melting Pot: The Negroes, Puerto Ricans, Jews, Italians and Irish of New York City.* Cambridge, Mass.: M.I.T. Press, 1970.

Glazier, Ira, and Michael Tepper, eds. *Famine Immigrants: Lists of Irish Immigrants Arriving at the Port of New York, 1846–51,* 6 volumes. Baltimore: Genealogical Publishing Company, Inc., 1983.

___, and Luigi De Rosa, eds., *Migration Across Time and Nations: Population Mobility in Historical Contexts.* New York and London: Holmes and Meier Publishers, 1986.

Glazier, Michael, ed. *The Encyclopedia of the Irish in America.* South Bend, Indiana: Notre Dame University Press, 1999.

Glazier, Michael, and Thomas J. Shelley, eds. *The Encyclopedia of American Catholic History.* New York: The Liturgical Press, 1998.

Golway, Terry. *Irish Rebel: John Devoy and America's Fight for Ireland's Freedom.* New York: St. Martin's Griffin, 1999.

Gordon, Michael. *The Orange Riots: Irish Political Violence in New York City, 1870 and 1871.* Ithaca: Cornell University Press, 1993.

Gordon, Milton. *Assimilation in American Life: The Role of Race, Religion and National Origins.* Oxford and New York: Oxford University Press, 1964.

Gray, Tony. *The Orange Order.* London: The Bodley Head, 1972.

Greeley, Andrew. *That Most Distressful Nation: The Taming of the American Irish.* Chicago: Quadrangle Books, 1972.

___. *Ethnicity in the United States: A Preliminary Reconnaissance.* New York: Wiley, 1974.

___. *An Ugly Little Secret: Anti-Catholicism in North America*. Kansas City: Sheed, Andrews and McMeel, 1977.

___. *The American Catholic: A Social Portrait*. New York: Basic Books, 1977.

___. *The Irish-Americans, The Rise to Money and Power*. New York: Harper and Row, 1981.

___. *A Book of Irish American Blessings & Prayers*. Allen, TX: Thomas More Press, 1991.

Gribben, Arthur, ed. *The Great Famine and the Irish Diaspora in America*. Amherst: University of Massachusetts Press, 1999.

Griffin, William D. *A Portrait of the Irish in America*. New York: Scribner, 1981.

___. *The Book of Irish Americans*. New York: Times Books, 1990.

___. *Irish Americans: The Immigrant Experience*. Westport, CT: Hugh Lauter Levin Associates, 1998.

Groneman, Carol. "The 'Bloody Ould Sixth:' A Social Analysis of a New York City Working-Class Community in the Mid-Nineteenth Century." Unpubl. Ph.D. diss., University of Rochester, 1973.

Gronowicz, Anthony. *Race and Class Politics in New York City before the Civil War*. Boston: Northeastern University Press, 1997.

Hachey, Thomas and Lawrence McCaffrey, eds. *Perspectives on Irish Nationalism*. Lexington, Kentucky: University Press of Kentucky, 1989.

Hackett, James D. *Bishops of the United States of Irish Birth or Descent*. New York: American Irish Historical Society, 1936.

Hammond, J.L. *Gladstone and the Irish Nation*. London and New York: Longmans, Green and Company, 1938.

Handlin, Oscar, *Boston's Immigrants, A Study in Acculturation*. Cambridge, Mass.: Harvard University Press, 1941.

___. *The Uprooted*. Boston: Little, Brown and Company, 1951.

___. ed. *Immigration as a Factor in American History*. Englewood Cliffs, NJ: Prentice-Hall, 1959.

___. *Children of the Uprooted*. New York: G. Braziller, 1966.

Hansen, Marcus Lee. *The Atlantic Migration*. Cambridge, Mass.: Harvard University Press, 1940.

___. *The Immigrant in American History; Edited With Foreword by Arthur Schlesinger*. Cambridge, Mass.: Harvard University Press, 1940.

Harlow, Alvin. *Old Bowery Days: The Chronicles of a Famous Street*. New York: Appleton & Co., 1931.

Haverty, Anne. *Constance Markievicz: An Independent Life*. London and San Francisco: Pandora Press, 1988.

Healy, Kathleen, ed. *Sisters of Mercy, Spirituality in America, 1843–1900*. New York: Paulist Press, 1992.

Hearne, Dana, ed. *The Tale of a Great Sham*. Dublin: Arlen House, 1986.

Henkin, David M. *City Reading: Written Words and Public Spaces in Antebellum New York*. New York: Columbia University Press, 1998.

Hennessy, Bernard. *Public Opinion*. Berkeley: University of California Press, 1985.

Herlihy, Kevin, ed. *The Politics of Irish Dissent, 1650–1840*. Dublin: Four Courts Press, 1997.

Higham, John. *Strangers in the Land, Patterns of American Nativism 1860–1925*. New York: Atheneum, 1955. Repr. New Brusnwick: Rutgers University Press, 1988.

___. *Send These To Me: Jews and Other Immigrants in Urban America*. New York: Atheneum, 1975. Repr. Baltimore: Johns Hopkins University Press, 1984.

Hill, Jacqueline. *From Patriots to Unionists: Dublin Civic Politics and Irish Protestant Patriotism, 1660–1840*. Oxford and New York: Oxford University Press, 1997.

Himber, Alan, ed. *The Letters of John Quinn to William Butler Yeats*. Ann Arbor, Michigan: University of Michigan Press, 1983.

Hodges, Graham. *New York City Cartmen, 1667–1850*. New York: New York University Press, 1986.

Homberger, Eric. *Scenes from the Life of a City: Corruption and Conscience in Old New York*. New Haven: Yale University Press, 1994.

___. *Mrs. Astor's New York: Money and Power in a Gilded Age*. New Haven: Yale University Press, 2002.

Houston, Cecil, and William Smyth. *The Sash Canada Wore: A Historical Geography of the Orange Order in Canada,* Toronto: University of Toronto Press, 1980.

Howe, Stephen. *Ireland and Empire: Colonial Legacies in Irish History and Culture.* Oxford and New York: Oxford University Press, 2000.

Hueston, Robert. *The Catholic Press and Nativism, 1840–1860.* New York: Arno Press, 1976.

Hurley, Michael J., ed. *Irish Anglicanism 1869–1969.* Dublin: Allen Figgis, 1970.

Hutchinson, John. *The Dynamics of Cultural Nationalism: The Gaelic Revival and the Creation of the Irish Nation State.* London: Allen and Unwin, 1987.

Hutton, Sean, and Paul Stewart, eds. *Ireland's Histories: Aspects of State, Society and Ideology.* London: Penguin, 1991.

Ignatiev, Noel. *How the Irish Became White.* New York: Routledge, 1995.

Innes, C. L. *Woman and Nation in Irish Literature and Society, 1880–1935.* Athens: University of Georgia Press, 1993.

Ireland After The Union: Proceedings of the Second Joint Meeting of the Royal Irish Academy and the British Academy. Introduction by Lord Blake. Oxford and New York: Oxford University Press, 1989.

Isacsson, Alfred. *Irish Letters in the New York Carmelites Archives.* Middletown, New York: Vestigium Press, 1988.

Jackson, Alvin. *Ireland 1798–1998, Politics and War.* Oxford: Blackwell Publishers, 1999.

Jackson, Kenneth T., ed. *The Encyclopedia of New York City.* New Haven: Yale University Press, and the New York Historical Society, 1995.

___ and David S. Dunbar, eds. *Empire City: New York Through the Centuries.* New York: Columbia University Press, 2002.

Jacobson, Matthew Frye. *Special Sorrows: The Diasporic Imagination of Irish, Polish, and Jewish Immigrants in the United States.* Cambridge, Mass: Harvard University Press, 1995.

___. *Whiteness of a Different Color: European Immigrants and the Alchemy of Race.* Cambridge, Mass.: Harvard University Press, 1998.

Jacoby, George Paul. *Catholic Child Care in Nineteenth Century New York, With a Correlated Summary of Public and Protestant Child Welfare.* Washington: The Catholic University of America, 1941.

Jenkins, Keith. *On 'What is History?' From Carr and Elton to Rorty and White.* London: Routledge, 1995.

Jones, H. Lloyd, V. Pearl, and B. Worden, eds. *History and Imagination: Essays in Honour of H.R. Trevor-Roper.* New York: Holmes and Meier Publishers, 1981.

Joyce, William. *Editors and Ethnicity: The Irish-American Press, 1858–83.* New York: Arno Press, 1976.

Katz, Michael B. *In the Shadow of the Poorhouse; A Social History of Welfare in America.* New York: Basic Books, 1986.

Kearns, Caledonia, ed. *Cabbage and Bones: An Anthology of Irish-American Women's Fiction.* New York: Henry Holt, 1997.

___, ed. *Motherland: Writings by Irish American Women About Mothers and Daughters.* Fairfield, NJ: William Morrow & Company, 1999.

Kee, Robert. *The Green Flag: A History of Irish Nationalism.* London: Penguin, 1972.

___. *The Laurel and the Ivy: The Story of Charles Stewart Parnell and Irish Nationalism.* London: Hamish Hamilton, 1993.

Keller, Morton. *The Art and Politics of Thomas Nast.* Oxford and New York: Oxford University Press, 1968.

Kenneally, Michael, ed. *Cultural Contexts and Literary Idioms in Contemporary Irish Literature.* New Jersey: Barnes and Noble Books, 1988.

Kennedy, Jr., Robert E. *The Irish: Emigration, Marriage and Fertility.* Berkeley: University of California Press, 1973.

Kenny, Kevin. *The American Irish: A History.* New York: Pearson Education Limited, 2000.

___, ed. *New Directions in Irish-American History.* Madison: University of Wisconsin Press, 2003.

Kiberd, Declan. *Inventing Ireland: The Literature of the Modern Nation*. Cambridge, Mass.: Harvard University Press, 1995.

Kivisto, Peter, and Dag Blanck, eds. *American Immigrants and their Generations: Studies and Commentaries on the Hansen Thesis After 50 Years*. Urbana: University of Illinois Press, 1990.

Knoble, Dale. *Paddy and The Republic: Ethnicity and Nationality in Ante-bellum America*. Middleton, Connecticut: Wesleyan University Press, 1986.

Kolko, Gabriel. *Main Currents in American History*. New York: Harper and Row, 1976.

Krase, Jerome, and Charles La Cerra. *Ethnicity and Machine Politics*. Lanham: University Press of America, 1991.

Kroessler, Jeffrey A. *New York Year by Year: A Chronology of the Great Metropolis*. New York: New York University Press, 2002.

Lankevich, George. *American Metropolis: A History of New York City*. New York: New York University Press, 1998.

Larkin, Emmet. *The Roman Catholic Church and the Creation of the Modern Irish State, 1878–1886*. Philadelphia: American Philosophical Society, 1975.

___. *The Historical Dimensions of Irish Catholicism*. New York: Arno Press, 1976.

___. *The Making of the Roman Catholic Church in Ireland, 1850–1860*. Chapel Hill: University of North Carolina Press, 1980.

___. *The Consolidation of the Roman Catholic Church in Ireland 1860–1870*. Chapel Hill: University of North Carolina Press, 1987.

Lenox-Conyngham, Melosina, ed., *Diaries of Ireland: An Anthology, 1590–1987*. Dublin: Lilliput Press, 1998.

Levenson, Leah and Jerry H. Natterstad. *Hanna Sheehy-Skeffington, Irish Feminist*. Syracuse: Syracuse University Press, 1986.

Linton, Ralph, ed. *The Science of Man in the World Crisis*. New York: Columbia University Press, 1945.

Liptak, Dolores. A *Church of Many Cultures: Selected Historical Essays on Ethnic American Catholicism*. New York: Garland Publishing, 1988.

___. *Immigrants and Their Church*. New York: Macmillan; Collier Macmillan Publishers, 1989.

___. *Pioneer Healers: The History of Women Religious in American Health Care*. New York: Crossroad, 1989.

Lloyd, David. *Nationalism and Minor Literature: James Clarence Mangan and the Emergence of Irish Cultural Nationalism*. Berkeley: University of California Press, 1987.

___. *Anomalous States: Irish Writing and the Post-Colonial Moment*. Durham: Duke University Press, 1993.

Llywellyn, Morgan. *100 Essential Books for Irish-American Readers*. Secaucus, NJ: Carol Publishing Group, 1998.

Londraville, Janis and Richard, eds. *The Letters of Maud Gonne and John Quinn: Too Long a Sacrifice*. Selinsgrove, PA: Susquehanna University Press, 1999.

___, eds. *John Quinn: Selected Irish Writers from his Library*. West Cornwall, CT: Locust Hill Press, 2001.

Luddy, Maria. *Women and Philanthropy in Nineteenth-Century Ireland*. Cambridge, Mass. and New York: Cambridge University Press, 1995.

___, and Cliona Murphy, eds. *Women Surviving, Studies in Irish Women's History in the 19th and 20th Centuries*. Dublin: Poolbeg, 1990.

Lydon, James. *The Making of Ireland From Ancient Times to the Present*. London and New York: Routledge, 1998.

Lyons, F.S.L. *Ireland Since the Famine*. London: Fontana, 1973.

___ and R. A. J. Hawkins, eds. *Ireland Under the Union: Varieties of Tensions, Essays in Honour of T. W. Moody*. Oxford and New York: Oxford University Press, 1980.

MacLysaght, Edward. *Irish Life in the Seventeenth Century: After Cromwell*. Dublin: Irish University Press, 1939.

Malcolmson, A.P.W. *The Pursuit of the Heiress: Aristocratic Marriage in Ireland 1750–1820.* Belfast: Public Relations Office of Northern Ireland, 1962.

___. *John Foster: The Politics of the Anglo-Irish Ascendancy.* Oxford and New York: Oxford University Press, 1978.

Martin, Augustine. *The Works of James Clarence Mangan.* Dublin: Irish Academic Press, 1998.

McBride, Ian. *The Siege of Derry in Ulster Protestant Mythology.* Dublin: Four Courts Press, 1997.

McCaffrey, Lawrence, *The Irish Diaspora in America.* Bloomington: Indiana University Press, 1976.

___, Ellen Skerrett, Michael F. Funchion, Charles Fanning, eds. *The Irish in Chicago.* Urbana: University of Illinois Press, 1987.

McCartan, Patrick. *With DeValera in America.* New York: Brentano, 1932.

McCarthy, Margaret. *A Cathedral of Suitable Magnificence: St. Patrick's Cathedral, New York.* Wilmington, DE: Michael Glazier, Inc., 1984.

McCarthy, Mary Peter. *Old St. Patrick's, New York's First Cathedral.* New York: U.S. Catholic Historical Society, 1947.

McColgan, Daniel T. *A Century of Charity; the First One Hundred Years of the Society of St. Vincent de Paul in the United States.* Milwaukee: Bruce Publishing Co., 1951.

McDannell, Colleen. *American Catholic Women: A Historical Exploration.* New York: Macmillan Publishing Co., 1989.

McDowell, R.B. *Public Opinion and Government Policy in Ireland, 1801–1846.* London: Faber and Faber, 1952.

___. *Ireland in the Age of Imperialism and Revolution 1760–1801.* Oxford and New York: Oxford University Press, 1979.

___ and D. A. Webb. *Trinity College, Dublin, 1592–1952: An Academic History.* Cambridge: Cambridge University Press, 1982.

McFarland, E. W. *Ireland and Scotland in the Age of Revolution: Planting the Green Bough.* Edinburgh: Edinburgh University Press, 1994.

McIver, Joan. *30 Irish American Women Who Changed Our World: From Mother Jones to Grace Kelly.* Secaucus, NJ: Carol Publishing Group, 1999.

McLeod, Hugh. *Piety and Poverty: Working-Class Religion in Berlin, London and New York 1870–1914.* New York: Holmes & Meier, 1996.

McLoughlin, Dympna. "Shoveling Out Paupers: Female Emigration from Irish Workhouses, 1840–1870." Ph.D. diss., Syracuse University, 1988.

___. *Women, Subsistence and Emigration, 1840–1870.* Dublin: Irish Academic Press, 2000.

Meagher, Timothy J., ed. *From Paddy to Studs: Irish-American Communities in the Turn of the Century Era, 1880 to 1920.* Connecticut: Greenwood Press, 1986.

___, ed. *Urban American Catholicism, The Culture and Identity of The American Catholic People.* New York: Garland, 1988.

___. *Inventing Irish America: Generation, Class and Ethnic Identity in a New England City, 1880–1928.* Indiana: Notre Dame University Press, 2001.

Metress, Seamus P. *The American Irish and Irish Nationalism: A Sociohistorical Introduction.* Lanham: University Press of America, 1995.

Miller, Kerby. *Emigrants and Exiles: Ireland and the Irish Exodus to North America.* Oxford and New York: Oxford University Press, 1985.

___. *Out of Ireland: The Story of Irish Emigration to America.* Washington, D.C.: Elliot and Clark, 1994.

___ and Patricia Mulholland Miller. *Journey of Hope: The Story of Irish Immigration to America.* San Francisco: Chronicle Books, 2001.

Mishkin, Tracy. *The Harlem and Irish Renaissances: Language, Identity, and Representation.* Gainesville: University Press of Florida, 1998.

Mokyr, Joel. *Why Ireland Starved: A Quantitative and Analytical History of the Irish Economy, 1800–1850.* London and Boston: Allen and Unwin, 1983.

Monaghan, Patricia, ed. *The Next Parish Over: A Collection of Irish-American Writing.* Minneapolis: New Rivers Press, 1993.

Montgomery, David. *The Irish Influence in the American Labor Movement.* Notre Dame: Hibernian Lecture, 1984.

Moody, T. W., ed. *The Fenian Movement.* Cork and Dublin: Irish University Press, 1968.

___, F. X. Martin, and F. J. Byrne, eds. *A New History of Ireland, Vol. III; Early Modern Ireland 1534–1691.* Oxford and New York: Oxford University Press, 1976.

___, and W.E. Vaughn, eds. *A New History of Ireland, Vol. IV; Eighteenth-Century Ireland 1691–1800.* Oxford and New York: Oxford University Press, 1986.

Mooney-Eichacker, Joanne. *Varieties of Irish Republican Womanhood: Lectures During their United States Tours, 1916–1925.* Dublin: Irish Academic Press, 2000.

Morris, Charles. *American Catholic: The Saints and Sinners Who Built America's Most Powerful Church.* New York: Times Books, 1997.

Murphy, Charles Kavanagh. *The Spirit of the Society of St. Vincent de Paul.* New York: Longmans Green, 1940.

Murphy, Maureen, ed. *Annals of the Famine in Ireland/Asenath Nicholson.* Dublin: Lilliput Press, 1998.

Murphy, Richard, and Lawrence J. Mannion. *The History of the Society of the Friendly Sons of Saint Patrick in the City of New York, 1784–1955.* New York: Fordham University Press, 1960.

Mushkat, Jerome. *Tammany: The Evolution of a Political Machine, 1789–1865.* Syracuse: Syracuse University Press, 1971.

___. *The Reconstruction of the New York Democracy, 1861–1874.* Rutherford, NJ: Fairleigh Dickinson University Press, 1981.

___. *Fernando Wood, A Political Biography.* Ohio: Kent State University Press, 1990.

Ni Bhroimeil, Una. *Building Irish Identity in America, 1870–1915: The Gaelic Revival.* Dublin: Four Courts Press, 2003.

Niehaus, Earl. *The Irish in New Orleans 1800–1860.* Baton Rouge: Louisiana State University Press, 1965.

Nolan, Janet. *Ourselves Alone: Female Emigration From Ireland 1825–1920.* Lexington, Kentucky: University Press of Kentucky, 1989.

Norman, Diana. *Terrible Beauty: A Life of Constance Markievicz, 1868–192.* London: Hodder and Stoughton, 1987.

Oates, Mary. *Higher Education for Catholic Women: An Historical Anthology,* New York: Garland Publishing, 1987.

___. *The Catholic Philanthropic Tradition in America.* Bloomington, Indiana: Indiana University Press, 1995.

Obelkevich, Jim, Lyndal Roper, and Raphael Samuel, eds. *Disciplines of Faith: Studies in Religion, Politics and Patriarchy.* London: Routledge & Kegan Paul Ltd., 1987.

O'Brien, Mary Agnes. "History and Development of Catholic Secondary Education in the Archdiocese of New York." Unpubl. M.A. thesis, Brooklyn College, CUNY, 1949.

O'Brien, William, and Desmond Ryan, eds. *Devoy's Post Bag, 1871–1928.* Dublin: C.J. Fallon Ltd., 1948.

O'Broin, Leon. *Fenian Fever: An Anglo-American Dilemma.* New York: New York University Press, 1971.

O'Carroll, Ide. *Models for Movers, Irish Women's Emigration to America.* Dublin: Attic Press, 1990.

O'Conner, Rebecca. *Jenny Mitchel Young Irelander: A Biography.* Minnesota: Irish Books and Media, 1985. Repr. Tuscon: Trust Publishers, 1988.

O'Connor, Thomas H. *The Boston Irish: A Political History.* Boston: Northeastern University Press, 1995. Repr., Boston: Little, Brown & Company, 1997.

O'Connor Wibberly, Leonard P. *The Coming of the Green*. New York: Henry Holt and Company, 1958.

O'Dowd, Mary, and Sabine Wichert, eds. *Chattel, Servant or Citizen: Women's Status in Church, State and Society*. Belfast: The Institute of Irish Studies, 1995.

O'Faolain, Sean. *Constance Markievicz, or The Average Revolutionary, A Biography*. London: Cresset Library, 1987.

O'Ferrall, Fergus. *Catholic Emancipation: Daniel O'Connell and the Birth of Irish Democracy, 1820–1830*. Dublin: Gill and Macmillan, 1985.

O'Hanlon, Ray. *The New Irish Americans*. Boulder, CO: Roberts Rinehart Publishing, 1998.

Oiuiroga, Virginia. *Poor Mothers and Babies: A Social History of Childbirth and Childcare in Nineteenth Century New York City*. New York: Garland Publishing, 1989.

O'Leary, Philip. *The Prose Literature of the Gaelic Revival 1881–1921: Ideology and Innovation*. Philadelphia: Pennsylvania State University Press, 1994.

Oppel, Frank. *Gaslight New York Revisited*. Secaucus, NJ: Castle Books, 1989.

Orsi, Robert. *The Madonna of 115th Street: Faith and Community in Italian Harlem, 1880–1950*. New Haven: Yale University Press, 1988.

O'Sullivan, Patrick, ed. *The Irish in the New Communities; The Irish World Wide: History, Heritage, Identity*. Leicester and London: Leicester University Press, 1992.

___, ed., *Irish Women and Irish Migration; The Irish World Wide: History, Heritage, Identity*. London and New York: Leicester University Press, 1995.

O'Tuathaigh, Gearoid. *Ireland Before the Famine 1798–1848*. Dublin: Gill and Macmillan, 1972.

Padden, Michael, and Robert Sullivan, eds. *May the Road Rise to Meet You: Everything You Need to Know About Irish American History*. New York: Plumsock Mesoamerican Studies, 1999.

Park, Robert E., and Ernest W. Burgess, *Introduction to the Science of Sociology*. Chicago: University of Chicago Press, 1921.

Patterson, Jerry E. *Fifth Avenue, The Best Address*. New York: Rizzoli International Publications, 1998.

Pencak, William, Selma Berrol and Randall M. Miller, eds. *Immigration to New York*. Philadelphia: The Balch Institute, 1991.

Potter, George. *To The Golden Door: The Story of the Irish in Ireland and America*. Boston: Little, Brown and Company, 1960.

Pratt, John W. *Religion, Politics and Diversity: The Church State Theme in New York History*. Ithaca: Cornell University Press, 1967.

Rafferty, Oliver P. *The Church, the State, and the Fenian Threat, 1861–75*. New York: St. Martin's Press, 1999.

Ravitch, Diane. *The Great School Wars: A History of the New York City Public Schools 1805–1973*. New York: Basic Books, 1974.

Reedy, George. *From the Ward to the White House: The Irish in American Politics*. New York: Scribner's Sons, 1991.

Reid, Benjamin. *The Man From New York: John Quinn and his Friends*. Oxford and New York: Oxford University Press, 1968.

Ridge, John T. *The History of the Ancient Order of Hibernians and Ladies' Auxiliary of Brooklyn*. Brooklyn: Ancient Order of Hibernians, 1973. Repr., Brooklyn: Ancient Order of Hibernians, 1985.

___. *The St. Patrick's Day Parade in New York*. New York: St. Patrick's Day Committee, 1988.

Rodechko, James. *Patrick Ford and his Search for America, A Case Study of Irish-American Journalism, 1870–1913*. New York: Arno Press, 1968.

Rosenweig, Roy, and Elizabeth Blackmar. *The Park and the People: A History of Central Park*. Ithaca: Cornell University Press, 1992.

Ryan, Desmond. *The Fenian Chief, A Biography of James Stephens*. Dublin: Gill and Son, 1967.

Sarna, Jonathan D., and David G. Dalin. *Religion and State in the American Jewish Experience* South Bend: Notre Dame University Press, 1997.

Scally, Robert James. *The End of Hidden Ireland*. Oxford and New York: Oxford University Press, 1995.

Scherzer, Kenneth. *The Unbounded Community: Neighborhood Life and Social Structure in New York City 1830–1875*. Durham: Duke University Press, 1992.

Schoener, Allon. *New York: An Illustrated History of the People*. New York: W. W. Norton & Company, 1998.

Sebestyan, Amanda, ed. *Prison Letters of Countess Markievicz*. London: Virago Press, 1987.

Seidler, Murray B. *Norman Thomas: Respectable Rebel*. Syracuse: Syracuse University Press, 1961.

Senior, Hereward. *Orangeism in Ireland and Britain, 1795–1836*. London: Routledge and Kegan Paul, 1966.

Shannon, William V. *The American-Irish*. New York: Macmillan, 1963.

Shea, Ann M. and Marion R. Casey, eds. *The Irish Experience in New York City: A Select Bibliography*. New York: New York Irish History Roundtable, 1995.

Shepard, Leslie. *The Broadside Ballad: A Study in Origins and Meaning*. London: Herbert Jenkins, 1962.

Shulman, Harry M. *The Slums of New York, Rotary Club of New York Study, 1931, 1932*. New York: Albert and Charles Boni, Inc., 1938.

Simms, J. G. *Jacobite Ireland 1685–91*. London: Routledge and K. Paul, 1969.

Skelton, Josephine. *The Ardent Exile: The Life and Times of Thomas D'Arcy McGee*. Toronto: Macmillan and Company of Canada, 1951.

___. *The Ballad of D'Arcy McGee; Rebel in Exile*. Toronto: Macmillan and Company of Canada, 1967.

Smith, Anthony D. *National Identity: Ethnonationalism in Comparative Perspective*. Reno, Las Vegas: University of Nevada Press, 1992.

Smith, Dennis. *A Song For Mary: An Irish-American Memory*. New York: Warner Books, 1999.

Spann, Edward K. *The New Metropolis: New York City, 1840–1860*. New York: Columbia University Press, 1981.

___. *Gotham at War: New York City, 1860–1865*. Wilmington: SR Books, 2002.

Stansell, Christine. *City of Women: Sex and Class in New York, 1789–1860*. New York: Knopf, 1986. Repr. Urbana: University of Illinois Press, 1987.

Stephens, Michael G. *Green Dreams: Essays Under the Influence of the Irish*. Atlanta: University of Georgia Press, 1994.

Stewart, A.T.Q. *The Summer Soldiers: The 1798 Rebellion in Antrim and Down*. Belfast: Blackstaff Press, 1995.

Stewart, George C. Jr. *Marvels of Charity: History of American Sisters and Nuns*. Huntington, In.: Our Sunday Visitor, Inc., 1994.

St. Hill, Thomas Nast. *Thomas Nast: Cartoons and Illustrations*. New York: Dover Publications, 1974.

Super, R. H., ed. *The Complete Prose Works of Matthew Arnold, Vol. 3, Lectures in Essays and Criticism*. Ann Arbor: University of Michigan Press, 1962.

Tansill, Charles. *America and the Fight for Irish Freedom 1866–1922: An Old Story Based Upon New Data*. New York: Devin-Adair, 1957.

Taylor, William. *In Pursuit of Gotham: Culture and Commerce in New York*. Oxford and New York: Oxford University Press, 1992.

Thernstrom, Stephan, ed. *The Harvard Encyclopedia of American Ethnic Groups*. Cambridge, Mass.: Belknap Press of Harvard University, 1980.

Thuente, Mary Helen. *The Harp Re-strung: The United Irishmen and the Rise of Irish Literary Nationalism*. Syracuse: Syracuse University Press, 1994.

Touhill, Blanche, ed. *Varieties of Ireland: Varieties of Irish-America*. St. Louis: University of Missouri Press, 1976.

___. *William Smith O'Brien and his Irish Revolutionary Companions in Penal Exile*. Columbia: University of Missouri, 1981.

Van Voris, Jacqueline. *Constance de Markievicz: In the Cause of Ireland*. Boston: University of Massachusetts Press, 1967.

Vaughn, W. E., and A. J. Fitzpatrick, eds. *Irish Historical Statistics: Population, 1821–1971*. Dublin: Royal Irish Academy, 1978.

___, ed. *A New History of Ireland, Vol. V, Ireland Under the Union, I, 1801–70*. Oxford: Clarendon Press, 1989.

Walsh, Sister Margaret. *History of the Sisters of Charity of New York, 1809–1959*. New York: Fordham University Press, 1960.

Ward, David. *Poverty, Ethnicity and the American City, 1840–1925*. New York: Cambridge University Press, 1989.

Ward, Margaret. *Unmanageable Revolutionaries: Women and Irish Nationalism*. London: Pluto Press, 1983.

___. *Maud Gonne: A Life*. London and San Francisco: Pandora Press, 1990.

Ward, Patrick. *Exile, Emigration and Irish Writing*. Dublin: Irish Academic Press, 2002.

Warner, Lloyd, and Leo Srole. *The Social Systems of American Ethnic Groups*. New Haven: Yale University Press, 1945.

White, Joseph P., ed. *The American Catholic Religious Life*. New York: Garland Press, 1988.

Widmer, Edward L. *Young America: The Flowering of Democracy in New York City*. Oxford and New York: Oxford University Press, 1999.

Wiebe, Robert H. *The Search For Order, 1877–1920*. New York: Hill and Wang, 1967.

Williams, William H.A. *'Twas Only an Irishman's Dream: The Image of Ireland and the Irish in American Popular Song Lyrics, 1800–1920*. Urbana: University of Illinois Press, 1996.

Wilson, David A. *United Irishmen, United States: Immigrant Radicals in the Early Republic*. Ithaca: Cornell University Press, 1998.

Winslow, Calvin, ed. *Studies in Waterfront Labor History*. Urbana: University of Illinois Press, 1998.

Wittke, Carl. *We Who Built America, The Saga of The Immigrant*. New York: Columbia University Press, 1939.

___. *The Irish in America*. Baton Rouge: Louisiana State University Press, 1956.

Wokeck, Marianne. *Trade in Strangers: The Beginnings of Mass Migration to North America*. University Park: Pennsylvania State University Press, 1999.

Woodham Smith, Cecil. *The Great Hunger: Ireland 1845–1849*. London: R. Hamilton, 1962.

Wyndham, Horace. *Speranza, A Biography of Lady Wilde*. New York: Philosophical Library Inc., 1951.

Yans-McLoughlin, Virginia, ed. *Immigration Reconsidered: History, Sociology and Politics*. Oxford and New York: Oxford University Press, 1990.

Index